"*The Complexities of Authority in the Classroom* shifts the questions of classroom climate away from classroom management and behaviour control toward a much more holistic and integral understanding of how human beings learn and how that learning is best facilitated. The term *authority* is reclaimed for teachers as something that is earned, modelled, embodied, and integral and that operates in the space created by the relationships between people. Education for too long has focused on the top-down transmission and assessment of content knowledge: this book is a refreshingly simple, yet profound re-balancing of this equation to an *inside-out* model that privileges authenticity, listening, relationships, engaging curricula and student self-leadership. Written by practitioners, this volume offers needed insights into how effective classrooms work and how the students in those classrooms can engage more meaningfully in their own learning narratives."

Ruth Crick, *Founder and Director, WILD Learning Sciences, Professor of Learning Analytics and Educational Leadership, University of Technology, Sydney, Australia*

"Authority is far too often framed as 'discipline.' This exciting and interesting book helps teachers and teacher educators take other perspectives. A range of high quality chapters give insight into theoretical and practical issues related to the core business of teaching, namely cultivating relational spaces in which pupils can learn to take their own responsibility. The authors unravel the complicated job of teachers of both authorizing themselves to teach and authorizing students to learn. This book will undoubtedly be of great value for teacher-training and for post-initial training. I recommend it to all teachers who are searching for new insights and practical tools for their everyday job."

Bram de Muynck, *Professor of Education at Driestar Christian University, Gouda, the Netherlands*

"Badley and Patrick have curated a collection of stories, theories, and research notes that is both brilliant and authentic. The central ideas of being authorized to teach by self and others, and the consent to learn, are concepts that all educators confront yet too often fail to articulate and thoughtfully address with their practice. Teaching is done with, rather than done to. An exchange occurs between teacher and learner that transforms classrooms into places of learning. It is magical and yet it can be analyzed. The authors in this text contribute to that analysis adeptly and address a wide variety of aspects and contexts, such as substitute teaching, early career teaching, special needs teaching, cross-cultural teaching, and the list goes on. Addressing issues of true authorization and honest consent, every chapter hits the nails on the heads. As Badley notes, teaching requires guts, which in turn calls for courage and hope. The consent only learners can grant to their teachers constitutes the difference between trying and truly teaching. Every university teacher preparation program owes this book to their students as part of a required text list. Teaching careers and student trajectories demand as much."

Jay Mathisen, *Superintendent, Jefferson County School District, Oregon, USA*

"For many reasons, *The Complexities of Authority in Classroom* should find its way into the personal libraries of all teachers. This book is about relationships first, and it pushes managing the classroom far down the list. In that regard, I think the philosophy at the foundation of the book is spot-on."

Jim Parsons, *Professor Emeritus, Faculty of Education, University of Alberta, Canada*

THE COMPLEXITIES OF AUTHORITY IN THE CLASSROOM

This book argues that democratic classroom management is not a stand-alone issue but is deeply intertwined with classroom climate and requires a thoughtful, grounded understanding of classroom authority. Contributors explore the sources, nature, and extent of teacher authority, as they distinguish authority from authoritarianism, and describe how classroom authority is ultimately a shared endeavor between teachers and students. By drawing on a variety of contexts and perspectives, chapters in this volume contend with the complexities inherent in classroom authority through the lenses of gender, urban versus rural contexts, and within elementary and secondary classrooms.

Ken Badley, PhD, lives in Edmonton, Alberta, and teaches foundations of education at Tyndale University in Toronto, Ontario. He has taught in secondary, undergraduate, graduate, and doctoral programs in Canada and the United States and has worked extensively with teachers in Kenya. He is the author of many books and articles related to curriculum, instruction, and the teaching vocation.

Margaretta Patrick, PhD, taught high school for 12 years before getting her PhD and then joining the Faculty of Education at The King's University (Edmonton, Alberta). At the time of writing, she is in her 13th year of teaching at King's. While Margaretta's research focuses on how secondary social studies teachers in public schools teach about religion, teaching a course on classroom management for the past 10 years has generated its own research questions.

THE COMPLEXITIES OF AUTHORITY IN THE CLASSROOM

Fostering Democracy for Student Learning

Edited by
Ken Badley
Margaretta Patrick
Illustrations by Kristen Badley

NEW YORK AND LONDON

Cover image: Kristen Badley

First published 2022
by Routledge
605 Third Avenue, New York, NY 10158

and by Routledge
4 Park Square, Milton Park, Abingdon, Oxon, OX14 4RN

Routledge is an imprint of the Taylor & Francis Group, an informa business

© 2022 selection and editorial matter, Ken Badley and Margaretta Patrick; individual chapters, the contributors

The right of Ken Badley and Margaretta Patrick to be identified as the authors of the editorial material, and of the authors for their individual chapters, has been asserted in accordance with sections 77 and 78 of the Copyright, Designs and Patents Act 1988.

All rights reserved. No part of this book may be reprinted or reproduced or utilised in any form or by any electronic, mechanical, or other means, now known or hereafter invented, including photocopying and recording, or in any information storage or retrieval system, without permission in writing from the publishers.

Trademark notice: Product or corporate names may be trademarks or registered trademarks, and are used only for identification and explanation without intent to infringe.

Library of Congress Cataloging-in-Publication Data
Names: Badley, Kenneth Rea, 1951– editor. | Patrick, Margaretta, editor.
Title: The complexities of authority in the classroom : fostering democracy for student learning / [edited by] Ken Badley, Margaretta Patrick ; illustrations by Kristen Bradley.
Description: New York, NY : Routledge, 2022. | Includes bibliographical references and index.
Identifiers: LCCN 2021053592 (print) | LCCN 2021053593 (ebook) | ISBN 9780367691998 (hardback) | ISBN 9780367691981 (paperback) | ISBN 9781003140849 (ebook)
Subjects: LCSH: Classroom management. | Classroom environment. | Teacher-student relationships.
Classification: LCC LB3013 .C5597 2022 (print) | LCC LB3013 (ebook) | DDC 371.102/4—dc23/eng/20211109
LC record available at https://lccn.loc.gov/2021053592
LC ebook record available at https://lccn.loc.gov/2021053593

ISBN: 978-0-367-69199-8 (hbk)
ISBN: 978-0-367-69198-1 (pbk)
ISBN: 978-1-003-14084-9 (ebk)

DOI: 10.4324/9781003140849

Typeset in Bembo
by Apex CoVantage, LLC

We dedicate this book to all the In-Service Teachers who work every day to share authority with their students and to all the Pre-Service Teachers who plan to do so.

CONTENTS

Preface   xii
Acknowledgments   xiv
List of Contributors   xvii

1 Introduction   1
   Margaretta Patrick and Ken Badley

2 Classroom Management: A Dialogue With Larger Social
   Questions   17
   Margaretta Patrick

PART 1
Gaining Classroom Authority Introduction   33

3 Authorizing Yourself to Teach   35
   Ken Badley and Michelle C. Hughes

4 Good to Go: Teaching by Our Students' Consent   44
   Ken Badley

5 Being All There: Teacher Presence and Teacher Authority   55
   Ken Badley

6 The Importance and Impact of Listening Well   71
Emily Robinson and Shae Nimmo

7 Invitational Theory: A Theoretical Foundation for
Establishing a Positive Classroom Ethos   82
Sean Schat

8 School of Rock   92
Mason Steinke

9 Case Study: A Turn-Around in a High-Needs Classroom   95
Nadine Ayer

PART 2
Authorizing Students   105

10 A Sense of Place and Student Consent   107
Jacqueline Filipek

11 Authorizing Students Through Inquiry and Assessment   118
Reanna Jordan and Ken Badley

12 Authorizing Students Through Relationships   126
Iriel Jaroslavsky Rindlisbacher

13 On Authority and Dignity   132
Paige Ray

14 Situating Classroom Management in English Language
Arts, Math, and Social Studies   141
Jacqueline Filipek, Margaretta Patrick, and Wendy Stienstra

PART 3
Teacher Authority and Diversity   155

15 Teacher Authority and Culturally Responsive Teaching   157
Margaretta Patrick

16 Male Authority: Assumption Busting   175
Genie Kim

17 Look Who's Talking: Gender, Teacher Authority, and
the Use of Linguistic Space   187
Allyson Jule

18 Interrogating the Relationship Between a Teacher's Race
and Classroom Authority   201
Malini Sivasubramaniam

PART 4
Narratives From the Field and Special Situations   **209**

19 The Student Teacher's Relationships: Mentor Teachers
and Students   211
Rebecca Clarke, Tiffany Chung, and Maegahn Smith

20 Reflections of a Beginning Teacher: Who Am
I Going to Be?   222
Ashley Ryl

21 Establishing Yourself as a Teacher in a Foreign Setting   228
Nicola Campbell

22 Succeeding as a Substitute Teacher   234
Bina Ali and Douglas Laing

23 Creating Positive Classroom Climate in Remote Settings   238
Kristen Tjostheim

24 The Challenges and Rewards of Teaching in Remote
Settings   248
Dena Palmaymesa and Natasha Steenhof Bakker

25 Reflections of a Veteran Secondary Teacher   259
Ron McIntyre

Conclusion   267
Margaretta Patrick and Ken Badley

Index   273

PREFACE

Our first encounter was when Margaretta (Margie) read one of Ken's early writings on teacher authority. A few years later, we met at a working conference where we discovered our mutual interest in helping teachers understand classroom authority. At some point about 2018, this mutual interest grew into discussions of writing a book proposal. We began to envision an edited book that would include voices from many kinds of classrooms, from veteran teachers, from induction teachers, and from teacher educators.

As the conversation evolved, the question of the book's audience inevitably rose to the surface. Who most needs a book like this? The answer came easily: education students who need to understand what many veteran teachers have learned about the complexities of classroom authority. Both of us teach in education programs, and thus we know some of the questions education students have about what has traditionally been called classroom management. This book is meant to answer not only some of those questions but also the larger human questions that are present in every classroom and in the heart of every teacher: how do we communicate with each other, how do we live together well, and how do we care for each other in classroom spaces? The book also addresses some misperceptions about teacher authority, especially that it is not about power. In fact, teacher authority is undermined when implemented through power. Instead, it is about attitudes and dispositions and gaining student consent.

Both of us have extensive experience in K-12 classrooms, as do the contributors to this volume. They know the complexities of classroom authority. In different ways, all of them reflect on teacher authority, sometimes by engaging in the literature and often through the stories of their own practice. The combination of theory and practice here will be valuable to In-Service and Pre-Service Teachers alike because all teachers make decisions regarding the classroom ethos or climate they wish to establish in their classrooms, consider how they are going to gain classroom authority, determine the degree to which they are going to authorize their students, and explore the ways in which they will respond to and interact with the diversity of their classrooms and communities. Additionally, some may move to new settings or contexts, and they will undoubtedly learn from the authors in this book who recount their experiences of teaching in new and sometimes challenging settings. Readers will detect a consistent theme in the words of our contributors; in every situation in which they have found themselves they have learned, and they have taken with them new insights about who they are as teachers, about teacher authority, and about how authorizing students can happen in any context.

There is something in this book for every teacher. Classrooms are dynamic and vibrant places, and teachers both shape those places and are shaped by them. Within such dynamic and formative places, there are no prescriptions for becoming a successful teacher, for gaining teacher authority, or for authorizing students. There are no cookie-cutter approaches. Instead, we invite you to read the essays and stories offered by teachers. Sit with them for a while, and if you encounter an idea, practice, or disposition with which you resonate, feel free to adapt it into your own teaching practice. It is our fervent hope that all teachers, but especially those beginning their teaching journey, will benefit from the wisdom offered by the authors in this text.

Margaretta Patrick
Edmonton, Alberta
Ken Badley
Calgary, Alberta
October 2021

ACKNOWLEDGMENTS

We begin by acknowledging the many colleagues who have contributed chapters to this volume. We were thrilled to receive their "yes" answers when we asked about their interest in being part of this project. All our contributors are busy educators who serve in a wide variety of contexts in two countries, Canada and the United States. Some became new parents during the writing of this book. Others changed cities. Some changed jobs or took on new responsibilities in the schools and universities where they work. All dealt with the COVID-19 pandemic during the months of writing.

Our contributors responded with grace to our many editorial requests and suggestions. They helped us think more deeply about our perspectives on teaching and classroom authority.

Because this book would never have come to fruition without these colleagues, it is with deep gratitude that we acknowledge their work.

Together, we are grateful as well for the encouragement and guidance of Matthew Friberg at Routledge and Jessica Cooke at Taylor & Francis. As we said about our contributors, this book would not have come into being without them. We also acknowledge the work of the editors, typesetters, and designers at Routledge who worked behind the scenes to bring our work to fruition.

Margie Patrick

I still remember my first day and first year of teaching, 25 years ago. Even though I poured my heart and soul into my preparations and stayed up late every night getting everything ready for the next day, I wasn't a particularly good teacher. Did my students learn some content? I think so, but I didn't really connect with them. I was too focused on content and too uptight about making a mistake to connect on a personal level. I never welcomed a summer break as much as I did at the end of that first year.

The following fall I returned, not sure how my year would go. Unexpectedly, I was blessed with a wonderful group of students who oozed character, who engaged with their teachers, and who had fun together. I can still picture most of their names and faces in my mind. That group of students gave me the gift of joy, the joy of teaching, the joy of delighting in the hilarity of 17-year-olds, and the joy of discussing together the tough stuff of life. While I didn't have the language at the time to describe what was happening, those students consented to have me teach them. Their consent provided me with the confidence to believe that I belonged in the classroom, that I was a teacher, and that I could engage with high school students. I authorized myself, which I could not, or did not, do in my first year. Year 2 was a completely different experience than year 1.

Years later, when I was a newly minted PhD starting my first university position, I read an article by Ken on teacher authority, student consent, and teachers authorizing their students. His words resonated with me; they gave me the framework to explain my teaching experiences. I used that early article in my classroom management course to reassure Pre-Service Teachers that they didn't have to be the Lone Ranger in their future classrooms. I assured them that if they took the time to dignify and care for their students and even authorize their students to be classroom leaders and to be the experts on the topics they loved, they did not have to fear classroom management.

Several years later, when Ken suggested writing a book to expand on his earlier ideas, I jumped at the opportunity. Throughout this project, I have been in awe of Ken's editorial and writing gifts, the way in which he can create magic with words. On more than one occasion over the past year, I have said, "I am sending this to you so you can work your magic." I have learned a lot from Ken and count him esteemed among my friends.

I have especially enjoyed reading the chapters by the contributing authors. At times I was moved to tears as I read their stories. Sometimes I had to stop reading and ponder an insight. At other times I nodded my head as I read, able to relate to a particular event or way of thinking. All the authors have my immense gratitude for sharing their wisdom, for being vulnerable, and for being great teachers.

As noted, this book came together during a pandemic year. Time was in short supply for our authors as well as for Ken and me. If it wasn't for my husband Mike, I am not sure we would have eaten during these last few months, as the book demanded an increasing amount of time. I am grateful for his willingness to pick up all the pieces on the home front, for his encouragement, and his reminders that everyone needs sleep. Mike, I couldn't have done this without you.

Ken Badley

As always, I am grateful to the members of Team Ken who encouraged me to keep going on this project. You know who you are. I am grateful as well to

Kristen Badley, who produced the powerful cover and the internal graphics for this book. I daily have gratitude for my wife, K. Jo-Ann Badley, whose influence runs through all my thinking about education and whose insights appear uncredited in this volume. Without her encouragement, I might be sitting in a coffee shop every morning pretending to solve world problems but actually just complaining about the government.

I acknowledge the role of my BEd students at both Tyndale University in Toronto and Mount Royal University in Calgary who, over the last several years, have inspired me to keep looking for new ways to share authority with them. Together, we have journeyed to discover what Parker Palmer calls the heart of teaching. Part of that journey has involved laughing with them at my pedagogical flops and then carrying on. But another part has been that they have taken the openings I have offered and produced academic papers, songs, spoken word performances, social initiatives, a book about flourishing during practicum, board games adapted to curriculum units, videos, and websites of resources for teachers. I shared classroom authority with them, and they shared their abundant talents with their classmates and with me. To complete their course requirements, they have done real work for a real audience in the real world. We are all richer for what they have brought. We have truly feasted together, both literally and metaphorically. For that, I will always remain grateful. Regardless of how much we enjoyed our shared work on campus, they have inevitably graduated and gone on to realize the dreams they had when they came to campus in the first place. They have continued to give me joy as I have watched them develop as competent and visionary professional educators who want to authorize their students.

Finally, I acknowledge the brilliance, patience, hard work, great writing, and organizational skills that my colleague Margie Patrick, of The King's University in Edmonton, has brought to this project. I first presented on classroom authority at a conference in Chicago in 1995. Because of her, 26 years later, this project is now done, not finished, but done.

CONTRIBUTORS

Bina Ali graduated with a Bachelor of Arts degree in sociology from Simon Fraser University in Burnaby, British Columbia, in 2012 and completed her BEd in elementary education at Tyndale University in Toronto in 2015. She currently teaches grade 1/2 in Ontario and has experience teaching in person and online.

Nadine Ayer completed a Bachelor of Fine Arts degree focused in the dramatic arts and Bachelor of Education at the University of Lethbridge in 2012. Since graduating, she has taught in Calgary, primarily in an elementary setting but has taught grades 1–9. Nadine has focused on arts-centered learning, mainly through visual arts integration into curriculum. Nadine is passionate about building strong student relationships and resilient communities of learners who feel free to express themselves as individuals.

Natasha Steenhof Bakker lives in Terrace, British Columbia, and completed her teaching degree at The King's University in Edmonton. Although she is a trained high school teacher who taught grades 8–12 in her first years, Natasha is currently an elementary homeroom teacher. She has taught in both public and independent schools in a variety of urban centers and rural areas.

Nicola Campbell began her teaching career abroad after completing her Bachelor of Education at Mount Royal University in 2018. After her first year of teaching, Nicola returned to Calgary, Alberta, and taught in multiple K-6 classrooms before moving to a grade 3 generalist position at a local independent school. Now in her fourth year of teaching, Nicola is enjoying fostering student leaders in her school, and she continues to explore ways through which her students can be active citizens in their community and take their learning beyond the classroom.

Tiffany Chung began her journey as an educator when she homeschooled her eldest son and daughter. She went on to become a presenter with Scientists in School. Shortly after finishing the Bachelor of Education program at Tyndale University, she began teaching at Peoples Christian Academy in Markham, Ontario. She currently teaches middle school Mathematics, Science, and Technology and has experience teaching in face-to-face, online, and hybrid learning environments.

Rebecca Clarke attended Mount Royal University and obtained her teaching degree with the graduating class of 2020. Since then, she has moved to Seattle, Washington, where she serves as a teacher in elementary education. Her greatest passions in teaching are celebrating diversity and building a strong classroom community where her students know that their voices are valued and that each of them plays an important role within their community. She believes that learning can happen only when strong relationships are formed, both between student to student and teacher to student.

Angela Farrington-Thompson began her journey toward teaching by becoming a volunteer in the grade 8 classroom at the elementary school her six children attended. The adventure led to her first college diploma in writing and publishing, a certificate in teaching effectiveness, a degree in history and global studies, and finally, to the Bachelor of Education program at Tyndale University. Balancing family and studies, she went from volunteer to lunchroom supervisor, to educational assistant, and finally to a teacher specializing in history and language. In the fall of 2021, she began a new journey as a grade 4 teacher at Westminster Classical Christian Academy. She sees teaching as not only a gift and a privilege, but also a calling—the call to serve her students, be refined by them, and to be taught *by* them.

Jacqueline Filipek, PhD, is Assistant Professor at The King's University in Edmonton, Alberta. She teaches courses in literacy, language arts curriculum, and technologies in education. Her research interests include digital and transliteracies in elementary contexts as well as how place contributes to learning. She received her PhD in language and literacy from the University of Alberta.

Michelle C. Hughes, EdD, is a veteran educator who has taught junior high school English and served as a high school administrator. Since 2009, Michelle has embraced sharing her passion for the teaching profession and K-12 education with Westmont College students and the larger educational community. She is Associate Professor of Education at Westmont College in Santa Barbara,

California, as well as Chair of the Education Department. She embraces the challenge of equipping students to serve in public and independent schools. Michelle is also the co-editor of *Joyful Resilience as Educational Practice: Turning Challenges Into Opportunities* (Routledge, 2022) with Ken Badley.

Reanna Jordan graduated with a Bachelor of Education degree from Mount Royal University in 2018. She has worked as a teacher in the St. Thomas Aquinas Roman Catholic School division near Edmonton, Alberta, for four years. During this time, she has taught grade 4, grade 1, and grade 1 online during the COVID-19 pandemic. At the time of writing, Reanna is teaching grade 2.

Allyson Jule, PhD, is Professor of Education and Dean of the School of Education at University of the Fraser Valley in, Abbotsford, BC, Canada. She is also Associate of the University of Oxford's International Gender Studies Centre (Lady Margaret Hall). Jule was awarded Canada's 3M Teaching Fellowship for 2016, a prestigious fellowship honoring excellence in teaching in higher education. She has written widely on the topic of language use alongside gender and has particular research interests in the area of gender, language, and silence in the classroom and workplace as well as gender and language alongside religious identity. She currently chairs the Association of British Columbia Deans of Education.

Genie Kim, PhD, has extensive teaching experience, working with both high school and elementary students. Her time as a teacher was predominantly spent in inner-city schools, where she experienced immense joy working with marginalized and disadvantaged students. She is currently teaching aspiring educators at Tyndale University's Bachelor of Education program in Toronto. Her doctoral dissertation focused on effective mathematics pedagogy. Genie's greatest passions are in the areas of social justice, leadership, effective teacher praxes, mentorship, and classroom management. She aims to empower future teachers to become transformational agents of change within education.

Douglas Laing has been teaching in Airdrie, Alberta, since graduating from the Mount Royal University Bachelor of Education program in 2018. He currently works for the Rocky View School Division in a substitute teaching role. Substitute teaching has granted Doug many opportunities to experience different classroom management and instructional styles, as well as chances to meet different teachers, administrators, and, most importantly, students with diverse learning needs. Although working primarily in elementary schools, he has experience at each grade level and is looking forward to the continuous learning that is uniquely available to a Substitute Teacher, as no two days are the same.

Ron McIntyre was a teacher for over 30 years in Edmonton Public Schools. During that time, he coached rugby and football at the secondary and university levels as well as served as Department Head of Social Studies and Department Head of Student Leadership. His most gratifying moments in education were in building teams on the playing field, in the classroom, and in the various social studies departments he was a part of. In his retirement, Ron has served as a consultant with teams in the Western Hockey League, Canadian University Sport, and the Delta Hockey Academy.

Shae Nimmo graduated in 2018 from the Bachelor of Education program at Mount Royal University in Calgary, Alberta. Shae acted professionally before entering teaching and has studied with acting coach Stanford Meisner, whose method helps workshop participants focus on listening as a way of being present. Shae now teaches elementary school with the Calgary Board of Education.

Dena Palmaymesa, EdD, has taught in her rural Oregon, K-8 setting for well over a decade. In her 25-year career, she has taught multi-grade settings in rural Appalachia and in a girls' detention center in Knoxville, TN. She has led single-grade classes in both independent and public elementary schools, as well as spent a season leading Pre-Service Teachers at Oregon State University. While in her current rural setting, she completed her Doctorate of Education degree through George Fox University.

Paige A. Ray currently serves as Associate Professor of English at College of the Ozarks, where she teaches in the Composition Sequence and instructs Pre-Service Teachers in secondary English education. Before coming to the College of the Ozarks, Paige taught for several years at the secondary level. She sees her combined experience in both high school and undergraduate classrooms as essential to the preparation of teacher candidates.

Iriel Jaroslavsky Rindlisbacher lives in Chestermere, Alberta. She has been teaching in Calgary since receiving her BEd from St. Mary's University in 2016. She has taught grades 4 and 5 in a Spanish Bilingual program with Calgary Catholic School District. At the time of writing, she is working as a Diverse Learning Coordinating Teacher, where she enjoys building relationships with students and fostering teacher capacity through collaboration. In the summer of 2021, Iriel began working on her Master of Education degree at the University of Calgary.

Emily Robinson, DNP, has worked as a nurse for 17 years. She worked in hospitals, schools, and overseas at a U.S. embassy as a Bachelor's prepared nurse before returning to school at the University of Washington in 2012 to complete her practice doctorate. After graduating with her doctorate in 2015, she began working as a Primary Care Nurse Practitioner, which she continues to do today. She is passionate about providing Gender Affirming Care for transgender and non-binary people and is returning to school to pursue additional certification as a psychiatric/mental health nurse practitioner.

Ashley Ryl is a recent graduate of The King's University Bachelor of Education program. She completed a Bachelor of Arts degree in English at the same university. After graduation, Ashley obtained a position in a rural, northern Alberta community. She hopes to have a long career in education and strives for professional growth.

Sean Schat, PhD, is an assistant professor in the School of Education at Redeemer University in Ancaster, Ontario. Prior to his work at Redeemer, he taught at the elementary, secondary, undergraduate, and graduate levels in Ontario and also served as an educational leader (Director of Program, Director of Staff Development, Vice Principal, and Principal). Sean's research interests focus on interpersonal relationships in education. His dissertation research study explored the offering and successful communication of educational care.

Malini Sivasubramaniam, PhD, studied at the University of Toronto, Canada, with a specialization in Comparative, International, and Development Education. Her dissertation examined household decision-making in low-fee private schools in Kenya. For seven years, she taught a course on Diversity and Equity issues in Education to teacher candidates at Tyndale University, Canada, and has co-taught and supervised teacher candidates at the Ontario Institute for Studies in Education (OISE). Malini has published various reports and articles on equity issues in education and has co-edited a book on *Religion and Education: Comparative and International Perspectives*. She is currently an independent research consultant. Her research interests include diversity, social justice and equity issues in education, school choice and equity for marginalized communities, and non-state, philanthropic, and faith-based actors in education.

Maegahn Smith completed her teaching degree at Mount Royal University in Calgary. She has experience teaching in K-12 classrooms, both in person and online. She is currently teaching high school music in Cochrane, AB, fulfilling a lifelong dream of getting to hold the conductor's baton. Her primary focus over the last few years has been on developing applicable strategies for forming student–teacher relationships that teachers can easily implement in any classroom setting and sharing them with other teachers whenever possible.

Mason Steinke began teaching in Calgary, Alberta, since he received his BEd degree from Mount Royal University in 2018. He has taught in a wide range of positions, including grades 5–9 Health and Physical Education, a grade 5 generalist, and, currently, as a K-6 Music teacher. He has been with the Calgary Board of Education for the duration of his professional career. Mason has committed to memory "The Man" monologue from the movie, *The School of Rock*.

Wendy Stienstra, PhD, has taught at The King's University for the past 14 years. Her area of expertise and research is mathematics education. While she began her more than 30 years career as a high school mathematics teacher, her experience also includes teaching in upper elementary and junior high settings. She has worked with Pre-Service Teachers in a variety of settings for over 20 years. These range from courses in mathematics content and methods, and curriculum planning, to facilitation of student teaching practice.

Kristen Tjostheim started her career by teaching for seven years in a remote Alberta K-12 school. During that time, she taught a variety of subjects in multi-grade classrooms and classrooms where students participated via video conferencing. She further served her school community as an assistant principal for five years, during which time she collaborated with other school leaders and teachers to implement classroom strategies for student success.

1
INTRODUCTION

Margaretta Patrick and Ken Badley

We begin this book and this chapter not with a definition but with an important question. Why should students follow their teacher's lead or do what their teacher asks or tells them to do? We call this question important because successful schools and classrooms depend on students' recognition of their teachers' authority. Teachers without legitimate authority end up with chaotic classrooms or classrooms full of sullen and resistant students. In such classrooms, if learning does take place, it may be along negative and cynical lines. Students may say, "I've learned that I hate school," or "I've learned that my teacher doesn't care about me," or "I've learned that my teacher is stupid." On the other hand, classrooms where rich learning happens and students flourish are led by teachers who have and who share what, throughout this book, we call *classroom authority*. We will nuance that phrase throughout the book but, for now, please accept our assertion that the classrooms most teachers and students want to work in have this feature: the teachers in those classrooms have earned the right to teach, in part by sharing the authority others have entrusted to them. In short, educators need to understand classroom authority.

Among the wide variety of kinds of authority, what comes to mind when teachers or students think about authority? Sociologists and political scientists have identified traditional authority, a kind of deference because of age or long experience (a grandparent), and legal authority where through appointment or election someone has been assigned oversight (a president). Add moral authority where someone has gained the goodwill of others (Oprah), raw power (an earthmoving machine), the authority of expertise (your mechanic or doctor), and contractual authority (the teacher hired by a school board). This partial list of types of authority may help explain why classroom authority warrants

DOI: 10.4324/9781003140849-1

examination. What kind or what combination of kinds of authority do classroom teachers have or need?

Almost everyone intuitively grasps the importance of teachers' authority, but many people miss its complexity. Even the way we worded the question in the first paragraph reveals some of that complexity: *why should students follow their teacher's lead or do what their teacher asks or tells them to do?* The first part of the question clearly asks about what most observers call *authority*, while the second connects more with what many call *power*. The differences between the words *asks* and *tells* in the second part of the question denote different degrees of power. What do classroom teachers need: authority, or power, or both? If they need authority—and all the contributors to this book believe they do—what kind of authority do they need and how do they earn it? In short, classroom authority is complex.

Four Misunderstandings About Classroom Authority

Both beginning and veteran teachers can misunderstand classroom authority or misidentify its sources. For example, some confuse or conflate the two concepts we just distinguished: authority and power. They think that the teacher's request or wish will become the students' command. Recognizably, to a degree, most teachers can coerce most students to complete certain assignments and to behave in specified ways. Centuries ago, in *Leviathan* (1651 [2017]), Thomas Hobbes labeled this kind of coercive power as *command*, where a person can expect obedience without having to supply reasons. Hobbes distinguished the power to command from what he called *counsel*, where leaders must supply reasons why those whom they serve should follow their leadership. Teachers who mistake their authority for power will not see students engage in learning the way they do with teachers who recognize the need for what Hobbes called counsel. Educator Kenneth Benne (1943) observed nearly a century ago that understanding authority as power not only does not help but actually undermines the teacher's genuine authority. He wrote as follows:

> The stupidity that often inheres in the use of coercive sanctions, by established bearers of authority, in and out of the schoolroom, is not that their use establishes and preserves authority. It is rather that they prevent the establishment of an organic moral order adequate and congenial to the stabilization and guidance of the social process underway—an order morally accepted in some measure as rightful by all participants in the process. In other words, they are to be condemned as defeating rather than serving the development of an adequate authority.
>
> (p. 149)

Benne has gone beyond the distinction we called for in the previous paragraph. Note his use of the phrase *organic moral order*. In his view and that of other observers

(Metz, 1978), power actively sabotages the organic moral order required for learning. On these accounts, power is inimical to legitimate authority.

A second misunderstanding, one that beginning teachers make more frequently than veteran teachers, is to try to become friends with students. Teachers who follow this path think that chumminess will lead students to like them and then willingly join them in the learning journey they have planned. In fact, this mistake has in it a seed of logic: the teacher's instructional program can only benefit if students *are on the teacher's side*, so to speak, a conclusion in accord with the views of all the contributors to this book. Still, we label this a confusion because, as generations of teachers have learned, students want to learn in a classroom led by a professional not by a "big friend or cheer leader" (Bantock, 1966, p. 22).

Another misunderstanding relates to what for many decades was called *classroom management*. Some mistakenly believe that the teacher's authority relates only to classroom management and to the appropriate responses to specific misbehaviors and discrete discipline problems. On this account, classroom management becomes a stand-alone question, one focused more on control of the learning environment and less on learning itself. This misunderstanding is grounded in at least two errors. First, the goal of understanding our authority as teachers is not primarily to address aberrant behavior (even if we must do so periodically) but is to create an ethos in which students succeed in learning. We are mistaken if we think that our authority relates only to controlling behaviors. Second, the teacher's authority has more to do with the teaching–learning relationship than it does with classroom management. As Patrick traces in Chapter 2, the classroom management conversation has shifted dramatically in the last century and even in the last few decades and now reflects much more the need to create a classroom climate that encourages cooperation and learning. Although having that climate in place does not mean that some students at some points will not have bad days or bad moments, we still distinguish classroom climate from classroom management. Our use of the term *classroom climate* expands the notion of classroom management beyond relationships and coaching for pro-social behavior, as important as they are, to include instructional planning, mastering and employing a wide repertoire of instructional methods appropriate to contents and students' ages and abilities, promoting and assessing student learning, developing record-keeping and paper-flow systems, interacting with students in a friendly yet professional way throughout each workday, and so on. In other words, classroom climate has to do with our whole program; it goes far beyond simply maintaining order or dealing with misbehaviors and episodes.

Fourth, and finally, some mistake the three basic necessary conditions—expertise, teaching certificate, and employment contract—for sufficient conditions to run a classroom program. Obviously, teachers do gain some authority when they meet these three basic conditions; in fact, thousands of beginning teachers go to their first jobs every school year possessing only those three things. At that time, beginning teachers have less expertise than they will have five years later; regarding pedagogical expertise, they will likely enter the profession at the level of *competent beginner*. Both beginning and veteran teachers also gain some room to move from traditional assumptions about classroom roles. But teachers—beginning teachers especially—can make the mistake of relying too heavily on traditional expectations and assumptions about the teacher's right to control the electronics in the room, or to determine seating plans, to stand or sit when and where they see fit, and to carry out a hundred other ordinary classroom functions.

These confusions are not the only mistakes educators make related to authority, but they point to the truth that both experienced and beginning teachers need a more nuanced understanding of classroom authority. We share with all the contributors to this book the view that teachers can understand their own authority in ways that will help them sustain an inviting classroom program from year to year if they can avoid the confusions we have touched on here and understand the varieties of soil from which legitimate classroom authority grows.

To conclude this section, we have identified two things that classroom authority is not. It is not the power to make students do whatever we want. Granted, some learning may occur in authoritarian classrooms where most students grant their teachers only a kind of grudging compliance, but that learning will be characterized only rarely by either joy or flow (Csikszentmihalyi, 1982, 1990, 2002; Steeg-Thornhill & Badley, 2021). Second, teacher authority or classroom authority is not classroom management. In our most utopian picture of a classroom, the learning ethos is so positive and powerful that the teacher never needs to make a classroom management intervention. We know that few such classrooms exist in the real world. Nevertheless, we have argued here that the classroom ethos encompasses something much larger and more substantial than classroom management and that in classrooms grounded on the kind of consent we describe here, students desire to learn and they engage more fully in their teacher's program.

Structure of the Book

Ken Badley starts this chapter with a question: why should students follow their teacher's lead or do what their teacher asks or tells them to do? His responses to teacher authority and student consent are the themes of this book. All the authors unpack in some fashion the nature of those two terms and what they look like in a classroom. They start by understanding teacher authority holistically, as establishing a classroom ethos in which student learning and flourishing occur. They agree that teacher authority goes beyond the formal qualifications, such as a degree and a contract, which, to use Ken's later words, only bring the teacher to the classroom but do not ensure that they are successful in it. Success happens when teachers authorize themselves to teach and students consent to learn with the teacher and within the learning community established in the classroom.

Students cannot be coerced into learning, and teachers cannot use power to force students to learn. Instead, a relationship is cultivated in which both teachers and students authorize each other and learn from each other. How this occurs is highly complex, thus requiring a book to tease out its multifaceted angles and surfaces. Some authors will examine the research while others pose a theory. Still others tell stories; in fact, many tell stories, their stories from the classroom as they learned how to authorize themselves and their students, even those challenging students. The stories are from the heart, and they are sometimes heartrending in their honesty, but they always open the heart to new ways of caring for every student in one's class.

Badley insists that teacher authority is related to classroom management but cannot be reduced to classroom management. The connection is apparent in many chapters, as authors discuss their challenges, experiences, and successes with teacher authority within the context of classroom management. Thus, the second chapter of the introduction provides an overview of the field of classroom management.

It is Margaretta Patrick's contention that the development of the field over time is three Rindlisbacher dimensional. On one surface, we find the story of a movement away from corporal punishment toward a recognition that students need to learn social-emotional skills and practices, as well as academic content and skills. On another surface are the underlying principles, the social ideas, and visions that undergird the various approaches to classroom management, implying that classroom management is never merely a set of tools or strategies. Rather, all classroom management approaches contain specific views of students, highlighting their capacity for doing good, their ability to commit harm, or perhaps a combination of both. They also advance specific purposes of education, such as the development of democratic citizenship or the creation of consumers for a society deeply influenced by neoliberal economics. On the third surface are the critical theorists who raise questions about the power and coercion they see involved in managing students. They question the degree to which rules and expectations of behavior are White, middle-class values being enforced through power.

The rest of the chapters are organized into four themes. Part 1 begins with the teacher and how teachers authorize themselves to teach. Classrooms are complicated micro-communities and unpacking the nature of teacher authority within them takes intentional effort. Authors in this section probe the need for teacher authority, how we define teacher authority, and how teacher authority can be learned. They explore the need for teachers to authorize themselves, to believe that they belong in the classroom, and then enter the classroom community as one who forms and is formed by it, as one who self-authorizes and is authorized by students. Teachers are present to their students and in the process learn about student needs and how they can meet those needs. Contrary to popular culture, where leaders are consistently portrayed as individuals with single-minded intentions to right the ship, to re-set the course, teacher leaders who self-authorize and seek the consent of their students share their authority.

As easy as these words are to write and read, they are difficult to enact. The dispositions and attitudes needed to create democratic and trusting communities of learning are forged in fire, in the failures, disappointments, and general tough stuff of what can happen in a classroom. In the early years of teaching, some, perhaps many teachers employ the mantra "fake it till you make it." At times they are sleep deprived and are only one step ahead of their students. They sometimes forget that students do not know that their teachers are barely holding on and feeling out of their depth, nor do students need to know. But no matter how physically tired beginning teachers might be and how tired they are from the effort of faking it, they need to show up every day, even if the previous day was difficult. They need to develop understandings of teacher authority which come only with practice. But there is always hope because the story in the final chapter of this section describes a turnaround that occurred when a teacher shifted their attitude toward some students and the class in general. Change is possible. In fact, the overarching theme of this book is that change is always possible, which teachers and students are always able to put a better foot forward tomorrow.

While Part 1 focuses on the teacher component of the classroom relationship, Part 2 examines the student element of the relationship. Students are not passive actors in a classroom; rather, they consciously or unconsciously authorize or deauthorize their teachers to teach. To employ an over-used term, the relationship is iterative. Teachers and students respond to each other's initiatives, attitudes, words, gestures, and authorizing. If students believe that they have a place in the classroom, if the space has meaning because of what happens in it, if students are given real choice and control over some aspects of their education, and if students have dignity, they are more likely to authorize their teacher, to acknowledge their teacher's right and ability to teach and their own ability to participate in and even direct their own learning. This section suggests important and authentic ways in which teachers can authorize students, from pedagogical and assessment strategies to treating students with dignity, to planning for differentiation and grouping. As teachers authorize students, classroom space becomes a place of significance and rich learning.

When teachers authorize their students to be active participants in their learning and when students have some power and control over what happens to them in the classroom, they flourish. As psychiatrist and educator Rudolf Dreikurs (1974) insisted, authorizing students in this way does not imply chaos, a lack of structure, or a lack of consequences for student choices. But neither does it mean that students sit quietly in rows, all doing the same thing. Equally important, authors in this section insist that shared authority with students does not diminish teacher authority. Rather, it expands the space for teaching and learning.

Space and place are important for all students, but especially so for students and teachers in diverse classrooms, the topic for Part 3. The research literature for most western countries shows that while classrooms have increasingly diverse student populations, the teaching profession remains largely White, resulting in what some have termed a cultural mismatch between the teacher and their students. Research on the type of teachers who teach well in multicultural contexts began in earnest in the early 1970s and continues to develop to this day. Nevertheless, significant inequities continue in school systems, which perpetuate the privileging of White, western European cultural and social values. The resulting discrimination can be obvious or subtle, and many teachers are not aware of the discrimination that exists in their assumptions of what is "good" and "bad" behavior, of how teaching materials depict and essentialize groups of people, usually in a negative manner, and how their language codes disempower some students.

Racial and cultural differences are not the only issue of diversity investigated in Part 3. Gender issues abound throughout educational institutions, including assumptions that teacher authority is linked to gender, i.e., male teachers are perceived as more able to command authority and gender speech patterns in classrooms. The scenarios discussed in these chapters reveal the serious problems that arise in classrooms and for students when the conceptions (see Badley's Chapter 5) of teacher authority and student consent are either not acknowledged or not taken seriously.

Democratic and shared conceptions of teacher authority are taken seriously by the authors in Part 4. These authors are all teachers who discuss teacher authority from their unique places and special situations. By telling their own stories, they highlight what teacher authority looks like throughout a teacher's career, from the days in practicum placements to reflections from a perspective of retirement.

When Pre-Service Teachers (PSTs) enter a Mentor Teachers' (MTs) classroom, they share authority with the MT. The space has been created and imbued with meaning by someone else. PSTs enter as a learner and a mentee. In most cases, they will continue the expectations and routines that in part shape the meaning of the space, but they inevitably introduce their own dispositions and practices, further developing that meaning. These beginning teachers do what every teacher must do: find ways to authorize themselves and to gain the consent of their students.

When teachers begin their first position, or change schools, they enter the school space as a place with established norms and understandings and then set about injecting their own meaning into their specific classroom space and eventually the larger school. For those moving from an urban to a rural location, or to a remote context, or to another country to teach, the challenges of creating place are even larger. Clearly, teachers never stop learning and good teachers do not wish to stop learning.

Chapter Synopsis

Part 1: Gaining Classroom Authority

This section of the book explores the nature of teacher authorization and emphasizes the importance of teachers authorizing themselves to teach. In Chapter 3, Ken Badley and Michelle C. Hughes focus on how teachers authorize themselves in the day-to-day activities in the classroom. In essence, teachers must show up and teach. If this sounds easy, it isn't. To show up and teach, teachers need to rely on their internal resources, develop resiliency, get out of bed every morning, and return to the classroom. There is nothing easy about returning after a bad day or facing a difficult day, but a significant component of self-authorization is courage, of digging deep and finding, in the words of the authors, "the inner strength to power through, to keep going, to persevere." Teachers around the world demonstrated courage when they pivoted to online teaching during the COVID-19 pandemic. Suddenly, they faced unexpected and unknown circumstances and had to devise new ways of teaching, but they did it. Courage sustained them.

Badley continues the conversation about authorization in Chapter 4, "Good to Go," in which he examines *consent*, a concept political philosopher John Locke introduced over three centuries ago. Locke distinguished consent—or legitimacy—from raw power, and Chapter 4 uses that distinction to explore the reasons students do or do not engage with their teachers. Teachers who want to teach effectively know that they need to earn the consent of their students. Gaining students' consent to teach requires that the teacher be good, in both the moral and professional senses of that word. Because education students take multiple courses focused on professional competence or *good*ness, this chapter focuses on the other, moral, sense of being good. In most cases, students engage most fully with consent to be taught by—teachers who show care, respect, fairness, hospitality, and humility. Chapter 4 mentions the need for teachers to listen and to have presence, topics dealt with in more detail in the two following chapters.

One component of teacher self-authorization that most educators agree is important is teacher presence, but there is no common understanding of what it is. Badley takes this on in Chapter 5, asking three questions: 1) Is having presence necessary to establish oneself as a teacher with authority, as a teacher worthy of being in charge of a classroom? 2) Is teacher presence definable or is it some kind of X-factor, some mysterious quality that cannot be defined but that people recognize when they see it? 3) Can teacher presence be learned? After establishing the importance of presence, Badley criticizes some of the portrayals of presence offered by Hollywood in "reel" teacher movies: the enigmatic teacher, the charismatic teacher, the dead boring teacher, and the scary teacher. He prefers those cinematic portrayals of the warmly attentive teachers and teachers who represent tough love. Presence can be learned, insists Badley (but not so much from Hollywood), and he suggests that presence can be expressed and realized in effort and enthusiasm, listening and conversation, humor, and authenticity. Helpful to all teachers is the fact that they can incorporate the components of presence by caring about their students, listening to them, and treating them as real people.

In fact, listening is the subject of Chapter 6, in which a teacher and a nurse practitioner share their experiences and insights about listening. In this chapter, Emily Robinson and Shae Nimmo use two lenses to examine the importance of listening, the affects of listening, and some ways that teachers can learn to listen. Robinson writes from the perspective of a medical professional who listens carefully to patients' stories of their lives and descriptions of their symptoms. Nimmo brings insights into listening both from her personal experience of not being heard and from her training and work as an actor. They offer teachers new insights into why and how to listen to students.

Being present and listening contribute to teacher authority by creating a positive classroom ethos, which is essential to the Invitation Theory, "a theoretical model that challenges communities to ensure that they are inviting places that promote the well-being and flourishing of community members and guests." In his overview of the theory in Chapter 7, Sean Schat highlights the view of human nature underlying the theory. Developed by William Purkey and others, the theory acknowledges that all people have the potential for both the amazing and the not-so-amazing, that all are capable of good and all are flawed. Promoters of the Invitation Theory can be both idealistic and realistic about their students, able to recognize the very high value of each student and retain a belief in their ability to learn and change behavior as well as be held responsible for their actions. The significance of the model, suggests Schat, is that it can shape a teacher's vision for the classroom community and for all the relationships that occur within it. Indeed, Schat elaborates how the theory lays the groundwork for a classroom discipline sequence that promotes community, remains invitational, and recognizes the space for the choices and actions of both teachers and students.

In Chapter 8, Mason Steinke offers an example of invitational theory put into action, albeit in a university setting. After convincing an education professor to allow him to create a presentation linking the movie *The School of Rock* (Linklater, 2003) to the idea of teacher authority, Steinke asked fellow students how a "washed up, wannabe rock star with zero educational credentials or teaching experience" could develop teaching authority in the classroom. After watching the clips chosen by Steinke, his peers could point to incidences of the "fake" teacher authorizing his students to do their best work. The opportunity to teach this lesson to several university classes enabled Steinke to become more aware of teacher authority and of the need to authorize students as an aspect of teacher authority in his own classroom.

This section concludes with the story of an educator who initially struggled to assume teacher authority in a grade 4 classroom and, as a result, could not authorize her students. In return, the students did not consent to her teacher's authority. In Chapter 9, Nadine Ayer describes how she desperately wanted to do right by her students, but the difficult behavior and high needs of the students left her demoralized and resorting to punitive responses. A discussion with an administrator shifted this teacher's perspective of her students, and she saw them in a new light. Recognizing the need for herself and her students to start over, she authorized herself to be the teacher her students needed her to be. She implemented strategies that valued the students and slowly helped them revise how they viewed themselves.

Part 2: Authorizing Students

As the earlier paragraphs make clear, teachers do not authorize only themselves. They also authorize their students—to be leaders in the classroom, to learn, to be experts on a topic, to have and develop skills, and to be contributors to the class community. Ayer's story about her shifting attitudes toward a group of students labeled as "difficult" and even "bad" is a story about how a teacher came to authorize their students. Authorizing students is about shared authority, and as contributors to this section argue, shared authority does not diminish teacher authority. Rather, in the words of Reanna Jordan in Chapter 11, it opens "the door to more opportunities for learning and will help foster a positive relationship between the teacher and students and among the students themselves."

In Chapter 10, Jacqueline Filipek argues that theories of place help frame student consent. As teachers and students work with and relate to each other within a physical space, the space becomes meaningful because of the relationships and experiences within it. In meaningful places, students experience a sense of belonging, and relationships are iterative inasmuch as communication goes in both directions. In a classroom, rules, routines, and resources can be used to "shape classrooms into good places," a process that has such positive implications for students as positive status, experiences in leadership and choice, space to be creative, and peer bonding. Based on an eight-month ethnographic research project in a grade 3 classroom, Filipek identifies how the teacher enacted specific structures such as rules, routines, and resources, as well as relationships to make the classroom a meaningful place in which students consented to being there, engaged in their learning, and joined to their classroom community.

The "everyday" in a classroom involves pedagogy and assessment, the themes of Chapter 11. Just as a teacher can use routines and relationships to create good things for students, they can also use inquiry learning. Reanna Jordan explains how inquiry-based learning need not be limited to curriculum studies but can be expanded to the "everyday aspects of human life, including effective decision-making, promoting kindness, and fostering independence." When students problem-solve everyday experiences, such as conflicts on the playground, they gain a sense of control and confidence. When they do the work of thinking through the tough questions and making choices, they gain a greater sense of belonging. When students believe their teacher wants to help them grow and succeed, they feel authorized to become the best they can be.

In the same chapter, Ken Badley examines how teachers can authorize their students by providing choices for how students demonstrate their learning. Not all students learn the same way, and thus not all students can demonstrate their learning in the same manner. Taking a junior high social studies unit on Democracy in Ancient Athens as an example, Badley suggests how teachers can provide students with numerous options for how to demonstrate their learning. The options allow students to play to their strengths. This is not an academic exercise for Badley, who gave such choices to his students when he taught high school. From those experiences, he learned that sometimes students knew more than he did on a topic, enabling him to learn from his students and thereby to model what life-long learning might look like. Offering students choice increased student engagement, which in turn led to fewer behavioral issues. And like Jordan, Badley believes that providing choice gives students a sense of control, or authority, over their lives. The work they do in school thus becomes less about doing what the teacher wants and more about exploring what is meaningful to them.

Iriel Jaroslavsky Rindlisbacher offers more strategies for authorizing students in Chapter 12. An elementary educator, Jaroslavsky Rindlisbacher recalls a class of nine-year-olds with diverse learning needs and several students who had experienced trauma. After some initial frustrations experienced by both teacher and students, Jaroslavsky Rindlisbacher tried a new strategy in which students worked independently through subjects in addition to participating in daily conferences and whole group mini-lessons. Each day Jaroslavsky Rindlisbacher supported a different subject area. Student choice about which subject to work on when (some rules that ensured students covered all the subjects over time) fostered their problem-solving and communication skills as well as internal motivation. Additionally, it deepened the relationships in the classroom. Ultimately, students were authorized to be kids and to be "human beings who are going on a journey."

Behind these strategies of authorizing students is the desire to "see" students rather than manage them. This is the assertion of Paige Ray in Chapter 13. Life-giving authority occurs naturally in classrooms, contends Ray, when "teachers invite students to recognize and live into their own dignity." For Ray, teachers recognize their students' dignity when they see problematic behavior as symptoms of unmet needs and evidence of students who are "unsure of their place in the classroom." Teacher responses that dignify their students can include the use of a restorative justice model and enacting democratic ideals, which ask educators to explore how educational practices replicate social inequities. For example, schools serving working-class communities tend to emphasize obedience, whereas those serving upper-class communities emphasize freedom and independent thought. Drawing on her own experience of teaching a university English writing class to students from rural and often underprivileged areas, many of whom were the first in their family to attend college, Ray describes how she dignified her students' literacies, critically explored with them conceptions of literacies, and thus affirmed "their agency in expanding those repertoires."

The last chapter in this section is written by three professors in an education faculty who describe how they prepare teachers to authorize their students in ways that have positive impacts on classroom management. First, PSTs experience and learn the value of student-centered pedagogies, which involves learning to trust students and letting go of control. Preparing for student-based pedagogy is time and knowledge intensive and requires detailed planning. Student-based pedagogy is still structured; it is not a student free-for-all, and each instructor provides an example from their subject area of mathematics, English language arts, or social studies. Second, PSTs learn all the planning involved when authorizing students, from considering differentiation to planning grouping strategies. The third section examines the iterative relationships between classroom management and assessment practices, arguing for increased teacher assessment literacy.

Part 3: Teacher Authority and Diversity

This section addresses the reality of diversity present in every classroom. Diversity is examined in different ways in each chapter, and each chapter is relevant to every teacher. Margaretta Patrick opens the section in Chapter 15 by exploring teacher authority in multicultural classrooms, often retelling stories from the research to demonstrate such concepts as warm demanders and culturally responsive teaching. Teachers can lose classroom authority if they are not aware of their own cultural assumptions, do not teach with warmth, do not teach about power, do not recognize the power that resides in language codes or how power is used to disempower some while enhancing others, and do not engage with cultural literacy.

In Chapter 16, Genie Kim intertwines her own story with those of several other female and male teachers to confront the pervasive assumption that female teachers do not manage their students as well as their male counterparts. Using the stories, Kim dispels the notion that there is a direct relationship between a teacher's gender and their ability to "manage" a classroom.

Allyson Jule also examines gender differences, but the focus in Chapter 17 is how teachers and university professors respond to their male and female students. Jule focuses on the gendered speech patterns in three classrooms, a grade 2 classroom and two university classrooms. Jule conducted research in each of these classrooms for the year or semester, and in each one, the teacher did most of the talking (far less surprising in the university classes than in the grade 2 classroom). When students spoke, the male students did so more often, and the teacher engaged with the male student responses in more meaningful ways than they did with female student responses. In the college lecture classes, female students were virtually absent in the question periods. Jule observed that in all three contexts, the speaking aloud of male students was valued, while female students learned the skills of being attentive and quiet "and to be sure to give space and attention to the teachers and/or males speaking around them." As Jule concludes, if girls do not speak in public spaces like classrooms, public discourse is diminished.

Malini Sivasubramaniam closes this section with Chapter 18, in which she examines some of the connections between race and teachers' authority. She argues that teachers' race has the potential to have impacts on their authority in the classroom in divergent ways. In classrooms where students identify with the teacher's race, teachers can yield and command an authority that creates a space for meaningful teaching and learning. However, the same classroom context can also impede teacher authority and sometimes set up unrealistic expectations on the part of students when students expect differential treatment because they identify with the teacher's race.

Part 4: Narratives From the Field and Special Situations

This section consists of stories from teachers who work in contexts where teacher authority and student consent may take longer to develop. In Chapter 19, Rebecca Clarke, Tiffany Chung, and Maegahn Smith discuss teacher authority within the context of a practicum experience. Clark emphasizes the importance of the relationship between the PST and MT urging PSTs to enter the classroom with humility. Communication is essential to the relationship, and Clark provides several additional strategies that help ensure a successful practicum experience. In preparation for her practicum, and especially the classroom management element, Chung developed a 3Cs approach consisting of competence (connecting with the MT well ahead of time to discuss teaching styles and learning goals), confidence (knowing the curriculum and the students), and care (intentionally caring for the whole child).

Maegahn Smith identifies four components of mutual trust-based relationships that will support PSTs as they enter new classrooms. First, predictable teachers who remain calm and level-headed in all classroom situations put students at ease. Second, showing interest in students' lives through questions and conversations facilitates the building of relationships as teachers learn about their students. Third, honesty is essential in all relationships, and in the teacher–student relationship, this implies honesty in how teachers represent themselves, especially when they make a mistake. And fourth is the importance of ensuring strong communication processes, such as conversations and journaling.

Ashley Ryl's story in Chapter 20 of discovering her identity as a teacher began in the first practicum of her Bachelor of Education program. Her MT during the first-year practicum was a successful male teacher who had developed strong classroom management skills. Ryl discovered that she was very different from the MT and she struggled to find an approach with which she was comfortable. The second-year practicum in a large, urban high school went much better, and Ryl was able to develop more confidence in her abilities to manage a classroom in a manner that felt authentic. Her first teaching position took her to a small rural community, but Ryl felt the pressure to become like the other teachers, of being someone other than who she was. The feelings of frustration and being inauthentic returned, but fortunately, the chance remark of a colleague gave Ryl the confidence to stay true to who she was, and the relationships with her students flourished.

Nicola Campbell had a different first-year teaching experience. In Chapter 21, Campbell recounts her first teaching job, which occurred in an overseas context. Campbell describes navigating school policies, practices, and values that were markedly different from those she had developed as a PST and how difficult navigating those processes was because in some instances they required that she put aside, at least temporarily, some of her foundational educational visions and values. For example, the behavioral policies were strict and Campbell felt that they sometimes got in the way of building relationships with her students. Teachers had little input into either curriculum or pedagogy, and the focus on high academic standards resulted in a lot of transmission teaching. Yet students thrived and, over time, Campbell identified some of the strengths in the program she was teaching. When Campbell returned home, she took with her an expanded set of understandings and strategies and a different mindset.

Some beginning teachers spend their first years teaching as a Substitute Teacher, also known as a Supply Teacher. In Chapter 22, Bina Ali shares her experiences and the wisdom of incorporating certain practices into one's substitute teaching. Walking into a new school without knowing the school practices and policies or any of the students can be daunting, so Ali suggests getting to the school early to familiarize oneself with policies, especially the safety protocols. Ali prepares for classroom management in the same manner as she prepares to teach curricular content; she is flexible and prepared. She reminds her readers that all communication is self-advocacy, meaning that notes, reports, leaving a business card, and cleaning up the classroom at the end of the day are all ways of providing principals and teachers with reasons to call you back into their school again.

Teaching in rural or remote locations offers a different kind of challenge. As described in Chapter 23, Kristen Tjostheim's first job was in a small, isolated, tightly knit community, a place where she "received several crash-course lessons on classroom management." Because students knew each other well, part of classroom management entailed teaching them what behavior was appropriate in the school and how to ensure that their behavior was respectful toward everyone, including newcomers to the community. Tjostheim learned how to focus on student strengths rather than deficits and thus enjoyed such "extraordinary gifts" as the students' strong work ethic and ethical code. Interestingly, she applied the Universal Design for Learning (UDL) model to classroom management to build engagement and trust, and she found ways to engage students online when students from other remote schools joined her students via a video conferencing suite (in pre-pandemic days). Tjostheim concludes that classroom management in remote communities is not all that different from any other location inasmuch as it still depends on trusting relationships, clear expectations, and consistent implementation.

Two other teachers tell their stories of teaching in rural and remote communities. In Chapter 24, Dena Palmaymesa describes with delight the *gifts of simplicity* she discovered when she worked as a one-room schoolteacher (nine grades!). It wasn't always that way; being the new person in the community was difficult at first and it took time to gain her students' trust. They did not like the changes proposed by the newcomer teacher. But, over time, attitudes shifted, especially when Palmaymesa decided to *host* the classroom rather than *manage* it, which meant authorizing students to "take charge of their learning and voice how they work best." She witnessed students caring for each other, playing with each other, and creating together, all with the simplest materials and supports.

Natasha Steenhof Bakker's context was similar in that she went to a small community, albeit one larger than the one described by Palmaymesa. Bakker's secondary practicum experiences were in a large urban setting, and her first teaching position was a temporary position in the community in which she grew up. In contrast to the practicum experiences, students had pre-existing relationships with Bakker and her family members, and students were much more inquisitive about her private life. Bakker found herself valuing the tight-knit student and community relationships but discovered that she was always "on," that there "was no space between workplace and my home life." When she accepted a position in another small independent school, this time as an elementary teacher, Bakker valued both the way that she could build relationships with the small group of students in her classroom and the school-wide focus on community building. The pursuit of healthy relationships in the classroom, maintains Bakker, is the key to classroom management in any context.

The authors of Chapters 19–24 all describe settings where they worked as PSTs, as teachers relatively new to the profession, or as teachers new to particular locations. By contrast, the last contributor to this section writes from the other end of his career. Ron McIntyre, the author of Chapter 25, is a retired teacher who also coached various sports for 38 years. McIntyre offers his reflections on successful classroom management, which involve three aspects. First, be a purposeful leader, which "fosters the emotional growth of the student and delivers the curriculum through strong unit and lesson planning." Second, be optimistic, retaining a growth mindset regarding student behavior. Third, use humor, which draws students and teachers together in a common experience.

Conclusion

Several recurring themes run through this overview. First, teacher authority is deeply dependent on teacher–student relationships. No matter the situation or context, the importance of relationships is paramount in many of the teacher stories and theories. This emphasis reinforces the association between teacher authority and teacher authorization of students; one cannot occur without the other. Second, the connection between teacher authority and place-based theory is evident in the narrative sketched earlier. As teachers authorize themselves and their students, and as students authorize their teachers, richer learning occurs in the classroom space, imbuing that space with meaning. When teachers authorize their students, the space becomes a place that is safe for them to take cognitive risks, to pursue their interests, and to develop their empathy. And third, we hear the reminder that both individually and collectively, we still have much to learn, as made clear by the chapters in Part 3. Only a few issues were discussed in this section, and we know there are so many more diverse student groups who are in classrooms across the country whose voices are diminished or even non-existent. Taking the conceptions of teacher authority and the authorization of students seriously is an important first step in assuring the dignity of all students.

References

Bantock, G. H. (1966). *Freedom and authority in education*. Faber and Faber.
Benne, K. D. (1943). *A conception of authority: An introductory study*. Teachers College Press.
Csikszentmihalyi, M. (1982). *Flow: The psychology of optimal experience*. Harper and Row.
Csikszentmihalyi, M. (1990). Intrinsic motivation and effective teaching: A flow analysis. In J. L. Bess (Ed.), *Motivating professors to teach effectively* (pp. 72–89). Jossey-Bass.
Csikszentmihalyi, M. (2002). *Motivating people to learn*. Edutopia. www.edutopia.org/mihaly-csikszentmihalyi-motivating-people-learn
Dreikurs, R. (1974). *Child guidance and education: Collected papers of Rudolf Dreikurs, M.D.* Alfred Adler Institute of Chicago.
Linklater, R. (Director). (2003). *School of rock*. Paramount Pictures.
Metz, M. H. (1978). *Classrooms and corridors: The crises of authority in desegregated secondary schools*. University of California Press.
Steeg-Thornhill, S. M., & Badley, K. (2021). *Generating tact and flow for effective teaching and learning*. Routledge.

2
CLASSROOM MANAGEMENT
A Dialogue With Larger Social Questions

Margaretta Patrick

In recalling their experiences of teaching in New York during the 1920s, female teachers used such words as "brutal, unforgiving, and isolated" to describe their working conditions (Rousmaniere, 1994, p. 49). They encountered many of the problems one would expect with rapid urbanization: large classes, diverse student abilities, social complexity, economic disparity, and behavioral issues (Rousmaniere, 1994). At the time, maintaining order was paramount and the inability to do so was a major cause of teacher dismissal in the United States (Johnson, 1952). Yet by 1952, Henry Johnson could write that school discipline was the educational aspect most changed in Canada, and by definition in the United States, as many educational ideas in Canada originated in the United States. Such change could not occur without social and structural transformations in the intervening decades.

Yet disruptive student behavior remains a challenge, especially for beginning teachers. The National Council on Teacher Quality (Greenberg et al., 2014) in the United States claimed that accumulated teacher wisdom and extensive research studies provide teachers with the knowledge and skills to implement strong management practices. One problem lies with the teacher preparation programs, charged the NCTQ, particularly their insufficient attention to the "Big Five" management strategies that have emerged from authoritative research: establishing and teaching rules, creating routines, using praise to reinforce positive behavior, imposing consequences for misbehavior, and fostering student engagement.

The preceding two paragraphs provide two distinct but related foci in the classroom management literature: those who study the social ideas and visions behind classroom discipline and management approaches and those who advance strategies or programs they believe develop just and efficacious classroom management

DOI: 10.4324/9781003140849-2

practices. The two foci are related in that strategies are never independent of philosophy and vision, but the latter are often implicit or a secondary emphasis within the models and strategies. This chapter explores both foci to demonstrate both the connectedness of the two strands and how the field of classroom management has emerged from ongoing conversations about larger social and religious beliefs concerning human nature, who students are, and how they learn. Views of teacher authority and student consent are rooted in these larger human questions.

The big picture questions are foregrounded in the first section, which examines the shift within classroom discipline away from authoritarian punishment toward progressivist and democratic alternatives and traces how the shift reflected changing societal and religious beliefs in western societies. As several scholars have already documented this narrative, especially the curtailment of corporal punishment in public schools, this first section builds on several histories already published.

The curtailment of corporal punishment and the rise of other educational visions did not end the contestations surrounding teacher authority. As the second section demonstrates, during the mid to late 20th century, the field developed with two parallel views of teacher authority. One view was evidenced in the *Assertive Discipline* program developed by Lee and Marlene Canter and the other by scholars who built upon the research of Rudolf Dreikurs and Jacob Kounin. The section concludes with a critique of the various reform movements, including some progressivist approaches, and how they failed to embody a democratic social vision.

The final section highlights contemporary themes as classroom management established itself as an educational specialization. Original disagreements about what comprised classroom management gradually developed into an understanding that classroom management is an expansive field that goes beyond discipline to include classroom and school learning and social environments. Scholars collated the research, engaged in a meta-analysis, and developed programs. However, the larger social issues remained, as several critical theorists raised concerns about the influences of neoliberalism they observed in management practices. They are especially worried about what they perceive to be the ongoing preoccupation of classroom management theories with control and modifications of student behavior.

Discipline: Corporal Punishment and Alternatives

Limiting Corporal Punishment

As public education became accessible to more families throughout the 19th century, many teachers used corporal punishment to maintain order and control in their classrooms. Evidence suggests excessive use of such punishment as early as the late 18th century. For example, students in the English city of Winchester mutinied in protest several times between 1775 and 1793 (Johnson, 1952).

While such stories do not describe all schools and teachers, they were ubiquitous. James Jewett's (1952) history of American opposition to corporal punishment began with the following vignette, first published in 1876 by Henry K. Oliver.

> Corporal chastisement was in full tide of successful experiment. Of the eight different teachers under whose care I fell before I entered college, but one of them possessed any bowels of mercy. He hit me, but in a single instance, and that was for the crime of having left my leg a little out in the passageway between the desks. This was done with a stoutish piece of rattan, though the flogging instruments mostly in use were the cowhide and the ferrule.
>
> *(as quoted on p. 1 from* The American Journal of Education, XXVI, *212)*

Jewett noted that such discipline served the dual purposes of maintaining order and developing moral education.

In Canada, a teacher in Niagara (Ontario) was said to have "hit a pupil on the head with a round ruler, knocking him insensible and to have revived him in a snowbank" (Johnson, 1952, p. 31). Most teachers were men, as only men were thought capable of handling the rough and rowdy children of pioneer immigrants, some of whom were older than the teachers. Several inspectors noted the bad teaching practices of many teachers at the time and deduced that the use of corporal punishment did not improve classroom order.

Scholars writing about this era agree that the common religious views of the time regarding the human person contributed to the harsh discipline. Whether it was the obedience-minded views of John Wesley or the heightened sense of Calvinist natural depravity imbued in Puritan New England (Johnson, 1952), students were thought to require strict guidance and admonition. Jewett (1952) posed the American debate about corporal punishment as revolving around two central religious issues. The first concerned human nature: if humans are born in sin, they are in constant need of correction, but if they are innately good, corporal punishment is harmful. The second issue revolved around the afterlife; if there is a divine system of rewards and punishments in which humans receive the consequences of their earthly actions, then severe punishment is helpful and even necessary. But if the afterlife does not involve such rewards and punishments, then there is no need for them in this life either. On these questions, the educational reformers split with the traditional religious views, evidenced most clearly in the 1845 debate between Horace Mann (1796–1859), then Secretary of the Massachusetts Board of Education, and the 31 Boston schoolmasters.

Appointed as Secretary in 1837, Mann traveled to Europe in 1843 to visit western European public schools. In his published account of the trip, Mann's appreciation for Prussian schools was apparent. He recounted how one superintendent explained that his reliance on "active occupations, music, and Christian love" (Mann & Hodgson, 1846, p. 87) was the key to his success in transforming the lives of orphans. Mann further celebrated the role Prussian moral teachers had on their students, especially on those who had previously engaged in criminal behavior. When describing these students, Mann tended to link their behavior to the evils of society rather than any inherent wickedness. In summarizing the success of Prussian schools, Mann wrote, "A teacher who cannot rule by love, must do so by fear. A teacher who cannot supply material for the activity of his pupils' minds by his talent, must put down that activity by force" (p. 155). For proof, Mann noted that throughout his six weeks in Europe, he observed no punishment of children and, further, that no child demonstrated any fear of punishment.

When Mann published his report in 1845, the Boston schoolmasters perceived it as an indictment on their work, and 31 of them rebutted Mann's conclusions. They presented themselves as learned and experienced and criticized Mann for never having visited a Boston school and thus unfamiliar with what happened in them. While Mann was surprised by the critique and personally offended, the controversy engendered greater public support for his ideas and recommendations (Winship, 1925).

Indeed, the schoolmasters had misread the times. While the debate about corporal punishment was fierce, it was relatively short lived, as opposition was soon widespread among educational theorits. Although enactment into practice came more slowly, by the outbreak of the American Civil War (1861), the practice was catching up to theory due to the humanitarian movement influencing American society, particularly its impact on moral education (Jewett, 1952). As morality came to rest with the sentiments, and thus emotions and feelings, educational reformers separated character training from intellectual instruction. The increased valuation of students' inner life and beliefs led many to conclude that harsh punishment negatively impacted students' moral character by hardening their obstinacy (Jewett, 1952; Johnson, 1952).

Legislation in North America, however, fell behind Europe. Already in their report, Mann (Mann & Hodgson, 1846) noted that the Dutch had replaced corporal punishment with school expulsion. Mann attributed its continued use in English schools, along with some instances of solitary confinement, to the country's lack of a national system of education. It was not until 1883 that the London School Board formally limited teachers' use of corporal punishment (Johnson, 1952).

In North America, New Jersey was the first jurisdiction to abolish corporal punishment, in 1867, with Massachusetts the second American state to do so in 1972 (Axelrod, 2011). Canadian prohibitions followed a similarly long path. One of the earliest opponents was Egerton Ryerson (1803–1882), a Methodist minister who established common schools and founded a teachers' college in what is now the province of Ontario. Today Egerton is widely condemned for his role in the creation of Residential Schools, which caused tremendous trauma for Indigenous families and communities across Canada, the effects of which continue today. Like Mann, Ryerson valued the German education system (Ryerson, 2000 [1847]) and his Methodist background led him to oppose corporal punishment (Johnson, 1952). In addition to Ryerson, Johnson (1952) recorded some initial opposition in 1832 and noted that official limitations were first imposed in British Columbia in 1872. Johnson additionally documented teachers' decreased use of corporal punishment beginning in 1850, and their preference for withholding privileges, giving detentions, suspensions, or demerits, calling home, depriving students of recess, or having a student sit alone, among other practices. As Paul Axelrod (2011) recounted, the Toronto Board of Education banned the practice in 1971, with several provinces following between 1989 and 1997 and the Supreme Court of Canada prohibiting its use in all Canadian schools in 2004.

Alternatives and Implications

In a study of alternative disciplinary practices and visions of education, Alan Cumming (1969) acknowledged that one's conceptions about human nature and process of intellectual formation impact one's evaluations of educational theories and views of teacher authority. Cumming argued that while the term *discipline* historically involved classroom order through such means as control and obedience, it also needed to encompass the progressive ideal of self-discipline. Although "education commenced with coercion" (p. 366), alternatives existed, such as the Jesuit *Ratio Studiorum*, which emphasized personal contact, emulation (imitation), rivalry, and awarded prizes (Schwickerath, 1911). However, Cumming criticized the Jesuits for excessive surveillance, competition, and control of their students. But coercion was not the exclusive domain of the Jesuits, with Cumming also critiquing the withdrawal forms of discipline that replaced corporal punishment, such as withholding privileges and employing mockery and humiliation. (For more on how shaming techniques replaced corporal punishment in North America, see Stearns & Stearns, 2017.) The underlying principles of such "discipline[s] of constraint," contended Cumming (1969, p. 368), were the Protestant and particularly Calvinist beliefs in the fallen nature of all human beings as well as the belief that obedience is a virtue.

Cumming (1969) preferred the progressive and democratic alternative developed by Dewey that sought to instill self-governance and self-discipline within students, learned through experience and discretely guided by the teacher. Given the importance of the teacher–student mentoring relationship in such schools, Cumming highlighted the importance of teachers' personalities and their ability to use their personal authority to shape students. Indeed, contended Cumming, without these types of teacher leaders, experiments in democratic education quickly descend into chaos. For positive examples, Cumming pointed to the Montessori schools, with their child-centered focus on self-expression and creativity, and the Scouting movement.

Cumming also praised the schools established by Dr. Cecil Reddie in England. When Patrick Geddes (1905) formally reviewed Reddie's school for boys at Abbotsholme, Debyshire, he said he witnessed the union of labor and culture when he observed students haying a field, weeding, attending to a bee farm, and engaging in light machinery repair, as well as participating in daily chapels, swimming lessons, and music recitals, all while being capably led by older students. The stated purpose behind these practices was intelligent action and citizenship, developed via a code of laws not imposed but iteratively developed with the students through experience. Geddes thought the school was a wonderful introduction to sensible and orderly democracy.

While such progressivist education was one result of the humanization of education, the feminization of education was another (Rousmaniere, 1994). Building on the ideas of Rousseau and Pestalozzi, educational reformers perceived women as embodying the vision of humanized teachers as sensitive, moral, and restrained—and they could be paid less than male teachers. But the female teachers in the burgeoning New York schools interviewed by Rousmaniere (1994) decades later reported this humanized vision to be rudderless. As school officials called for stricter discipline and blamed progressive ideas for the chaos in their schools, they did not provide teachers with the necessary instruction on how to achieve more discipline. In fact, the lack of discipline was perceived as the female teachers' fault, their struggles thought to arise from their gender, and their own lack of moral order rather than embedded in the complexities of the student population and structures of the system.

Events and social beliefs continued to unfold, and the next influence came from science. In his contribution to the *Sage Encyclopedia of Classroom Management*, W. George Scarlett (2015) traced how the new faith in science during the first half of the 20th century led to two new movements in classroom discipline: child study and mental hygiene. Child study examined the developmental needs of students and called upon educational systems to fit students' needs rather than the reverse. The mental hygiene movement originated from the caring professions and linked students' emotional needs with their behavior in school. Movement leaders counseled teachers to take students' needs and inner lives into consideration when contemplating discipline.

Various social movements also impacted classrooms. In the United States, the civil rights movement and desegregation of schools following *Brown v. Board of Education* (1954) led to greater diversity within classrooms. Significant migration changed school populations. Social changes arising from the 1960s shifted attitudes against institutions and those in authority positions. Over the following decades, teachers reported greater violence and drug use among older students (Weinstein, 1999). Fearing the loss of authority and control, many teachers turned to the popular behaviorist discipline program by Lee and Marlene Canter titled *Assertive Discipline: A Take-Charge Approach for Today's Educator.*

Teacher Authority: Development of Parallel Conceptions

The Explosion of Research and Approaches

In *Assertive Discipline*, first published in 1976 and revised several times thereafter, the Canters stated that the purpose of assertive discipline was to "help teachers increase their influence in their classroom by becoming more *assertive*" (Canter & Canter, 1976, p. 9, italics in original). The original version of the book opened with the words "You, the teacher, must be able to get your needs met in the classroom" (p. 2). The authors then outlined several reasons for decreased teacher influence and asserted that students needed teachers who set "consistent, firm, positive limits in the classroom" (p. 7). Ultimately, the book helped teachers take responsibility by developing assertive discipline.

Over time, the Canters discovered that some educators reduced their program to focusing on negative student behavior and writing names on the board when students misbehaved. Such reductions totally missed the mark, claimed Lee Canter in 1989. The key instead was "catching students being good" (p. 58), with teachers teaching, modeling, and repeating the required student behaviors, such as those needed in transitions from large to small groups or in group work.

Perhaps in response to some of these mischaracterizations, the Canters rewrote the goal of *Assertive Discipline* in the revised edition (Canter & Canter, 1992) to read "teach[ing] students to choose responsible behavior and in so doing raise their self-esteem and increase their academic success" (p. xiii). The focus on students was also evident in the text, with the opening sentence now reading "As a teacher, you want the optimal classroom environment in which you can teach and your students can learn" (p. 3). Weinstein (1999) attributed the changes to the "process-product" research that had occurred in the 1980s, which examined how teacher behaviors such as classroom organization (e.g., beginning of the year practices, how rules and procedures are introduced, taught, practiced, and reinforced) impact student outcomes.

Despite the revisions, however, critics continued to characterize the Canters' program as overly teacher focused, control oriented, and based on power (Weinstein, 1999). Brophy (1999) noted the lack of evidence regarding the efficacy of the Canters' program to influence student behavior. Several critics called for a new paradigm in a book edited by Jerome Freiberg (1999a) titled *Beyond Behaviorism: Changing the Classroom Management Paradigm.* In rejecting behaviorism, Freiberg (1999b) contended that the authors also rejected the negative view of the student embedded in it. If one views students as destructive, then they are not to be trusted, need to be monitored, and must be bribed with rewards to comply. But if students are viewed as good, they can be given some responsibility, are capable of self-discipline, and can be active learners. Freiberg had previously described the new paradigm as "person-centred," imbued with caring and cooperation as much as administration and oversight.

The person-centered paradigm of *Beyond Behaviorism* had roots within the research of several earlier 20th-century scholars, beginning with psychiatrist and educator Rudolf Dreikurs. Writing since the 1950s, Dreikurs (1974) insisted that children's actions are purposeful, with the child's purpose being to incorporate themself into the group. Misbehavior is equally goal oriented, such as a mistaken self-concept developed to address an educational difficulty, perhaps with reading. When children are unable to establish their social position or encounter challenges, they engage in what Dreikurs identified as one of the four families of "disturbing" behavior: attention-getting, power, revenge, or flaunting inability.

Dreikurs (1974) advocated for new approaches to child rearing and teaching given the "democratic evolution" that provided children with increased status and voice. Rather than feeling as if they had lost their ability to control students, Dreikurs encouraged parents and teachers to dig beneath the behavior to discern a child's needs. A student disturbing the class must be understood as unhappy and in need of encouragement rather than punishment. Taking care to avoid being seen as permissive, Dreikurs emphasized not only the need to unearth unconscious means of control being imposed on the child by those in authority (especially parents but also teachers) but also the need for children to experience natural consequences of their actions.

Concurrently, Jacob Kounin (1977) published *Discipline and Group Management in Classrooms* in 1970. Kounin investigated teacher actions in successful classrooms, those classrooms in which students were engaged in their work and there was little student "deviancy." Based on evidence collected from video-recorded elementary classrooms, Kounin concluded that the key was how effective teacher behaviors prevented student misbehavior as they managed the group. Preventative teacher actions included *withitness*, typically described as teachers having eyes in the back of their heads so that they always know what is going on, overlapping, or being able to pay attention to two issues at the same time, transition smoothness, thus avoiding behaviors that impede movement between lesson elements, and utilizing a variety of student work types. These techniques are not ends in and of themselves, cautioned Kounin, but group management techniques that free up teachers to focus on aspects of teaching other than managing behavior.

The Re-Emergence of the Big Social Questions

Despite these significant theoretical advances in child behavior, not all educational organizations took notice. Ronald Butchart (1994), in his presidential address to the American Educational Studies Association (AESA), stated that "Discipline is a dirty word in foundations circles" because of its connection to power and manipulation. The consequence is the under-theorizing of classroom relationships, which left "teachers to face a barrage of slickly marketed, ideologically loaded discipline packages" (p. 166). Butchart then sketched the landscape of the "slender" literature available (p. 168) and lamented its overemphasis on corporal punishment. The real issues, he contested, were the various constructions of authority within competing views of discipline, the use of power, and an examination of what Butchart called "disciplinary structures."

Tracing the evolution of classroom management from the "traditional" approaches of the 18th century through the 19th-century reforms of Lancasterian schools and New England pedagogy and the progressive era of the early 20th century, Butchart found each of the management innovations created their own disciplinary structures. Structures such as procedures, processes, reward systems, standardized exams, grade promotions, and the proliferation of school administration all embedded "disciplinary technologies" that enabled greater surveillance of students and eventually, over teachers.

Butchart (1994) thought progressivism continued and even enhanced some of the disciplinary structures first enacted by previous reform movements. While some progressive elements advocated for child-centered pedagogy and mental hygiene, others "fetishized efficiency and routine in all classroom activities" (p. 175). What worried Butchart the most, however, were the disciplinary structures of the market now embedded in educational structures. Evident in the earlier movements as well, Butchart highlighted such structures in the child-centered wing of progressivism, which presented to students "a world shorn of conflict and power, one in which narcissistic self-expression, unlimited individual ambition, and expert adjustment of environments constituted the ends of modern life" (p. 178). The failure to address impulse control and social responsibility produced students suited to a market geared to impulse and desire. For Butchart, the lack of social consciousness and support of possessive individualism betrayed a democratic view of classroom discipline.

Other scholars engaged with similar ideas, albeit from different angles. Scarlett (2015) observed how Dewey's constructivism "had been misinterpreted so many times—mostly by those who thought that progressive education meant giving children little or no structure at all" (p. 378)—that teachers adopted behaviorist models to regain control amidst the chaos. Robert Carson (1996) made a similar point to Butchart, noting that a false binary had emerged in the literature between behaviorism and being permissive and that too often the management literature based on constructivist methods lacked sufficient philosophical foundations. Building on the work of Dreikurs, Dewey, and others, Carson insisted that in addition to not being permissive, democratic classrooms were committed to *all* students developing the social skills to solve problems accompanied by high standards, accountability, and responsibility for each other, meaning all must find their place within the group, that all belong. In other words, discipline must always be connected to a larger social vision. When it is not, discipline is seen as punitive action or manipulative control by the teacher or both.

Carson's desire to situate discipline within a larger social vision echoed Butchart (1994), who was alarmed by the lack of social vision he found in the classroom management literature that had emerged since the 1950s. Rather than explicated visions or ends, Butchart found the literature overly focused on strategies that relied on behaviorism and control. He interpreted the search for control and discipline as a frantic attempt to counter the character traits promoted by a consumerist culture that promoted possessive individualism and banished impulse control, meaning that educational theory helped create a problem that classroom management approaches then tried to mitigate.

Others interpreted the literature differently. Prior to the publication of Butchart's article, Daniel Duke and Vernon Jones (1984) attempted to clarify the parameters of the emerging field of classroom management.

Classroom Management as an Educational Specialization

Titling their article "Two Decades of Discipline—Assessing the Development of an Educational Specialization," Duke and Jones (1984) reviewed the reality of teachers' struggles to cope with diverse student populations, the explosion of literature emerging from that reality, and the public perception of a discipline crisis in public schools. They noted how the phrase *classroom management* had become increasingly popular and how it was used to describe "teacher efforts to control student behavior in class" (p. 25). Duke and Jones categorized research-based strategies into models (plans of action), paradigms (conceptual frameworks such as behavioral modification), and systems (composed of recommendations emerging from research and practice). They further identified the many challenges found in the new field of research, such as the lack of a common definition of *classroom management*, various and problematic data sources, and lack of agreement regarding the goals of and best approaches to classroom management (for example, regarding the use and effectiveness of punishments). These authors expressed hope in the then-current teacher instruction about classroom management and the formalization of classroom procedures.

Fifteen years later, writing within the paradigm of "person-centred" management, Brophy (1999) expanded the definition of classroom management as "actions taken to create and maintain a learning environment conducive to successful instruction (arranging the physical environment of the class, establishing rules and procedures, maintaining attention to lessons and engagement in academic activities)" (p. 43). Brophy distinguished classroom management from "disciplinary interventions," defined as compelling changes in student behavior when their behavior does not meet expectations (p. 43). Particularly helpful was Brophy's identification of three emerging principles of classroom management: 1) that clearly establishing expectations and teaching students how to meet them is likely more effective than focusing on misbehavior; 2) that management paradigms must support the chosen instructional system (a behaviorist classroom management program would not support social constructivist learning, for example); and 3) that planning for management begins with the articulation of learning goals and consideration of the knowledge, skills, and behavioral dispositions students require to achieve those goals, a process that informs the management system.

Contemporary Themes

As research continued, it was spread across a variety of fields, published in numerous journals, and not always identified as classroom management (Evertson & Weinstein, 2006b). Several theorists attempted to pull the research together, including Robert Marzano, who published *Classroom Management that Works: Research-based Strategies for Every Teacher* in 2003. Uniquely, Marzano applied the research methodology of meta-analysis to classroom management, which enabled him to make recommendations with a greater degree of certitude regarding their efficacy. Chapters centered on rules and procedures, disciplinary interventions, teacher–student relations, and mental set (how a teacher thinks and behaves). For each chapter, Marzano provided the research data, related programs, and recommendations encompassed in what he called *action steps*.

Just three years later, Carolyn Evertson and Carol Weinstein (2006a) co-edited the *Handbook on Classroom Management*, described as late as 2013 as "the largest collection of scholarship on classroom management in a single volume" (Casey et al., 2013, p. 48). Evertson and Weinstein (2006b) drew on the work of others when defining "classroom management as the actions teachers take to create an environment that supports and facilitates both academic and social-emotional learning" (p. 4). They highlighted how their definition included both the classroom environment and students' "social and moral growth" (p. 4). Brophy (2006) noted how researchers such as Kounin, Evertson, and Edmund Emmer had shifted the research regarding students "from good conduct to engagement in learning activities" and regarding teachers "from dealing with disruptions to establishing effective learning structures and routines" (p. 38). Common research themes identified in the *Handbook* included: 1) the importance of student-teacher relationships; 2) the social and moral functioning of classroom management found in, for example, practices of self-regulation, social skill development, learning to engage with the classroom community, and promotion of a democratic society; 3) the negative repercussions of external rewards and punishments; and 4) the importance of individual characteristics such as ethnicity, culture, age, and socioeconomic status (Evertson & Weinstein, 2006b).

Research continued, as seen in the NCTQ's report on classroom management (Greenberg et al., 2014). Relying on three meta-analyses of the literature, the Council arrived at its "Big Five" of classroom management and supporting strategies. One of the meta-analyses referenced by the NCTQ was by Simonsen et al. (2008), who had evaluated the literature using evidence-based criteria. Simonsen et al. (2015) later elaborated their research-based strategies when they grouped teacher interventions into the categories of foundational, preventive, and responsive strategies. Despite the abundance of research and succinctly summarized best practices, the research indicated that teachers were not implementing the practices at recommended levels.

Some research suggested that the sheer number of strategies might be overwhelming teachers, prompting Collier-Meek et al. (2019) to discern the core strategies that would improve elementary teacher implementation and student academic engagement. In their study, Collier-Meek and their colleagues discovered lower-than-recommended levels of the components they examined, although they found positive student engagement resulting from the preventive strategy of teacher references to routines and/or schedules as well as the response strategy of specific praise. Negative student engagement was associated with the teacher response strategy of correcting errors. Interestingly, teachers demonstrated low usage of the less intensive responses to unproductive behavior, such as proximity and planned ignoring. As Collier-Meek and their co-researchers noted, their focus on core strategies was a new research direction.

The Larger Social Questions Remain

Critical educators seek to uncover the philosophical commitments of theories, models, paradigms, and systems, meaning they often address issues of power and control. This was the case with a 2013 cultural-historical study of the term *management* (Casey et al., 2013) and its links with present-day neoliberalism. Like others, the authors traced the concept of management to the early days of American settlement and plantations and the colonization of Africa by European empires to demonstrate how management has been explicitly racialized. They followed the concept as the scientific management of factories was applied to education, which bequeathed many of the now-familiar aspects of schools: bells, the traditional physical structures of schools, grades, and subject areas. The principles of scientific management shaped the social efficiency educators, who sought to eliminate wasteful practices and prepare students for the industrialized job market. Casey et al. noted the racialization of the social efficiency movement, which established skills training programs for Black and Indigenous students considered by some to be developmentally unprepared for "regular" classes.

It was the contention of Casey et al. (2013) that classroom management retains many of these earlier features of management. They asserted that at its heart classroom management continues to be concerned with control and modifying student behavior via procedures, rules, and even the management of the physical space. Echoing others, they noted that evaluations of "good" and "bad" behavior are ideological constructs.

Educational mirroring of societal management continues, argued Casey et al. (2013), as schools now reflect the "harmonious human relationship" emphasis of corporations (p. 43). And just as colonial educational practices and structures coerced and managed the lives of those in the colonies in racialized ways, so neoliberal practices and structures continue to regulate students' bodies and their lives, at least partly by imposing capitalist and corporatist logic. Classroom management "is part of the process for ensuring that students believe that their educational success is due to merit" (p. 47).

As evidence of the degree to which American neoliberal views of management permeate educational systems around the world, Casey et al. (2013) pointed to the 2006 *Handbook* co-edited by Evertson and Weinstein (discussed earlier). They criticized how "Pedagogically, management is an attempt to separate curriculum from human interaction" (p. 50), which may sound a bit strange given the focus of management definitions on creating a learning environment conducive to student learning. But the authors returned to Dewey, who they claimed, "likens the learning that takes place in management-based educational environments to students either choosing to find intellectual stimulation in the routine and process of schooling, or simply choosing to feign interest over the consequences of punishment" (p. 50). Nor can defenders of classroom management point to the culturally responsive approaches developed to promote social justice for all students (Chapter 15), contended Casey et al. Understanding one's students in and of itself is not problematic; it becomes so for Casey et al. when it is removed from its pedagogical and learning roots and positioned within the framework of classroom management, which now serves neoliberal ends. On the one hand, a key purpose of classroom management is to establish the rules of conduct or behavior (and for Casey et al., these too often are White, middle-class codes) and on the other hand, the goal of culturally responsive classroom management is to teach about power with the intention of transforming existing cultures of power. For the authors, it is because classroom management *manages* students and thus retains the racialized and technical production foci of the factory and of neo-liberalism, it can never be utilized for social justice.

Conclusion

When teachers confront change, some adopt behaviorist management techniques that they believe will shore up their teacher authority. But such techniques are only the tip of an iceberg; they come with a range of beliefs that lie below the surface. Beliefs and practices cannot be isolated from each other. Indeed, the very language we use to discuss classroom practices carries embedded beliefs. As Casey et al. (2013) argued, the term "management" has a racially ugly history. Thus, after reviewing the critical theory literature, Ellen Brantlinger and Scot Danforth (2006) employed the term "classroom climate and organization" rather than classroom management (p. 166).

The dialogue between those who engage in classroom management as an area of specialization and the critical theorists who examine classroom management within the larger social questions of power and control highlights the difficulties of defining and describing what teacher authority and student consent look like in a classroom. Much depends on one's prior understandings regarding human nature (whether we are fundamentally good or bad), who students are (whether they can provide consent, have the capacity to make "good" or "right" choices, can be trusted, etc.), and how they learn (whether students are responsible for their learning, if learning occurs best in democratic or highly structured and ordered classrooms, whether these two options are mutually exclusive, and whether behaviorism is a valid management approach). Teachers must consider additional beliefs regarding power (whether it is always bad) and authority (how one gains legitimate authority and if it can be shared). All these terms and ideas are contested, but as this chapter makes clear, they are critically important in the development of classroom management as a field of study and as a teacher concern within the classroom.

References

Axelrod, P. (2011). Banning the strap: The end of corporal punishment in Canadian schools. *Education Canada, 51*(1). www.edcan.ca/magazine/winter-2011/

Brantlinger, E., & Danforth, S. (2006). Critical theory perspective on social class, race, gender, and classroom. In C. M. Evertson & C. S. Weinstein (Eds.), *Handbook of classroom management: Research, practice, and contemporary issues* (pp. 157–179). Routledge.

Brophy, J. (1999). Perspectives of classroom management: Yesterday, today, and tomorrow. In H. J. Freiberg (Ed.), *Beyond behaviorism: Changing the classroom management paradigm* (pp. 43–56). Allyn and Bacon.

Brophy, J. (2006). History of research on classroom management. In C. M. Evertson & C. S. Weinstein (Eds.), *Handbook of classroom management: Research, practice, and contemporary issues* (pp. 17–43). Routledge.

Butchart, R. E. (1994). Discipline, dignity, and democracy: Reflections on the history of classroom management. *Educational Studies, 26*(3), 165–184. https://doi.org/10.1207/s15326993es2603_1

Canter, L. (1989). Assertive discipline: More than names on the board and marbles in a jar. *The Phi Delta Kappan, 71*(1), 57–61.

Canter, L., & Canter, M. (1976). *Assertive discipline: A take-charge approach for today's educator*. Lee Canter & Associates.

Canter, L., & Canter, M. (1992). *Assertive discipline: Positive behavior management for today's classroom*. Lee Canter & Associates.

Carson, R. N. (1996). Reaction to presidential address of Ronald Butchart. *Educational Studies, 27*(3), 207–216. https://doi.org/10.1207/s15326993es2703_1

Casey, Z. A., Lozenski, B. D., & McManimon, S. K. (2013). From neoliberal policy to neoliberal pedagogy: Racializing and historicising classroom management. *Journal of Pedagogy, 4*(1), 36–58. https://doi.org/10.2478/jped-2013-0003

Collier-Meek, M. A., Johnson, A. H., Sanetti, L. H., & Minami, T. (2019). Identifying critical components of classroom management implementation. *School Psychology Review, 48*(4), 348–361. https://doi.org/10.17105/SPR-2018-0026.V48-4

Cumming, A. (1969). Discipline: An historical examination. *Paedagogica Historica, 9*(1–2), 366–379. https://doi.org/10.1080/0030923690090113

Dreikurs, R. (1974). *Child guidance and education: Collected papers of Rudolf Dreikurs, M.D.* Alfred Adler Institute of Chicago.

Duke, D. L., & Jones, V. F. (1984). Two decades of discipline—Assessing the development of an educational specialization. *Journal of Research and Development in Education, 17*(4), 25–35. https://doi.org/10.1016/0738-0593(84)90024-5

Evertson, C. M., & Weinstein, C. S. (Eds.). (2006a). *Handbook of classroom management: Research, practice, and contemporary issues.* Routledge.

Evertson, C. M., & Weinstein, C. S. (2006b). Classroom management as a field of inquiry. In C. M. Evertson & C. S. Weinstein (Eds.), *Handbook of classroom management: Research, practice, and contemporary issues* (pp. 3–15). Routledge.

Freiberg, H. J. (Ed.). (1999a). *Beyond behaviorism: Changing the classroom management paradigm.* Allyn and Bacon.

Freiberg, H. J. (1999b). Beyond behaviorism. In H. J. Freiberg (Ed.), *Beyond behaviorism: Changing the classroom management paradigm* (pp. 3–20). Allyn and Bacon.

Geddes, P. (1905). The school at Abbotsholme, conducted by Dr. Cecil Reddie. *The Elementary School Teacher, V*(6), 321–333. https://doi.org/10.1086/453460

Greenberg, J., Putman, H., & Walsh, K. (2014). *Training our future teachers: Classroom management, revised.* National Council of Teacher Quality. https://eric.ed.gov/?id=ED556312

Jewett, J. P. (1952). The fight against corporal punishment in American schools. *History of Education Journal, 4*(1), 1–10.

Johnson, F. H. (1952). *Changing conceptions of discipline and pupil-teacher relations in Canadian schools* (Thesis, D. Paed.), University of Toronto. https://archive.org/details/changingconcepti00johnuoft/page/n5/mode/2up

Kounin, J. S. (1977, 1970). *Discipline and group management in classrooms.* Robert E. Krieger Publishing Company.

Mann, H., & Hodgson, W. B. (1846). *Report of an educational tour in Germany, and parts of Great Britain and Ireland, being part of the seventh annual report of Horace Mann, esq., secretary of the Board of Education, Mass., U.S., 1844, with preface and notes* [electronic resource]. Simpkin, Marshall, and Company [etc., etc.]. https://babel.hathitrust.org/cgi/pt?id=mdp.39015003458174&view=1up&seq=11

Marzano, R. J. (2003). *Classroom management that works: Research-based strategies for every teacher.* Association for Supervision and Curriculum Development.

Rousmaniere, K. (1994). Losing patience and staying professional: Women teachers and the problem of classroom discipline in New York City schools in the 1920s. *History of Education Quarterly, 34*(1), 49–68. https://doi.org/10.2307/369228

Ryerson, E. (2000, 1847). *Special report of the measures which have been adopted for the establishment of a normal school: And for carrying into effect generally, the Common School Act, 9th Vict. cap. XX, with an appendix.* E-book. Lovell and Gibson.

Scarlett, W. G. (2015). History of classroom management. *The Sage encyclopedia of Classroom management.* eBook. https://doi.org/10.4135/9781483346243

Schwickerath, R. (1911). Ratio studiorum. In *The catholic encyclopedia.* Robert Appleton Company. New Advent www.newadvent.org/cathen/12654a.htm

Simonsen, B., Fairbanks, S., Briesch, A., Myers, D., & Sugai, G. (2008). Evidence-based practices in classroom management: Considerations for research to practice. *Education and Treatment of Children, 31*(3), 351–380. https://doi.org/10.1353/etc.0.0007

Simonsen, B., Freeman, J., Goodman, S., Mitchell, B., Swain-Bradway, J., Flannery, B., Sugai, G., George, H., & Putnam, B. (2015). *Supporting and responding to student behavior: Evidence-based classroom strategies for teachers.* OSEP Technical Assistance Brief. www.pbis.org/resource/supporting-and-responding-to-behavior-evidence-based-classroom-strategies-for-teachers

Stearns, P. N., & Stearns, C. (2017). American schools and the uses of shame: An ambiguous history. *History of Education, 46*(1), 58–75. http://dx.doi.org/10.1080/0046760X.2016.1185671

Weinstein, C. S. (1999). Reflections on best practices and promising programs: Beyond assertive classroom discipline. In H. Jerome Freiberg (Ed.), *Beyond behaviorism: Changing the classroom management paradigm* (pp. 147–163). Allyn and Bacon.

Winship, A. E. (1925). Horace Mann, personally and professionally. *The Journal of Education, 101*(6), 149–172. https://doi.org/10.1177/002205742410002102

PART 1
Gaining Classroom Authority Introduction

Discussions regarding the nature of teacher authority are not new. One need only think of the different types of authority identified by Max Weber to realize the myriad ways available to authorize teachers (Badley, 2009). What is under-researched is the notion of teacher self-authorization. As Badley reports, because the research investigating how teachers authorize themselves is slim, the film industry has stepped into the gap to define both successful teaching and teacher authorization, creating unrealistic and overly romanticized visions in the process.

The authors in this section offer more reasonable visions based on teacher experiences and theory. H.G. Ginott recalled in *Teacher and Child: A Book for Parents and Teachers* (1972) how he had arrived at "a frightening conclusion. I am the decisive element in the classroom. It is my personal approach that creates the climate" (p. 15). How teachers authorize themselves will have a significant impact on how their classrooms operate and on their students' learning experiences, implying that teacher self-authorization is very important. As we learn from the chapter on invitational theory, how "one looks at something often exercises a profound impact on how one acts in response." Thus, the manner in which teachers view authority and their role in the classroom has impacts on how they interact with students, on the ethos they establish in the classroom, on how they define "good" and "bad" behavior, and so much more.

As several authors in this volume note, it takes courage to be oneself in the classroom. Several describe trying to be someone else at some point in their career, trying to emulate someone else they thought was more successful than they were. And all discovered that such emulation was not possible. The insight of these authors is that self-authorization starts with the courage to dig deep and discern who one is. As Parker Palmer (2007) reminds us, we all teach who we are, and therefore teachers need to understand themselves if they are going to

DOI: 10.4324/9781003140849-3

authorize themselves to teach who they are. If they do so, they are better able to be present to their students, to listen to their students, and to believe in their students' capacity to behave in ways that support learning.

References

Badley, K. (2009). Coercion and consent: Helping pre-service teachers understand classroom authority. In *Faculty publications—school of education* (Paper 53). http://digitalcommons.georgefox.edu/soe_faculty/53

Ginott, H. G. (1972). *Teacher and child: A book for parents and teachers*. Palgrave Macmillan.

Palmer, P. J. (2007). *The courage to teach: Exploring the inner landscape of a teacher's life* (10th anniversary ed.). Jossey-Bass.

3
AUTHORIZING YOURSELF TO TEACH

Ken Badley and Michelle C. Hughes

The idea of *self-authorization* may be new to some readers, but it is a relatively simple concept: we need to permit ourselves to teach. In this chapter, we will highlight several aspects of self-authorization, beginning with the idea that teaching is a vocation and including such personal qualities as determination, caring, presence, and courage.

Self-Authorization: What, When, Why?

Many teachers torment themselves with vocational questions, sometimes for good reason. Some families consider the profession of teaching beneath (or above) them and consequently do not support their adult children's vocational desires and choices. Other teachers end up asking vocational questions because they struggle with the challenging combination of the sheer volume of hard work, the relatively modest salaries, and the criticism teachers regularly face from some politicians and members of the public who apparently believe that schools should be able to solve all society's ills in about six hours per day. Some question whether teaching is their vocation because students do not respond warmly to their teaching; they seem simply unable to make their classroom function as it should (a legitimate concern and one several authors in this volume address). In the face of criticisms and vocational doubts, teachers need to authorize themselves, by which we mean they need to be able to assert to themselves and to their family and most trusted friends, "I am going to teach." And they need to make this same assertion clear to their students, likely more by demonstration than with those precise words. Current and vernacular versions of the idea of authorizing oneself run more like "I've got this" or "You go girl!" In our view, if some form of the Nike slogan or the words of *The Little Engine that Could* (Watty Piper, 1930) gets

DOI: 10.4324/9781003140849-4

one out of bed in the morning and to school, then that is precisely what teachers should say. Teachers who would authorize themselves must rise above family expectations and workload, salary, public criticism, and environmental factors so that such considerations fade into a quiet backdrop to their important work.

The most obvious setting in which teachers need to authorize themselves and the one we focus on in this chapter is in their day-to-day work in their own classrooms with their students. They need to authorize themselves in this more direct way every time they start a class. In music and comedy, a *cold start* implies beginning one's song or sketch without an introduction by a host or master of ceremonies. Opera singers have to authorize themselves this way every time they sing; no one introduces them. They muster their confidence, courage, chutzpah, guts, pluck, or moxie—call it what you like—but when their turn to sing comes they stand up and they start singing. Apparently, the decision to begin a given episode of *Saturday Night Live* (SNL) with a cold start always entails a lot of discussion during the week. The big question at SNL is always whether the audience will go with the performer or performers who begin the show with a cold start. To be quite blunt, teachers do a cold start at the start of their first year in their first school, at the start of their first year in every school after that, at the start of every new school day, and, for that matter, at the start of every class in their career. Obviously, teaching gets easier, but our point is that teachers never (or rarely) have the luxury of a principal introducing them after warming the class up with a funny monologue. In the ordinary circumstances in which teachers work every day, they must authorize themselves to teach. Teachers start; it is what they do.

In addition to the day-to-day need to start teaching, situations sometimes arise in class where teachers must authorize themselves in another way. The film *Freedom Writers* (LaGravanese, 2007) has Hillary Swank portray real-life teacher Erin Gruwell facing strong opposition from her students who make it quite clear in one scene that they do not care one iota about her credentials, teaching license, contract, or educational ideals. In their view, she came to their side of town as another wannabe savior, do-gooder teacher. They planned to cut her no slack whatsoever. She had no choice but to authorize herself to teach them and she did that. Not to be cynical, but, of course, her story would never have made it to the screen had Erin Gruwell's students not ultimately authorized her as well, but our point here is that, to begin, she had to stand up—literally and figuratively— and authorize herself. As the story unfolds, we learn that her students ultimately authorized her partly because she had the courage to do just that. We also learn that she authorized them—in this case, to be literal authors—and that her authorizing them worked reciprocally, that her posture as a warm demander (Chapter 15), as a teacher who communicated high expectations led them to respect her more. Not all teachers face the antipathy Erin Gruwell had to overcome, but all teachers do have to authorize themselves.

Several teacher films other than *Freedom Writers* illustrate self-authorization. For example, *Stand and Deliver* (Menéndes, 1988) is based on Jay Matthews' 1986 book *Escalante: Best Teacher in America*. It contains parallels to *Freedom Writers* inasmuch as minority students need to be shown that their teacher—a newcomer—deserves their trust. *Mona Lisa Smile* (Newell, 2003) repeats the newcomer theme as it follows a professor through her first year of teaching at an élite women's college. She must work to gain her students' consent to be their professor. *Not One Less* (Zhang, 1999) follows the newcomer formula, but it tells the story of a girl of 13 who is pressed into service as the teacher in the elementary school in her remote Chinese village. Obviously, given her age, a major theme of the story will necessarily be about self-authorization. We expect that no readers of this book were required to take over a village classroom at age 13, but our thesis remains: teachers need to authorize themselves to teach. They have to demonstrate their authority to teach by standing up and starting.

The well-known teacher film *The School of Rock* (Linklater, 2003) illustrates that people not formally authorized to teach are also able to authorize themselves. Mason Steinke explores this film at length in Chapter 8 of this volume, so we simply mention it here. In the film, a licensed teacher's unqualified housemate (played by Jack Black) answers a school's phoned request for a Substitute Teacher and shows up at the school simply to get the work. In short, he authorizes himself to teach. Other films and books illustrate that such fraudulent self-authorizing happens in other fields of endeavor as well. For example, in *Catch Me if You Can* (Spielberg, 2002), different groups of people continue to grant a fraudster authority simply because he acts in expected ways as if he actually has formal or contractual authority to do what he is doing; he authorizes himself. In Anne Tyler's 1980 novel, *Morgan's Passing*, her protagonist regularly authorizes himself to step into circumstances and do what is needed at the moment, even pretending at one point to be a doctor and delivering a baby. As was the case with Frank Abagnale, the fraudster in *Catch Me if You Can*, Tyler's Morgan authorizes himself simply by acting in the ways people expect.

People's responses to the imposters portrayed in *Morgan's Passing* and *Catch Me if You Can* are important to our understanding of self-authorization. Morgan and Frank Abagnale both acted like people expect someone formally authorized to act. Because they acted that way, those around them assumed they were formally authorized and therefore granted them their consent. That is, expectations are a factor. Those who pay to attend the opera or the concert expect the singer to stand up and start. And students expect their teachers to teach. Teachers should not underestimate the importance of what social scientists call the *expectation effect* on students' behavior. We may go to school in the morning knowing that we have to authorize ourselves to teach. But, if we have done a few key things right, most of our students will come to school expecting to authorize us to teach.

In the introductory chapter of this book, we cataloged several kinds of authority and connected that catalog to classrooms and the ways teachers and students work together in those classrooms. The authors of all the chapters in this book recognize the three kinds of authority usually needed by teachers: a teaching degree, a license to teach (usually dependent on the teacher's having earned the degree by taking courses, completing internships successfully, and so on), and formal, legal authority, in the form of a contract with a school authority. We recognize those three necessities here and would never suggest that self-authorization is sufficient (except perhaps in the fantasy world of *School of Rock*). Rather, we are suggesting that these three kinds of authorization only get us **to** the classroom; self-authorization helps us become successful once we get there. At its most blunt, the person who cannot stand up and start teaching will not succeed as a teacher.

The Components of Self-Authorization

Self-authorization requires both attitudes and actions. We will explore those briefly here and then consider several other possible qualities and characteristics that likely contribute to teachers' efforts to authorize themselves.

Attitudes, Dispositions, Postures

Our references to teachers in film—what many call *reel teachers*—underline the importance of teachers' attitudes. One must have confidence that one can teach. We know that many of our readers have had days during their in-school placements when they wondered if they had what it apparently takes to do this challenging work. Veteran teachers have those days as well. When they start any year, or day, or individual class, some veteran teachers conduct a mental review of the teaching resources they have at hand, resources such as their degree, their expertise, and their years of classroom experience. Beginning teachers might think of what they have learned in their micro-teaching experiences in their first semesters of their education degree, their longer internships, their own subject-area expertise, and their deep desire to see children learn, to suggest a few examples. That kind of review of resources builds a teacher's confidence. Backpackers don't leave the trailhead without checking that they have what they need. Perhaps the same kinds of checks would reassure teachers that we have what we need to start and would give our confidence the boost we sometimes need.

Teachers who authorize themselves to teach share authority in the classroom. This may sound counterintuitive because sharing authority with others may sound like one's own supply or pool of authority necessarily shrinks. But sharing classroom authority with students takes the pressure off teachers to know everything and to be in control of everything that occurs in the classroom. The disposition at work here is openness to recognize one's own strengths and the strengths of one's students. Some students have the interest and experience to be an expert on some content, or they have the skills to lead a discussion or help plan an event.

Authorizing oneself recognizes that self is part of a community, and members of a community work together rather than alone. This recognition helps the teacher let go of some unrealistic expectations of control as described in

Chapter 14 but also models for, and develops within, students aspects of democratic education. Additionally, it demonstrates care for students, another disposition, by doing one's best to ensure that all students thrive and flourish throughout the year or semester that they are together with the teacher. The dispositions of sharing authority and caring for students are related, as many students can reach high school and not recognize that they have a particular gift, such as being able to sum up an argument's key points or identify the key issues in a controversial social debate or mediate conflict. When teachers share authority, students learn what they are good at and what their gifts are, and they gain support in their efforts to develop those gifts. When teachers help students identify their gifts, students grow in their self-knowledge. In both instances, there is a greater likelihood that students will flourish.

Actions

We have made repeated references in this chapter to singers for good reason: they stand up and start. We fully realize how obvious the parallel to that claim might be that teachers start teaching. But we state the obvious because, being that obvious, some might miss it. Teachers start teaching. Earlier, we noted what social scientists call the expectation effect. Briefly defined, people tend to adjust their behavior to suit what others expect of them. As Patrick notes in Chapter 15 (on multicultural classrooms), students come to school expecting their teachers to teach and, in most cases, adjust their behavior accordingly. Some decades ago, Phillip Schlechty (2011) introduced his schema of levels of student engagement. Many educators benefit from his insight that at any given moment students' postures in a class might range from full engagement to open rebellion. Notwithstanding that fact, students still expect teachers to teach. As teachers, we need to act accordingly. We need to start teaching.

Having given the earlier paragraph to the obvious, we now add that a key part of standing and starting—part of teaching—is that we do so prepared and with clear purposes. Again, professional singers have prepared, they know what song comes next, and they know the songs themselves, intimately. Even the apparently spontaneous encore at the end of a rock or pop concert is planned in advance. Likewise, the teacher comes to class prepared and starts by saying specific words and starting specific activities related to the learning outcomes for that class. The teacher knows what comes next and knows the content, intimately. The opera, rock, or pop singer's apparent ease and sense of control are the results of both preparation and experience. Likewise, the apparent ease with which great teachers teach roots itself in much preparation and, usually, much experience. We want to note an aspect of preparation that many teachers forget in the busyness of day-to-day preparation and teaching. While it may be true that a teacher prepared a given lesson the evening before or even over their lunch hour, it remains the case that teachers have been preparing for each class for years, possibly even from before they took their first education course at university. Certainly, they have been preparing since the first day of their first placement. With preparation framed that way, teachers may be able to respond to that nagging doubt, "I don't feel ready for this class," with self-talk more along the lines of "Heck, I've been getting ready for this class for years!," a much more positive thing to say if, in the rush of a busy work week, they did not manage to get every instructional minute planned in detail.

We list trust as an action, although it is arguably an attitude or posture. Why list trust as an action? As a teacher, you need to trust yourself. You need to trust your experience (even in your first year). You need to trust your preparation. You need to trust the process of interacting with students and colleagues. In our view, trusting the process implies not being afraid to learn. If a student challenges a teacher's instructions or teaching content, view it as an opportunity for dialogue, not as a threat to your authority. Responding to such a challenge with the power of your office (the degree, the license, the contract) actually diminishes student goodwill or what we call *moral authority* throughout this book. Such challenges require you to trust yourself and the process.

Self-Authorization: Other Factors

Several other factors connect with self-authorization. Presence, which Chapters 5 and 6 address in detail, is obviously a part of being able to *start* teaching on a given day or in a given class. In this chapter, we will not explore it at length, but we do want to note that those teachers who know they have presence have an easier time making the kind of cold start we talked about in the first page of this chapter.

"Good to Go" (Chapter 4) deals with the idea of student consent that students must authorize their teachers to teach. Among the several links to the idea of self-authorization, one of the most important is that the teacher who teaches for several years in the same school building earns a reputation of one kind or another. Good or bad, engaging or boring, tough or soft, that reputation contributes to students' expectations as siblings and students' friends in older grades tell younger students about different teachers, their preferred pedagogical styles, the kinds of assessments they use, and especially the climate in their classrooms. A good reputation in a school building increases the freedom teachers' have to authorize themselves with each incoming year's students. A bad reputation decreases that freedom.

The last factor we wish to note, before turning to an extended treatment of courage, is simple: it is the teacher's personality that drives the class. One of us (KB) served for several years on a committee that selected 20 finalists for outstanding teaching awards given annually by the Alberta Minister of Education. Reading through about 200 nominations over four days repeatedly confirmed what Haim Ginott (1972) wrote decades ago, that he had arrived at "a frightening conclusion. I am the decisive element in the classroom. It is my personal approach that creates the climate" (p. 15). The conversation among the members of the selection committee for those outstanding teacher awards was peppered with affirmations of the truth of Ginott's comment. Several times per day, someone would say aloud, "As goes the teacher, so goes the class." Ginott's frightening conclusion points to the importance and significance of teacher authority. Yes, there is one teacher and as many as 35 students in a class (depending on the setting), but the teacher's personality still drives the class; the teacher is the decisive element. If that personality or decisive element comes from a place of teachers' recognition of their rightful place in the classroom, recognition of their students' place, recognition of themselves as learners, and recognition of the need for community relationships rather than hierarchical ones, classrooms will feel and look very different from how they look when teachers rely on raw power or try to authorize themselves by virtue of their degree, license, contract, age, gender, stature, and so on.

Courage

Courage can be linked to self-authorization. Courage, often synonymous with bravery, can serve as strength during difficult times. Courage denotes mustering up some character and guts, pulling up your bootstraps, and finding the inner strength to power through, to keep going, and to persevere. Without taking a survey or doing years of intense research, most teachers have encountered classroom experiences that require courage and a measure, or many measures, of strength.

Most often, people think of courage as physical courage—like Superman lifting a two-ton truck off a damsel in distress or saving a child in danger. It must be remembered, though, that Superman, like most glorified superheroes, also summoned moral and emotional courage in his work saving the world. In my humble opinion, teachers are similar—they are superheroes in their own right; teachers need to tap into moral, physical, and emotional courage in the classroom. Whether teachers need to find a creative way to motivate a student or find the inner strength to deal with loss or grief in the classroom, teachers need to authorize and essentially give themselves permission to move forward and persevere through the day-in and day-out grind that they sometimes feel. And they may even experience an exceptional trauma such as a school shooting or a natural disaster. Hence, teachers self-authorize when they need to tackle a difficult issue at a school board meeting or disagree constructively with their principal. Regardless of the circumstances, teachers need courage each and every day.

Most recently, during the ongoing global COVID-19 pandemic, teachers were forced to tap into a well of courage. Sometimes courage is an option or a choice, yet during the pandemic, courage became a "get onboard or be left behind" mentality. The pandemic forced school districts, teachers, and administrators to make sweeping decisions for students and schools. Teachers needed to buy in and quickly find or muster up courage from within themselves. There wasn't time for grieving, digging their heels in, or considering not showing up. Teachers tapped into and found courage to teach in new ways whether they liked it or not.

By finding and exercising courage, a teacher builds confidence as both an individual and a professional. Parker Palmer (2004) calls this type of work *inner work* or *growing from the inside out*. As humans, teachers often doubt and are skeptical about their own strength and courage. Yet once a teacher exercises or demonstrates courage, there can be a sense of relief and even renewal. Just like when a person practices gratitude, practicing courage fosters a desire to develop more courage. Exercising courage strengthens a teacher's muscles for bravery and grows more courage.

Recently, a student of mine (MH) was nervous to teach a first lesson in clinical practice; she shared that she summoned a dose of courage and the new experience energized her to want to improve her lesson and delivery. Because this student took a risk and embraced the opportunity to teach and practice, she felt empowered by her actions and courage. The student's example demonstrates that taking time to identify courage and authorize courage produces more courage.

Palmer tells the story of a teacher who teaches beautifully one day and then the next day that teacher's lesson flops (1998). In order to teach again the following day, the teacher must reflect and find courage to get back in the game. Disney's famous teen movie *High School Musical* (Ortega, 2006) has a song that reminds the audience to "Get your head in the game, get your head, head, head in the game." The words to this song ring true for teachers as they self-authorize and get back in the game and the classroom when the going gets tough or when the next teaching day comes.

Likewise, Dweck's research (2007) on growth mindset posits that mindsets are incentives that inform behavior and choices. A growth mindset, rather than a fixed mindset, prompts an individual to push forward, to learn, to persevere, and to grow. Possessing a growth mindset helps teachers and all humans make choices and respond to situations, even those that require courage. Likewise, dispositions, such as resilience or courage, inform our responses, our decisions, and our actions as we teach, collaborate, and engage in classroom work (CAEP, 2016). Being open to growing and having a growth mindset takes courage and strength.

As teachers continue to navigate the changing landscape and never-ending pressures in education, there is an increased need to find, develop, and demonstrate courage as professionals. Teachers can make the conscious choice to authorize taking risks, to employ a growth mindset, and to grow professionally in order to acquire courage. As teachers, we do this every day. In the wise words of Superman, "You're much stronger than you think you are, trust me."

Conclusion

Authorizing oneself to teach is necessary if a teacher is going to be successful. As demonstrated here, self-authorization is an ongoing process. It begins on the first day of the Pre-Service Teacher's first school placement when facing one's first group of students with no reputation to support one's claim of authority. It continues (several times in one's career) on the day after a poorly-executed lesson the day before. To self-authorize, to show up and teach, becomes easier over time, but it always involves the same set of dispositions and actions: confidence, openness to learning, and courage. Importantly, teachers require courage in the face of new challenges, such as internal changes within a school or a tragedy that affects the whole school community, a group of students, or an individual family (such as Dena Palmaymesa recounts in Chapter 24). And as the section on courage makes clear, the more that a teacher self-authorizes, the more that they develop the courage to do so, the more courage they will develop to keep on doing so despite the challenges.

References

Council for the Accreditation of Educator Preparation Standards. (2016). *Vision, mission, strategic goals.* http://caepnet.org/about/vision-mission-goals
Dweck, C. (2007). *Mindset: The new psychology of success.* Ballantine.
Ginott, H. G. (1972). *Teacher and child: A book for parents and teachers.* Palgrave Macmillan.
LaGravanese, R. (Director). (2007). *Freedom writers.* Paramount Pictures.
Linklater, R. (Director). (2003). *School of rock.* Paramount Pictures.
Matthews, J. (Director). (1986). *Escalante: Best teacher in America.* Holt.
Menéndes, R. (Director). (1988). *Stand and deliver.* Warner Brothers.
Newell, M. (Director). (2003). *Mona Lisa smile.* Columbia Pictures.
Ortega, K. (2006). *High school musical.* Disney.
Palmer, P. (1998). *The courage to teach.* Jossey-Bass.
Palmer, P. (2004). *A hidden wholeness.* Jossey-Bass.
Piper, W. (1930). *The little engine that could.* Platt and Munk.
Schlechty, P. (2011). *Engaging students: The next level of working on the work.* Jossey-Bass
Spielberg, S. (Director). (2002). *Catch me if you can.* DreamWorks Pictures.
Tyler, A. (1980). *Morgan's passing.* Fawcett.
Zhang, Y. (Director). (1999). *Not one less.* Sony Pictures.

4
GOOD TO GO
Teaching by Our Students' Consent

Ken Badley

In this chapter, I argue that teachers need to demonstrate the kinds of moral and professional qualities that will lead their students to consent to the teacher's leadership in the classroom. Teachers need to be *good* in the moral sense of that term, as demonstrated by their consistent efforts to show care and respect to their students and to act with fairness in all their dealings with students. In other words, student consent has a moral foundation, the root of one of the senses of the word *good* in our title and the focus of this chapter. Teachers need to be *good* in the professional sense as well. That is, they need to be good at what they do, to be competent at teaching. Specifically, this professional goodness expresses itself in three (four?) ways. They know their subject area. They use a variety of appropriate instructional strategies day to day. They come to class prepared. They use assessments that allow students to show authentically what they have learned. Although professional competence is not my focus in this chapter, I must nevertheless keep it in view because professional competence—being a good teacher, not just a good person—is essential to earning our students' consent to teach.

The contemporary phrase *good to go* connotes that everything is in order and an activity can proceed. The software is now installed correctly. The car is packed for the trip. The team members have put on their game face. By assigning the title "Good to Go" to this chapter, I wish to catch the sense that teachers who demonstrate the kinds of moral and professional qualities I listed will be able to carry out their classroom program with their students' consent. When teachers meet the necessary conditions, their students will grant them the right to teach, what some call *moral authority*.

The phrase *good to go* is a relatively recent addition to the English lexicon. But the word *consent* goes back centuries. In 1689, political philosopher John Locke wrote in *Two Treatises of Government* that governments rule by the consent of their citizens. In his understanding, a government ruling without the consent of citizens is illegitimate and is likely governed by power alone. Locke's distinction between legitimate authority (consent) and illegitimate authority lies at the foundation of every part of this book. When I assert that teachers need their students' consent to teach, I do not mean that teachers can ignore the formal, threshold requirements of the degree, the license, and the contract. Rather, I am saying that the three typical elements of formal authorization are only the starting point for the teacher's authority; they are required for the teacher to secure a teaching position, but they do not guarantee long-term success. The degree, license, and employment contract imply, for example, that the teacher possesses a level of expertise. But students want to know if their teachers can be trusted, if they care, if they're fair. When teachers meet such additional criteria, most students will grant them their consent to teach. Locke addresses his 1689 volume to questions of the state and its government, not to classrooms. But I use his language here because his arguments clearly do apply to classrooms.

The Three Starting Conditions

In the introduction, I lumped together expertise, a teaching certificate, and a contract as *three threshold conditions* for teaching. Briefly, I want to return to these three basics. I noted that some mistake these necessities for sufficient conditions, that is, thinking that a teacher not only can start teaching but also can continue through the school year with these alone. No doubt, in most cases, the teacher needs these three, but they are not sufficient and therefore they warrant our attention. I recognize that teachers in millions of formal and in formal learning settings share their expertise without a certificate or a contract. With those caveats in view, I return to the fact that most school authorities take the certificate issued by a teacher certification agency as evidence of expertise; they trust the other authorities involved in the teaching, assessing, and credentialing processes of teacher candidates. With the certificate in hand, the new teacher has applied to a school or school authority and has received an offer of employment. Thus, the contract implies certification, and certification implies at least a beginning level of expertise. Except during teacher shortages, most schools view the expertise and certificate as necessities before they will issue the contract. Nevertheless, almost every certified teacher with a contract has discovered that, while necessary, these three qualifications are not sufficient to execute a classroom program month to month and year to year.

The Degree

Connecting authority and certification is also important for our understanding of professorial authority. Many professions establish systems of certification so that the paying public can save themselves the trouble of having to judge expertise which is, in fact, beyond their own expertise to judge. Indeed, some recognize this credentialing function as the telling mark of a profession. It is interesting here to compare the grounds on which one is appointed and the grounds on which one excels in various professions. It is in answering this question that the teacher's credentials differ in at least one important respect from those of other professionals. For example, I may forgive lawyers for being ill-mannered as long as they are competent, but I will likely not stay with a doctor for long if I think she does not care, regardless of her level of competence. In both cases, the certification process is meant to guarantee an entry level of expertise. Beyond that, both doctors and lawyers gain reputations as good or bad doctors or lawyers. I choose doctors and lawyers primarily on the basis of that competence, but I may add the condition of care in the case of a doctor (as Emily Robinson notes in Chapter 6).

When I think of teachers, however, I see that the grounds on which I am appointed are only a beginning part of what I need to be successful in the profession, it is an entry-level necessary condition. Habits of class preparation, standards of fairness, and a disposition toward caring are not guaranteed by certification. In effect, the degree, license, and contract give the average teacher the authority to walk into a room on the first day of the term. From that day on, teachers must earn the right to teach. They must, in effect, prove the wisdom of the appointment (and implicitly even the wisdom of having been granted a teaching degree and license).

We need to add one codicil to the claim that the degree indicates expertise. As a teacher educator, I believe that graduating from an education program usually does indicate a level of pedagogical competence one would ordinarily expect from a beginning teacher. I also believe that I live in a particular cultural moment when expertise of all kinds has come under attack. Consider these three beliefs as examples: that the earth is flat, that climate change is not real, and that COVID-19 is a hoax. To put it at its starkest, and using COVID-19 as an example, thanks to Dr. Google, Dr. Reddit, and Dr. Facebook, everyone can do their own "research" on COVID now, and they can ignore the conclusions of trained researchers with a budget larger than the GDP of some nations (U.S. Centers for Disease Control 2021 budget of US$15.4 billion). In *The Death of Expertise*, Tom Nichols (2017) traces the roots of this rejection of expertise and catalogs some of its effects. In defense of credentials and the expertise they represent, he writes, "While some of the most determined opponents of established knowledge deride [degrees and licenses] as mere 'credentialism,' these degrees and licenses are tangible signs of achievement and important markers that help the rest of us separate hobbyists (or charlatans) from true experts" (p. 31). I stand with Nichols on this point; a teaching credential implies expertise that non-teachers usually do not have.

In fact, teachers may face more questions about their expertise than some other professionals. In his 1975 sociological study of teaching, Dan Lortie used the phrase "apprenticeship of observation" (p. 31) to name the reality that most people have gone to school and therefore have an opinion of how classrooms and teaching ought to work. Few of us have been close-up witnesses to the finer details of the work that lawyers, welders, or doctors do, and so I may trust them to do their professional work (although Nichols has observed declines even in those areas). But all of us have been close-up witnesses to the work of teachers. Lortie was particularly interested in how this apprenticeship shapes the expectations of would-be teachers and how, during their teacher education, they learn or do not learn new understandings of curriculum and instructional strategies they have not seen before. I note it here in the context of Nichols' lament about the death of expertise; combine the apprenticeship of observation with a cultural shift by which everyone is now an expert, and teachers' actual expertise will likely be regarded with less deference than it was a century ago. That is, our authority has suffered a decline, even while the requirements for entering the teaching profession have risen.

The License

As is the university degree, the teaching certificate or license remains in place as a prerequisite for most teaching posts. Ordinarily, an administrative officer in the education program at the university forwards to the Teacher Certification Branch of the respective Department or Ministry of Education a list of students who have met all the requirements for the teaching degree. Next, staff in that branch of government mail teaching licenses to all the freshly graduated teachers whose names the universities have provided them. Most new teachers receive some kind of initial or conditional teaching license and receive a permanent license after two or three years of successful teaching and possibly the completion of some additional courses or attendance at professional development workshops. I already noted (with reference to the degree) that this government-issued certificate or license is necessary to move into the teaching profession, but it is not sufficient for success in that profession.

The Contract

With an education degree and initial teaching license in hand, the new teacher then must find a job. I know our readers know that. Without repeating what I have said in the earlier two sub-sections, my point here is simple: the contract is necessary for starting into the teaching profession, but it does not guarantee that students will engage with the new teacher. New teachers—what some call induction teachers—must still earn their students' consent.

Conclusion: The Three Starting Conditions

To conclude this brief discussion of these three initial requirements, I want to reiterate that in almost all formal settings, the degree, license, and contract are necessary. Furthermore, I believe that these three forms or sources of authority imply that the new teacher has levels of knowledge and expertise that one ordinarily expects of a competent beginning teacher. I expect new teachers to have some subject-area expertise and to possess at least a beginning repertoire of teaching methods and understanding of how high-functioning classrooms work.

We also want to reiterate that teachers who believe that these three forms of legal or formal authority are sufficient to exercise classroom authority will likely not work as hard at earning students' consent as those teachers who understand the fundamental necessity of consent. Furthermore, teachers believing these three forms of authority to be sufficient are less likely to look to those whom they serve for subtle clues or even advice regarding how to exercise their authority. Finally, such teachers may be surprised and then suspicious of those students who do not grant them the authority they assumed followed naturally on the designation of a formal teaching degree. This brief catalog of negative possibilities is not the end; I now turn to the kinds of authority that teachers earn and, implicitly, some of the ways they earn that authority.

Moral Authority

Having noted the necessity of three kinds of formal authority to get into a classroom, I turn now to the matter of gaining students' consent to teach so that one might keep returning to that classroom. Students usually give their consent to those teachers who establish over time that they are good people and who demonstrate the professionalism one ordinarily expects of educators. As I noted in the first paragraph of the chapter, the word *good* in the chapter title refers to both these aspects. In what follows, I focus on moral authority, by which I mean getting the consent of one's students by establishing over time that one is a good person.

Those who have studied authority have defined moral authority in a variety of ways. Some speak of legitimacy or legitimate authority. Many join John Locke and use the word *consent* in their definitions as a way to distinguish legitimate authority from raw power. In fact, the distinction between consent and power has remained in place in philosophy and political science from Locke's time to our own. In our view, teachers need to remember that distinction every day they teach, in part because teachers who rely on their power—on the authority that comes with their *office*, so to speak—likely will find their moral authority eroded (Yariv, 2009; Koutrouba et al., 2012). How can teachers gain the consent of their students? I turn to that question now.

Gaining Moral Authority

How do teachers gain their students' consent to conduct their classroom program, a program that requires students to do hard work? In most situations where someone has gained legitimate authority, a number of features are typically present. I want to be clear that these are not behavioral techniques the teacher can implement; they are not steps to follow in a specified order. Rather, these are *postures* that arise from deep within the teacher's own self. Before turning to the qualities themselves, let me suggest two conditions. First, I believe that people can grow into postures or develop dispositions by engaging in the practices that ordinarily arise from them. I deal with that learning and growth at the end of Chapter 5. Second, I list these postures and dispositions fully aware that, in each case, I am only touching the surface; each of the following small sections represents robust areas of research. With that condition in place, I want to suggest seven postures necessary for teachers to gain their students' consent: showing care, acting with fairness, showing respect, showing humility, being hospitable, having presence, and listening. I begin with care.

Care

For several decades, the research literature on care in education has grown, sparked in part by the philosophical work of Nel Noddings (1984, 1992, 2007). If I may generalize the conclusions of several earlier researchers, caring is a necessary component of good teaching and it is connected to students' acceptance of their teachers' authority (Miller, 2021; Noblit, 1991; Rogers & Webb, 1991; Wentzel, 1997; Baker et al., 1997). Later research, such as that conducted by Keyes (2019), continues to reveal the connection. With a few exceptions, for example, Mastel-Smith et al. (2015), most research into caring does not make direct connections to moral authority. However, if, as I argue, moral authority is essential to student learning, much of the research on care supports our thesis.

Respect

The history of research into respect has followed a similar trajectory to the research into care. For decades, researchers (Stone, 1995; Nuckles, 2000; Vella, 2002, 2008; O'Grady, 2015; Miller et al., 2017) have asked students about the characteristics, postures, and practices of those teachers whose classes they enjoy taking. The list of desirable traits and practices is long, but, predictably, *shows respect for students* appears consistently. This should not surprise us; in life outside of school buildings, I give my respect—grant authority—to other people for any number of reasons, among them that they have shown respect to me. I recognize that respect and moral authority are not synonymous. However, with reference to educators' need for students to grant them the room to teach, the overlaps between these two concepts are obvious. That is why I list respect as one of the essential postures for teachers to adopt.

Max Van Manen (2016) has approached respect, albeit from a different angle. Based on years of observations in K-12 classrooms, he has identified what he calls the four fears of students: failure, ridicule, rejection, and punishment (p. 94). Notice that the second, ridicule, is precluded by respect. Multiple films illustrate Van Manen's concern. In the feature film *Ten Things I Hate About You* (Junger, 1999), a teacher insults a secondary student (played by Julie Stiles) and demands that she leave the classroom. She does as he asks, but her complete lack of respect for him is clear from her facial expression and body language. In the language of this chapter, in losing her respect for her teacher, her teacher lost his authority; his demand that she leave the classroom was simply an exercise in power. Although the majority of real teachers in the world do show respect to their students, I find it interesting that the cliché of the insulting teacher who uses power persists in television and film.

PRESENCE AND HUMILITY

Angela Farrington-Thompson

Humility is a necessity in the classroom. And, because showing humility is a means of demonstrating confidence, it fits with the idea of presence. It is also woven into the idea of students' ownership of their learning.

Curriculum documents from departments of education often remind teachers to recognize the knowledge and experience that every student brings into the classroom. Lesson plan templates, for example, encourage educators to open a lesson with an activity that will bring prior knowledge and experience to the forefront of students' thinking. This has the obvious function of allowing the teacher to ascertain what students already know about a topic and thereby determine what still needs to be taught. But kind of exploration opens another door: the possibility that the teacher will discover students in the classroom who have more experience or understanding of a topic than they do.

This has happened to me, particularly in instances where I have been called on to teach a subject or topic that is not my forte, a situation that generalists encounter regularly. Three paths are usually open to a teacher in this circumstance. First, they can bluster and fall back on their position of authority in the classroom, silencing or stifling the input of the students who know more than they do. Second, they can latch on to the expertise of these students and in some sense give over the classroom to them. This path may or may not be wise, depending on the dynamic of the class. Third, they can welcome the contributions of such students in an attitude of teamwork and *mutual learning*. For example, "You know what, Taylor, you have a lot of background knowledge on this and it's clear you've done a lot of research. I think **we** can learn a lot from that!" "Is it alright if I call on you as we work through this topic and invite your input? You can even spice it up a bit for us!"

The teacher who takes this second/third course of action is not surrendering their position of responsibility and guidance or their voice of organization and direction. Instead, they are acknowledging that they don't know everything, that in some areas, in fact, they might not know more than the basics. And that they too are learners. They are also modeling the kind of attitude they want students to have toward their teachers and toward their peers: respectful, open, positive, and growth oriented. It encourages students in their areas of strength and fosters the kind of collaboration most teachers desire. But it takes humility.

Fairness

We turn now to fairness. I just noted here that (Silver et al., 2014) when students identify the qualities of the teachers they respect—the teachers to whom they grant the authority to teach—they list respect. They also list fairness, consistently (Clayson, 1999; Gipps 1984, 1994; Gipps & Stobart, 2016). I note here that at an early age most humans have developed quite sensitive antennae for unfairness, especially when they consider themselves the victim of that unfairness. I also note something that most veteran teachers already know: fairness and the perception of fairness are not always the same thing (Chory, 2007). Teachers may do their best to treat all their students with fairness as they grade a set of assignments fairly, but some students—frequently and anxiously asking their classmates, "What did you get?"—will consider themselves unfairly treated. The takeaway here is obvious: I must take as many steps as possible to persuade students that I grade fairly. Many teachers, for example, ask students not to sign their work but to assign only a random number to their work. That way, the teacher can grade without knowing the identity of the students and match the assignments to names after completing the grading (I know that this approach has its own problems).

Fairness in education has at least two aspects. First is the one I just discussed that the teacher treats students with fairness not only in relation to each other, especially regarding assessment and grades but also, of course, in relation to classroom behavior. Education students are more likely to hear about the second aspect during a course on assessment in their education program. That is, the teacher uses assessment instruments that assess students' work authentically. This second sense is one of fit; it focuses on the need for assessments to allow those students who know the material to show that they know it and to allow the teacher to see who has not learned the material (and, implicitly, what the teacher may not have taught effectively). Assessments and assignments must fit the learning outcomes for the curriculum and instruction being assessed.

Hospitality

As was the case with care, a growing number of writers have begun to address hospitality in the classroom (Palmer et al., 2010; Kapuscinski, 2008, Marmon, 2008). This area of research and writing is relatively new compared to care, respect, and fairness, but it is rich with implications for teachers who wish to gain the consent of their students. A central theme in this conversation is that the teacher welcomes the student as a guest to the classroom. Not to dwell too much on the obvious, but hospitality has the power to shift the teacher's focus from *covering ground*, as Neil Postman (Postman & Weingartner, 1969) used to call the curriculum-focused teacher's goal, toward learning with students. Hospitality shows itself in simple acts, such as welcoming students by name at the classroom door (as Nadine Ayer recounts in Chapter 9) or bringing snacks to the classroom, as many teachers do.

Smith and Carvill have pointed to an important metaphor that lies in classroom hospitality (2000). The classroom can be a place where teachers offer an intellectual feast to their students. Students do not have to partake of the snacks or drinks a teacher might put on the counter at the side of the room. And they do not have to enjoy the learning feast that their teacher has planned. But both those kinds of sustenance are on offer, and students are invited to enjoy what is there.

Presence, the theme of Chapter 5, could also appear in this treatment of teacher qualities needed to gain students' consent to teach. Because I treat it at length there, I will simply mention it here. Likewise, listening, the focus of Chapter 6, could appear here. Emily Robinson and Shae Nimmo, two colleagues, offer a thorough treatment thereof listening, and so here I will say simply that teachers who want their students' consent to teach need to learn to listen.

Conclusion

Several sources of the teacher's authority are simply missing from the chapter. For example, what role does age play? Some students grant more authority to the young teacher whom they consider cool; others respect the older teacher whom they consider wise (although these qualities are neither guaranteed among nor restricted to those respective age groups). I have not dealt here with how a good reputation developed over years in a single school building increases the authority each new cohort of students grants their teacher (I do deal with this briefly in Chapter 5). Nor have I discussed how accomplishments outside the classroom—in business, sports, the arts, government, or religion and philanthropy, for example—may induce some students to grant their classroom teacher more authority. Chapters 10–14 in this volume explore the idea of authorizing students. The authors of those chapters all hold the view that authorizing students—making them authorities—actually increases the degree to which they grant their teachers more authority. I have not asked in this chapter how students will view their teachers' expertise as the Internet becomes more ubiquitous. For that matter, how will teachers frame our own expertise and how will we work with the changes brought by ubiquitous technology? These questions remain.

Teachers are human beings, complete with strengths and weaknesses. Our students know that about us. But we need to possess some combination of the qualities I have listed in this chapter if we want students to grant us what musicians call *the room to move*—the authority to teach in our classrooms. If we grow into these dispositions and postures, we can end up discovering the authority has become more mutual than we might at first have predicted. Not only will we have room to move with our students, but they will also begin to have a say in what we do. Many of our students will become partners with us in the learning journey we want to lead them on. They will grant us the consent to teach.

References

Baker, J. A., Terry, T., Bridger, R., & Winsor, A. (1997). Schools as caring communities: A relational approach to school reform. *The School Psychology Review, 26*(4), 586–602.

Chory, R. M. (2007). Enhancing student perceptions of fairness: The relationship between instructor credibility and classroom justice. *Communication Education, 56*(1), 89–105.

Clayson, D. E. (1999, April). Students' evaluation of teaching effectiveness: Some implications of stability, *Journal of Marketing Education, 21*, 68–75.

Gipps, C. V. (1984). *Testing children: Standardized testing in local education authorities and schools*. Heinemann.

Gipps, C. V. (1994). *Fair test? Assessment, achievement and equity*. Open University Press.

Gipps, C. V., & Stobart, G. (2016). Fairness in assessment. In N. J. Dorans & L. L. Cook (Eds.), *Educational assessment in the 21st century* (pp. 105–118). Springer.

Junger, G. (Dir). (1999). *Ten things I hate about you*. Touchstone Pictures.

Kapuscinski, R. (2008). *The other*. Verso.

Keyes, T. S. (2019). A qualitative inquiry: Factors that promote classroom belonging and engagement among high school students. *School Community Journal, 29*(1), 171–200.

Koutrouba, K., Baxevanou, E., & Koutroumpas, A. (2012). High school students' perceptions of and attitudes towards teacher power in the classroom. *International Education Studies, 5*(5), 185–198.

Locke, J. (1689 [1988]). *Two treatises of government*. Cambridge University Press.

Lortie, D. C. (1975). *Schoolteacher: A sociological study*. University of Chicago Press.

Marmon, E. L. (2008). Teaching as hospitality. *Asbury Journal, 63*(2), 33–39.

Mastel-Smith, B., Post, J., & Lake, P. (2015). Online teaching: "Are you there, and do you care?" *Journal of Nursing Education, 54*(3), 145–151. https://doi.org/10.3928/01484834-20150218-18.

Miller, A. D., Ramiriz, E. M., & Murdock, T. B. (2017, May). The influence of teachers' self-efficacy on perceptions: Perceived teacher competence and respect and student effort and achievement. *Teaching and Teacher Education, 64*, 260–269. https://doi.org/10.1016/j.tate.2017.02.008

Miller, K. E. (2021). A light in students' lives: K-12 teachers' experiences (re)building caring relationships during remote learning. *Online Teaching Journal, 25*(1), 115–134.

Nichols, T. (2017). *The death of expertise*. Oxford University Press.

Noblit, G. W. (1991, April). *Power and caring.* Paper presented at the American Educational Research Association.

Noddings, N. (1984). *Caring: A feminine approach to ethics and moral education.* University of California Press.

Noddings, N. (1992). *The challenge to care in schools.* Teachers College Press.

Noddings, N. (2007). Caring as relation and virtue in teaching. In R. Walker & P. Ivanhoe (Eds.), *Working virtue: Virtue ethics and contemporary moral problems* (pp. 41–60). Oxford University Press.

Nuckles, C. R. (2000). Student-centered teaching: Making it work. *Adult Learning, 11*(4), 5–6.

O'Grady, E. (2015). Establishing respectful educative relationships: A study of newly qualified teachers in Ireland. *Cambridge Journal of Education 45*(2), 167–185.

Palmer, P., Zajonc, A., & Scribner, M. (2010). *The heart of higher education: A call to renewal.* Jossey-Bass.

Postman, N., & Weingartner, C. (1969). *Teaching as a subversive activity.* Delacorte.

Rogers, D., & Webb, J. (1991), The ethic of caring in teacher education. *Journal of Teacher Education, 42*(3), 173–180.

Smith, D. I., & Carvill, B. (2000). *The gift of the stranger: Faith, hospitality and foreign language learning.* Eerdmans.

Stone, S. J. (1995). Teaching strategies: Empowering teachers, empowering children. *Childhood Education, 71*(5), 294–295.

Van Manen, M. (2016). *Pedagogical tact: Knowing what to do when you don't know what to do.* Routledge.

Vella, J. (2002). *Learning to listen, learning to teach: The power of dialogue in teaching adults.* Jossey-Bass.

Vella, J. (2008). *On teaching and learning: Putting the principles and practices of dialogue education into action.* Jossey-Bass.

Wentzel, K. R. (1997). Student motivation in middle school: The role of perceived pedagogical caring. *Journal of Educational Psychology, 89*(3), 411–419. https://doi.org/10.1037/0022-0663.89.3.411

Yariv, E. (2009). Students' attitudes on the boundaries of teachers' authority. *School Psychology International, 30*(1), 92–111.

5
BEING ALL THERE
Teacher Presence and Teacher Authority

Ken Badley

Chris Rock, a friend (but not the comedian), regularly reminds his students that if they are going to be physically present in class, they might as well engage their thinking as well. To make his point, he repeats the sentence, "If you're going to be present, you might as well be present." In my view, the same is true of teachers. If we are going to be there, we need to be fully there. To use a popular phrase, we can't simply phone it in. We need to be present. In fact, our authority as teachers depends on our being present. But what does being present mean for teachers?

Three questions give shape to this chapter. First, is having presence or being present necessary to establish oneself as a teacher with authority, as a teacher worthy of being in charge of a classroom? Second, is teacher presence definable or is it some kind of X-factor, some mysterious quality that cannot be defined but that people recognize when they see? The task of identifying teacher or teaching presence is made slightly more difficult in our time by cinematic portrayals of teachers because they tend to show the successful teacher as more enigmatic, charismatic, troubled, or brilliant than most of us actually are. The third question—the practical question—is this: whether presence is necessary to a teacher's authority or not, whether it can be defined or not, can it be learned? These are three important questions, especially for Pre-Service Teachers who, legitimately, want to have some idea of their likelihood of succeeding as teachers.

In the first, relatively short section of the chapter, I argue that presence is important to one's gaining and maintaining authority as a teacher. To use contemporary vernacular language, our students want to know (and they deserve to know) if we are really *there* for them. My argument that presence is important comes with an important qualifying question that I deal with in the second section of the chapter: when I say that presence is important, what do I mean by presence? How do I define it? We agree that psychotherapists need to be present

DOI: 10.4324/9781003140849-6

to their clients and that medical professionals need to be present to their patients. What do we mean when we say that teachers need to be present to their students? As I noted, defining presence turns out to be challenging, in part because teacher films, which significantly shape our culture's images of good teaching and teacher presence, turn out to offer a variety of conflicting portrayals of teacher presence. In the last major section of the chapter, I discuss several of the most common qualities and aspects of teacher presence, closing by asserting that teachers can learn to be present by adopting the practices that characterize presence.

Is Presence Important?

I began the second paragraph of this chapter by asking this question: Is having presence or being present necessary to establish oneself as a teacher with authority, as a teacher worthy of being given charge of a classroom? The short answer to that question is yes, as hundreds of educational researchers have concluded from their studies of classrooms, as thousands of teachers have discovered in their professional practice, and as millions of students have made clear in their formal and informal evaluations of their teachers.

A very brief sampling of the academic research on presence reveals some consistent themes and also the varied ways educators and students understand presence. Students pick up cues from their teachers' facial expressions, their body language, and their tone of voice (Farber, 2008). They want to see what enthusiasm their teachers bring to teaching and what energy or effort their teachers expend in planning, instruction, and carrying out other classroom tasks (Farber, 2008; Intrator, 2004; Rodenburg, 2017; Shea et al., 2010). Participants in Rossetti and Fox's (2009) research associated presence with enthusiasm and the promotion of learning. Bigatel et al. (2012) associated presence with student success, which they defined as increased students' understanding of curricular content. This sampling of research, while brief, illustrates the difficulty of defining teacher presence; some themes appear and reappear in the research, but researchers offer a wide variety of understandings. In the last decade or two, researchers focusing on teaching presence have given substantial effort to understand the meaning of presence in online teaching (Anderson et al., 2001; Gurley, 2018; Shea et al., 2010; Cole et al., 2017). This relatively recent shift in focus obviously may enrich the experience of those who learn and teach online, but it also has the potential to shed new light on face-to-face teaching. Most researchers concur that whether one is teaching online or face-to-face there is a strong connection between teacher presence and student engagement and success. So, is presence important? Again, yes, it is.

Can Presence Be Defined?

The second question I asked at the start of this chapter relates to how we define presence. I noted in the paragraph where I raised that question that cinematic portrayals of teachers and teaching have made presence a bit more difficult to define. Three ways to define or understand presence offer themselves. First, we could review in depth the kinds of research I mentioned in the previous section. Second, we could check one or more dictionaries. Third, we could examine some images of teacher presence currently popular in our culture.

If one followed the first course of action I listed—reviewing the research on effective teaching and presence—one could arrive at a definition of the concept of presence. Teachers can be present by developing these dispositions, adopting these postures, developing these practices, and avoiding these behaviors. In fact, in the last section of the chapter, I will return to some of the research on presence and will review some of these dispositions, postures, and practices suggested by researchers.

If one took the second course of action and looked up the word *presence* in a dictionary, one would likely find many overlaps with what educational researchers have concluded. Of course, one would also find differences. A general dictionary would offer a general definition, not one specifically related to teacher presence. A dictionary of education, if it included a definition of presence, might list some of the same components or aspects of presence that researchers have listed. However, relying on a dictionary to understand a concept such as presence can lead one astray. To explain how a dictionary can lead astray, I will very briefly distinguish a concept from a conception. The word *concept* ordinarily means something along the lines of idea, notion, or principle. I want to distinguish the concept of presence, as the dictionary might report it, from various conceptions of presence. Gerald Dworkin, one of the few writers to address the concept-conception distinction directly, calls a conception the "filling out of an abstract concept with . . . different content" usually to address a particular "set of problems and questions" (1988, p. 10). Gallie (1962) noted that concepts such as *democracy*, *justice*, and *peace* are more subject to conception-building—what he called being contested—than are terms such as *shelf* or *water*. I suggest that teacher presence, given its importance in the world of education, is likely to have different educators assign to it different content or to be contested. In short, it will not be easy to define. But in an attempt to get at what presence is, we will examine various conceptions of presence. We will see some of the different ways people have filled out this concept with different content (Dworkin, 1988).

To survey some of those conceptions, I want to go to the movies and remind you of some of the images of teachers we see on screen, what many writers about teachers in film call *reel teachers*. These images range from warmly attentive, to enigmatic, to charismatic, to funny, to scary, to dead (seriously). I proceed this way for a couple reasons. First, for years, I have used clips from many of these films with Pre-Service and In-Service Teachers to open up discussion about images of teachers in our culture. I use clips to facilitate those discussions for the second reason I explore films here: reel teachers have become powerful shapers of what is expected of teachers by students, by the general public, and even by teachers ourselves.

The Enigmatic Teacher

Some films present the enigmatic teacher as the one who engages students. For example, in one of the most famous teacher films, *Dead Poets Society* (Wier, 1989), actor Robin Williams plays Mr. John Keating, a teacher who raises difficult and even unanswerable questions for students used to rote learning and complying with their élite academy's upper-class expectations. Watch the engaging interactions between Mr. Keating and his students by typing "rip it Dead Poets" or "Oh Captain my Captain Robin Williams" into YouTube and see a teacher go far beyond the dictionary's definition of *lesson*. Those scenes portray a conception of the lesson where the teacher engages the students by challenging their assumptions about themselves, about poetry, and (in the one case) even about damaging school property. Those scenes from *Dead Poets Society* are noteworthy for anyone thinking about teacher presence. The film portrays a teacher very present to his students, a portrayal that has served for decades as a model for many who teach or wished to teach.

Teachers inspired by the conception of teacher presence in *Dead Poets Society* may not know or may forget that a team of writers worked on a screenplay for months before shooting began and that they continued to revise that screenplay day-to-day during filming. Teachers may not know that dozens of crew members worked for hours to get the lighting right for each scene and to identify the best locations for the actors, set furniture, and microphones. Teachers may not know that a whole day's work on set typically produces only a few minutes of the final product. Teachers may even forget that Robin Williams was an actor and comedian, not a teacher. I don't list these caveats to spoil the film, which has inspired generations of teachers. Rather, I list them to help us scale back our expectations for ourselves as teachers. Without a team of screenwriters, without a crew of four or five dozen professionals, without a group of professional actors, our classes may be less engaging than those we see in films. As real teachers, we may be less enigmatic than reel teachers such as Mr. Keating in *Dead Poets Society*.

The Charismatic Teacher

The image of the charismatic teacher has been with us for decades, both on screen and in educational research (Milojkovic, 1982). In fact, it may be the best example of what Barlowe and Cook (2015) called a "perennially misleading" image of teachers perpetuated by the film (p. 25). I turn to *School of Rock* (Linklater, 2003) and *To Sir with Love* (Clavell, 1967) to illustrate this cinematic conception of teacher presence, the charismatic teacher. In another chapter in this book (Chapter 8), Mason Steinke deals at greater length with *School of Rock* to explore the question of a teacher's authority. Here, I want simply to note that, as in one of the oldest teacher films, *To Sir with Love*, the actor in the teacher role in *School of Rock* is, not incidentally, a charismatic actor. Sidney Poitier was a famous actor of his time, as is Jack Black in our own time. On screen, they exude confidence and ease. On screen, one is flamboyant and the other is calm and determined, but both have undeniable charisma. (Even people who dislike Jack Black's characters admit that.)

On-screen portrayals of teachers shape our expectations and, in these two cases, they have helped shape the expectation that teachers should be confident and charismatic. I will argue in the last section of this chapter that confidence is a necessary part of teacher presence. But I will also argue that charisma is not.

The Dead Boring Teacher

Dozens of films include a scene of bored students in a class being taught by a stultifying teacher. In one of the most famous such scenes in film history, from *Ferris Bueller's Day Off* (Hughes, 1986), a mortifyingly boring economics teacher asks if anyone knows the two-word answer to the question he is posing. Type "anyone, anyone, Bueller" into YouTube to laugh or cry in response to this cringe-worthy scene of a teacher who is simply not present to his students. He knows clearly what curriculum contents he wants to teach, but he apparently has given no thought to how students learn. In *Teachers*, a relatively unknown and somewhat comical teacher film from the same era (Hiller, 1984), a teacher dies at his desk, but no one actually knows for several hours because—whether dead or alive—he always looked and acted the same way, slouched behind his desk with a newspaper. And he used only one pedagogical strategy if it can be called that. He printed worksheets for every class. His students picked them up off his desk on their way in to the class and deposited them there on their way out. For years, his students and teaching colleagues had called him by the nickname *Ditto* because of his exclusive use of photocopied worksheets. His eventual demise is discovered only because he fails to appear in the staff room at the end of the teaching day. Talk about a lack of presence. Type "Ditto's class" into YouTube to see this bleakly comic counter-example of teacher presence.

Teachers in *Ferris Bueller's Day Off* and *Teachers* represent what presence is not. To their credit, they do not engender confusion about what presence is. In the final section of the chapter where I catalog some of the components or aspects of presence, I will give some attention to the opposites of dead and boring. First, I will survey several other cinematic portrayals of teachers.

The Warmly Attentive Teacher

Miss Honey, the elementary school teacher in *Matilda* (DeVito, 1996), is perhaps more a caricature than a believable character. Either way, she has an outsized influence on children's views of what teachers are like or should be like. Furthermore, a good number of my own education students regularly identify her as one of the reasons they wanted to become teachers. Throughout *Matilda*, Miss Honey lives up to her sweet name, even crossing professional boundaries in her effort to see Matilda, her protégé, flourish academically and in life. Dialing Miss Honey's sweetness back from eleven, we might consider middle school teacher Jess Day, played by Zooey Deschanel in the television series *New Girl* (Meriwether, 2011), which, after running for seven seasons, ended in 2018. Although *New Girl* is essentially another repeat of the formula series about young adults trying to make their way in the big city, it periodically includes scenes set in Miss Day's school. In those scenes, she is consistently portrayed as warmly attentive, thus possibly offering viewers a confirmation that Miss Honey was on the right track in how she approached students.

Tough Love

If one end of a continuum can appropriately be sub-titled *boring to dead*, the other end of that continuum could be labeled *tough love to scary*. Several reel teachers fit the tough love category. The film *Lean on Me* (Avildsen, 1989) tells the story of real-world principal Joe Carter's efforts to turn a failing inner-city school around. *Lean on Me* has Morgan Freeman portraying principal, Joe Clark. He makes clear as he stands at the front of his year-opening assembly that he has not come to Eastside High to pass the time. Type "lean on me you are dismissed" into YouTube to hear a voice that does not sound like someone gently narrating the migration patterns of penguins. This is Morgan Freeman portraying someone who seriously means business. Is he present? Yes, he is. Is his threatening voice the sole component or source of that presence? No, it is not. To anticipate the language of Chapter 15, Joe Clark is a warm demander; he sets the bar high, but he cares deeply.

Throughout this chapter, we want to argue that teacher presence typically derives from multiple sources. *Meaning business*, as the common phrase has it, may be a useful component part of teacher presence. Those who take the time to watch the whole of *Lean on Me* will see that Morgan Freeman's character's presence has many sources besides the indignation one sees in the YouTube clip I suggested.

Tough love films—films showing warm demanders—are too numerous to offer detailed analysis here. But I will offer four titles as examples of the genre, all of them based on real-life teachers. *Music of the Heart* (Craven, 1999) has Meryl Streep portray the work of Brooklyn violin teacher Roberta Guaspari. Guaspari demanded much of both herself and her music students, and they learned more than they ever thought they could. *Stand and Deliver* (Menendez, 1998) retells the story of Jaime Escalante, first told in Jay Matthews' (1986) book, *Escalante, Best teacher in America*. It shows another class where students learned more than they ever thought they could. The third feature film based on a real-life teacher, *Freedom Writers* (LaGravanese, 2007), has Hillary Swank play the role of real-life teacher, Erin Gruwell, who helped her minority writing students achieve far more than they ever thought they could. I end my short offering of titles with one documentary film, *Pressure Cooker* (Becker & Grausman, 2009), shot in and out of cooking teacher Wilma Stephenson's Philadelphia classroom. All four of these films portray warm demanders who were fully present to their students and whose students achieved great things. In all four cases, viewers cannot help but connect these teachers' presence to their students' success.

The Scary Teacher

Films such as those I named earlier portray warm demanders, but warm demanders are not the endpoint of the continuum of portrayals of teacher presence. I want briefly to explore the complete opposite of dead and boring: the scary educator. Two characters come to mind to illustrate the scary end of my continuum. First, I offer Trunchbull, Miss Honey's school principal in *Matilda* (DeVito, 1996). Another character that will come to many readers' minds, of course, is Professor Snape of Hogwarts, played by Alan Rickman in the two *Harry Potter and the Deathly Hallows* films (Yates, 2010, 2011). In the same way that the much earlier Trunchbull, the nasty caricature in *Matilda* lived up to her surname, Professor Snape lived up to his given name, Severus; he was severe. Trunchbull and Snape both fit the teacher film stereotype that school buildings, while populated by caring and warm educators such as Miss Honey in *Matilda*, also contain nasty educators. In these two cases, we see extreme versions of this negative teacher film stereotype.

With sadness, many of us can admit that as educators or students we have met characters on the nastier end of the scale, educators who we perhaps wish would have found employment elsewhere. The educator who has read Albert Bandura's work on student self-efficacy (Bandura, 1977, 1997) knows that students need to believe they can succeed. Neuroscientific research on how we respond to fear—increased cortisol, adrenaline, blood pressure, and heart rate—shows us that fear, while it enhances our survival instinct does not enhance learning. Our responses to fear diminish our capacity to learn, implying that the student afraid is not the student who can gain new insights into a sonnet or grasp a new concept in grammar or chemistry. In short, if a school hires someone on the tough end of the continuum, they should also hire a warm demander, someone like the four teachers I mentioned in the previous paragraph, someone who can temper their toughness with great care and an unshakeable belief that all their students can succeed.

Can Teachers Learn Presence?

We turn now to the third question I asked at the beginning of the chapter, what I called the practical question. Given the portrayals of presence in teacher films, this question takes on special importance for Pre-Service Teachers who wonder if they have what it takes to enter the teaching profession and to flourish in it for several decades. The short answer to that important question is yes, a teacher can learn to be present. In what follows immediately, I briefly explore what presence is by noting three things it is not.

What Presence Is Not

As they have done with presence, researchers have also offered portrayals of what presence is not. Farber (2008) suggests connections to absence, distance, automatism, and lifelessness. Hollis (2003), a Jungian psychoanalyst, argues that presence cannot arise from what he calls the divided self, a theme Parker Palmer follows in several of his works (1983, 1998, 2004). In *The Courage to Teach*, Parker Palmer (1998) offers the image of teachers so divided within themselves or disconnected from their work that their words appear to their students as bubbles in front of their faces, the same way that cartoonists picture their characters' dialogue or thoughts. Halonen's (2013) participants listed monotone delivery, a lack of energy, and absence of emotion as indicators of a lack of presence and lack of enjoyment of teaching. For her participants, showing indifference toward students or, worse, making crude and insulting comments demonstrate a lack of presence. Arrogance, boasting, pomposity, self-absorption, superiority, unfairness, lack of preparation, impatience, and complacency comprise a portion of the bundle of attitudes and postures that Halonen's subjects identified as postures and practices by which some educators diminish their teaching presence and erect between themselves and their students.

While dull, monotone delivery ("Beuller, Beuller?") indicates a lack of presence and dampens students' desire to learn, its opposites—spectacle and performance—typically do not indicate the kind of teacher presence that leads to deep student learning. Without doubt, rock and pop stars project or illustrate presence when they perform. Should teachers aspire to bring that kind of energy or that level of spectacle to their teaching (even if they had access to the Boeing 747 air freighters typically required to transport a major star's equipment for a stadium tour)? Would such energy enhance learning? Intrator (2004) found that students value their teachers' authenticity more than their ability to entertain. Given the typical teacher's budget, I will argue that the answer to the question about whether spectacle and entertainment enhance learning really doesn't matter because the likelihood of its happening is so slim. But let us consider some important differences between an ordinary teacher's classroom program and any major rocker or pop star's performance. Without doubt, any teacher with a boatload of musical talent and several jumbo jets loaded with sound and lighting equipment could make learning more exciting. But most teachers, besides the time they spend preparing and grading, deal directly with students from five to six hours per day, longer than any concert. And teachers don't have a staff of 50–60 (typical numbers for a major star) handling logistics and setting up so they can perform. Because we live in a culture where keeping up with the Kardashians is for some actually a worthwhile ideal, teachers may be tempted to think that if they can be more entertaining, they might be able to engage their students more readily. To a tiny degree, research bears this conclusion out, but, as I will note shortly, such entertainment must be authentic.

To conclude this brief excursion into what presence is not, I want to mention briefly the matter of introversion and extraversion. This common distinction between personality types has the potential to result in misunderstandings of classroom presence. Some people associate introversion or quietness with a lack of presence, despite the fact that we have all met quiet and apparently unpossessing teachers who are fully present to their students and who operate highly successful classrooms where every student respects their authority. Note the corollary misconception as well that the flamboyant teacher who gets in students' faces will not always be successful, Jack Black's character in *School of Rock* notwithstanding. Flamboyance does not guarantee student engagement.

Although a substantial body of research shows that extraverts come to most workplaces with an advantage (Zelenski et al., 2012; Smillie, 2013), one meta-analysis of 97 scholarly papers concluded that the extravert's advantage is actually slim (Wilmot et al., 2019). Comparatively few researchers have studied introversion and extraversion among educators and the possible connections of this dimension of personality to classroom presence and success. Although such research is not plentiful, what there is bears out the claim that introverts can experience teaching success (Balsari-Palsule Little, 2020; Eryilmaz, 2014).

The Qualities of Presence

We move now to what researchers, students, and teachers themselves have identified as the properties or qualities of presence, beginning with effort. I list nine qualities in this section but am certain that someone else would list some I have omitted and likely omit some I have listed. These qualities or properties are as follows: effort, enthusiasm, listening and conversation, empathy, humor, authenticity, self-awareness, tact, and professionalism.

Please understand that I do not consider these all to be necessary conditions for presence. Rather, they are typical of those educators who have presence. Any given teacher is likely to have and show a combination of some of these qualities. Obviously, some teachers will possess all the qualities. No one should go into despair on seeing the list that follows; it is not meant as a checklist. Rather it is meant to give people direction, especially those of us wondering if we have the presence required to teach.

Effort

Participants in a study of teacher presence (Shea et al., 2010) identified teacher effort as a factor. Some may consider this finding obvious, but it bears examination. Teachers who are neither as charismatic as Jack Black's character in *School of Rock* nor as enigmatic as Robin Williams' character in *Dead Poets Society* may wonder if they have what it takes to teach. It turns out that plain old effort may be more important than being charismatic or enigmatic.

One way to show effort is to use instructional strategies you have never used before. Doing so shows your students that you are still learning and that you are thinking about how to improve the class. Continually trying new strategies (and adjusting as you see what to do and what not to do) is one way to ensure that you will keep your brain alive and that you will flourish long term in the teaching profession. Participants in Hosler and Arend's (2012) research viewed effort put toward course design as a signifier of teacher presence, anticipating the conclusion Arinto (2013) came to a year later, as well as the conclusions I drew myself in my work on taking a design approach to curriculum and unit planning (Badley, 2018).

Enthusiasm

To carry out her research on presence, Halonen (2013) asked students for their descriptions of teachers who demonstrated presence. Among the answers her participants gave her was that teacher presence implied energy and excitement for students, for the subject area at hand, and for life itself. This should not surprise us. Research on enthusiasm in teaching, often treated in concert with its near-synonym, passion goes back decades (Greene, 1986; Intrator, 2004) and has continued to the time of this writing (Pottenger, 2021).

Listening and Conversation

Students and research alike identify conversation between teachers and students as an important aspect of presence. Meijer et al. (2009), for example, suggest that teachers engage in individual conversation with students not only during class but before and after class as well. Teachers need to create the opportunities for such conversation. How? Walk among the students, even sit in an empty seat among them, a practice consistent with Halonen's university participants' having identified the podium as a physical barrier that keeps educators from being present with their students (Halonen, 2013). Liberating oneself from the idea that teaching is what happens mainly at the front of the classroom initially takes courage and creativity, but thousands of teachers have done it and found it to be an effective way to be more present with their students.

A strategy some teachers use both to listen and to demonstrate that they listen is to refer to things specific students said on previous days. Doing so creates a kind of conversational thread connecting the curriculum contents and instruction from one day to the next. Creating this kind of thread can be as simple as saying, "This connects to Taylor's question last Friday." "Do you remember

Anthony's comment last week about this?" Some teachers make posters with students' comments on them and hang them on the classroom wall. If Jason said, "You can remember the whole biology course just by remembering these two words: botany and zoology," then make a *Jason's Law* poster. If when Jason said that in class, Isabella retorted, "Are you sure? There are lot of other words that go with those words and some of them are in Latin," produce an *Isabella's Corollary* poster as well and hang the two posters side by side on the classroom wall. Students beam with pride when they enter a room to find themselves the authors of posters. Teachers who produce such posters authorize their students literally; they make them into authors.

Empathy

Empathy obviously connects to listening (Evans-Palmer, 2016), but I will leave that connection to my colleagues Shae Nimmo, a teacher colleague who has acted professionally, and Emily Robinson, nurse practitioner, who treat listening and empathy at length in the following chapter.

Humor

Students regularly identify humor as a quality of teachers whom they consider present. A substantial body of research on humor in teaching supports the claim that, used correctly, humor helps establish a teachers' presence (Evans-Palmer, 2016; Halonen, 2013; Silver et al., 2015; Tomlinson, 2015; Ziv, 1988). Humor helps build relationships between teachers and students, and it improves students' attitudes toward their teachers and their academic work.

But, as with classroom entertainment, humor needs to be authentic; it needs to arise out of the teacher's own person and not look like an attempt to be as funny as the latest popular comedian. I say this for two important reasons. First, professional comedians spend hours writing the few minutes of the performance we see, and some pay professional writers. Second, they may have rehearsed or performed the routine we see dozens or even hundreds of times before we see it. We simply don't have the writing resources or the time (and most of us likely don't have the talent). Teachers who happen to be exceptionally talented in the comedic arts and who can keep a class at a kind of rolling boil may find that students don't learn the curriculum materials any more thoroughly in their classrooms than the students down the hallway learn the same contents in classrooms led by mere mortals. Second, as happens in comedy clubs, comedic teachers may find themselves competing for comedic space because their own overuse of a performance mode induces would-be comedians in their classroom to try to carve out space for themselves. In short, teaching is noble and important work; rather than try to be comedians, we should be teachers.

Authenticity

Authentic implies letting your students know about you (Intrator, 2004). Sports, hobbies, favorite television shows or internet sites, places you have traveled or want to travel, the team you cheer for—these topics are all appropriate. One outstanding teacher I know exclaims to at least one class every day, "You know what I learned on the internet last night?" Her students now expect this from her and they know her as a person, not just as their teacher, in part because she lets them know what excites her. Another teacher I know keeps his guitar in his classroom and spontaneously composes goofy songs related to course contents or students' comments. In both cases, these teachers' openness with their discoveries on the web or their musical talents are not forced; they are genuine. Although neither of these teachers has likely the conclusions Lisa Gurley (2018) drew from her research into teacher presence, they are both following her advice; they are letting their students see them as real persons. Gurley's conclusions actually align with those of Smillie (2013) and Zelenski et al. (2012) who suggest in the plainest English that teachers should be who they are.

Obviously, with topics such as your own family, your religious views, and your politics, sensibilities vary in a classroom, implying that what one person considers appropriate for a classroom another might consider an overshare. Thus, it is best to steer well clear of where you think the professional boundaries are with these topics. Those limits still leave lots of room for teachers to be who they are and to let their students see who they are.

Self-Awareness and Connectedness

Self-awareness has obvious links to authenticity. Decades ago, educational philosopher Maxine Greene (1973) defined presence as wide-awakeness. Decades later, Rodenburg (2017) talked about "full connection between people so we can understand something of the other's story" (p. 4). Farber recalls having observed teachers who are "right there *with* the rest of us in the room; others seem imprisoned in their own space, on the far side of an unbridgeable gulf" (2008, p. 215). With reference to online teaching specifically, Shin (2002) sees two component parts to presence: connectedness and availability. Rossetti and Fox (2009) identified presence as one of the four factors students typically associate with outstanding teaching (along with the promotion of learning, teachers as learners, and enthusiasm). Other related concepts or wordings include being mindful (Brown & Ryan, 2003) and being aware (Mingyur Rinpoche, 2007). Some stipulate that one must be of oneself as a pre-condition to being aware of the other (Rodgers & Raider-Roth, 2006; Meijer et al., 2009). If these researchers are correct, then learning to be present to one's students likely cannot be reduced to steps. And, second, if they are correct, the teacher who would have presence will need to be self-aware.

Teacher Tact

In his elaborations of what he calls *teacher tact*, Max van Manen offers another perspective on presence (1991, 1995, 2016), which one of us has worked with at length in another book (Steeg-Thornhill & Badley, 2020) and will simply summarize here. The most common sense of *tact* today relates to having the interpersonal skills to know how to approach a touchy situation or the ability to choose the right words while raising a sensitive topic. With the word *tact*, van Manen refers to some teachers' deep and apparently intuitive knowledge of the currents and undercurrents at work in classrooms at any given moment. Real-life illustrations of high degrees of tact are easy to find in sports. For example, Simone Biles looks like she was born to gymnastics. Hockey great Wayne Gretzky is reputed to have said that the good hockey player always knows where the puck is, and the great hockey player always knows where the puck is going to be. It may seem unfair to pick *la crème de la crème* of the world of sport to illustrate an educational concept, but, in my view, these examples serve this good purpose: by being extreme, they make clear the kind of intuitive knowing—the kind of presence in a classroom—that van Manen is describing.

Professionalism

This list of ten qualities ends with an echo of one of the arguments in Chapter 4: students expect their teachers to be professionals. I need not repeat what and I suggested in Chapter 4. If a teacher is a competent professional, it will show. Students will see it. Language, use of classroom time, preparation, purposefulness, even one's manner of dress—these all send a message to students. Decades ago, in *Teaching as a Subversive Activity*, Postman and Weingartner (1969) argued that teachers should send the unmistakable message to students: we are going to do important, special work here today in this room.

Conclusion

I repeat the question: **can teachers learn presence?** My short answer is yes. First, and bluntly, the qualities and characteristic postures I've cataloged in this chapter are not X-factor stuff. These are things teachers can learn to do and postures teachers can adopt. Second, I believe, with Aristotle, that we can learn dispositions, we can adapt postures. About 340 BC, Aristotle wrote in *The Ethics* (2012) that we could learn—grow into—a disposition by practicing the behavior that would ordinarily result from having that disposition. I tested his claim in my own classroom. For the first 15 years of my career, I taught from the front of the room. Then I came across an interview with Parker Palmer (referred to by several in this volume) in which he said he had learned to circulate among his students. I decided to try it but was overcome with apprehensions. "What would my students think was going on?" "What if this or that happened?" But one day, I tried it. Over some months, I learned how to do it. By practicing the behavior, I grew into the attitude; eventually, I found it easy to circulate. I now find the podium a barrier to the kind of connections I wrote about with reference to listening and to self-awareness. I learned how to be present with my students and, by doing so, increased my presence in the classroom.

In conclusion, let me remind you that another writer would almost certainly offer a different list from the one I have offered here. Second, let me encourage you to practice the behaviors that would ordinarily flow from the dispositions or qualities where you suspect you may have a deficit. I learned how to walk out from behind the podium. And I believe you can learn to be present. Finally, let me remind you that teacher presence will always remain a key condition if students are to grant their teachers their consent to teach.

References

Anderson, T., Liam, R., Garrison, D. R., & Archer, W. (2001). Assessing teaching presence in a computer conferencing context. *Journal of Asynchronous Learning Networks*, 5(2)1–17.

Arinto, P. B. (2013). A framework for developing competencies in open and distance learning. *The International Review of Research in Open and Distance Learning*, 14(1), 167–185.

Aristotle. (2012, unknown original date). *Nicomachean ethics* (S. D. Collins, Trans.). University of Chicago.

Avildsen, J. G. (Director). (1989). *Lean on me*. Warner Brothers.

Badley, K. (2018). *Curriculum planning with design language: Building elegant courses and units*. Routledge.

Balsari-Palsule, S., & Little, B. R. (2020). Quiet strengths: Adaptable introversion in the workplace. In L. A. Schmidt & K. L. Poole (Eds.), *Adaptive shyness: Multiple perspectives on behavior and development* (pp. 181–197). Springer.

Bandura, A. (1977). Self-efficacy: Toward a unifying theory of behavioral change. *Psychological Review*, 84(2), 191–215.

Bandura, A. (1997). *Self-efficacy: The exercise of control*. Freeman.

Barlowe, A., & Cook, A. (2015). From blackboard to Smartboard: Hollywood's perennially misleading teacher heroes. In D. P. Liston & A. P. Renga (Eds.), *Teaching, learning and schooling in film* (pp. 25–40). Routledge.

Becker, M., & Grausman, J. (2009). *Pressure cooker*. Participant Media.

Bigatel, P. M., Ragan, L. C., Kennan, S. S., May, J., & Redmond, B. F. (2012). The identification of competencies for online teaching success. *Journal of Asynchronous Learning Networks*, 16(1), 59–77.

Brown, K. W., & Ryan, R. M. (2003). The benefit of being present: Mindfulness and its role in psychological well-being. *Journal of Personality and Social Psychology*, 84, 822–848.

Clavell, J. (Director). (1967). *To sir with love*. Columbia Pictures.

Cole, A., Anderson, C., Bunton, T., & Cherney, M. (2017). Student predisposition to instructor feedback and perceptions of teaching presence predict motivation toward online courses. *Online Learning Journal*, 21(4), 245–262.

Craven, W. (1999). *Music of the heart*. Miramax.

DeVito, D. (Director). (1996). *Matilda*. TriStar Pictures.
Dworkin, G. (1988). *The theory and practice of autonomy*. Cambridge University Press, 1988.
Eryilmaz, A. (2014). Perceived personality traits and types of teachers and their relationship to the subjective well-being and academic achievements of adolescents. *Educational Sciences: Theory & Practice, 14*(6), 2049–2062.
Evans-Palmer, T. (2016). Building dispositions and self-efficacy in preservice art teachers. *Studies in Art Education, 57*(3), 265–278.
Farber, J. (2008). Teaching and presence. *Pedagogy, 8*(2), 215–225.
Gallie, W. B. (1962). Essentially contested concepts. In M. Black (Ed.), *The importance of language* (pp. 121–146). Prentice-Hall.
Greene, M. (1973). *Teacher as stranger*. Wadsworth.
Greene, M. (1986). Reflection and passion in teaching. *Journal of Curriculum and Supervision, 2*(1), 68–81.
Gurley, L. E. (2018). Educators' preparation to teach, perceived teaching presence, and perceived teaching presence behaviors in blended and online learning environments. *Online Learning, 22*(2), 197–220.
Halonen, J. (2013). Classroom presence. In S. Davis & W. Buskist (Eds.), *The teaching of psychology: Essays in honor of Wilbert J. McKeachie and Charles L. Brewer* (pp. 41–55). Psychology Press.
Hiller, A. (Director). (1984). *Teachers*. Metro-Goldwyn-Mayer.
Hollis, J. (2003). *On this journey we call our life: Living the questions*. Inner City Books.
Hosler, K. A., & Arend, B. D. (2012). The importance of course design, feedback, and facilitation: Student perceptions of the relationship between teaching presence and cognitive presence. *Educational Media International, 49*(3), 217–229.
Hughes, J. (Director). (1986). *Ferris Bueller's day off*. Paramount Pictures.
Intrator, S. (2004). The engaged classroom. *Educational Leadership, 62*(1), 20–24.
LaGravanese, R. (Director). (2007). *Freedom writers*. MTV Films.
Linklater, R. (Director). (2003). *School of rock*. Paramount Pictures.
Matthews, J. (1986). *Escalante: Best teacher in America*. Holt.
Meijer, P., Korthagen, F., & Vasalos, A. (2009). Supporting presence in teacher education: The connection between the personal and professional aspects of teaching. *Teaching and Teacher Education: An International Journal of Research and Studies, 25*(2), 297–308.
Menendez, R. (Director). (1998). *Stand and deliver*. Warner Brothers.
Meriwether, E. (Creator). (2011–2018). *New girl*. Fox Broadcasting.
Milojkovic, J. D. (1982). *Teaching with charisma* (Paper 15). Professional and Organizational Development Network in Higher Education. https://digitalcommons.unl.edu/podnetwork/
Mingyur-Rinpoche, Y. (2007). *The joy of living*. Harmony Books.
Palmer, P. J. (1983). *To know as we are known: A spirituality of education*. Harper.
Palmer, P. J. (1998). *The courage to teach*. Jossey-Bass.
Palmer, P. J. (2004). *A hidden wholeness: The journey toward an undivided life*. Jossey-Bass.
Postman, N., & Weingartner, C. (1969). *Teaching as a subversive activity*. Delacorte.
Pottenger, K. (2021). A passion for teaching and a vision for change. *New Labor Forum, 30*(2), 100–104. https://doi.org/10.1177/10957960211004851
Rodenburg, P. (2017). *The second circle: How to use positive energy for success in every situation*. Norton.
Rodgers, C. R., & Raider-Roth, M. B. (2006). Presence in teaching. *Teachers and Teaching: Theory and Practice, 12*(3), 265–287.

Rossetti, J., & Fox, P. (2009). Factors related to successful teaching by outstanding professors: An interpretive study. *Journal of Nursing Education, 48*(1), 11–16.

Shea, P., Hayes, S., & Vickers, J. (2010). Online instructional effort measured through the lens of teaching presence in the community of inquiry framework: A re-examination of measures and approach. *International Review of Research in Open and Distributed Learning, 11*(3), 127–154.

Shin, N. (2002). Beyond interaction: The relational construct of "transactional presence." *Open Learning, 17*(2), 121–137.

Silver, D., Berckemeyer, J. C., & Baenen, J. (2015). *Deliberate optimism: Reclaiming the joy in education.* Corwin.

Smillie, L. D. (2013). Why does it feel good to act like an extravert? *Social and Personality Psychology Compass, 7*(12), 878–887. https://doi.org/10.1111/spc3.12077

Steeg-Thornhill, S., & Badley, K. (2020). *Generating tact and flow for effective teaching and learning.* Routledge.

Tomlinson, C. A. (2015). Being human in the classroom. *Educational Leadership, 73*(2), 74–77.

van Manen, M. (1991). *The tact of teaching: The meaning of pedagogical thoughtfulness.* SUNY Press.

van Manen, M. (1995). On the epistemology of reflective practice. *Theory and Practice, 1*(1), 33–50.

van Manen, M. (2016). *Pedagogical tact: Knowing what to do when you don't know what to do.* Routledge.

Wier, P. (Director). (1989). *Dead poets society.* Touchstone Pictures.

Wilmot, M. P., Wanberg, C. R., Kammeyer-Mueller, J. D., & Ones, D. S. (2019). Extraversion advantages at work: A quantitative review and synthesis of the meta-analytic evidence. *Journal of Applied Psychology, 104*(12), 1447–1470. https://doi.org/10.1037/apl0000415

Yates, D. (Director). (2010). *Harry Potter and the deathly hallows—Part 1.* Warner Brothers.

Yates, D. (Director). (2011). *Harry Potter and the deathly hallows—Part 2.* Warner Brothers.

Zelenski, J. M., Santoro, M. S., & Whelan, D. C. (2012). Would introverts be better off if they acted more like extraverts? Exploring emotional and cognitive consequences of counter-dispositional behavior. *Emotion, 12*(2), 290–303. https://doi.org/10.1037/a0025169

Ziv, A. (1988). Teaching and learning with humor: Experiment and replication. *The Journal of Experimental Education, 57*(1), 5–15.

6
THE IMPORTANCE AND IMPACT OF LISTENING WELL

Emily Robinson and Shae Nimmo

Listening is about more than information gathering. Listening is relational, it is dynamic, and it is a practice. To say that something is a practice is to encourage an attitude of humility and a recognition that there is no destination, there is no magical place of perfected proficiency. We can only hope to improve our skills over time. There is always more to learn and more to notice. While the practice of listening comes more naturally to some than others, it demands of everyone knowledge, intention, and a humble posture. The latter lets us know when we've reached the edge of our ability to listen well, and it alerts us to the need to build a broader, more robust listening capacity. The nature and scope of one's capacity for listening look different in different contexts. There is no one-size-fits-all way of listening.

In this chapter, the authors, an elementary teacher (Shae) and a family nurse practitioner (Emily), combine their experience and knowledge of listening in the hopes of scaffolding the listening practice of others. The type of listening we discuss in this chapter extends beyond the mere hearing of words and sounds. It is the act of truly hearing another with our hearts and minds without the need to change or alter what we observe. Think of the person in your life with whom you feel the most heard or seen. What is it about that person that makes you feel heard? Most likely, it is their authentic honoring of who you are, just as you are, without any additional narration, or judgment painted over you. This kind of listening is a beautiful gift both to give and to receive. As teachers, you have the opportunity to listen deeply to 20–30 young people every year. We invite you to consider the impacts your listening can have on each student.

Throughout this chapter, we share stories from our personal and professional lives to illustrate the various components involved in the practice of listening. We begin with a story from Shae, a story that demonstrates the gift of being heard, and then we move on to describe what is involved when we prepare to listen. The sections following explore the mindful presence and the elements of listening, for which both Emily and Shae provide professional examples. We then examine roadblocks to listening well before concluding with a section on power and privilege, drawing on an example from Emily's experience in the health care profession.

The Gift of Being Heard (Shae Nimmo)

The impact of listening well can be profound. Beginning around the age of 16, I began suffering from debilitating stomach pain. This pain profoundly affected my ability to work and be successful in school. It was years before I finally received a diagnosis and appropriate treatment. As I navigated the health care system, no matter how I presented my concerns, I continued to get the same unhelpful responses from both my family doctor and the emergency room (ER) doctors I encountered. I eventually stopped asking questions and stopped seeking treatment. Coping with pain became my life for eight years. During one particularly bad episode of pain, my now husband took me to the ER despite my protests. I had an amazing doctor that day. She asked questions no one had ever asked; she looked at me when I told her what the pain felt like, her brow furrowed to match mine in empathy. She ran new tests. I went home that day without answers but with an entirely new sense of hope. I finally felt like someone was listening to me. The symptoms I had been dealing with for years were being validated. That ER visit led to a follow-up visit with another doctor who ended up diagnosing me with severe Crohn's disease. I have now been treated, and I experience only infrequent pain or bothersome symptoms. The act of listening well by that ER doctor changed my life.

As I think about listening in a classroom, I hold this story as a constant reminder of the importance and power of listening well. I learned firsthand about the impact listening well can have on a person's psyche, on their sense of self, and on their ability to trust their own feelings.

When we think of the mechanics of listening, it may seem like a docile task requiring one to be quiet and still, but the word "listen" is a verb requiring both action and reaction. By listening well, one can be fully present to the other person and react to the non-verbal and verbal cues in an interaction. When we truly listen, we are invited into a greater sense of empathy toward the person speaking, which strengthens the sense of trust in a relationship.

Last, as we consider how to listen, we must also consider to whom we are listening. Teachers are required to listen not only to students but also to their parents. One of the most common responses I receive when asking a colleague for insight on a challenging parent is that "they just want to be heard." Listening is the first step in building a strong and healthy relationship with anyone, including students' families. Believe it or not, most parents just want to see their child happy, healthy, and fulfilled. At the core of my teaching philosophy is the recognition that my students are human beings first and students second. But it took time for me to consider that parents are also human beings first and parents second. My understanding of my students' parents was a corrective to my earlier assumption that I cared more for their child at that moment than the parent did. This is where I started to work on my own sense of humility and on gaining knowledge about the boundaries inherent in my role as the teacher. I came to understand that the degree to which we feel heard has an impact on our actions, an insight that pertains to parents, teachers, and students.

Preparing to Listen

Listening requires one to be in the present moment, which takes practice. In a conversation with students, we may expect to hear the same thing we always hear about their having forgotten their homework or about another weekend of gaming with their friends. It takes time to develop our capacity to listen without anticipating the conversation ahead of time. Allowing ourselves to respond specifically to the needs, voices, and feelings of each particular student in a given moment is a skill that takes time and intention to develop. This kind of listening is called "mindful" or "present moment" listening. This section explores how we can prepare to deliver this kind of listening.

Listening happens from within your physical body. The most involved system in the act of listening is your nervous system. A calm and engaged or well-regulated nervous system enhances our capacity for listening well. Mindfulness is a kind of meditation and happens to be an excellent, evidence-based stress management technique that, practiced regularly, can have profound effects on our nervous system's ability to self-regulate (Keng et al., 2011). It is also becoming popularized in the classroom through social-emotional learning (SEL) programs (Lawson et al., 2019). Mindfulness was born out of the meditation practices of Buddhism and was brought to the Western world by Jon Kabat-Zinn, a microbiologist at the University of Massachusetts Medical School. When Kabat-Zinn noticed the positive impacts of mediation on stress, he created Mindfulness-Based Stress Reduction (MBSR), a particular set of mindfulness skills. Kabat-Zinn defined mindfulness as an "awareness that arises through paying attention, on purpose, in the present moment, non-judgmentally" (Mindful Staff, 2017). Read that definition once more. Listening in this way can be life changing for both the person listening and the person being listened to. The skills of mindfulness are geared toward establishing yourself in the present moment so that you can be present with whatever is happening without needing to label it as good or bad or tell a story about it. The skills of mindfulness allow us to maintain a calm, attentive stance so that we can listen well in the midst of the stressful, busy classroom environment. Discussion on how to practice mindfulness is outside the scope of this chapter, but there are a multitude of apps and websites that support the development of one's own practice. Kabat-Zinn and Tara Brach are two excellent teachers (Brach, 2021; Kornfield, 2021).

We often think of listening as something we must do with another person, but before we can listen well to others, we must learn to listen to ourselves, our own minds and bodies, to determine what we may need in any given situation. Mindfulness through the lens of Social-Emotional Learning in the classroom is an invitation to do some self-reflection or self-noticing. A student practicing mindfulness might say, "I am not in a 'ready to learn' place right now, what do I need to get myself back to a place where I am calm and ready to learn?" A teacher might say, "I am not in a 'ready to teach and listen place' right now, what do I need to get myself back to a place where I am calm and ready to teach and listen?" This practice asks that we learn what circumstances set us up to remain calm and attentive in order to listen well. Most of us can start with ensuring we are meeting our body's needs for food, water, sleep, movement, and healthy stress management techniques. Meeting our own physical and psychological needs before we show up to the classroom is part of preparing to listen.

Mindful Presence (Shae Nimmo)

Before I was a teacher, I was an actor. I began acting when I was 12 years old and continued with the profession for the next ten. After high school, I attended an intensive master class program for a year that focused on voice and movement, film acting, and Meisner technique. Sanford Meisner is a storied acting coach who famously ran the Neighborhood Playhouse in NYC for several years. Meisner theory is rooted entirely in listening and being fully present, and it taught me to be an active, engaged, and thoughtful listener. An actor is provided a script. They know their lines, their cues, and most likely the lines of the other characters. In film acting, the camera is so close to your face that the slightest movement will be picked up on screen. So how does an actor react to things in the moment and not a second sooner? How do they not tip their hand to the audience? Put simply, they are present. They react moment to unanticipated moment. Teachers must do the same. As teachers, we write out lesson plans and, for many of us, teach the same lesson multiple times. How then, do we listen to the responses of our students and allow those impulses, conversations, and moments to guide our lesson in the most authentic way possible when we already have a predetermined outline of how things should go? How do we allow those perfectly unscripted moments to take our students' learning further? We are present. We react moment to unanticipated moment. And we do this through mindful, whole body listening. This stance must inform how we prepare our lesson plans so that they can bend and shift depending on what we hear from our students on a particular day. Practicing this kind of mindful presence can set us up to listen and react from moment to unanticipated moment.

Qualities of a Good Listener

A number of qualities make good companions on the road to listening well. According to Hughes and Read (2012), a good listener possesses these seven qualities: empathy, attunement and presence, warmth, respect for others, genuineness, sense of humor, sense of humility, and self-awareness. These can present in different ways. For example, we don't all have a loud, boisterous sense of humor. Each quality will come more naturally to some than others, so we encourage you to consider which of these qualities you possess easily, which require more intention, and what they look for you in particular. You might also query what each of these qualities would ask of you as a listener. Humility, for example, asks us to remember that we have as much to learn from our students as they do from us. Curiosity invites us to let go of our own tendency to anticipate or control what a student will say or feel and, instead, to listen without expectation or judgment. Some of these qualities are mentioned throughout the chapter and some are addressed elsewhere in this book. We invite you to keep them in mind as you consider how you might prepare to listen well. Like many skills, listening cannot be mastered overnight or really at all. We will all be poor listeners at times, and those times provide us an opportunity to get curious about what pulled us away from listening well, or what quality of a good listener might be missing, and work to build our capacity for listening well in the future.

The Elements of Listening

What Does Listening Look Like? (Emily Robinson)

There are several possible ways to approach the question of what listening well looks like. We will use active listening. Active listening is a specific communication skill set, based on the work of psychologist Carl Rogers. It involves giving free and undivided attention to the speaker. Active listening communicates that we are interested and concerned. The flip side is that poor listening communicates that we are not interested and do not care. The skill of active listening divides into three groups of skills: body language, following skills, and reflecting skills. We will also include the importance of empathy, curiosity, and humility as qualities that contribute to mindful listening (Robertson, 2005).

I suspect that you are familiar with how body language can communicate the degree to which a person is listening. Body language includes such components as eye contact, whether the listener's arms are crossed or open, whether they are leaning in or away, facial expressions, and so on. I have washed the feet of people experiencing homelessness or housing insecurity. These are people whose voices are rarely if ever heard. When I am physically below them, crouching down to wash their feet, it is amazing how much they share about their lives. My body language in this case is flipping a power dynamic on its head and saying, "you are important and I want to listen to your story." As mentioned in the chapter on presence (Chapter 5), where you place your physical body in the classroom influences whether students feel invited into the experience or are observers. Body language can communicate humility and empathy and can dilute the typical dynamics of authority and help students to feel more comfortable. Like all the elements of listening, this is an art that requires noticing what your tendencies are, being thoughtful about what they might communicate, and being curious about how shifting your body language might increase a sense of being heard by those to whom you are listening (Robertson, 2005).

The second set of skills in active listening is the skill of following. This skill set focuses on giving the speaker space to tell their story in their own way. As a part of this skill, Carl Rogers talked about the importance of listening to the feelings just under the surface of the words being spoken or the actions being taken (Morris, 2016). We listen with our whole bodies, with our eyes, our stance, our mind, and our imagination. When the skill of following is present, there is a sense that the story being told has space to breathe. It is not rushed or contained. Most of us spend a decent amount of time while someone is talking to us thinking about how we are going to respond, which pulls our attention away from what we are hearing. Mindful listening, in this case, invites us to notice the tendencies that pull us away from the act of listening, release them without judgment, and return to listening. This is not a once-and-done task. Most of us will need to do this several times a minute as we build our capacity to listen (Robertson, 2005).

The third skill involved in active listening is reflecting. Reflecting back on what you've just heard and witnessed, again without your own narration or judgments added, is a powerful validation tool. Reflection can be simply paraphrasing what was said and perhaps offering back what feelings you noticed just under the surface of the words being spoken. It is important to note that reflection does not indicate that you are condoning or agreeing with the perspective of the speaker.

A Health Care Example (Emily Robinson)

As a health care provider during the COVID-19 pandemic, I ask during every visit if my patients are vaccinated. If the answer is no, I ask if they are willing to share their thoughts and feelings concerning the vaccine. As a proponent of the vaccine, I already know that I will disagree with their logic, but that does not preclude listening well. One patient, in particular, comes to mind. She is the wife of an alcoholic, and she suffers from profound anxiety and codependency. The combination of a severely crooked spine and pronounced tremor means that she suffers daily from chronic pain. She shared her fear that the vaccine would worsen her tremor, causing her more pain and suffering, which she could not bear. While the risk of this is minuscule, to her the risk is terrifying and was causing her to have suicidal thoughts. I fell into a place of empathy as I imagined being in her situation. My job was to validate her fear, even though I disagreed with her decision not to get the vaccine. The practice of empathetic listening in this situation led me to provide her with a medical exemption letter for the vaccine, the only one of its kind I have done to date. The skill of reflecting does not require that you agree with the speaker; it simply communicates that you heard them and that their story matters to you.

An Education Example (Shae Nimmo)

How do you set up a classroom to support listening well? If you have set foot in any elementary classroom, you have likely heard at least one of the following statements: "Wow, I love how Johnny is showing me full body listening right now." "Sophie, I can't tell for sure if you are really listening to me if you are drawing on your paper." "Oops, I'll just wait until I have everybody's eyes AND ears." As teachers, we are constantly asking students to listen to us. We need to ensure that we are giving students clear messages about what listening is. This is best done by deciding WITH students what listening looks like. This may include *I can* statements and success criteria such as I can listen with my heart by looking the person who is speaking in the eye. I can listen by asking questions when I don't understand. These intentions can be unique to you and your students and can help us learn how our specific students feel heard.

Roadblocks to Listening Well (Emily Robinson)

Having written about what it looks like to listen well, we will now explore what might get in the way of listening well. Carl Roger's model of active listening calls these impediments "roadblocks" to listening. The first roadblock is judging. Imagine a courtroom with the judge seated above all others in the room. The seating arrangement in a courtroom is an accurate depiction of the power dynamics at play during a trial. The judge has the most power and is in fact responsible for judging the situation and delivering a verdict. The teacher in the classroom holds more power than anyone else. The temptation when we hold the power can be to hand out judgments, and the problem is that students will listen to our judgments and alter their words and actions to try and earn a favorable judgment. To students, judgments can look like criticizing, labeling, diagnosing, or praising evaluatively (Robertson, 2005). Lack of praise can also feel like a judgment. Perhaps a more appropriate image for the classroom is that of a team with the teacher as the coach. Everyone stands on the same level ground. In some ways, the coach has less power than the players because the coach is not on the field. Rather, they are on the sidelines offering guidance and wisdom as the players make the ultimate decision about how the game will play out. Embedded in this tendency to use our power to judge is our human inclination to evaluate what we hear and to do so from our own point of view. Mindfulness would have us notice when we are moving toward a judgment or evaluation and simply naming it as *judging*.

Active listening requires us to release judgment from our mind and return to an open, curious, and non-judgmental listening stance. Once again, this is a practice.

Suggesting solutions is the second roadblock to listening well. There is certainly a time and place for advice, but it is a place best visited infrequently. One thing I hate about the electronic charting system I use as a Nurse Practitioner is a feature called the "problem list." Every patient has a list of "problems" prominently displayed on the front page of their online profile. The issue with the problem list is that it guides us toward a grossly simplistic "problem and solution" view of people. There are certainly times when this approach is helpful, but in Family Practice, it is more often helpful to listen and let patients define what the "problem" or dilemma is from their point of view, as well as what possible solutions make sense to them. When I meet patients for the first time, I always say something like, "I see us as equals in this room. I bring the knowledge gained from years of schooling, but I don't know what it is like to be you in your body existing in the world. That is the knowledge that you bring, and I can't do my job without it. I don't see my job as telling you what to do, but rather walking through the options with you and following your lead."

In the classroom, mindful listening would invite us to remain curious about what ideas might emerge as the student or students consider a question or a dilemma from their own point of view. I was a school nurse for a brief period of time, and one of my first graders was hit in the face with a football. His lip immediately swelled up and when he presented in my office, I was worried he had knocked a tooth loose, so I asked him, "how do your teeth feel?" He thought for several seconds before replying, "like they have a really big pillow." He was approaching this dilemma from a very different point of view from my own. The same is true when talking to parents about difficult classroom dynamics involving their child. In the case of disruptive behavior, most likely, the parents have tried some solutions at home. To jump to offering solutions when discussing a student with their parents can feel like an insult. Starting with mindful, curious listening about what the parent's perception of the dilemma is and what has and has not been working at home shows the parents that you believe they are the expert on their own child and that you appreciate any insights they have to offer. Some warning signs that suggest we are stumbling into a place of offering solutions include asking excessive questions, especially when they are aimed at a particular answer, moralizing someone's story or answer, ranking answers or ideas, or offering advice without permission or invitation (Robertson, 2005).

Avoiding the other's concerns is the third roadblock Rogers identified. Reassurance or minimization can be such a tempting response when listening. This is especially true when the speaker's concerns or story do not make sense to us. I remember reading a memoir called *Inheritance* (Shapiro, 2020). It was recommended by a dear friend who loved it. I hated it. The author tells the story of finding out that her father is not her biological father. This is an earth-shattering truth for her because her father was Jewish and a large part of her own identity is tied to her Jewish heritage. The whole time I was reading the book I could not get over how whiny she sounded. I kept thinking, "get over it already." As this annoyance persisted, I got a little curious about it and realized that I was seeing her story through my own lens, which colored what I saw. My relationship with my own father was fraught with significant struggle and difficulty, so it would in some ways be a relief to discover that I wasn't biologically related to him. The more I sat with my annoyance and contextualized it, the more it softened and dissolved, and I grew to appreciate the author's journey. The opposite of minimizing and reassuring is validating from a place of empathy. When we step out of our own story and into another's, we have the opportunity to experience and offer empathy.

Power and Privilege

In a classroom, the teacher holds the most power. The teacher's own identity and perspectives can influence whose voices are magnified and whose are marginalized (as Jule shows in Chapter 17). Listening well requires a lifelong commitment to exploring one's own biases, blind spots, and privileges. We all gravitate toward stories that make sense to us or that resonate with a part of our own story. It is easier and more natural to celebrate and emphasize stories we identify with and to dismiss those stories that are not as obvious to us from within our own experience.

Backing up from classroom interactions, it is imperative that teachers know the stories they inherit as representatives of a system. In other words, we must be informed about how certain people have been marginalized, oppressed, or harmed by the educational system in the past and seek to uncover ways we might be participating in these dynamics today. It is also important to seek more awareness of the larger social context influencing students' varying experiences in the classroom (as Patrick notes in Chapter 15).

Racism in Health Care (Emily Robinson)

A patient I'll call Sarah has been under my care for six years. She is an African American woman who had not received the COVID vaccine, which I strongly recommend, when I last saw her. Her initial response to my invitation to share her thoughts and feelings included the fact that her family would be angry with her and that a lot of people in her community do not trust the vaccine. As we discussed her concerns further, she shared that, cognitively, she wanted to trust the vaccine, then said, "What about the syphilis experiments?" I knew she was referring to the 40-year study conducted on 600 non-consenting black males in the United States from 1932 to 1972. The purpose of the study was to track the natural progression of syphilis. The men were told that they were being treated for "bad blood." In 1947, penicillin became a known, effective treatment for syphilis. The treatment was withheld from the study participants, without their knowledge, in order to carry out the study (Tuskegee University, 2021). This story sits among many of how the system I represent has intentionally harmed certain people groups throughout its history and continues to harm or fail to help certain people groups today. For me to hear truly what Sarah was saying required knowledge of the history of racism in health care and acknowledgment that systemic racism continues to affect the health care system today. When Sarah mentioned the Tuskegee Experiment, I softened. I knew that as a white person, I could not fully understand the lens through which she was peering, but I could validate her experience through empathy by trusting her telling of the story through her own lens. I told her just that. And I told her that I would respect whatever decision she made.

Recognizing that individual conversations often occur within larger narratives, and also being aware of whose voices are generally magnified and whose are minimized, can help ensure that all voices are heard. Chapter 17 (on gender) reveals that female voices are heard less and validated less in classrooms. We would be remiss not to consider other groups whose voices are likely dismissed in the classroom because of race, ethnicity, gender identity, sexual orientation, age, ability or disability, or socioeconomic status. A commitment to study one's own perspective and biases continually and to practice mindful listening rooted in humility, curiosity, and empathy is absolutely essential to ensuring that each child is heard equitably.

Conclusion

The work it takes to learn how to listen well is worthwhile. We have introduced the idea that one must prepare to listen. Listening well is not something that comes naturally or something we can expect simply to happen when we step foot in a classroom or any other setting. It is an intention and a practice that we must decide to pursue. And it requires being present, in each moment, without anticipation, narration, or judgment. Mindfulness is one way to increase our ability to remain present and listen. You may find other tools along the way that work well for you as you embark on the journey of becoming a mindful listener.

Our discussion here of the elements of listening and roadblocks to listening can be a starting point, but they are certainly not an exhaustive exploration of what might hinder or help your own listening practice. With regular practice, you will discover what helps and hinders your specific listening practice. You may begin to notice subtle adjustments you can make to hone your listening skills. A commitment to uncovering your own implicit biases is necessary if you want to listen well to each individual voice that wants to be heard in your classroom.

The practice of listening well is a gift not only to those we hear, one that literally has the power to change lives, but is also a gift to ourselves. Truly hearing and allowing ourselves to be affected by the stories of those we encounter have a ripple effect in our own lives that spreads into the world around us. And that is worth practicing for.

References

Brach, T. (2021). *Tara Brach*. www.tarabrach.com/

Hughes, A., & Read, V. (2012). *Building positive relationships with parents of young children*. Routledge.

Keng, S. L., Smoski, M. J., & Robins, C. J. (2011). Effects of mindfulness on psychological health: A review of empirical studies. *Clinical Psychology Review, 31*(6), 1041–1056. https://doi.org/10.1016/j.cpr.2011.04.006

Kornfield, J. (2021). *Jack*. https://jackkornfield.com/

Lawson, G. M., McKenzie, M. E., Becker, K. D., Selby, L., & Hoover, S. A. (2019). The core components of evidence-based social emotional learning programs. *Prevention Science, 20*(4), 457–467.

Mindful Staff. (2017, January 11). *Jon-Kabat-Zinn: Defining mindfulness*. Mindful. www.mindful.org/jon-kabat-zinn-defining-mindfulness/

Morris, C. (2016, September 16). *Carl Rogers: Active listening*. www.youtube.com/watch?v=5RdDWIlBTE8

Robertson, K. (2005). Active listening: More than just paying attention. *Australian Family Physician, 34*(12), 1053–1055.

Shapiro, D. (2020). *Inheritance: A memoir of genealogy, paternity, and love*. Knopf Doubleary

Tuskegee University. (2021). *About the USPHS syphilis study*. www.tuskegee.edu/about-us/centers-of-excellence/bioethics-center/about-the-usphs-syphilis-study

7

INVITATIONAL THEORY

A Theoretical Foundation for Establishing a Positive Classroom Ethos

Sean Schat

The inviting approach is firmly rooted in an unwavering and unconditional belief in the capacity and potential of people. People are amazing. And they are capable of amazing things. On the other hand, people are also flawed. They can make mistakes and bad choices. The potential for amazing and not-so-amazing is constantly and simultaneously in play. This is why perception and stance matter. And this is what makes the inviting approach so important. A person with an inviting stance is able to be both *idealistic* and *realistic* at the same time, believing in the potential for others to be amazing and do amazing things, while also recognizing the potential for people to fall short, sometimes far short. Invitational theory recognizes that, when obstacles and challenges are addressed, each person is capable of making wise and appropriate choices and decisions.

Invitational theory is a theoretical model that challenges communities to ensure that they are inviting places that promote the well-being and flourishing of community members and guests. The model is built upon the foundational conviction that people are able, valuable, and responsible and should be treated accordingly. The theory was introduced by William Purkey (1978) and has been refined and extended (e.g., Purkey & Novak, 1984; Purkey & Novak, 1996; Novak & Purkey, 2001; Purkey & Novak, 2015; Purkey et al., 2020). The authors describe invitational theory as a *theory of practice* that promotes the development of inviting schools and workplaces, authentic communities that invite every community member and stakeholder to participate, contribute, and flourish. Purkey and Novak (2015) emphasize that "inviting is an ethical process involving continuous interactions among and between human beings" (p. 1). The theory has been applied in numerous settings, including businesses, counseling centers, and medical and government offices but has been particularly well received in educational settings. Indeed, the terms "Invitational Theory" and "Invitational Education" are often used interchangeably. However, *invitational theory* is the theoretical foundation, and it can be applied in many different contexts. *Invitational education* is the direct application of invitational theory in schools.

At the heart of the invitational vision are five principles that establish an essential ethical and relational foundation. In their invitational theory glossary, Shaw et al. (2013) provide definitions for each principle:

- **Trust:** Thoughts, behaviors, and beliefs based on reliability, consistency, personal authenticity, and honesty.
- **Respect:** A belief that all people are valuable, able, and responsible and should be treated accordingly.
- **Optimism:** An expectation of positive, realistic outcomes for self and others.
- **Care:** To demonstrate concern by sharing warmth, empathy, positive regard, and interest in others, specifically with the intention to help them reach their potential.
- **Integrity:** A belief underlying behavior with a purposeful direction and aim.

(p. 33)

Purkey and Strahan (2002) note that these principles "serve as a conceptual framework to assist teachers in their efforts to communicate their vision and to summon students to realize their potential as learners" (p. 8). This foundation is essential because the elements function as both signposts and touchstones, establishing a clear course and direction, while also providing a means for assessing choices and actions.

The theory also identifies five primary domains, known as the "5 Ps." Shaw et al. (2013) provide a helpful overview of the 5 Ps:

- **People:** Human beings.
- **Places:** The physical environment in which people typically interact.
- **Policies:** The rules, codes, and procedures used to regulate the ongoing functions of organizations.
- **Programs:** Organized activities that have a specific purpose or goal.
- **Processes:** A systematic series of actions directed to a particular end.

(p. 32)

These domains can be used to develop an invitational community and to assess the extent to which a community is truly inviting. The International Association for Invitational Education (IAIE) has developed resources for both assessment and implementation.

The foundational principles and primary domains provide a powerful conceptual framework for intentional and effective practice. As Purkey et al. (2020) noted recently,

> In the abstract, Invitational Education can sound too good to be true. It is a positive approach to working with people, and most educators can see a value to this mindset. In the often harsh realities of everyday practice, however, it takes persistence, resourcefulness, and courage to make the intentionally inviting stance a self-correcting way to work with oneself and others.
>
> *(p. 45)*

Invitational theory provides a vision and structure for working in community with others, seeking the flourishing of each individual and their shared community. The invitational education approach provides a powerful vision and helpful guidance and resources for applying the theory in schools.

The Inviting Approach and Classroom Ethos

In a previous chapter, Badley draws an important distinction between teacher authority and raw power by distinguishing between students who *follow the teacher's lead* and students who *do what the teacher tells them to do*. The difference is pivotal, but it is not always drawn by teachers and students. Ultimately, the distinction is a **perceptual** one: *it all depends on how one looks at things*. As others in this volume have reiterated, this distinction, which may seem minor, is a crucial one when it comes to student consent, student motivation, and student engagement. How do teachers perceive the nature and impact of their own choices and behaviors when it comes to student agency, autonomy, and self-efficacy? How do students perceive their own decision to follow the teacher's lead? There is a significant difference between compliance and consent.

The community classroom ethos that is the focus of this book should be characterized by invitation. Invitational teachers believe in their students and act in ways that demonstrate this belief. When students don't behave appropriately, teachers still assume they are capable of doing so. This has a significant impact on how teachers respond to mistakes and misbehavior. The teacher is the adult and direction setter in the room. They have a positional, personal, and ethical obligation to do the right thing. As significantly, they need to remind themselves consistently that they are modeling and teaching the inviting approach. Students are constantly in the process of becoming. They have not yet arrived. They need opportunities for both feedback and practice. As they are figuring this out for themselves, they need their teachers to continue to believe in them and to approach them with trust, respect, optimism, care, and intentionality. Teachers must maintain an inviting stance at all costs.

Students must be invited to engage and participate in the learning process. Students need to have the opportunity to develop self-direction and self-regulation skills and should be provided with opportunities to learn self-discipline and responsibility, which they are capable of, even when it appears otherwise. Students will learn to be more responsible when their teacher affirms their capacity for responsibility and holds them accountable for their actions.

The Three Foundations of Invitational Theory

Invitational theory is built on three firm foundations: the *perceptual tradition*, *self-concept theory*, and the *democratic ethos*. An authentic implementation of the theory requires a clear understanding of these foundations, as each contributes specific insights that intersect powerfully in the inviting approach. Teachers with an inviting stance are committed to ensuring that their students are truly invited to develop their capacity for autonomy, agency, and self-regulation, which can have profound implications in and beyond the classroom.

Foundation 1: The Perceptual Tradition

The *perceptual tradition* (Combs, 1999; Combs et al., 1976) suggests that all behavior is a symptom of the individual's perception. If you want to understand why someone behaves in a certain way, you must consider their point of view. This seems obvious in theory, of course. But it is surprisingly overlooked in practice. We tend to see and respond to behavior from our own point of view. Even when we try to see things from the perspective of another, we often tend toward *projective empathy* (e.g., imagining how we might perceive the situation if we were in their shoes), rather than *receptive empathy* (e.g., actually trying to find out how they perceive the situation).

Another central tenet of perceptual theory is that every behavior makes sense to the behaver in the moment of behaving. This is true even if the behavior seems ridiculous to others who are observing the behavior, or if the behaver may recognize their own behavior as strange or inappropriate moments later. At the time of their behavior, their actions made sense. If we are to support the flourishing and well-being of others, we must be aware of the relationship between perception and action. Their behavior is completely shaped by their perception of reality, not by reality as others may perceive it.

Importantly, perceptions are learned and shaped by experience. As a result, it is possible for an individual to consider their perceptions and to change them. This, too, is a central element of the perceptual approach. If you want to help someone to change their behavior, you need to focus on their underlying perceptions. You can't change someone else's behavior. But you can position them to change their perception, which may result in a behavioral change. This is a critical distinction for a focus on classroom ethos because it explains why it is essential to provide students with the opportunity to consider and manage their own actions and the consequences of their actions. By reflecting on their own perceptions and the perceptions of others, students will be positioned to have the opportunity to experience a change in behavior, potentially contributing to the development of important skills, such as self-regulation, autonomy, agency, and self-efficacy.

Foundation 2: Self-Concept Theory

Self-concept theory (Jourard, 1974; Purkey, 1970; Rogers, 1969) emphasizes that human identity is defined by how one relates to one's own environment, and it is constructed through interactions with others. The way the individual perceives "self" has a profound impact on their actions and choices. Radd (2006) points out that "Self-Talk/Self-Pictures is the process that allows 'what we say and believe' to be congruent with 'what we think and feel'" (p. 88). Humans seek a stable or consistent self-concept, and their experiences exercise a profound shaping impact. As Ellis (1990) notes, "A person seeks to maintain a consistent self-concept by assimilating or rejecting perceptions that do or do not fit preconceptions, but a person's self-concept can change and develop as a result of inviting or encouraging acts" (p. 3).

Purkey and Schmidt (1990) have identified three basic assumptions of self-concept. First, self-concept is *learned*, gradually emerging in the first few months of life, and shaped and reshaped through experiences and interactions with others. Second, self-concept is *dynamic*, an internal guidance system that shapes how the individual perceives reality and that directs their actions and behavior. Third, self-concept is *organized* and resists change, a stable force characterized by order and harmony. Purkey and Schmidt note that the "tendency toward internal organization appears to be a necessary feature of human personality. It provides the individual's entire being with internal balance, and sense of direction, and a feeling of stability" (p. 19). These dynamic and organized characteristics speak to the formative power of self-concept. The fact that self-concept is learned, however, provides an important opportunity to influence how students perceive themselves.

Radd (2006) identifies three central elements of self-concept development: truth, behavior, and accountability. (1) *Truth:* the process starts by recognizing the fundamental truth that every single person is unique and valuable. (2) *Behavior:* because every person matters, individuals have a responsibility to help and not harm themselves or others through their words and actions. (3) *Accountability:* as a result, each person is responsible and accountable to treat themselves and others as if they are important. These three elements can play a crucial role for teachers, who are well positioned to provide students with the opportunity to reflect on and refine their self-concept. While self-concept is a stable and change-resistant force, it is something that can be influenced. As Purkey and Schmidt observe,

> Invitational Learning takes the position that the most logical way to positively influence self-concept development is to explore and improve the myriad messages, formal and informal, witting and unwitting, that invite people to feel able, valuable, and responsible, and to reduce or eliminate those messages that inform them that they are unable, worthless, and irresponsible.
>
> *(p. 19)*

Foundation 3: The Democratic Ethos

"Democracy is a social ideal based on the conviction that all people matter and can grow through participation in self-governance" (Purkey & Novak, 2015, p. 2). The invitational approach provides opportunities for students to experience, practice, and learn what it means to be part of a democratic ethos. The approach underscores the importance of all community members participating in and contributing to their community. As Purkey and Novak (2015) note, "deeply embedded in this respect for persons is a commitment to the ideal that people who are affected by decisions should have a say in formulating those decisions" (p. 2). Students must be able to participate in decisions that impact them, even as they deal with the consequences of their actions and choices. In the most recent iteration of invitational theory, Purkey et al. (2020) observe that invitational theory

> is rooted in the aim of enabling people to live more fulfilling lives through positive, non-coercive means by being involved in doing- with relationships. Deep down, a commitment to creating a socially and emotionally safe place for people in schools is a commitment to the basic notion that all people matter. Individuals and communities have a need and a right to participate in deciding the principles, policies, and practices that guide their lives. This is a deep sense of the concept of democracy that goes beyond the customary conventions of voting for representatives in public elections and forming and participating in political parties.
>
> *(p. 27)*

Implications for Practice

This chapter concludes with three implications for practice, ideas, and resources that educators can use in their work with students. First, invitational theory itself provides an important theoretical foundation for a vision for classroom ethos and school community. Invitational theorists have also introduced two resources directly linked to classroom culture and relationships, *The Good Discipline Sequence* (Purkey & Strahan, 2002) and *The Six Cs Approach to Conflict Management* (Purkey & Novak, 1996; Purkey et al., 2010).

A Theory of Practice, a Vision for Classroom Ethos

Invitational theory's emphasis on perception underscores an essential distinction: the way one looks at something often exercises a profound impact on how one acts in response. The extent to which this happens is shaped by intentionality and reflective action. Invitational theory provides a conceptual framework that provides an opportunity to enact a powerful vision for community and relationships. The theory's emphasis on human potential and capacity can lead to powerful acts of invitation that authentically invite others to become part of the unfolding process and community. It truly can be a theory of practice that contributes to the formation of a significant and positive classroom ethos which, in turn, shapes the perception and behavior of community members.

The Good Discipline Sequence

In "Inviting Positive Classroom Discipline," Purkey and Strahan (2002) introduce what they describe as "the good discipline sequence," a three-stage approach to establishing an approach to classroom management and classroom relationships rooted in an invitational framework (see Figure 7.1).

The *Preparation* stage focuses on intentionally and proactively establishing an inviting and collaborative classroom ethos, rooted in a conviction that students will respond and engage. As they note, "By expecting good things of oneself and of students, the teacher is in an excellent position to invite positive classroom discipline" (p. 81). The *Initiating/Responding* stage begins to shift the locus of control to the student, providing them with opportunities to accept and maintain

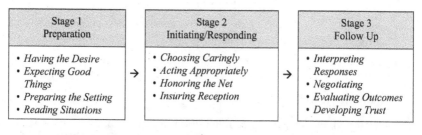

FIGURE 7.1 The Good Discipline Sequence (Purkey & Strahan, 2002, p. 79)

responsibility for their behavior. Students are expected to choose caringly and act appropriately. The teacher needs to "honor the net," the hypothetical and inviolable boundary between teacher and student "territory." Each needs to "own" their own territory and maintain responsibility for their own choices and actions. Purkey and Strahan (2002) observe that:

> In honoring the net, the teacher acknowledges the fact that he or she consists of only half of the sending/receiving process. No matter how much the teacher wishes for the student to accept his or her invitations, and, no matter how beneficial the opportunity, the teacher stays on one's own side of the net. In the final analysis, students are responsible for choosing their behaviors. It also follows that students are responsible for the logical consequences of their actions.
>
> (p. 90)

The *Follow-Up* stage provides theory-consistent opportunities for dialogue between teachers and students as they work together to co-construct community norms and patterns.

The three-stage approach is a potentially powerful one, because not only it is rooted in invitational principles but it also draws on systems theory. While the steps may not always appear to be interconnected, from the perspective of student perception and lived experience, the collective impact enacts a powerful vision for living and working in a community.

The 6 Cs Approach to Conflict Management

Conflict is normal, but students don't always know how to handle it. Neither do many adults. Students need the opportunity to practice managing conflict and to receive feedback from a trusted source. People have the right to assert their rights. They may not deny the rights of others. And they also need to ensure that their asserting is not perceived as hostility and aggression because that infringes on the rights of others. The entire process is rooted in individual perceptions but exercises powerful cultural impacts. Purkey and Novak (1996) developed an approach to managing conflict that is firmly planted in invitational principles. The 6 Cs approach identifies six levels, each beginning with the letter C: *Concern, Confer, Consult, Confront, Combat,* and *Conciliate* (see Figure 7.2). As Purkey and Strahan (2002) noted,

> The Rule of the Six C's provides a systematic framework for managing and resolving conflicts. This approach is practiced as teachers and administrators can manage conflicts at the lowest possible level while expending the least amount of energy. It is invitational in its emphasis on trust, intentionality,

C1	Concern	*Is this really a problem?*
C2	Confer	*Can we talk about this in private?*
C3	Consult	*Do we remember our responsibilities?*
C4	Confront	*How can we connect choices and consequences?*
C5	Combat	*How can we enforce the consequences?*
C6	Conciliate	*How can we re-establish a working relationship?*

FIGURE 7.2 The 6 Cs Approach to Conflict Management (Purkey & Novak, 1996; Purkey & Strahan, 2002)

respect, and optimism. Teaching this process to students gives them a practical, invitational strategy they can use to address concerns and conflict in their own lives, not only in school, but beyond.

(p. 114)

Indeed, the 6 Cs could be integrated into a school's curricular program, providing students with the opportunity to develop conflict management skills in the context of their learning. Purkey and Strahan (2002) point out that the six steps "lend themselves to almost any method of problem solving that teachers apply in language arts, health, math, science, the arts, social studies, or science" (p. 114).

Conclusion

The primary purpose of this chapter was to introduce invitational theory as a potential theoretical foundation for the book's focus on developing a positive classroom ethos rooted in an appropriate approach to issues such as authority, power, accountability, and responsibility. The theory provides a well-established conceptual framework, a lens through which teachers and educational leaders can develop and assess their school and classroom communities. It is a theory of practice, a theory that is both theoretical and practical. The literature contains a host of practical resources and helpful concepts that can collectively exercise a profound impact on classroom ethos (e.g., Purkey et al., 2020; Purkey & Strahan, 1995; Riner, 2003; Young, 2016; Young & Schoenlein, 2017). John Novak (2021) encapsulates this well: "Built on a defensible theory of practice, it provides a rationale, strategies, and examples of ways to develop and sustain exemplary schools, schools where people want to be, schools where people want to teach, learn, and work together" (p. 1).

References

Combs, A. W. (1999). *Being and becoming: A field approach to psychology*. Springer.
Combs, A. W., Richards, A. C., & Richards, F. (1976). *Perceptual psychology. A humanistic approach to the study of persons*. Harper & Row.

Ellis, T. I. (1990). *Invitational learning for counseling and development. Highlights: An ERIC/CAPS digest*. ERIC Clearinghouse on Counselling and Personal Services.

Jourard, S. M. (1974). *Healthy personality: An approach from the viewpoint of humanistic psychology*. Palgrave Macmillan.

Novak, J. M. (2021). Invitational education for a post pandemic world: A recap and a look forward. *Education Today*. www.educationtoday.com.au/news-detail/Invitational-Education-for-a-Post-Pandemic-World-5368#

Novak, J. M., & Purkey, W. W. (2001). *Invitational education. Fastback #488*. Kappa Educational Foundation. http://teacherlink.ed.usu.edu/yetcres/catalogs/reavis/488.pdf

Purkey, W. W. (1970). *Self-concept and school achievement*. Prentice-Hall.

Purkey, W. W. (1978). *Inviting school success: A self-concept approach to teaching and learning*. Wadsworth.

Purkey, W. W., & Novak, J. M. (1984). *Inviting school success: A self-concept approach to teaching and learning* (2nd ed.). Wadsworth.

Purkey, W. W., & Novak, J. M. (1996). *Inviting school success: A self-concept approach to teaching, learning and democratic practice* (3rd ed.). Wadsworth.

Purkey, W. W., & Novak, J. M. (2015). *An introduction to invitational theory*. www.invitationaleducation.org/wp-content/uploads/2019/04/art_intro_to_invitational_theory-1.pdf

Purkey, W. W., Novak, J. M., & Fretz, J. R. (2020). *Developing inviting schools: A beneficial framework for teaching*. Teachers College Press.

Purkey, W. W., & Schmidt, J. J. (1990). *Invitational learning for counseling and development*. ERIC Counseling and Personal Services Clearinghouse.

Purkey, W. W., Schmidt, J. J., & Novak, J. M. (2010). *From conflict to conciliation: How to defuse difficult situations*. Corwin Press.

Purkey, W. W., & Strahan, D. B. (1995). School transformation through invitational education. *Research in the Schools*, *2*(2), 1–6.

Purkey, W. W., & Strahan, D. B. (2002). *Inviting positive classroom discipline*. National Middle School Association.

Radd, T. (2006). Getting there: Creating inviting climates. In J. Novak, W. Rocca, & A. DiBiase (Eds.), *Creating inviting schools* (pp. 81–99). Caddo Gap Press.

Riner, P. S. (2003). The intimate correlation of invitational education and effective classroom management. *Journal of Invitational Theory and Practice*, *9*, 41–55.

Rogers, C. R. (1969). *Freedom to learn*. Charles E. Merrill.

Shaw, D. E., Siegel, B. L., & Schoenlein, A. (2013). The basic tenets of invitational theory and practice: An invitational glossary. *Journal of Invitational Theory & Practice*, *19*, 30–42.

Young, J. S. (2016). Making systems theories work through an invitational framework. *Education Today*, *1*(1), 12–14. www.educationtoday.com.au/_images/articles/pdf/article-pdf-1162.pdf

Young, J. S., & Schoenlein, A. (2017). School transformation made simple with the invitational education toolkit. *Education Today*, *1*(1), 10–12. www.educationtoday.com.au/_images/articles/pdf/article-pdf-1296.pdf

8
SCHOOL OF ROCK

Mason Steinke

Jack Black is always applicable. This was my exact thought when my education professor mentioned to an education class that Dewey Finn, Jack Black's character in *School of Rock* (Linklater, 2003) was irrelevant or impossible to connect to a professional discussion of teacher authority in the classroom. I was convinced that I could take on this project and, with little convincing, my professor agreed. One of my colleagues at the time saw my enthusiasm and asked to be a part of this far-fetched idea. So off we went creating this practical lesson plan related to the idea of teacher authority and Mr. Dewey Finn. I thought that submitting the final project would be the end of my work on *School of Rock*, but I quickly realized it was only the beginning. My professor presented us with our next challenge, suggesting we put our lesson to the test with his second-year education students, I immediately jumped at the opportunity and my colleague finally agreed. Since presenting our lesson for the first time, I have returned to my alma mater on two separate occasions and taught this particular lesson on my own.

Here is a brief summary of the film to put my lesson into context. In *School of Rock*, a failed rock musician (Jack Black) is down on his luck and in need of money. While trying to sell off some of his guitars, he receives a call from a principal looking for his best friend (a certified teacher) to sub at her school. Jack Black's character pretends to be his best friend and appears at a private middle school to serve as the Substitute Teacher. He devises a plan to teach the class music and create a new rock band to try and revive his dreams!

For the introduction of my lesson, I asked the students what authority meant to them. This sparked a class discussion, as many different opinions and perspectives were being shared. I then went on to explain the different types of

DOI: 10.4324/9781003140849-9

teacher authority, some of the more important ones which I have listed as follows.

- Credentialed or certified: a K-12 educator who holds a permanent teaching certificate and/or a continuous contract.
- Expertise: separated into two kinds, subject area and pedagogical. A combination between these two is usually expected within the teaching profession.
- Charismatic: the "fun" teacher, leading with enthusiasm.
- Coercion: using your position of power to make students live up to your expectations.
- Self-authorization: you take on your role comfortably; therefore, you stand up and start teaching.
- Passion: for teaching, for the subject area, for the curriculum, for students, and for life.
- Authorizing students: many times, teachers can actually gain authority by giving it up to their students. For example, adopting a servant attitude can show students that you take them seriously.

Once I had explained the many types of teacher authority, I had the students re-read the list either individually or in small groups. Most of this information would have been relatively new, so I wanted to ensure that they had an understanding of the content as it would be used during the focal point of the lesson. You may be asking yourself how this relates to Jack Black and *School of Rock*? Well, once I had established the groundwork of the lesson, I then incorporated the main idea; How is it possible for a washed-up, wannabe rock star with zero educational credentials or teaching experience to obtain teaching authority? Enter Mr. Dewey Finn!

After watching *School of Rock* twice through, I identified four different clips or scenes for students to dissect in light of the different types of teacher authority. Before showing the first clip, I gave the class this viewing prompt, "I want you to look and listen for possible types of teacher authority that Jack Black demonstrates or lacks." After each clip, we had a class discussion surrounding the task and, of course, the obvious was highlighted, "Jack Black definitely doesn't have credentialed authority," or "He possesses charismatic authority." However, after having taught this lesson on three separate occasions, I am surprised by what students noticed the first time I taught it. Again for context, in one clip I showed, Dewey Finn was asking a student what he was playing on the guitar. The student was hesitant at first but then mentioned it was a song he had written. Dewey Finn immediately assembled the band and went to work learning his student's song. What I did not show to the class was that this later became the song that they performed in the final Battle of the Bands. In response to this scene, one student, in particular, mentioned how Jack Black authorized his students in numerous subtle ways. This student's comment led to a deeper level of discussion, which enhanced students' and my own understanding of the importance of teacher authority. I used this same format with all four clips and, in each class I taught on *School of Rock*, I gave the students the opportunity to apply what they had learned to their own teaching.

As the class organized themselves into various groups, I presented them with another task. I wanted each group to produce a Venn diagram or some other visual representation of a comparison of the teaching authority of Jack Black's character to their practicum teacher. As a bonus, they could include themselves based on their teaching experience or what they think might work most effectively for them. Again, this generated a conversation, and throughout each of the three lessons I taught, there was at least one "aha" moment. During my second time through the lesson, a student in fourth year was completing the Venn diagram and came to the realization that her practicum teacher had an immense amount of authority based on professional expertise. This particular student had been placed in a specialized program, so it made sense; however, they later mentioned that they could not understand how their teacher was able to control such a diverse classroom until my lesson was presented to them. This is why we teach, because of moments like this!

Essentially, that is how I incorporated Jack Black into a teacher authority lesson. At the time of writing, as I step into my fourth year as an educator, I am immensely grateful for the opportunity my professor offered to me. I am grateful not only for the challenge of the assignment but also for being called back to my alma mater to reteach the lesson I had designed. By doing so, I learned what works and what doesn't work in terms of teacher authority and classroom management. In my own experience, I have quickly realized that sticking to one type of teaching authority will start to become challenging in your teaching practice. I have found success by applying different and new types of authority within the classroom. There is a place and time for everything. If you try to constantly portray the charismatic authority—aka the "fun teacher"—you will tend to burn out more quickly than expected. On the other hand, teaching with the authority of expertise may get you only so far. Again, in the little experience I've had as a teacher, I find that using multiple types of authority within the classroom will set you up for success. It is important to find that balance, but isn't that what teaching is all about? Who would have thought that *School of Rock* and Jack Black could help teachers with their authority within the classroom? I tip my hat to you, Mr. Dewey Finn!

Reference

Linklater, R. (Director). (2003). *School of rock*. Paramount Pictures.

9
CASE STUDY
A Turn-Around in a High-Needs Classroom

Nadine Ayer

Talkback, pushback, attitude, refusals, and the odd projectile here and there: if you have not had "that class" at least once in your career as an educator, it is safe to say that you will at some point. We are all familiar with "that class," the one that gets whispered about in the staff room, the one that Substitute Teachers refuse to come back to, and the one that requires so many after-school meetings, phone calls, and strategy meetings. When you are the teacher entrusted with a class like that on a daily basis, the endless needs and learning disabilities, together with the academic and behavioral challenges, can feel insurmountable.

I am fortunate enough to have taught several years of "that class," and when I say fortunate, I mean it without irony. Such classes are undeniably challenging, and while teaching them, I often wondered whether the solution was simply to change careers altogether. However, when I was in the depths of burnout, I came across new perspectives that helped me see "problem" students differently. I became determined to create a community where these kids could feel safe and accepted because chances were that in the other areas of their lives they felt neither. I also felt determined to understand each student and to develop a relationship with them, no matter how tenuous it might be. As I will show, these shifts in perspective and approach radically changed the tone of my classroom and helped me form new goals for myself as an educator and as a person.

Background

In one of the classes I taught, I remember reading the class list and seeing multiple names that I had heard repeatedly in the staff room during previous years. When I told my colleagues which students I had in my class, I got looks of pity and I heard things like, "Good luck with Johnny; he was a nightmare to deal with,"

"Oh, you have Aiden? He is so disrespectful," and "James is one student that made me hate teaching." This class of students was notorious in the school; they regularly required parent meetings and phone calls home, and it was not uncommon for their teachers to end up in tears or even go on stress leave.

The impression I had of these students put me on the defensive before any of them set foot in my classroom. I was already in a deficit, which meant that I was harsher than I needed to be. From the very beginning of the school year, I was trying to control behaviors and attitudes. In some cases, the very first encounter I had with a student involved my sending them out of the classroom because I disliked the attitude I was getting from them. If I received even the slightest sniff of disrespect from a student, I would send that student to the office. There were so many behaviors to manage in my class that I was overwhelmed. As far as I could tell at the time, some of these behaviors might have been born of deep-seated anxiety, but others were simple expressions of outright disrespect.

There were also several students in my class with moderate to severe learning disabilities. Some of my students were coping with heartbreaking trauma. I had students who had been bullied or who were bullies. I had students who had awful home lives and students who came to school hungry. I also had quiet students who were often overlooked because so many of their classmates demanded attention all the time. How was I going to help all of them? How was I going to get any teaching done, let alone prepare them for provincial achievement tests?

Unsuccessful Approaches—Compliance and Control

In the years I spent teaching these challenging classes, there were a few moments during which I felt such desperation to gain control that I spent hours each evening researching behavior and classroom-management strategies. (While I was at it, I also researched alternative career paths.) I looked endlessly at Pinterest-perfect classrooms and tried every Pinterest-worthy classroom-management technique, with little success. I tried many approaches that I read about online as well as techniques that other teachers suggested, based on their own experiences.

My first instinct was to get much harsher with my students. The old adage "Don't smile before Christmas" was running through my mind: first, let the students know that you mean business and are not to be messed with, and then later show them that you care. This clearly backfired; in response to that approach, I received more pushback, more disrespect, more talk-back, and more frequent outbursts. One student would ignore everything I asked, while others would become so upset by seemingly small things that they would "turtle." Often, I could not even figure out what had made them upset. It was common for me to hear phrases like "You can't tell me what to do" or "I don't have to do what you tell me," and I would respond by becoming angry, standing up taller, wagging my finger at the student who had talked back, and threatening to send them to the office unless they did as I instructed. In short, I reacted with little compassion or empathy, demanded that students leave my class, and then called the office for reinforcements.

I continued to feel out of control as these difficult behaviors intensified. There were so many different behaviors to manage in my class that my students started to feed off each other, and as the chaos grew, my desperation to maintain authority in my own classroom grew until I felt out of control completely. Unfortunately, my response to my own lack of control was to rely on shame-based tactics: "I am so disappointed in you," "I can't believe you are like this," and "You're being incredibly rude" became familiar refrains from the front of the classroom. By that point, I was taking the behavior personally, which meant that I was no longer curious about why my students were struggling in the first place. I admit that there were times when I cried in front of my students and was so frustrated that I told them that they made my job harder. There were times when I was not gracious in the least and did not have the compassion that I should have had. In a last-ditch effort, I took away privileges and sent letters home. Those tactics have their place, but I was not using them logically in response to specific behaviors; instead, I was grasping at any thread of control I thought I had. With the benefit of hindsight, I can say that I was forcing compliance rather than fostering community.

Difficult Realizations

I had numerous conversations with my administrator during this phase of my career. Some of these conversations were helpful, while others were humbling and uncomfortable. I was forced to look deep into myself to address certain inadequacies I had as a teacher. This is also how I learned to advocate for myself, because I felt like I was drowning, and I did not know what to do anymore. One particularly hard conversation with my administrator, for which I will forever be grateful, brought to light how my students feared that I was going to abandon them. They felt like they were always being punished and that they were going to cause me to leave teaching. I had been feeling completely burnt out, but when I heard that they were feeling abandoned, something shifted in me.

I realized at that moment that in their time at the school, they had always been "that class." They had had teachers leave before. They had teachers who abandoned them and who had cut them down during all the time they had been in school. When I realized that, I burst into tears. The guilt I felt at that moment was overwhelming. I even thought that I needed to quit teaching because I was not cut out for it: I wanted to be a teacher to help kids, to lift them up, but instead, I was tearing them down and creating a community of distrust. Because of the way I was interacting with them, I was affirming in their little hearts and minds that they were bad kids, even though that was not what I actually believed about them. I needed a paradigm shift. I needed to start from scratch. This became the biggest uphill battle of my career, but during that battle, I was at my most determined, and I can be proud of that now.

Fostering Connection—Carrington

After that illuminating conversation with my administrator, I read the book *Kids These Days: A Game Plan for (Re)Connecting with Those We Teach, Lead, & Love* (2019) by Jody Carrington, a child psychologist. As a staff, we read through the book for professional development, and the words leaped off the page at me. Every page had a new thought, a new angle on how to connect with and view the children in my classes. Carrington's book, along with her social media accounts and the talk I heard her give in person, gave me renewed hope for my practice. Her approach facilitated a seemingly simple shift in thinking.

Carrington repeatedly emphasized that "kids are not 'attention seeking,' they are 'connection seeking'" (71). This phrase became a sort of mantra as I entered my classroom each day. It was the lens through which I tried to view each child when I felt frustrated by the behavior I was seeing. I began to ask myself, "What is the need I have to meet?" and "What is this behavior telling me about the child?" After all, when it comes to connection, the "kids who need it the most are the hardest to give it to" (51).

When I took a step back and thought about the students placed in my care, and when I diligently asked questions and read files, I began to see them in a different light. I began to shift my thinking about student behavior. This is not to say that I did nothing about unwanted behavior or that everything was permissible, because students still did need to respect themselves, their peers, the staff, and the space, but I did think about why the behavior was happening, and I approached it differently.

As I moved forward, I looked for ways to make connections with my students. Every day was a fresh start. This was hard at first because it is not easy to let go of the big emotions from the previous day's outburst, but we all make mistakes. Starting fresh every day was vital to my students. They needed to know that the past was in the past because for so long their past had followed them; every bad decision was a link in a chain they were dragging behind them as they came to school. I needed to break that chain and ensure that each student knew that each morning signaled a new beginning. This also meant teaching them that each day was a fresh start with each other because up to that point, they had also broken trust with each other, not just with me. We all needed a fresh start; we needed to build a new community from the ground up.

I started simple. Sometimes the solution was as simple as feeding them. I began stocking a bowl on my desk with apples and granola bars. Another strategy was something I had first learned in teacher training: standing at the classroom door at the start of the day to greet each student. I did not understand why this was important until this class. I would welcome each student into my class by name, and while doing so, I would quietly observe how they arrived. Who came in full of energy, with big smiles on their faces? Who came in quietly but content? Who seemed frazzled or out of sorts? Did I spot some tear-stained faces? Who was always arriving late? The five to ten minutes during which I stood at my door and welcomed students gave me a good idea of how the morning might go. It told me who I needed to connect with immediately and who might need a little extra grace and compassion that day. I also started each day with a quiet, simple activity for students to start as they came in the door, such as sitting and listening to music, journaling in response to a prompt, or looking at a piece of art. This quiet activity gave me the space and time to connect with key students in the first minutes of the day.

There was one student in particular for whom this was incredibly important. This student was often outright defiant and knew how to push everyone's buttons with little jabs or brags. This student would ignore teacher requests, not complete work, and get into regular confrontations with peers and staff. I slowly realized that this student was playing a role because they were told so often that they were a bad kid that it was easier to just be the bad kid than to try to reinvent themselves because no one would ever give them the chance. I made the conscious decision to connect with this student first thing every day. I would casually walk over, get down at eye level, quietly greet them, and ask how it was going. Over the course of a couple of weeks, I got to know this student better. I already knew that this student loved giraffes, so I would ask as many giraffe-related questions as I could. Then I began to learn new things. I learned how compassionate this student was, how talented they were in art, and how thoughtful they were.

As I learned new things, I ran with them. I built my students up in any way I could whenever I saw the opportunity. I gave out praise for each thing I saw that was good, whether it was a positive interaction with a peer or a piece of artwork done well. I also assigned important jobs in the classroom. I called home and sent emails about things that were going well (never underestimate the power of a positive email home to parents about their kids; it helps to bring them on side much more effectively than a negative email does). Slowly, I saw classroom behavior shift. My students started to trust that I wanted the best for each of them and that I believed they were good kids with great potential. My students began to change how they interacted with each other and started to develop more meaningful friendships. Were there still bumps in this road? Absolutely. There were steps backward, but the conversations around the negative behavior shifted, too.

Managing "Lid-Flipping"—Siegel and Bryson

These conversations shifted because, through Carrington's work, I was led to the work of Daniel J. Siegel, a child and family psychiatrist, who with psychotherapist Tina Payne Bryson, wrote *The Whole-Brain Child: 12 Proven Strategies to Nurture Your Child's Developing Mind* (2012). Siegel and Bryson discuss self-regulation and how a child's developing brain reacts to difficult situations and emotions. The key piece I took away from this work was the idea of "flipping our lid" (43). In simple terms, this is when a person ceases to be rational or regulated in their emotional responses. For a toddler, this might happen because you gave them the blue cup instead of a yellow one, while for a 10-year-old, this might happen because they do not understand the assignment you have given them.

Siegel and Bryson offer several ways to help students after they have flipped their lid. Interestingly, keeping the lid on is not the goal; this is because children need to flip their lid in order to learn how to manage and regulate their emotions. Rather, once a child has flipped their lid, the most important thing is to stay regulated yourself. Ways to do this include taking some deep breaths and trying not to engage in the heat of the moment. Once you know that you can stay regulated, name the emotion with which you think the student is struggling. For example, say, "It looks like you are feeling frustrated." The next step is the most important one: Validate the emotion they are feeling. So, to continue within the same example, say, "It's okay to feel frustrated."

Here is what a hypothetical encounter with a student used to look like compared to what it looked after I shifted my approach.

Previous approach
A student throws a book.
ME: "Don't throw the book. That's incredibly disrespectful to the book and our space."
STUDENT: "I don't care."
ME: "It's important to care about our space. You need to be respectful."
STUDENT: "It's a stupid book! Who cares?!"
ME: "Go to the hall, and we will talk about this later."

New approach
A student throws a book.
ME: *[Takes a deep breath and gets down on the student's level.]* "It looks like you are feeling frustrated. It's okay to feel frustrated. What's going on?"
STUDENT: "I don't understand what I am supposed to do with the poem; it doesn't make any sense."
ME: "Let's talk about it together. It's okay to be frustrated by the assignment, but it's not okay to throw the book. Ask me for help instead. I would hate for that book to have hit someone accidentally because you were frustrated."

Emotions were often not permissible in my previous approach, but the new approach anticipated them and made room for them. This approach to "lid-flipping" continually reminded me that there is nothing bad about feeling emotions; it's what we do with the emotions that is important.

Other Strategies and Tactics

Once I absorbed ideas from Carrington, Siegel, and Bryson, my first instinct was no longer to banish students when they were dysregulated. I tried my best to connect and validate emotions and to have my students tell me what was going on before I jumped to conclusions. I learned how important it is to stay with a student who is emotionally dysregulated; after all, one of my students' top fears was abandonment, so why would I leave them alone when they were at their most vulnerable? I still often needed backup because I had a full class of other students who needed me, so the support I got from my administrator and my educational assistants (EAs) was especially helpful during this time. My administrator often gave me the choice to work with the dysregulated child or to return to the class and leave the student with the administrator. I would choose based on the situation the student and I were in. What was most important was that they were not alone.

Another way that I shifted was to recognize each student individually and have the whole class talk about all the amazing things they saw in each of their classmates. We called it "Student of the Day." One student would come up to the front of the class and sit in front of the whiteboard. I would write their name on the board, and then I would invite the class to tell me a word or short phrase that described their classmate, and I would write each suggestion on the board above the student's head. It took some practice to get away from things such as "She's pretty" or "He's good at soccer," but we eventually got down to the meaningful pieces such as "She is caring" or "He is encouraging." Once we had exhausted all words and phrases to describe the student of the day, I would take a photo and print two copies. One copy the student got to take home, and the other was displayed on a wall in our room. By the time each student had taken a turn, there was a wall full of pictures of the students with positive words and phrases that their classmates had said about them. This simple thing increased the empathy and community in my room in a short amount of time. Students began to be kinder to each other and more understanding of small transgressions.

One final change to our classroom community that I want to describe was such a small thing that I did not realize at the time how large its impact would be: the use of nicknames. One afternoon while the class was on the carpet, I called one student Ketchup. I made that decision in a moment, and I cannot remember the reason for it now. All I know is that in that instant of laughter from the class, I realized the power of positive nicknames. Immediately, every single student wanted a nickname. We had a discussion about how some nicknames are not kind, and we should only use nicknames if the person thinks it is okay, but nicknames often are terms of endearment. For instance, I do not use my son's nickname when I am frustrated or exasperated with him; I use his nickname when I am being playful. As a class, we talked about how a nickname could be a good way to lighten the mood in the class. Another benefit was that when I was cross and used their regular name, they had a clue that I was getting frustrated. All the students had input on what their nickname would be, and suddenly I had a pantry full of food-nicknamed students: papaya, mango, seaweed, pizza, and mushrooms—the list went on. to my heart's delight, they even gave me the nickname Mrs. Coffee. I started to invite each student into the room in the morning by their nickname and then dismiss each one by their nickname at the end of the day. The joy and lightness this brought to my class were immediate and palpable. My students needed to know that I cared about them; they needed to know that they were important. Nicknames communicated that in a way I never imagined.

New Goals

In the end, my marker of success changed. My goals changed with this class. Perfect compliance was never a realistic goal. Never having students talk back or give pushback was not the goal anymore, and neither was a perfect academic achievement. Instead, the goal was to build a community of learners who could safely express themselves to me and to each other. The goal was to foster a community of trust, respect, and understanding and to know that this would not always be perfect. The goal was to communicate as much as possible with my class, with school administration, and with parents. I still needed to give consequences, I still made phone calls and sent emails home, and I still needed support from my administration, but the conversations shifted. How I addressed unwanted behavior also shifted; consequences were logical and well considered, and the students were involved. They knew that if I was calling home, they would be included in parent meetings. Nothing was a surprise, and I always made sure that they knew that I wanted the best for them.

Conclusion

Challenging classes like these became a blessing when I realized how much they encouraged me to learn, grow, and develop as a teacher and as a person; they brought out the humanity in me. Difficult classes forced me to develop my empathy and to be quick to listen instead of quick to judge, and quick to ask questions rather than quick to lay down consequences. The simple shifts in perspective that Carrington, Siegel, and Bryson offered helped me to shift my approach. Once I made that shift, I was able to learn from these students that education is about the kid and not the content. Because these students chose not to fit the mold, I could break out of the mold that I had forced myself into as an educator.

References

Carrington, J. (2019). *Kids these days: A game plan for (re)connecting with those we teach, lead, & love.* Friesen Press.

Siegel, D. J., & Bryson, T. P. (2012). *The whole-brain child: 12 proven strategies to nurture your child's developing mind.* Little, Brown.

PART 2
Authorizing Students

As Badley laid out in Chapter 1, teacher self-authorization is one of several authorization processes that occur in a classroom. Another is that students authorize the teacher to teach, and teachers authorize students to learn. Elements of authorizing students include teaching them to respect themselves and each other, to work and create together, and to ensure a safe space for all. Essentially, it is about shared authority, a notion that is not new, as various educational theorists who promote democratic classrooms can attest. Where authority is shared, students are given a degree of decision-making power about what happens in the classroom. A classic example is that students participate in creating the rules for the classroom and what should occur when a student or the teacher violates those rules. The authors in this section extend the idea, involving students as co-creators of the curriculum, developing their decision-making skills with real-world problems in everyday life, and having students decide how best to demonstrate their learning. Teacher preparation programs are able to introduce Pre-Service Teachers to these shared authority practices when Pre-Service Teachers experience such student-focused practices in their own education.

Whatever the degree of shared authority, the point is to develop student feelings of belonging, a sense of control over their lives, and the development of citizenship practices. Place-based theory offers a window into how such classrooms are constructed. Spaces are imbued with meaning by what occurs in them, including group activities, the development of leadership skills, and healthy, supportive relationships.

The theory, strategies, and stories shared in this section all rely on the fundamental commitment to dignifying students. Some may openly profess a restorative justice model, while others identify, critique, and seek to uproot unjust societal inequities. The latter requires awareness of how educational and social structures privilege some cultural aspects, such as language codes, over others, thereby providing some students with cultural power while denying it to others. When teachers at all levels of education remain unaware of these realities, they reproduce the status quo. On the contrary, when teachers bring this awareness into the classroom, they authorize themselves and their students to work for change.

10
A SENSE OF PLACE AND STUDENT CONSENT

Jacqueline Filipek

Previous chapters have presented an expanded understanding of a classroom ethos beyond simplistic ideas of managing behaviors—an encompassing one including considerations for planning, instructional methods, assessment, record keeping, and interactions with and among students. The ethos of a classroom is developed in the shared and everyday life experiences of those who dwell there but is also connected to the beliefs, ideas, and thinking shaped by the agency of teachers in their pedagogical choices and allowances.

Teachers need the consent, or permission, of their students to carry out their instructional program in the classroom. In review, consent implies a position or relationship in which students willingly join the educational program. Consent requires a classroom ethos where students are engaged in learning and want to be there. This chapter offers theories of place as frames for thinking about how teachers can support a classroom *ethos of place* whereby student consent is attached to the meaningfulness of the classroom and to students' sense of self and sense of belonging. Ellis (2005), a researcher who studies place and education, writes that for students,

> be it positive or negative in nature, the classroom and school will acquire an emotional significance for them. As teachers who want students' classroom experience to be positive, we may wish to consider whether the classroom as a place—the whole experience of being there—affords social affiliation and belonging, creative self-development, and positive identities.
>
> (p. 60)

A Sense of Place

Throughout this chapter, the words *space* and *place* are used but not interchangeably. A space is simply an area, environmental context, or location that can be occupied by people. Place is the whole experience that results from people inhabiting a space. Ellis (2005) suggests that spaces become places when they are invested with meaning by those who spend time and engage in habitual activities there. She believes that meanings are derived from what people give to and receive from spaces, making places subjectively significant to their members. Crang (1998) suggests that "people do not simply locate themselves, they also define themselves through a sense of place . . . the place says something not only about where you live or come from but who you are" (pp. 102–103).

Through her extensive literature review of place-related theories and relation-to-place concepts, Sebastien (2020) developed a helpful framework for identifying the contributions to what is called a *sense of place*. She consolidated many years of conceptual and theoretical ideas into the visual representation in Figure 10.1, which highlights the many ways people see and interact with the spaces around them. The framework shows that a sense of place, that is, a personal connection to a place, develops from cognitive dimensions (beliefs and perceptions), affective dimensions (emotions and feelings), and conative dimensions (behavioral intentions and commitments) (Sebastien, 2020, p. 208).

As described in Sebastien's diagram in Figure 10.1, places hold meaning because of people's satisfaction within them as well as a result of the experiences they have there. People also develop attachments to places because of place dependence and place identity. For example, people can become dependent on a place because it is a source of security or human connections. Furthermore, in addition to contributing to the identities of the individual people in a place, the identity of the place itself can contribute to the place's meaningfulness for its inhabitants through the stories told of what happens there, the history situated within social contexts, and by the goods it contains or proximity to other places with goods or amenities (Crang, 1998). Places create a vital sense of belonging for those who inhabit them (Tuan, 1992) and offer opportunities for security, social affiliation, creative expression, and exploration (Ellis, 2005). People can develop psychological or emotional attachments to places (Chawla, 1992) as they are deeply rooted in identity and are an anchor of shared experiences between people over time (Crang, 1998).

Everyday Life in Classroom Places

Places "are defined less by unique locations, landscape, and communities than by the focusing of experiences and intentions onto particular settings. [They] are not abstractions or concepts but are directly experienced

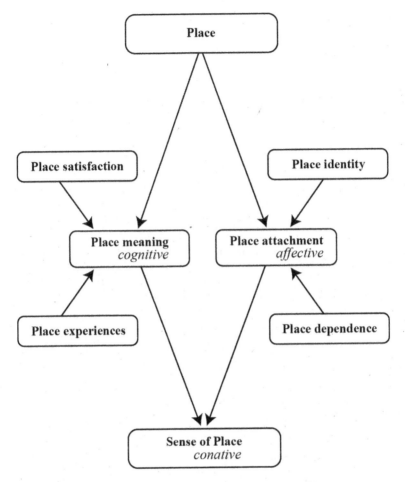

FIGURE 10.1 Framework Proposition for a Spatial Approach to Sense of Place

Source: From L. Sebastien (2020)

phenomena of the lived-world and hence are full with meanings, with real objects, and with ongoing activities."

(Relph, 1976, p. 141)

Within places are specific cultural characteristics and patterns of behavior (Crang, 1998).

"People construct their places," writes Sebastien (2020), "at both the level of representation and materiality; at the same time places do have an impact on the human way of life. As such, places function as facilitators and mediators of certain social relations that condition identity formation and behaviour."

(p. 206)

Often when students talk about their class or their classroom their talk is connected to how they feel about it, their roles there, or to a spiritual or personal connection called the *genius loci*, or unique spirit of the place (Crang, 1998). Classrooms become more than spaces students visit each day to learn; they become meaningful places full of shared experiences and relationships.

Everyday life is a relevant concept in understanding the role of place in student consent and classroom management. It is within everyday life experiences that we can understand what contributes to making a classroom a meaningful place for students. Based on Eyles' (1989) theory of the structural formation of place, Ellis (2005) created a diagram (Figure 10.2) of the reciprocal relationship between place and the structures and relationships that can enable or constrain everyday

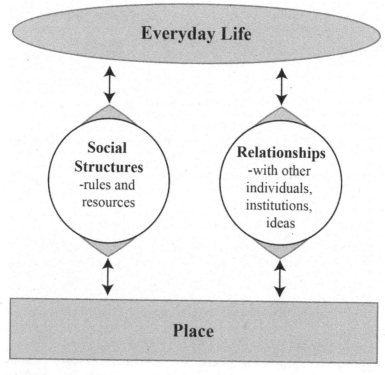

FIGURE 10.2 Structural Formations of Place Diagram

Source: From J. Ellis (2005)

life. She suggests students can develop a greater sense of place if their experiences in school and classrooms "are filled with familiar routines that build their confidence, if they know and become known by others, acquire intimate local knowledge, and learn the norms of the culture" (p. 60).

The concept of everyday life accounts for the ways in which people inhabit a space through present and available social structures and relationships. Eyles (1989) writes,

> Everyday life is, therefore, a taken-for-granted reality which provides the unquestioned background of meaning for the individual. It is a social construction which becomes a structure itself. Thus, through our actions in everyday life we build, maintain and reconstruct the very definitions, roles and motivations that shape our actions. . . . We both create and are created by society and these processes are played out within the context of everyday life. . . . From it we derive a sense of self, of identity, as living a real and meaningful biography.
>
> (p. 101)

The reciprocity between place and everyday life implies that structures and relationships within places are both a product of experiences and a medium through which people further shape their lives. This reciprocity suggests that teachers do play a role in establishing a sense of place in their classrooms.

Structures

Social structures, according to Eyles (1989), include the rules, routines, and available resources of a social system. Individuals cannot alter structures because structures are rooted in regular social practices and are produced within society through recurrent social practices and ideas. Research supports the conclusion that when people feel a part of the social structures and have developed relationships in a place, they are more likely to give their consent—to participate more fully in classroom life and activities (see Adeyemo, 2012; Alenazi, 2015; Djigic & Stojiljkovic, 2011; Hale & Robey, 2019).

To emphasize the relationship between place, consent, and classroom management, I draw on examples from an eight-month ethnographic study I carried out in a grade 3 classroom. The examples illustrate how teachers can foster relationships as well as implement structures such as rules, routines, and resources to shape classrooms into good places. Good places lead to positive things for students: feeling cared for and caring for others, contributing to the welfare of others in the classroom or for things that happen there, positive status and attention, positive experiences such as leadership, freedom, choice, and privacy, space for creative, autonomous, or self-expressive activities, and bonding with others in playful or adventurous exploration (Ellis, 2010b).

Teacher agency plays a large role in how classrooms are constructed, maintained, and reconstructed. Eyles (1989) writes that "agency is the essence of experience and everyday life" and sense of place is a manifestation of agency (p. 4). In the grade 3 classroom, Mrs. Carpenter, the teacher, worked hard to design social structures that both helped the classroom to function smoothly and fostered a collaborative atmosphere.

Rules

Rules occur in all parts of life and are social constructions resulting from shared social and cultural beliefs and values. In classrooms, rules are sometimes named *expectations* or *guidelines* but are essentially the same as rules in that they are meant to guide behavior. Most classrooms have rules that are specific to the class or are set by the school. They can be determined by the teacher or school administrators or constructed together with students. Rules are always a facet of place, whether they emerge from shared experiences or are set by someone, because rules help define places and the actions within them.

The grade 3 classroom had various rules. Mrs. Carpenter often invited students to share in making the rules, as doing so created an opportunity to discuss why specific rules should exist. Collaboratively setting rules allowed the students to take responsibility for their own learning and actions by contributing to what they thought their classroom should be like. Students are also more likely to follow classroom rules when they have actively participated in constructing them, which is also a defining characteristic of a good place. There were also rules to teach students to become more independent. For example, if students needed to use the bathroom, the rule was that they first determined if it was a good time to leave, then signed their name on a list, and then left on their own. Mrs. Carpenter trusted the students to make their own decisions but to let her know they were leaving by logging their short absence. There were times that she was busy with another student, so this policy not only limited interruptions but also established trust and helped develop the self-sufficiency of students.

Grade 3 students sometimes need support following rules or learning classroom expectations. Mrs. Carpenter helped students monitor their actions through a class money system where students were awarded fake coins for desirable actions, even interpersonal ones such as being kind to someone, and were asked to pay money for undesirable actions, like leaving a mess at their workspace. Students could then use the money they earned in the class store that was set up by the store leadership team each Friday. The students could purchase small items such as bookmarks or puzzles or choose to save their money for larger, more expensive purchases. Although this seemed like a behavioral reward system, Mrs. Carpenter explained that the money system connected to many curricular outcomes and taught the students lessons for future everyday life experiences. Good places have rules for and means of obtaining goods, such as through a currency system.

Mrs. Carpenter promoted place-making through the daily use of her money system while, at the same time, cultivating the expected behavior and actions described in their class rules.

Mrs. Carpenter also posted signs with important information rooted in classroom rules, such as criteria for independent reading, technology troubleshooting, and how to manage friendship conflicts. She directed students to use those signs to seek answers to some questions. When students are given ownership over the rules in a place or can take responsibility for some of their actions there, it helps them to feel like insiders and "gives them a strong centre for which to face the unknowns of the larger world" (Ellis, 2010b, p. 356).

Routines

One of the most effective aspects of the grade 3 classroom that contributed to place-making and, thus, increased student consent, was how Mrs. Carpenter created and utilized student leadership groups as part of the daily routines in the classroom. Very early in September, Mrs. Carpenter invited the students into a conversation about classroom responsibilities and ways they could all contribute. In asking the students their opinions, Mrs. Carpenter and the students co-constructed a shared sense of the responsibilities in the classroom. From there, the class discussed who could be responsible for each area and split into smaller groups of shared interest. Each group created a name and a list of responsibilities (see Table 10.1) which Mrs. Carpenter later typed and printed. In addition to physical tasks, students also added interpersonal responsibilities through phrases such as *be responsible and honest, use your manners, be helpful*, or *work together*. The students recognized that their responsibilities include both tasks and ways of acting with one another, a recognition which contributed to developing a culture of respect and helpfulness in how they carried out their group responsibilities.

Students were encouraged to join at least one group, but many wanted to join more than one—a sign that they were feeling a sense of care for their space and for each other. Each group was photographed, and the photo, group name, and list of responsibilities were posted on a bulletin board in the classroom. The students practiced their jobs with the teacher and eventually took complete control over them. They even corrected Mrs. Carpenter when she asked a student not in that group to do a class job. Not only did the classroom run smoothly because students were sharing in daily tasks, but each student shared in taking responsibility for the overall space and routines there. Crang (1998) believes that place is considered a set of cultural characteristics which extend beyond ideas of physical location and become "an anchor of shared experiences between people and continuity over time" (p. 103). Shared experiences create a vital sense of belonging; belonging contributes to consent and students' willingness to participate.

In addition to the routines for student leadership groups, students engaged in many other daily routines. Their routines involved putting away their coats and

TABLE 10.1 Leadership Groups in Grade 3

Group Name (created by the students)	Responsibilities (determined by the class and recorded by each small group)
Super Floor Cleaners (four members)	Pick up the garbage from the floor at the end of the day, be responsible, put left behind items on the purple table, be a role model to others in the class
Tables (two members)	Always keep the tables clean, use the washcloth properly, don't wash nametags, only spray the tables
Master Librarians (two members)	Check for library books every day, scan the books in, put the books in the return bin, bring the bin back to the class, be responsible
The Technology Smarties (four members)	Help others in the class, handle technology with care, carefully hand out Chromebooks and iPads and put them away, troubleshoot when needed, turn the SMART Board and document camera on and off when needed, change the batteries in the FM system
The Golden Phone (two members)	Answer the phone when it rings, use your manners, speak in a clear voice, take turns, be polite and responsible, take a message when needed
The Terrific Chairs	Stack chairs up at the end of the day, count the chairs per table, get chairs when needed, be safe
Mad Money Machines (four members)	Hand out morning money respectfully, be responsible and honest, pick money up off the floor and return it to Mrs. C's desk, make change or trade in money, set up, manage and clean up the store
Super Star Gym Helpers	Take equipment out of the storage room that Mrs. C. needs, return equipment to its proper place in the storage room, return keys to Mrs. C., be a leader with equipment, take turns with the key, be responsible and trustworthy
The B.A.D. Heroes	Help others when they are hurt, stay with the hurt person until they are feeling better, get a band-aid when needed, walk sick or hurt students to the office, get ice from the office, go to get help when needed

Source: From J. Filipek (2020)

backpacks in the morning, writing a morning message or note in their agendas, choosing a book for independent reading, and then having a class meeting about the day to come. Students also relied on a posted schedule and could use the clock to help track class changes. Students also had recess, lunch, and end-of-day routines. They learned routines in other classes, such as music or physical education, and they had procedures for lining up to leave and return to the classroom. The students also learned routines for retrieving and returning computer devices (with the help of the technology team). The class practiced their routines so that all students knew the expectations. Good places, where people feel they belong, have strong routines with shared responsibilities.

Resources

All good places have resources or provide access to resources. Resources can be physical or social and are accessible to members of the place. The grade 3 classroom resources included access to knowledgeable others, such as the teacher, peers, books, or Internet, had means of sharing information and ideas, had places for students to keep their personal belongings such as coat lockers and bins for extra supplies or notebooks, and spaces for group work, whole-class discussions, and learning centers. Mrs. Carpenter was deliberate about the resources she selected for the classroom so that her selections would reflect her intentions for teaching and learning. For example, Mrs. Carpenter used tables that could easily be rearranged into smaller circles, as she believed in collaborative learning. She also clearly labeled bins and containers so that objects could be easily found and returned to their places. Mrs. Carpenter encouraged students to bring in personal objects and had spaces for individual items that were not meant to be shared. Students sometimes set their own boundaries on sharing when they brought in their own things. Other available resources included books, a clock, a Canadian flag, an alphabet line, a number line, various posters with rules, a posted schedule, and inspirational quotations that students used in their everyday lives in the classroom.

Relationships

Places provide access to social affiliation through the relationships they offer. The word *relationships* refers to the "continuous flow of conduct, involving actual or contemplated causal interventions in the process of living" and is thought of as the essence of experience in everyday life (Eyles, 2013, p. 25). Relationships include how people interact with other individuals, institutions, and ideas.

The students participated socially in the classroom and took responsibility for their own relationships with and among each other. The teacher used various student grouping strategies to foster different relationships for academic or social learning. Mrs. Carpenter often used elements of the URStrong program (https://urstrong.com/) to teach students self and social awareness and to enhance their social-emotional well-being. Because of the program, the students had the skills to try to solve conflicts but, more importantly, felt capable, responsible, and open to dealing with them on their own. The troubleshooting guides, the plans for putting out friendship fires (conflicts), and the modeling by the teacher all contributed to students having the knowledge they needed—the sense of place in the classroom allowed the students to take ownership of their relationships.

Creating a classroom culture of respect and responsibility contributed to making it a place where students felt safe to stand up for themselves and others. It also created a collaborative place where students knew they could, and should, help one another, and that teaching and learning are not the responsibility of just the teacher. Ellis (2010a) claims that "without safety, social acceptance, and the absence of fear of ridicule or harassment, students cannot fully participate in or benefit from the learning activities they are invited into" (p. 393). Teachers need to establish the classroom as a safe place and can do so by enabling positive relationships, trust, and a sense of belonging among all the members of the classroom through active attention to relationship building.

Planning for Place-Making

This chapter and others in this book have offered examples of practices that support classroom management, but I want to leave you with a pathway to make your classroom a meaningful place for your students. Ellis (2009) proposed that teachers should think about their plans for teaching as plans for place-making. Planning for place-making implies uncovering the aspirations (see Table 10.2) you hold for your students and then finding ways for the parts of teaching—rules, routines, resources, and activities—to meet them.

As you consider your plans, keep in mind your role in place-making. If you want your students to consent to what happens in your classroom, then create opportunities for them to find or feel social affiliation, positive identity, belonging, security, meaning, autonomy, creative expression or self-development, and positive feelings through the social structures and relationships you create and foster in your classroom.

TABLE 10.2 Aspirations for Place-Making

Social affiliation: good access to like-minded peers, playmates, and friendly adults
Positive identity: feeling seen and appreciated for their gifts, talents, and abilities; personal characteristics are valued
Belonging, security, and meaning: caring for and feel cared for by others; contributing to the welfare of the class
Autonomy: making their own choices
Creative expression or self-development: space for students' interests, out-of-school knowledge or experience or relationships in assignments; being conceptually playful; opportunities to try new roles
Positive feelings: leadership opportunities; engaging in favorite activities

---

Source: From J. Ellis (2009)

References

Adeyemo, S. A. (2012). The relationship between effective classroom management and students' academic achievement. *European Journal of Educational Studies, 4*(3), 367–381.

Alenazi, S. S. (2015). A proposed perspective for effective classroom management based on Glasser model. *Proceeding: 1st International Conference on Teaching & Learning 2015, 14*, 9–12.

Chawla, L. (1992). Childhood place attachments. In I. Altman & S. M. Low (Eds.), *Place attachment (Human behavior and environment: Advances in research and theory* (Vol. 12, pp. 63–86). Plenum Press.

Crang, M. (1998). Place or space? In M. Crang (Ed.), *Cultural geography* (pp. 100–119). Routledge.

Djigic, G., & Stojiljkovic, S. (2011). Classroom management styles, classroom climate and school achievement. *Procedia-Social and Behavioral Sciences, 29*, 819–828.

Ellis, J. (2005). Place and identity for children in classrooms and schools. *Journal of the Canadian Association for Curriculum Studies, 3*(2), 55–73.

Ellis, J. (2009). "Planning for teaching" as "Planning for place-making." [Conference session]. West CAST 2009, University of Victoria.

Ellis, J. (2010a). The importance of attending to children and place. In G. S. Goodman (Ed.), *Educational psychology reader: The art and science of how people learn* (pp. 386–402). Peter Lang.

Ellis, J. (2010b). Researching children's place and space. In G. S. Goodman (Ed.), *Educational Psychology reader: The art and science of how people* (pp. 355–369). Peter Lang.

Eyles, J. (1989). The geography of everyday life. In D. Gregory & R. Walford (Eds.), *Horizons in human geography* (pp. 102–117). Palgrave Macmillan.

Eyles, J. (2013). *Senses of place* [eBook edition]. Society for Philosophy & Culture.

Filipek, J. (2020). *Shifting transliteracies in elementary school: Understanding how transliteracy practices contribute to grade three students' construction of meaning* (Unpublished Doctoral dissertation), University of Alberta.

Hale, J. V., & Robey, P. A. (2019). It all begins with relationships: The Glasser quality school model. In *Creating caring and supportive educational environments for meaningful learning* (pp. 20–35). IGI Global.

Relph, E. C. (1976). Preface & Prospects for places. In E. C. Relph (Ed.), *Place and placelessness* (pp. i–iii, 141–147). Pion.

Sebastien, L. (2020). The power of place in understanding place attachments and meanings. *Geoforum, 108*, 204–216.

Tuan, Y. (1992). Place and culture: Analeptic for individuality and the world's indifference. In W. Franklin & M. Steiner (Eds.), *Mapping American culture* (pp. 27–50). University of Iowa Press.

11
AUTHORIZING STUDENTS THROUGH INQUIRY AND ASSESSMENT

Reanna Jordan and Ken Badley

Teachers everywhere have found creative ways to authorize their students, by which we mean they find ways to give their students more agency as persons, more control over their emotions and their learning, and more choice in how they show that they have met learning outcomes. In this chapter, two teachers describe how they have authorized students.

Authorizing Students Through Inquiry Learning
Reanna Jordan

My teaching experience thus far has taught me two very important things; first, your classroom authority is only as strong and effective as the relationships you develop in your classroom and, second, teaching children to become advocates for their own well-being is the most important thing you can teach. By implementing these understandings together rather than viewing them as mutually exclusive ideals, and by using inquiry principles to teach decision-making, I have witnessed students flourish in the amount of respect they exhibit toward their teacher and one another in the school setting.

Children need to learn how to become decision-makers, and who will teach them? One of the best ways to help children become decision-makers is to have them explore the situations they face in everyday life. In a classroom context, teachers can encourage students to engage in deeper thinking by challenging them to ask tough, probing questions.

Encouraging students to engage in deeper thinking is an essential aspect of inquiry, as is the focus on everyday life. Inquiry-based learning does not have to focus solely on curricular outcomes but can also focus on everyday aspects of human life, including effective decision-making, promoting kindness, and fostering independence. In my classroom, every single day, I try to teach students how to be thoughtful and caring human beings. Teachers cannot teach children to be thoughtful and caring by using a cookie-cutter solution, such as telling a student they hurt another student's feelings; it must be done by allowing students opportunities to solve problems with guidance. When issues arise on the playground or in the classroom, asking children questions such as "Who was involved?," "Where were you?," and "What happened?" is just the starting point for helping to teach children how to be problem-solvers. Asking the more difficult questions entails giving children time to think. Questions like "Why do you think this happened?," "How did it make you feel?," "What do you wish would have happened instead?," and, the most important question of all, "How do you think you can solve this problem?" will encourage children to take control of the situation. Asking such questions encourages students to engage in higher levels of thinking, which results in higher levels of awareness and understanding of such situations. These questions also help prepare students for problem-solving in the future, given that all children will inevitably need to solve other problems down the road. Giving students the opportunity to make decisions not only helps them to become problem-solvers but also gives them a sense of control.

To illustrate, a student telling another student in the classroom to "shut up" provides an opportunity for learning as well as for building meaningful connections: the teacher, as the presumptive authority figure, might say something like, "Please don't use those words toward others because doing so could hurt their feelings." However, with an inquiry approach to everyday problem-solving and a willingness to share authority in the classroom, the teacher might ask questions along these lines: "How did it make you feel?," "Why do you think they said that?," "What do you wish would have happened instead?," and "How can you solve this problem?" With such questions, the teacher transfers some power to the student and guides that student toward the most effective solution to the problem. In these situations, the teacher, the authority figure in the classroom, releases some of their authority to the student, who then will have the opportunity to take the learning into their own hands. However, teachers who take this approach do not lose their authority; rather, they share it, and in the process, students learn that they have the power to make a difference. They have the power to stand up for themselves. They have the opportunity to teach someone else right from wrong. The teacher can guide students toward realizing their potential, but it is the students who must put what they learn into action.

The teacher who wants to pursue an inquiry approach should not hand solutions to students on a silver platter. Students themselves must put in some effort. They will learn more from working through problems and answering the kinds of tough questions that promote higher-level thinking. If students are to engage fully with such questions, they need time to process them and to think through the implications of their answers. As teachers, we must let students be problem-solvers and build confidence in their ability to make important decisions. Because most children naturally want to do what is right when they know there is someone watching, we need to observe their course of action and when necessary guide them toward appropriate decisions. Students become their own beacons of light when given the tools, the guidance, and the encouragement to make their own choices. This is the kind of authority that all children should be given so that they can succeed in life. When students are given the power to make their own choices and have the supports in place to make good choices, they will have a more powerful sense of belonging in the classroom as team members rather than constantly being told what to do by an authority figure. When teachers share authority throughout the classroom rather than holding it all themselves, they help build meaningful relationships between themselves and their students.

Children love to have control over situations. They are also far more likely to make good choices and be effective decision-makers in the future when they learn to do so in an environment that promotes confidence and success at a young age. Imagine the gains that would be made if children believed they had control over their own learning and over their own success. Sharing the decision-making in the classroom and on the playground will not diminish the teacher's authority. Rather, it will open the door to more opportunities for learning and will help foster a positive relationship between the teacher and students and among the students themselves. Classroom authority is based on strong relationships and connections made with students rather than being built on the expectation that students must listen to their teacher because the teacher is an adult and holds the power.

I have observed as an elementary school teacher that students love to be trusted. They love to take learning into their own hands and to be in control. For this reason, they also love to be given the opportunity to make decisions. As the teacher, you are not there to control the students and make every decision for them. My advice to any new teacher entering the profession is not to walk into the classroom demanding or expecting everyone's attention but, instead, work to captivate the students' attention by helping them realize that, as their teacher, you are there to help them succeed, you are there to help them grow, and you are there to help them realize the possibilities that lie ahead. This is done most effectively by allowing all students to share their voice and to share their potential with the classroom community of which they are a part.

Authorizing Students Through Choice in Assessment
Ken Badley

States, provinces, school districts, and schools expect students to meet specific standards and learning outcomes. The language may vary from place to place—*curriculum standards*, *learning outcomes*, and *learning objectives*—but the message is consistent: students are not simply to attend school; rather, by specific stages in their development, they are to have learned specific things and be able to do employ certain skills. They should be able to spell their name by this point, read by this point, multiply fractions by this point, understand the concept of *valence* by this point, list several important causes of the French Revolution by this point, and so on. The ages by which various nations, states, and provinces specify that students achieve these outcomes may vary and some of the contents may vary, but, roughly speaking, these expectations are consistent. In fact, on matters such as when a child should be able to read, the expectations are nearly uniform.

With such consistency in view, non-educators might be surprised to learn that in most of the world's classrooms, teachers are not told **how** to achieve their goals; they have the liberty to use a wide variety of instructional approaches to help their students meet the relevant standards. Furthermore, they may use a wide variety of assessments to establish whether their students have learned what they were supposed to learn. I will illustrate in this part of the chapter how offering students some choice among a variety of assessments increases their sense of control over their learning. That is, it increases their authority as learners. Many classroom teachers offer their students the kind of flexibility I describe here, and many educational researchers have studied the means and the results of implementing choice in assessment (Birdsell et al., 2009; Brubaker, 2010, 2012; Pretorius et al., 2017). As an illustration of assessment choice, I will work initially with a junior high social studies unit titled Democracy in Ancient Athens, but the principles behind the example apply in all subjects and at all grade levels.

Assessing whether students have met a typical learning outcome illustrates how teachers can authorize students. At some point in their lives, many students must be able to list some important characteristics or features of the democratic government of ancient Athens. Here are some ways students might demonstrate their having learned some of these important characteristics:

- A class presentation.
- A mock civic debate about extending the vote to foreigners.
- Poster presentation showing differences between Athens and the country in which students live.
- A test on the Greece unit's contents.
- Observation of students' classroom conversation.
- Conversations with individual students.

- The creation of a council and its bylaws that incorporate as many aspects of ancient Athenian democracy as possible.
- A mock trial for the council of 500, with each student assigned a role and given a script. The teacher hands out cards that say: Citizen, Metic, or Slave. Students are given questions that they care about and receive instructions regarding who is allowed to participate and who is not.
- Using the same cards (as in the earlier activity), the final assessment asks students to write a postcard to their current selves from their "character" in Ancient Greece. Students need to explain who they are and what a typical day is like for them. They must also describe the type and extent of their participation within the government. This activity assesses the degree to which students understand how social class affected daily life, as well as how citizens participated in government.

Obviously, this list could be extended. If a dozen creative teachers met for one hour—whether or not they had taught this unit—they could add several dozen more assessment strategies to the few I have listed here. (Full disclosure, I have never taught a unit on ancient Greece, and I compiled this list with the help of other teachers.)

Offering students some choice in how they demonstrate that they have learned what they were supposed to learn in a given unit fits with the work of Howard Gardner (1983, 1999) on intelligence and the many educators who have contributed to our understanding of learning styles (Carbo et al., 1986; Dunn, 1992; Kolb, 1984). For an important reason, I list these references from decades ago. At the time of my writing this chapter section, the learning styles and multiple intelligences conversations are approaching their 40th birthdays, but the message that teachers can assess student learning in varied ways has yet to become universally accepted. Whether they are aware of the contours of the learning styles conversation or Gardner's work or not, teachers the world over know from experience that some students make better drawings and maps than others, that some students can memorize dates and facts better than others, that some students understand the structure of the typical paragraph better than others, and that some students can do mental math and others cannot. If we take differences in ability and learning style seriously, we will invite our students to play to their strengths, we will offer them the opportunity to choose among several ways of demonstrating that they understand some of the key features of democracy as the ancient Athenians practiced it. Indeed, doing so is a fitting way to realize the ideal of the differentiated classroom.

Returning to the bulleted list of possible ways to assess student learning in the Greek democracy unit, consider this assessment scenario. What if the grades for that unit were apportioned so that students all completed some common work and all were required to complete some work selected from a list of choices? Table 11.1 illustrates this scenario (for a junior high classroom).

TABLE 11.1

Assignment/assessment	Grading weight/50
Common assessment: create a diagram showing the organization of the Athenian council.	15
Common assessment: complete a 200-word written comparison of Athenian democracy to democracy in contemporary Japan.	15
Choice in the culminating assessment: select one of the assignments from the bulleted list.	20

Obviously, the table does not take into account that some students in the room will likely need accommodations or adaptations because they have individual learning plans. Second, it does not represent how much work a typical junior high student would complete in a unit lasting three to six weeks. Third, I provided the grading allocations simply to illustrate, not to suggest that a culminating assignment should carry 40% of the weight in a unit. But the table does illustrate my point that teachers can offer students choice in how they demonstrate that they have met some of the learning objectives for a unit on Greek democracy.

The example I have worked with here arises from a social studies classroom. Reflecting individual differences and learning styles may appear to be easier in social studies and language arts classrooms, but it is also possible in science and mathematics. I have not taught in those two subject areas, but my quick search of *teaching science multiple intelligences* yielded 2.5 million records. Without checking them all, I conjecture that many would be relevant to my argument in this chapter. The few I did check revealed that there is pedagogical gold there, including some sites completely focused on implementing Gardner's ideas into science teaching. In short, teachers who want to implement more flexibility in assessment can find support.

Teachers know from experience that many students will consistently incline toward those assignments where they can shine. And why not? Most students want to earn good grades, and we should therefore expect them to play to their strengths. We want them to be able to shine. But by requiring work common to the whole class, we also push our students to develop other strengths.

Authorizing Students by Giving Them Choices

Over several decades, I have watched students' responses to my giving them choices in how they could demonstrate that they had learned what I wanted them to learn. From watching them, I have learned several things myself, five of which I wish to mention here.

First, I began to learn with them because some of them would produce work related to topics about which they knew more than I knew. Through some combination of their prior interest and their careful research, they taught me. Half a century ago, Carl Rogers (1969) suggested that educators become what he called *co-learners* with our students. I will note that teachers wanting to become co-learners with their students need to adopt a receptive posture to such learning. To use a metaphor of electrical power production, in some models of classroom authority, the teacher operates as the only source of power—of learning power—in the room. In this power metaphor, the teacher functions like a nuclear power plant or a hydro dam feeding an electrical network. Reframing classroom learning and classroom authority with the teacher as a co-learner implies that learning power can be generated all over the classroom, parallel to an electric utility allowing those who install rooftop solar to contribute their surplus to the grid. By viewing myself as only one source of learning, I have received innumerable gifts from my students.

A second benefit to teachers is that grading tasks become far more interesting. When students have a choice among several assessment modes and formats, the teacher will need to assess a variety of kinds of work. Imagine that the culminating assignment in a unit on ancient Greece was a 400–500 word comparison of Athenian democracy to contemporary democracy in Japan. Imagine reading 30 of those comparisons. Compare that task to assessing work ranging from student-written songs and spoken word performances, mock debates, posters and displays, Legomation and other video genres, written essays, student-authored contributions to the Wikipedia article on ancient Athens, and charts showing the results of classroom or school-wide polls. Aside from the ways students benefit when they have a choice, teachers benefit as well. We benefit because assessment tasks become more interesting. The variety of assignments I regularly read as a K-12 teacher and now read as a professor has helped me keep my brain alive, even though evaluating a set of varied assignments takes longer than grading a set of identical assignments. In the next paragraph, I recommend to all teachers that they give students more choice in assessment because doing so increases student engagement. I recommend it here for a different reason: to help teachers stay vital through each school year and through their whole teaching career.

Third, students' engagement increases when they are able to work in vital modes and on subjects that interest them. I do not need to repeat what others have argued elsewhere in this book, but, in summary, when student engagement increases, what has traditionally been labeled classroom management becomes easier. Viewed in this light, increasing student choice clearly relates to classroom authority and its complexities.

My fourth observation relates to student engagement and connects centrally to the point of this chapter: when students have choices, they sense that they have increased control—authority—over their learning. Of course, this response makes sense because they do have more authority. That is, they feel authorized, like authors. Teachers who have built this kind of flexibility and choice into their assessment of students' work have witnessed this increased sense of control among their students. As with increased engagement, so with increased authority.

Students who see what they are learning more as learning and less as necessary tasks their teachers assign them put more effort into their learning.

My last observation follows on the fourth. My students began to reframe the work they did in school. Rather than viewing me as someone making them learn things, I wanted them to learn, they came to see me as someone who wanted to help them learn what (like it or not) the provincial department of education had specified that they learn. Ideally—in what I call *kentopia*—students even begin to view what they learn as useful for their lives outside school. I cherished the days students told me that was happening. As their teacher, I wanted to become their coach or supporter. They and I begin to share the task of achieving the learning objectives for the respective units in that year's curriculum.

Simply put, sharing classroom authority by giving students some choice in how they demonstrate their having met the learning outcomes specified for a given portion of the curriculum increases their engagement with the course materials. Sharing classroom authority, while it authorizes students, does not diminish the teacher's authority. Teachers whom students view as members of their team, as their supporters, actually end up with a deeper pool of goodwill—of moral authority—than those teachers whom students view as their taskmasters. That is, teachers who authorize students and thereby give authority away actually end up with more authority than those teachers who keep the authority all to themselves.

References

Armstrong, T. (1987). *In their own way: Discovering and encouraging your child's personal learning style.* Jeremy Tarcher.

Birdsell, B., Ream, S., Seyller, A., & Zobott, P. (2009). *Motivating students by increasing student choice.* St. Xavier University, School of Education. https://eric.ed.gov/?id=ED504816

Brubaker, N. D. (2010). Negotiating authority by designing individualized grading contracts. *Studying Teacher Education, 6*(3), 257–267.

Brubaker, N. D. (2012). Negotiating authority through jointly constructing the course curriculum. *Teachers and Teaching, 18*(2), 159–180.

Carbo, M., Dunn, R. S., & Dunn, K. (1986). *Teaching students to read through their individual learning styles.* Prentice-Hall.

Dunn, R. (1992). *Teaching elementary students through their individual learning styles: Practical approaches for grades 3–6.* Pearson.

Gardner, H. (1983). *Frames of mind: The theory of multiple intelligences.* Basic.

Gardner, H. (1999). *Intelligence reframed: Multiple intelligences for the 21st century.* Basic.

Kolb, D. A. (1984). *Experiential learning: Experience as the source of learning and development.* Prentice Hall.

Pretorius, L., van Mourik, G., & Barratt, C. (2017). Student choice and higher-order thinking: Using a novel flexible assessment regime combined with critical thinking activities to encourage the development of higher order thinking. *Journal of Teaching and Learning in Higher Education 29*(2), 389–401.

Rogers, C. (1969). *Freedom to learn.* Merrill.

12
AUTHORIZING STUDENTS THROUGH RELATIONSHIPS

Iriel Jaroslavsky Rindlisbacher

One thing that I have learned throughout my career in education thus far, from both theory and practice, is that children learn at different speeds and in different ways. Although some suggest that learning styles theory does not have much support (Davis & Francis, 2021), my experiences in the classroom have convinced me that most learners do indeed prefer one approach over another. The second thing I have learned is more important than the first: the importance of the relationships students build with their teachers and peers.

It makes sense that relationships are an important aspect of teaching because, after all, we are human. Educators focus more on the whole student now than they did decades ago, reflecting a shift toward viewing the child as a social, psychological being. Educators once used more direct instruction and focused more on curriculum contents. In some traditional settings, education was based more on fear than on positive classroom relationships. The contemporary increase of awareness of the importance of relationships (Sparks, 2013; Veldman et al., 2013) has come about in part because our whole society has come to realize more fully the importance of relationships, including in educational settings. Today there is more awareness about trauma and the need for trauma-informed practice. Educators have more awareness of neuroscience research that shows how our state of mind is interconnected with our disposition to learn (Flueckiger et al., 2014). Now, educators are much more aware of research in neuroscience and trauma.

Relationships also provide opportunities for teachers to authorize students, as I discovered in an experience I had as an elementary educator. In this case, I had a typical class in Alberta, with neurodiverse students whose literacy and numeracy abilities spanned three grade levels. In my class, I also had ELL students (English

DOI: 10.4324/9781003140849-14

Language Learners), students with ADHD, students on the autism spectrum, students with various other learning disorders, and a handful of students who had experienced various kinds of trauma.

At the time, I could not find an instructional strategy that worked for all my students. I spent time in professional development and with experts to try and find a guide for how to teach my students. What I learned, of course, is that addressing the whole person in education means that no one student is going to be just like any other student. The idea that each student is unique is obvious; however, as teachers, we have our toolbox in which we carry general strategies that in a typical situation engage students and produce a specific outcome. The simplistic approach leads us to believe that if the instruction is clear and concise, then the end product should be somewhere close to what the teacher expects.

This class, however, did not respond to any of the tools I had available. They did well with direct teaching as long as the length of instruction was 10 minutes or less. Finding a strategy for student learning that worked for everyone proved difficult, and my most challenging discovery was that adopting a specific style of teaching for one group of students had the potential to trigger negative reactions from a second group of students. I should clarify that I am aware that not every student will be happy at every given moment during the teaching day. Teaching is in the business of people, and people are not happy all day, every day. We spent months trying on new habits and routines. Throughout the process, students didn't have a sense of responsibility for their learning.

After a conversation with a couple of colleagues, I created checklists. Our class was starting new units across most subjects, and the timing to try a new strategy worked well. I planned new units for each subject and determined what students needed to learn and what they needed to show me to prove they had grasped the concepts. I realized that the order in which they showed me they had met the learning objectives did not affect their learning; what was important was that they achieved the learning outcomes. Each student had their own checklist for each subject, and the rules were quite simple:

- Students could not do the same subject twice in a day.
- They could not skip a subject for more than one day.
- A maximum of five students could work on one subject at one time.

We started each day with a class conference or meeting, followed by a whole-group mini-lesson explaining any one aspect they needed me to clarify for them. After our mini-lesson, students would sign up on the board for a specific subject. Then, off they went to work on that subject. I would choose a specific subject at the beginning of the day and make that my focus for the day. For example, I would teach just math for the day while my students were working independently across the different subjects. When I had an educational assistant, she would also choose a subject to support student learning. In this model, students had the opportunity to participate in lessons with only four other peers and a teacher. Having an extra set of hands was a blessing because there were times when ten students were taken care of with small group instruction and the other ten students would be working independently. Each student would meet with me for a one-on-one conference every week; I would cycle through my class list and use these meetings to clear up any outstanding questions and ensure they were progressing.

For the most part, this worked well because it gave students autonomy and more choice. Some might argue that I gave more much choice than nine-year-old students can handle, and they would be partly correct. Some of my students did find this much choice overwhelming, so we had conversations and I made the choice for them. Most students, however, took ownership of their learning. As a result, I was able to focus my energy as a teacher on students' learning and productivity, not on managing behavior. My students became excited about their projects, designed purposefully for high engagement. These projects were all individual, although students could help each other and work with peers.

Using these planned units, I aimed for simplicity. For example, in the Social Studies projects related to provincial parks, I wanted students to recognize the diversity of parks across the province and the historical significance of different parks for the province. How my students presented what they had learned was up to them. I provided them links to websites and various printed resources, but then I let them go in whatever directions they chose. Similarly with math, I focused the small group mini-lessons on area, perimeter, budgeting—any skills that they needed to know and practice. More specifically, I developed units related to these ideas:

Social Studies (Alberta Education, 2006)
4.1.2 Examine, critically, the physical geography of Alberta by exploring and reflecting upon the following questions and issues:

- *How are Alberta's provincial parks and protected areas and the national parks in Alberta important to the sustainability of Alberta's natural environment?*

Students had to create an advertising campaign. They had to research about Alberta Parks, using available technology, such as Google Maps/Earth and Tour Builder (when it was available). They could choose how to show me what they had learned. All students had common and specific information that they had to address (resources, wildlife, historical significance, and so on) about the provincial parks, but the rest was up to them. They could present by producing a poster, a video advertisement with props and a green screen, a digital or print brochure, a website, a presentation, or an interactive tour.

Math (Alberta Education, 2016)
Shape and Space: Use direct and indirect measurement to solve problems
3. Demonstrate an understanding of area of regular and irregular 2-D shapes by:

- *Estimating area, using referents for cm^2 or m^2*
- *Determining and recording area (cm^2 or m^2)*

Students had to demonstrate an understanding of perimeter and area, so I had them create a blueprint of their house. They had to create a couple of drafts, measure, and give me the area and perimeter of each room in their house. Students also had to add furniture and decorate one room of their choosing. As part of the project, students had a budget to work within for furnishing their house. We collected furniture catalogs, and students created lists of items they would need while practicing mental math skills, addition, and subtraction of three- and four-digit numbers with two decimal places. For those students who needed an extra challenge, I would teach them how to calculate the provincial tax.

The result of this experiment was that the relationships I had built with my students throughout the year allowed them to trust me through the mayhem of self-directed study in grade 4. At times, my classroom was a little chaotic. Anyone who walked into my classroom would probably question my sanity, but I was so proud of my students. At any given moment, students were working on five or six different activities, collaborating, and helping each other. They strengthened their problem-solving skills, their adaptability, their communication skills, patience, and self-advocacy.

As a teacher, I found it highly satisfying to see students participate in classroom activities that enriched their learning so dramatically. These activities provided a sense in the classroom of what Mihaly Csikszentmihalyi called *flow* (1990). My personal goal as an educator has always been to foster internal motivation, one of the pre-conditions of flow Csikszentmihalyi consistently listed in his work (1982, 1990, 2002). With children, when we develop relationships and then present them with choices, we authorize them to be learners, to be autonomous, to be responsible, and to show what they have learned. My classroom was no longer one project they all worked on at the same time because that was not what these students needed at the time. I provided them options, and in doing so, I authorized them to choose.

Allowing students to take learning into their own hands was one of the richest experiences I have had as a teacher. Through this experience, I discovered that students engaged best with their learning after I learned their story, used the trauma-informed framework, and understood what they needed. Once I understood these approaches, I was able to provide students with choices, guide them through problem-solving approaches, and understand themselves better as learners.

Teaching in the way I have described here is not something I would recommend throughout the whole year because it gives too much responsibility to some students; it provides too much choice, possibly producing the opposite effect from what the teacher desires (depending in part on the students and their circumstances at the time). Still, I encourage educators to design opportunities for students to feel that they have control over their learning. To illustrate, I had a student who would say, "Sometimes I just really feel like I can't do math, I don't know why, but I just can't." We would check in and talk regularly, and she ended up doing well in mathematics. She finished her project and was able to demonstrate her understanding. I later discovered that the issue had not been about understanding the math at all but rather the pressure to succeed she felt from home. Authorizing her not to do math some days gave her the breathing room she needed to have a sense of control over her choices.

I have always thought and said to my students that we should think of our interactions as meetings and to imagine they were at work just like I was. I would ask my students to observe my behavior throughout the day. I would pick a day where I was feeling particularly fidgety, and I would start the day by saying "I would like you to observe my behavior today." I wouldn't give them any other prompt, and then I would check in with them at the end of the day. Throughout my day, I sat down, I stood up, I walked around, I worked at my table, standing, on the opposite side from usual, I had my coffee with me most of the day, and I had snacks at random times. I made mistakes on the board; I told students I didn't know an answer and we Googled it together. I also asked Siri to help me spell words with which I was not too familiar. At the end of the day, I would ask them what they noticed, and I frequently got comments about how many times I used the washroom or left the classroom because I forgot something. They noted my coffee consumption; they commented that I told students, "Don't ask me yet, I haven't finished my coffee!" I would then ask them the following—if I am an adult, and I am doing all this, then how can I expect my 9-year-olds to sit quietly and follow instructions for 6 hours straight? If I can't sit at my desk for 6 hours straight, then why would I expect that from children?

I would also say to them, I have never in my life had someone ask me in a job interview, "What did you learn in grade 4 social studies?" or "What was the grade you received in your second math quiz in grade 5?" Students would look at me like I had two heads and realize it would be ridiculous for them to ask. This was an exercise to relieve the pressure students put on themselves. Students need to succeed in assessments during elementary and not learn to regurgitate facts. Success in my classroom implies that students learned study skills, they learned resilience, and they learned to understand different points of view and to think critically. As teachers, we must understand that one piece of assessment or one way of learning does not encompass the whole student. Once we realize this, we can create room for children to realize that it is okay for them to need help or to need more opportunities to show their understanding. By creating this kind of room, we teach our students to persevere.

Authorizing students to learn and authorizing students to be people seems simple, but our actions as educators must be intentional. Our students are human beings who are going on a journey—highly individual journeys—and we do not really know what is going on in their lives before they come to our classrooms. Providing students with choice, providing them options and opportunities for ownership in a world that does not give them much is especially valuable. Children do not often get to choose; instead, adults usually choose for them. Why not provide students with the authority to become problem-solvers, to recognize what will be better for them? Ultimately, children need to be seen for who they are. Through relationships and trauma-informed practice, we can find out so much about what our students need, and we can then create space for them to develop as people and as learners. Once students are safe and feel safe, they will be able to make educated choices. Once they choose, their self-worth, their self-esteem, and advocacy skills improve, allowing them to flourish.

References

Alberta Education. (2006). *Social studies: Kindergarten to grade 12*. Alberta Education. https://education.alberta.ca/media/159595/program-of-studies-gr-4.pdf

Alberta Education. (2016). *Mathematics: Kindergarten to grade 9*. Alberta Education. https://education.alberta.ca/media/3115252/2016_k_to_9_math_pos.pdf

Csikszentmihalyi, M. (1982). Intrinsic motivation and effective teaching: A flow analysis. In J. Bess (Ed.), *Motivating professors to teach effectively* (pp. 15–26). Jossey-Bass.

Csikszentmihalyi, M. (1990). *Flow*. HarperCollins.

Csikszentmihalyi, M. (2002). *Motivating people to learn*. Edutopia. www.edutopia.org/mihaly-csikszentmihalyi-motivating-people-learn

Davis, B., & Francis, K. (2021). Learning styles theories. In *Discourses on learning in education*. https://learningdiscourses.com.

Flueckiger, L., Lieb, R., Meyer, A. H., & Mata, J. (2014). How health behaviours relate to academic performance via affect: An intensive longitudinal study. *PLoS One, 9*(10), e111080. doi:10.1371/journal.pone.0111080

Sparks, D. (Ed.). (2013). *Leading for results: Transforming teaching, learning and relationships in schools*. Corwin.

Veldman, L., van Tartwijk, J., Brekelmans, N., & Wubbels, T. (2013, May). Job satisfaction and teacher-student relationships across the teaching career: Four case studies. *Teaching and Teacher Education, 32*, 55–65.

13
ON AUTHORITY AND DIGNITY

Paige Ray

I think we've all seen it; the way students, when leaving the classrooms of certain teachers, have a glow about them. Most of us have been in the shoes of the students in this scenario. It is a glow we recognize for inspiring us to love learning more deeply and for inspiring us to become educators. Moreover, for two reasons, it is a glow worth examining in a chapter about teacher authority: the glow effect is complex, and the teacher authority that supports it is not what we think of first when we see students love learning in this way.

Educators and students alike might attribute the master teacher's magical impact to long years and the sage wisdom of a Gandalf figure. And while I agree that this sort of teacherly presence usually comes after some years of maturing, the crux of it is not so mysterious or magical. In these classrooms, under the wisdom of master teachers, there is a little struggle to establish and maintain authority. This teacher moves beyond the behaviorist perception of students as mere reactors to environmental stimuli. Recognizing that students often desire less than they deserve, the teacher marches right past what students think they want and shows them the greater possibility of fulfillment in community membership and revelatory learning. This teacher views students as agents in their own development and invites each student to step fully into their own dignity. There is no quibbling over distracting behavior or the "management" of the classroom because each student feels seen and senses the fact that the work of this learning community affirms their inherent worth.

Authority and Dignity

In 1964, James Raths offered a short treatise entitled "The Dignity of Man in the Classroom." In this two-page artifact, Raths called upon the vast population of educators as a unified people who surely believe in the dignity of all persons, but he confronted readers, including us, with the reality that still "many children suffer indignities at the hands of teachers" (1964). He first referenced Dickens' *Hard Times* and the terrible Mr. Gradgrind who regularly (and maybe happily) degraded students. The image of the demoralized and demoralizing old school master of the 1800s does not surprise us. Such scenes depict a time well-before nation and state-wide standards by which new teachers are now trained and evaluated before teacher education programs began cultivating empathy in Pre-Service Teachers and a vision of a classroom that hosts a community of learners. But the sad truth, as Raths reminds us, is that despite our best training, students still face moments in classrooms that do not affirm their dignity but negate it.

My son is a senior in high school this year. During his years growing up, I asked him every afternoon how the school had gone and what they had done during their day of learning. And every day, he responded predictably, "It was fine, mom; we did stuff." Over the past 12 years, my son has not shared many pivotal or watershed moments from his classroom life. But he did recently share a memory from elementary school. In pairs, the students had worked on composing a "Veteran's Day Letter" with an illustration. My son recounted his careful work on the letter, and he explained that somehow he and his partner had colored the entire American flag red. The teacher, a substitute that day, looked at their illustration, appalled. She took my son's hand, raised it in front of the class, and announced him "a disgrace to America." I do not mean to make this scene more dramatic by the fact that it happened to my son. What is of great importance though, is that he represents every student—as all have been exposed to moments that either encourage learning, trust, and openness or that stunt learning and defeat the learner.

That day, my son shed a few tears and he has since recovered. In fact, much of his recovery is due to his homeroom teacher that same year who convinced him not only that he was not a disgrace, but that he was a valuable member of his classroom, a lesson that eventually informed his view of himself in the larger community.

This narrative moment isolates my son as an individual learner, an important paradigm, for the authority granted to teachers by the school is enough to halt the momentum of the individual student. I want to look, though, at how the dignifying work of classroom authority deals not only with the "individual as learner" but with the "individual as member." In this chapter, I argue that the most effective expression of teacher authority develops as a natural byproduct in classrooms where teachers confer upon students their dignity in the classroom and the academy. This often means seeing student behaviors, emotional reactions, and the motivations they present as symptomatic of the deeper, unrealized needs of a learner unsure of their place in the classroom or broader educational context. Students do school because they must. But what does it mean for students to embrace and inhabit the space of their membership in the classroom? In many contexts, this is the work of restorative justice.

Restorative Justice, Democracy, and Demographics

Synthesizing current iterations of restorative justice in education, Reimer (2019) defined it as "a philosophical and pedagogic approach that addresses the individual needs of students in the social context of their relationships with each other, as well as with teachers, administrators and others" (p. 51). And, as a broader response to Freire's (2009) call for Critical Pedagogy, restorative justice "directs participants into the complex social, cultural, ethical and historical realities that form and inform classroom environments and the students within them" (Reimer, 2019, p. 51). Put more plainly, teachers who operate their classrooms in modes of restorative justice look beyond punitive responses to problematic student behavior and focus on reconciliation and relationships. And they do this because restorative justice in the classroom mirrors (and models for students) the ways in which social justice can be identified, problematized, and restored in larger contexts outside the school walls.

Thus, while a restorative justice model in the classroom is meant to help with individual student offenses and student-to-student or student-to-teacher conflict, the momentum of critical theory and pedagogy has broadened educators' use of the model. Widening the lenses by which we view student behavior helps us see both the individual learner and their broader context at once. Reimer (2019) suggested that this "commitment to more just and equitable societies involves providing students with the opportunity to engage with the ideas and practice of voice, participatory citizenship and transformative agency" (p. 52). Though we do not usually think of the voice and agency of the individual student when we consider teacher authority, these democratic ideals contribute to cultures of justice and the affirmation of authority in the classroom by creating communities of buy-in and participation.

Arguably, the democratic approach to classroom management complements the proposal that effective teacher authority stems from the work of dignifying students. Drawing from critical theory, the democratic perspective emphasizes "how schooling practices replicate larger social inequalities, particularly in terms of race and class" (Graham, 2018, p. 496). In his exploration of this approach, Graham (2018) observed that according to critical theory, our "everyday practices reproduce social hierarchies along the lines of race, class, gender, etc."; these practices include the daily goings on of classroom activities. In fact, if we view the classroom as a microcosm of society, where the work of honoring members' dignity allows freedom and agency, then the classroom becomes a key space for unearthing and rewriting "hidden" curriculums that teach students about their place inside and outside of school (Graham, 2018, p. 496).

While the larger institution of education exists to counter social injustice and inequities, if schools and individual teachers do not intentionally counter the injustices of social stratification and cultural marginalization, we risk unintentionally perpetuating them. Graham points out instances in which "schools serving working-class students emphasize obedience and rule-following, while schools serving upper-class students encourage freedom, independent thought, and self-management" (Graham, 2018, p. 496). Graham's work centered on his teaching context in an urban, predominantly African-American school. He wrestled with the tensions between the democratic ideals of teacher education programs and the highly punitive systems implemented in school settings like his. For teachers in diverse, urban contexts, questions about authority must encounter the implications of race and class.

Graham's argument and experience are reflected in teacher films. Films set in élite schools, such as *Dead Poets Society* (Weir, 1989), *Mona Lisa Smile* (Newell, 2003), and *School of Rock* (Linklater, 2003), tend to portray teachers who work to liberate their students from the strictures of society. Films portraying working-class or minority settings, such as *Stand and Deliver* (Menéndez, 1988), *Freedom Writers* (LaGravenese, 2007), and *Music of the Heart* (Craven, 1999), tend to show teachers telling their students that if they want to succeed, they are going to have to learn to work within the parameters of the curriculum and within the structures of society.

Somewhat unexpectedly, Graham's application of critical theory also applies to my own teaching context in the rural Midwest. I work with students from primarily rural and often underprivileged backgrounds. The students who arrive on our campus and enter my classroom come from farms big and small, quiet hill towns, spreading forested regions, and deep river valleys. They are in touch with the land but separated topographically and demographically from literacies more prevalent in urban settings and cultural hubs. Many are first-generation college students eager to earn degree status and social mobility.

The research on rural communities points to a population that is culturally marginalized on issues that include limited language use and literacy (see Donehower and Webb-Sunderhaus's 2015 volume on *Rereading Appalachia*, and Donehower et al. in *Reclaiming the Rural* (2011). In a case study of rural, Appalachian students, Snyder (2015) found strong patterns of what he termed *pioneer rhetoric*—a rhetorical self-positioning of students who feel that if and when they make the move to college, "they are entering unchartered academic territory" (p. 87). While they perceive faculty and other students as native to the social, linguistic, and cultural prism of the academy, they see themselves as alien, lacking the necessary capital and know-how to establish a sense of coherent identity as natural participants. Donehower (2015) deepened these insights, explaining that the tensions that rural, college-bound students experience center around assumptions of literacy and illiteracy (as traditionally defined by the academy) and how such a stark and limited conception of literacy determines image, identity, and possibility.

In the field of sociolinguistics, we expect certain populations of English language learners to feel ostracized by academic English. But the experience of this linguistic tension applies also to native English speakers of diverse regions and dialects. With the great American push to go to college, we find that students of varied contexts move to campuses where, because they are native English speakers (NES), instructors expect instant proficiency in academic writing and literacy. The glaring gap between expectation and performance is problematic. The academy does not know how to respond to the NES student whose language exposure and experiences (including differences as obvious as regional dialect and as elusive as value systems) deviate from those of privileged academic English.

While the rural students I work with experience intimidation in other college courses, their sense of inadequacy is intensified in the writing classroom. For this population, confronting academic English means also confronting their long-established doubts about wielding such language. During the past several years, I have witnessed students who, doubting that they belong in the college writing class or that they can succeed there, rely on habits of behavior that seem like challenges to authority, both my teacher authority and the authority of the institution that has designed liberal arts curricula and programming for their good.

I remember a student from a few years ago. I will call him Jake. From the beginning of our semester, he made a point to sit in the front row, just a few spots to my left. As I engaged a class full of students and delivered instruction, he made ongoing, subtle comments. Under his breath, he uttered playful jokes and quips, and when I glanced in his direction, he was consistently looking for eye contact. His remarks were not snide or negative. In fact, he was attempting to engage me with his charm. Despite the presence of 20 or so other students, he felt confident in his ability to make a personal connection with me.

What became clear to me was the work Jake was doing to avoid his insecurities about college writing and college work by using a well-crafted, disarming small-town charm. During his years in K-12, he had learned that a playful rapport could often earn him passing grades. Many teachers have had students like this and might initially see Jake as lazy or averse to the work of learning in an area of weakness. But a few weeks in, I had the opportunity for more pointed conversations with Jake, during which he dropped his charming veneer to reveal the fear that he was underprepared for college thinking and writing. As a first-generation college student, he was overwhelmed with the responsibility of forging new literacies in new spaces, not only the literacy of academic English but also a challenging educational experience with which his family (and many in his hometown) could not identify. Though his behaviors initially irritated and distracted me, I realized that Jake was using charisma and play not to challenge my authority but as a survival tactic in a realm where he felt foreign and disoriented. Dealing with Jake's behavior meant calling him to move beyond his old patterns of survival. Jake wanted to sidestep the seemingly impossible tasks of college writing. But if I had let him do the sidestepping, I would have allowed him to continue in patterns that short-change his worth. As Delpit (1995) argued, teachers in schools with diverse student populations need to both value students' cultural language styles and prepare their students to participate in the dominant culture. Gatekeeping points exist, Delpit insisted, and to ignore them is to perpetuate the status quo of power.

Self-doubt and frustration inevitably surface in other, less cheerful ways. Sam, a student from my early years, wore bitterness visibly on his shoulders. When he scored poorly on his first writing assignments, he was appalled and pointed to problems in the curriculum and in my teaching; he sought to condemn the class experience entirely. Sam felt that either his K-12 education had failed in training him for college writing or that the college expectations were too high. While his frustrations about the gap between high school and college writing were legitimate, they were system-wide issues that neither he nor I could answer or remediate during his one-semester journey. The injustice consumed him so much so that he rejected my attempts to help him move forward. But the truth I asked Sam to step into was the belief that despite problems in the systems of education (which plague us all), the learning he could do in our writing course offered a worthy fulfillment of his dignity as a student and as a thinking being. I could not restore justice to an imperfect bureaucracy, but we could together work toward the justice of his own flourishing. Such work required that he share in the authority of our coursework.

Sarah's challenges were different still. And even now, I remember the look of angst and self-condemnation on her face as she entered the classroom on the first day. While students found their seats, Sarah whimpered dramatically about her certain failure in the class. She stated frankly, "I can't do this kind of English." Sarah had left her home community and come to college to study agricultural science, an area in which she had much hands-on experience. But the discourses of her home and community made composing college-level essays feel like an impossible task. Establishing my authority in Sarah's eyes meant gaining her trust—trust in my confidence that with some work and grit she could acquire the necessary discourse for success in our class, and trust that, as a member of our learning community, her dignity and belonging were already affirmed, whether or not she felt like a successful writer.

In each of the previous situations, students were paralyzed in their frustrations and insecurities. And they were not free to move forward until they each agreed to share in the work of moving forward, of learning and growing, and ultimately of contributing to the realization of their dignity as people who belong to and show up for the community of the classroom.

Framing the Collaborative Work of Authority

This semester, I began my course with an introductory, community-forming activity, requesting that students share an example of a special literacy they have acquired. One student shared his fly-fishing literacy and another her literacies in working with resin. Several claimed literacies in dairy and beef farming, while others spoke of their hunting skills—including the literacy involved in such practical and text-based aspects as laws and permits, as well as the sensory-based literacies of reading the environment and animal behaviors.

These few moments of hearing and validating each other's literacies granted students instant credibility and did something, however small, toward integrating their various identities into our classroom space. We practiced a critical stance toward conceptions of literacy, who we are, and why we each delight in gaining literacies. The exercise was immediately freeing for them (an important feat at the start of a writing course), and it was freeing, too, for me. It may, in fact, free many composition course instructors to perceive students of such disparate but rich home and community discourses as highly literate.

By framing our semester work with this activity, I used my authority as one who understands the worth of diverse literacies as a means of dignifying students, calling their attention to their often-impressive literacy repertoires, and affirming their agency in expanding those repertoires. However, helping students carry this buy-in through the semester always takes ongoing work on my part.

A teacher's desire to establish this collaborative authority and extend it through the course involves continued attention to three key elements: trust, boundaries, and the practice of realization. Each of these three key elements has several aspects, as shown in the following.

Confronting students with the weight of their dignity:

- Trust
    - The teacher's trust in I
    - Students' trust in the teacher
    - Students' trust in themselves

- Boundaries
    - Boundaries around what we must give attention to as the work and purpose of the classroom—and how that meets student dignity
    - Boundaries that dictate what we cannot humor or give attention to as it detracts from student dignity
    - Boundaries that protect the work of the classroom are the same boundaries that protect student dignity.

- Realization
    - Engaging students in the work that affirms their dignity.

The trust required for effective authority requires first that the teacher trusts themselves to identify students' emotional and developmental needs and has the means to address those needs both in curricular design and in the way they structure classroom interactions. Keeping Jake after class to talk with him and move past his humorous deflections allowed us both to discover his insecurities. Making that progress with Jake required that I trust my intuition and see that his use of that humor concealed a deeper problem. Additionally, I had to earn Jake's trust. This was accomplished by addressing his behavior with curiosity instead of judgment. Finally, I was able to use Jake's confidence in me as a teacher who has guided many students through the joys and difficulties of learning, in order to help him trust himself. In some instances, this takes work to convince students of their inherent internal dignity, a quality that not all students have recognized before.

Most conversations about teacher authority involve systems of classroom discipline. But as the implementation of discipline varies at different levels of education, I find it helpful to use the term *boundaries*. And again, whether in elementary, secondary, or college contexts, the boundaries that will support a teacher's authority, as well as the shared authority with students, must move beyond mere behavior. As outlined earlier, the teacher must establish boundaries to protect the work of the classroom and the realization of learning outcomes. The second boundary supports that focus. In my interactions with Sam, I sympathized with his frustrations about the flaws in the education system, but I could not sit with him very long in that frustration, for it was unproductive and it would have inhibited him from moving into the dignifying work of learning.

In the wake of established trust and boundaries, authority is solidified as we work with students to realize further human flourishing in the classroom. Earlier, I referred to the classroom as a microcosm of a larger society. In the same way, though a student's time in a class lasts only a year or a semester, the authority of each healthy classroom does restorative work, calling students into the sort of flourishing available to them as thinking beings. I hope to run my college writing class not as a place to ostracize students who come with diverse linguistic exposure and experience and varying levels of literacy but as a place that affirms such diversity and empowers students toward new literacies.

References

Craven, W. (Director). (1999). *Music of the heart* [Film]. Craven/Maddalena Productions, Miramax Films.

Delpit, L. (1995). *Other people's children: Cultural conflict in the classroom.* The New Press.

Donehower, K. (2015). "How to reread Appalachian literacy research. In K. Donehower & S. Webb-Sunderhaus (Eds.), *Rereading Appalachia: Literacy, place, and cultural resistance* (pp. 13–31). The University Press of Kentucky. EBSCOhost, search.ebscohost.com/login.aspx?direct=true&db=nlebk&AN=985540&site=ehost-live.

Donehower, K., Hogg, C., & Schell, E. E. (2011). *Reclaiming the rural: Essays on literacy, rhetoric, and pedagogy.* Southern Illinois University Press.

Donehower, K., & Webb-Sunderhaus, S. (Eds.). (2015). *Rereading appalachia: Literacy, place, and cultural resistance.* The University Press of Kentucky.

Freire, P. (2009). *Pedagogy of the oppressed* (30th Anniversary ed.). Continuum.
Graham, E. (2018). Authority or democracy? Integrating two perspectives on equitable classroom management in urban schools. *The Urban Review, 50*. doi:10.1007/s11256-017-0443-8
LaGravenese, R. (Director). (2007). *Freedom writers*. MTV Films, Jersey Films, 2S Films.
Linklater, R. (Director). (2003). *School of rock*. Paramount Pictures.
Menéndez, R. (Director). (1988). *Stand and deliver*. Tom Musca.
Newell, M. (Director). (2003). *Mona Lisa smile*. Columbia Pictures, Revolution Studies, Red Om Films Productions.
Raths, J. (1964). The dignity of man in the classroom. *Childhood Education, 40*(7), 339–340. doi:10.1080/00094056.1964.10728844
Reimer, K. E. (2019). Relationships of control and relationships of engagement: How educator intentions intersect with student experiences of restorative justice. *Journal of Peace Education, 16*(1), 49–77. doi:10.1080/17400201.2018.1472070
Snyder, T. (2015). The transition to college for first-generation students from extractive industry Appalachia. In K. Donehower & S. Webb-Sunderhaus (Eds.), *Rereading Appalachia: Literacy, place, and cultural resistance* (pp. 77–98). The University Press of Kentucky. EBSCOhost, search.ebscohost.com/login.aspx?direct=true&db=nlebk&AN=985540&site=ehost-live
Weir, P. (Director). (1989). *Dead poets society*. Touchstone Pictures, Silver Screen Partners IV.

14
SITUATING CLASSROOM MANAGEMENT IN ENGLISH LANGUAGE ARTS, MATH, AND SOCIAL STUDIES

Jacqueline Filipek, Margaretta Patrick, and Wendy Stienstra

When beginning teachers study theory and engage in practice, they begin the journey of examining their beliefs. We believe an effective way to have an impact on K-12 classrooms is to engage teachers in an examination of their teacher beliefs such as their teaching philosophy, pedagogy, who students are, what makes a "good" student, and what they consider "controversial." As beginning teachers engage in learning experiences and reflection, they encounter the ecological nature of classrooms, which emphasizes the various interactions among classroom elements that contribute to learning (Lekwa et al., 2019). Using theory and examples from our own Pre-Service Teacher (PST) classrooms, we relate teacher authority and student consent with student-based learning, planning, and student achievement.

Student-Based Learning: Developing the Trust and Self-Authorization to Let Go

Over the past decades, educational theory has shifted from a behaviorist theory of learning to a (social) constructivist perspective with a goal of adaptive competence (de Corte, 2010). As teacher educators, we recognize the importance of actively engaging students as they construct their understanding of teaching. We support student-centered pedagogies, which focus on meaning making, inquiry, and authentic activities, as integral parts of effective classrooms (Dumont et al., 2010). Despite learning a variety of student-centered teaching and learning strategies in their PST education, many beginning teachers often struggle with classroom management when trying to implement them (Barron & Darling-Hammond, 2010; Makar & Fielding-Wells, 2018). Beginning teachers tend to focus on rules and discipline, while more experienced teachers recognize their role in hampering or increasing student learning (Wolff et al., 2017). Thus, beginning teachers need help in learning to see how their actions can "create an environment that supports and facilitates . . . learning" (Evertson & Weinstein, 2006, p. 4).

There are a variety of student-based instructional approaches, such as cooperative learning, classroom discussion, inquiry-based learning, project-based learning, problem-based learning, problem-solving, role playing, and experiential learning. Classroom management with these approaches can be significantly more challenging than it would be for direct instruction (Barron & Darling-Hammond, 2010; Makar & Fielding-Wells, 2018). If teachers do not fully understand the complexity of these pedagogies, they may not provide the scaffolding necessary for students to engage fully in the activity. Similarly, if students do not have the necessary background knowledge or skills required for the activity, they may not be able to work productively together or maintain motivation (Barron & Darling-Hammond, 2010). Student-centered approaches often take more time than direct instruction. Teachers have to balance the need for students to struggle productively with the inquiry process and the need for teacher feedback and modeling (Barron & Darling-Hammond, 2010). Finally, for these approaches to be successful, teachers must learn how to push their students beyond merely going through the motions of the activity to a deeper and critical engagement with the learning process (Inoue et al., 2019).

These challenges are not insurmountable for beginning teachers. By attending to the following four elements to create classroom environments that facilitate learning, they can begin to address management issues associated with student-based approaches. First, student-based approaches require teachers to have a deeper understanding of the content and connections than they would if they were using direct instruction. Coupled with this is the paradoxical notion that the teacher cannot know everything and must be okay with students gaining new insights or connections. This can be disconcerting for beginning teachers because they need to let go of the idea that they are the conduit of all knowledge. Second, clear learning goals, supported by a well-thought-out process, help to focus the activity (Barron & Darling-Hammond, 2010; Mergendoller et al., 2006). Being student-based does not mean unstructured. By designing clear structures for the task, materials, and collaboration, teachers help students attend to what is important. Teachers will also be more prepared to respond in-the-moment to students if they have anticipated the possible outcomes of students' work in their planning.

Third, teachers need to establish classroom norms for participation, collaboration, and accountability (Barron & Darling-Hammond, 2010; Makar & Fielding-Wells, 2018). For example, teachers may expect that in discussions, students go beyond a "show and tell" of their answer and examine the diverse ideas (Inoue et al., 2019). This can be daunting for beginning teachers. Here they will need to let go of being the sole judge of right and wrong to support the development of student reasoning. Finally, ongoing support of students, individually and in various groupings, through scaffolding, assessment, and possible redirection becomes critical (Barron & Darling-Hammond, 2010). This means that while circulating through the room and checking in with the various groups, the teacher intentionally assesses students' progress and understanding. Based on this ongoing assessment, teachers can make decisions regarding the need for redirection, structuring presentations, or consolidation of ideas.

Elementary Mathematics

Elementary PSTs begin their mathematics methods course with a problem-solving experience, which is accessible to upper elementary students. Working with a partner, they must determine which will give more money, the value of their height in quarters laid end to end or in nickels stacked on top of each other. Students are provided with manipulatives. They must use their prior knowledge to determine a strategy that makes sense to them and then place their finished work on chart paper to be shared with the class. Many are frustrated because they are not given a specific method or procedure. They struggle to remember basic math concepts, such as working with decimals. Through the process of being a mathematics student, the PSTs begin to understand some of the challenges and struggles their future students will encounter. One of their main takeaways is that they can employ many different strategies to solve the same problem.

In the debrief of the lesson, we go beyond their experience of the problem-solving context to unpack the teacher moves in planning and managing student engagement in the learning process. These PSTs readily recognize the importance of establishing a safe learning environment so that students can risk making mistakes. Yet, the deeper aspects of planning and management take time to develop. As PSTs become more confident in their math content knowledge, they are better able to think about how to engage students in making sense of mathematics. Through this problem-solving experience, they begin to shift their understanding of managing the math classroom to include how to engage student reasoning through active participation.

Junior High English Language Arts

PSTs created cross-disciplinary book clubs to bridge social studies content with ELA understandings and reading strategies. In their book club planning project, the PSTs considered which curricular outcomes could be achieved but also learned to balance teacher and student decision-making in book clubs. Book clubs generally use interest groups whereby students can select the book they will read—usually from a controlled set selected by the teacher; however, book or group selection also requires contingency planning if the groups are not naturally balanced. Groups that are too big or too small can have an impact on the quality of discussion when they meet.

Book clubs require a schedule for meeting times (usually weekly or biweekly), with a reasonable amount of time allocated for student-led group discussions. Because book clubs are meant to give space for students to express their own connections to the text and how they are making sense of what they are reading, teachers have to be willing to let students have and run their own book club discussions. It is helpful to practice what a discussion could look and sound like so students are aware of the expectations when they are on their own. Teachers can also teach conversation moves to aid respectful discussion and together the class can set behavioral expectations for meetings.

Secondary Social Studies

Secondary social studies PSTs recognize that social studies is often perceived as being about dates, coloring maps, and studying old dead White guys. To demonstrate alternative approaches, PSTs engage in an inquiry-based lesson that engages their critical thinking skills. They receive the following scenario:

> You work for Global Affairs Canada. The federal government is embarking on a new program to expand its foreign (financial) relationships, and thus influence, in Northern Africa. Your small working group is tasked with providing recommendations about which country Canada should increase its financial relationship with: Tunisia or Egypt.

The class collectively establishes the criteria to make such a recommendation and then in groups find the information to make their recommendations. To get them started, they are given some websites which address human rights, trade relationships, and bilateral aid. Toward the end of class, each group presents their recommendations and provides a rationale regarding how the recommendations meet the criteria established at the beginning of class. The exercise demonstrates how much students can learn when presented with a well-structured critical challenge and if the teacher lets go.

Planning: Considering Differentiation and Grouping

Research supports the idea that implementation of classroom management strategies improves when teachers make a concerted effort to plan for them (Sanetti et al., 2018). Teachers can consider countless elements of planning that have impacts on classroom management; however, they must recognize that planning is never neutral—what happens in classrooms is always situated in larger sociocultural contexts, beliefs, and practices. Thus, teachers plan based on mandated curriculum, academic goals of the school or district, the teacher's own classroom ideals, and the individual needs of the students in the classroom.

Two overlooked or oversimplified aspects of planning include thinking about differentiated learning and diversity and using various grouping strategies. Thoughtfully integrated, both can have significant impacts on classroom management (Blatchford & Russell, 2019).

Differentiation and Diversity

Tomlinson (2000) describes differentiation as "the efforts of teachers to respond to variance among learners in the classroom" (p. 2). She suggests that teachers can differentiate in four areas:

1. Content: what the student needs to learn or how they will get access to the information
2. Process: student activities to help students make sense of or master the content
3. Products: culminating projects that exemplify or extend learning
4. Learning environment: the way the classroom works or feels

Darling-Hammond and Cook-Harvey (2018) write that variation in human development and learning is the norm, not the exception. Planning for diversity through differentiated instruction is a consideration for all students because each has differences in strengths and areas of need. Tomlinson's elements of differentiation (listed earlier) encourage teachers to find many ways to meet needs, by considering that not all students need to (or can) learn the same things, at the same time, and in the same way. Classroom teachers and educational researchers have widely agreed that the components of student success, such as motivation, feeling visible and valued, and experiencing various learning methods, depend on high expectations for learning coupled with how well individual needs—including social and cultural—are acknowledged and met (Lew & Nelson, 2016; Williams, 2019).

Student Grouping Strategies

Intentional grouping is another way to consider differentiation in the classroom. Group work is a relevant means of meeting needs and interests; however, ability should not always guide how teachers make groups. Students need each other's experiences and ideas to further their own and to have space to learn with a variety of people. Within any grade, students can be grouped in the following ways:

1. Ability groups: grouping students with similar strengths and needs. Teachers often use ability groups for directed literacy instruction or reading/writing groups.

2. Mixed ability groups: students purposefully grouped so that there is a range of abilities.
3. Interest groups: grouping students based on shared interests.
4. Self-selected groups: students select their own group.
5. Random groups: groups randomly selected. Teachers can use online random list generators, can select names "from a hat," can assign numbers randomly, or can set a parameter (e.g., birth month).

Teachers can incorporate many types of grouping practices regularly to promote opportunities for student-based learning and differentiation. When grouping by ability, teachers should avoid language or group names that suggest high or low abilities and should use ability grouping only when needed to support specific academic needs. Teachers can save time by pre-preparing groups and posting the group member names in a visible place. If the teacher is using a random or self-selected strategy, they can plan for and share with students how that will happen. In addition to determining the composition of the groups, teachers can also discuss with students where groups can meet, taking on leadership roles within the group, retrieving required materials, and ways to conclude the group work at the end of class.

In summary, effective classroom management is strongly attributed to attentive planning. It makes sense; thoughtful planning leads to opportunities to think through potential challenges that might arise in classrooms and helps teachers consider how their plans for student grouping and differentiation improve classroom management.

Elementary English Language Arts

Because students read books at their instructional level, guided reading in elementary school is considered a highly effective strategy for improving literacy growth. PSTs learned about planning for guided reading at two levels: mini lesson plans for each reading session or book and the overall plan for giving time and space for guided reading. Guided reading typically happens alongside centers or independent reading time so that the teacher is freed to work with a small group.

Mini Lesson Planning

Teachers may carry out many guided reading lessons weekly; therefore, it works well to use a mini lesson plan format that includes some of the following elements: group members, reading plan (pages to read, comprehension stops, and waiting work), overall reading focus, comprehension focus, word work, assessment, and follow-up.

Overall plan

Guided reading typically uses ability grouping to help teachers focus the session on particular reading needs. Prior to running guided reading, teachers will need a process for determining groups, which typically involves teacher observation and informal reading inventories. Once groups are established, teachers require a plan for the other students not meeting for guided reading that day. Using rotating centers allows opportunities for students to work on their own literacy needs independently and offers space for teachers to provide differentiated practice activities for students. If using centers, teachers can plan their expectations for getting into groups, collecting and putting away materials, and selecting centers. Additionally, it is helpful to have signals to indicate the beginning and end of center time and to have clear instructions that students can listen to, view, or read at each center.

Junior High Mathematics

While mathematics is often considered to be a neutral subject, that is not the case. For example, there are sociocultural values embedded in the problems and examples that a textbook or teacher uses (e.g., many use the context of consumerism). As I was planning a problem-solving activity for a math methods course, I became aware that the problem I had used in the past did not take into account diversity. The problem stated:

> In a particular condominium community 2/3 of all of the men are married to 3/5 of all of the women. What fraction of the entire condominium community are married?

This problem assumes that there are no same-sex marriages. As a result, I decided to change the context of the problem to avoid these implicit assumptions and values. Inspired by local news stories, I made the following changes:

> During a recent cold spell, a particular social services agency provided winter outfits consisting of a pair of pants and a coat. On the first day, 2/3 of all of the pants were paired with 3/5 of all of the coats. What fraction of the entire winter clothes collection was distributed?

After presenting the problem to the PSTs, they worked on it with no further instructions from me other than the expectations regarding groupings and the presentation of written solutions. In this instance, I asked them to work in pairs, based on a 1–10 continuum activity regarding their feelings (not abilities) about mathematics we had done at the beginning of the course. They needed to choose a partner who was close to them on the continuum in hopes that they would have a common language to enter into the problem-solving process.

The debrief after the experience extended beyond the various solution strategies PSTs used. We discussed the pros and cons of the grouping strategy I employed. We also discussed my planning process and the decision to change the context of the problem. As a result, PSTs began to engage in the deeper aspects of planning for student engagement and learning.

Secondary Social Studies

Reading a series of BBC articles written by African writers inspired me to create a lesson on media literacy. In one article, Nigerian novelist Adoabi Tricia Nwaubani (2021) examined how the international media coverage of the Nigerian schoolgirls kidnapped by Boko Haram in 2014, inadvertently empowered Boko Haram. In class, I briefly presented some background information about Nigerian history, the rise of Boko Haram, the kidnapping, and some of the critiques regarding the media's role. In random groups, PSTs filled out charts about what they knew or had learned and things they wanted to know more about (a modified KWL chart).

Once we reviewed the charts, PSTs broke into new random groups. Working on a Google Jamboard, the groups further refined their inquiry question based on the interests of group members. Chosen group topics included the history of Christianity and Islam in Nigeria, an in-depth study of the media coverage of the kidnapping and subsequent partial releases, of whether Nigeria is becoming the new Middle East in terms of terrorist activity as one author suggested, the impacts of colonialism on Nigerian geography, and the effect of Boko Haram on education in Nigeria. Each group developed its inquiry differently, variously focused on source analysis, finding explanatory images, relating themes, teaching about bias, digging deep into the research, and/or mapping out a research plan. Not every group or individual needs to do the same thing, nor will they present their findings in the same manner, and that is okay.

Student Achievement: Relating Student Social Conduct and Assessment Practices

A growing body of research confirms the relationship between classroom management and student academic engagement (Lekwa et al., 2019), particularly the impact of student social conduct on academic achievement. For instance, disruptive behavior can negatively impact academic performance (Wenzel, 1993). To state the issue more positively, instruction in social and emotional skills, particularly related to cooperative work and problem-solving, is correlated with enhanced academic outcomes (Gerbino et al., 2018; Korpersoek et al., 2016;

Wenzel, 1993). Teachers understand this, for if students have the social skills to interact well with their peers and to self-regulate their emotions, they tend to exhibit fewer disruptive behaviors, providing the teacher with more time for instruction and use of instructional strategies, which in turn supports student achievement.

When students experience success, they feel greater competency and efficacy and thus pour more energy into their work. The opposite is also true: when students experience failure, they put in less effort. Experiencing too much failure may lead to withdrawal and perhaps dropping out of school (Archambault et al., 2012). Research suggests that when these experiences of failure combine with some combination of low socioeconomic status and low student achievement, even effective teachers can find it difficult to overcome such barriers (Archambault et al, 2012; Borman & Kimball, 2005).

Specific assessment practices are an integral aspect of classroom ecology. When teachers possess what is identified as "assessment literacy" (Lew & Nelson, 2016), they recognize when and how to use diverse assessment strategies to support student learning and how to align the assessment instruments with instructional goals and strategies. This literacy is not intuitive and often requires teacher instruction and professional development (Lew & Nelson, 2016).

When assessment literacy is not present, or students do not understand either the material or the nature and purpose of assessments, unproductive behavior may result, including passivity and apathy. The issue becomes cyclical with behavior linked to poor academic success. Structural issues may also marginalize some students as high stakes standardized tests often promote teaching to the test and can push teachers to move through the content at a faster rate than they would otherwise choose, which can negatively impact some students (Lew & Nelson, 2016). As a result, teachers rely on direct instruction with the consequence that there is less time for teachable moments. Unfortunately, students come to believe that learning is more about the test than meaningfully engaging with concepts and constructing meaning. Teacher self-authorization and student consent are both lost.

Elementary English Language Arts

As part of their English language arts curriculum courses, PSTs learn how kidwatching (Owocki & Goodman, 2002) is a powerful assessment strategy. Language arts curricula often include literacy skills, strategies, understandings, and dispositions which are difficult to assess through paper-based assessments. Kidwatching is a holistic approach that values all information teachers learn about their students, including observations, conversations, and products. Kidwatching requires a deep understanding of children and of the curriculum to be able to make sense of what students are learning. Kidwatchers often use anecdotal notes, field notes, checklists, self-evaluations, and family and other professional input to guide their instruction.

An activity I use to help PSTs see value in kidwatching is a field study with elementary-aged children. PSTs are required to have conversations with a child and their caregivers to develop an understanding of the child's literacy practices and beliefs, to listen to and record the child's reading, and to collect various writing samples. The PSTs then use the reading recording to do a miscue analysis and to collect other information such as fluency and strategies the child uses to read. The students must then use all their kidwatching observations to create a reading profile and individual plan for supporting the child's literacy development. In the field study, students learn to rely on all of the pieces and forms of assessment to fully understand the child as a reader and to create a comprehensive and appropriate plan. They learn that observation and conversation are as valid and necessary as are paper-based products and standardized tests in language arts assessment.

Junior High Mathematics

Assessment in mathematics focuses too often on determining if the final answer is correct. Unfortunately, this may not take into account what concepts the student actually knows. The process students use to solve the problem is equally important and gives insights into student thinking and understanding. One activity I use to help PSTs engage in a more holistic approach to assessment is a collaborative grading task. Using released samples of student work from various large-scale, provincial Grade 9 assessments, PSTs work in small groups to come to a consensus regarding the grade for student responses. The rationale for their decision must be based on a five-level scoring guide that identifies criteria relating to the provincial standards.

Once the groups have completed the task, we debrief both the process and the responses. As groups share their grades and rationale, we note how the differences reflect their priorities. When I provide the official responses and reasoning from the provincial exemplars, we discuss the differences between the PSTs' point of view and the official interpretations. Here PSTs identify how difficult it was for them to go beyond the final answer to look at the types of understanding the student work demonstrated. They also find it difficult to determine the important math concepts for each of the problems.

This task is very challenging for PSTs, yet very rewarding. It is an opportunity for them to engage in authentic teacher work. In the process, they need to re-evaluate their understanding of the nature of mathematics as well as their beliefs about what it means to teach and learn mathematics. When a teacher learns to value the process of learning and affirming student thinking, they support student self-efficacy. Students stay engaged in their learning and acknowledge the benefits of productive struggle. They begin to see that math is more than memorization.

Curriculum All Subjects

In a required course regarding the philosophy and design of curriculum planning, PSTs create a three-week unit that includes a philosophy of evaluation and summative assessment instrument. PSTs learn about evaluation issues in several classes and evaluate various types of test items, particularly multiple-choice questions. We discuss how to construct multiple choice questions, determine question validity, teach students strategies to respond, and more. I emphasize that good tests employ a variety of types of questions and engage higher-order thinking. For their unit's summative assessment, PSTs may choose to develop a test, although they are encouraged to create a performance assessment.

Previous experience leads most PSTs to believe that tests are the only way to assess learning. The program challenges this belief. In this course, the midterm is a performance assessment where the PSTs evaluate and critique a developed unit plan based on what they have learned in the course. PSTs receive the unit plan a week in advance and are encouraged to work with peers—we believe much of learning is social. They must, however, write the midterm at the appointed time independently, as each person needs to demonstrate their ability to synthesize what they have learned and apply it to a specific example. I share with PSTs that as a high school teacher I had occasionally conducted similar types of assessment with my secondary students.

Conclusion

The examples of our teaching practices highlight several elements of an ecological classroom. We described what is important for teachers to notice and attend to, both when creating an effective learning environment and when developing their teacher beliefs. As beginning teachers gain more experience, they will more thoroughly link theory and practice to understand how their beliefs have an impact on their instructional, differentiated, and assessment practices. The scenarios we have shared from our classrooms situate classroom management in the larger set of postures and practices.

References

Archambault, I., Janosz, M., & Choinard, R. (2012). Teacher beliefs as predictors of adolescents' cognitive engagement and achievement in mathematics. *The Journal of Educational Research, 105*(5), 319–328. http://dx.doi.org/10.1080/00220671.2011.629694

Barron, B., & Darling-Hammond, L. (2010). Prospects and challenges for inquiry-based approaches to learning. In D. Hanna et al. (Eds.), *The nature of learning: Using research to inspire practice* (pp. 199–225). OECD. https://doi.org/10.1787/9789264086487-11-en

Blatchford, P., & Russell, A. (2019). Class size, grouping practices and classroom management. *International Journal of Educational Research, 96*, 154–163.

Borman, G. D., & Kimball, S. M. (2005). Teacher quality and educational quality: Do teachers with high standards-based evaluation ratings close student achievement gaps? *The Elementary School Journal, 106*(1), 3–20.

Darling-Hammond, L., & Cook-Harvey, C. M. (2018). *Educating the whole child: Improving school climate to support student success*. Learning Policy Institute.

de Corte, E. (2010). Historical developments in the understanding of learning. In D. Hanna et al. (Eds.), *The nature of learning: Using research to inspire practice* (pp. 34–67). OECD. https://doi.org/10.1787/9789264086487-4-en

Dumont, H., Istance, D., & Benavides, F. (Eds.). (2010). *The nature of learning: Using research to inspire practice*. Educational Research and Innovation. OECD. https://doi.org/10.1787/9789264086487-en

Evertson, C., & Weinstein, C. (2006). Classroom management as a field of inquiry. In C. Evertson & C. Weinstein (Eds.), *Handbook of classroom management: Research, practice and contemporary issues* (pp. 3–16). Lawrence Erlbaum Associates.

Gerbino, M., Zuffiano, A., Eisenberg, N., Castellani, V., Kanacri, B. P. L., Pastorelli, C., & Caprara, G. V. (2018). Adolescents' prosocial behavior predicts good grades beyond intelligence and personality traits. *Journal of Personality*, 86(2), 247–260. https://doi.org/10.1111/jopy.12309

Inoue, N., Asada, T., Maeda, N., & Nakamura, S. (2019). Deconstructing teacher expertise for inquiry-based teaching: Looking into consensus building pedagogy in Japanese classrooms. *Teaching and Teacher Education*, 77, 366–377. https://doi.org/10.1016/j.tate.2018.10.016

Korpersoek, H., Harms, T., de Boer, H., van Kuijk, M., & Doolaard, S. (2016). A meta-analysis of the effects of classroom management strategies and classroom management programs on students' academic, behavioral, emotional, and motivational outcomes. *Review of Educational Research*, 86(3), 643–680. http://dx.doi.org/10.3102/0034654315626799

Lekwa, A. J., Reddy, L. A., & Shernoff, E. S. (2019). Measuring teacher practices and student academic engagement: A convergent validity study. *School Psychology*, 34(1), 109–118. http://dx.doi.org/10.1037/spq0000268

Lew, M. M., & Nelson, R. F. (2016). New teachers' challenges: How culturally responsive teaching, classroom management, and assessment literacy are intertwined. *Multicultural Education*, 23(3–4), 7–13.

Makar, K., & Fielding-Wells, J. (2018). Shifting more than the goal posts: Developing classroom norms of inquiry-based learning in mathematics. *Mathematics Education Research Journal*, 30, 53–63. https://doi.org/10.1007/s13394-017-0215-5

Mergendoller, J. R., Maxwell, N. L., & Bellisimo, Y. (2006). The effectiveness of problem-based instruction: A comparative study of instructional methods and student characteristics. *Interdisciplinary Journal of Problem-Based Learning*, 1(2), 49–69. https://doi.org/10.7771/1541-5015.1026

Nwaubani, A. T. (2021, January 13). Viewpoint: Global media's Nigeria abductions coverage 'wrong.' *BBC News*. www.bbc.com/news/world-africa-55572897

Owocki, G., & Goodman, Y. (2002). *Kidwatching: Documenting children's literacy development*. Heinemann.

Sanetti, L. M., Williamson, K. M., Long, A. C., & Kratochwill, T. R. (2018). Increasing in-service teacher implementation of classroom management practices through consultation, implementation planning, and participant modeling. *Journal of Positive Behavior Interventions*, 20(1), 43–59.

Tomlinson, C. A. (2000). *Differentiation of instruction in the elementary grades*. ERIC Digest.

Wenzel, K. R. (1993). Does being good make the grade? Social behavior and academic competence in middle school. *Journal of Educational Psychology*, 85(2), 357–364.

Williams, S. (2019). *The influence of differentiation on student behavior and achievement* (Master of Education Thesis). Milligan University, Milligan Digital Repository. http://hdl.handle.net/11558/4320

Wolff, C. E., Jarodzka, H., & Boshuizen, H. P. A. (2017). See and tell: Differences between expert and novice teachers' interpretations of problematic classroom management events. *Teaching and Teacher Education, 66*, 295–308. http://dx.doi.org/10.1016/j.tate.2017.04.015

PART 3
Teacher Authority and Diversity

Part 3 investigates teacher roles within contexts of diversity, and two types of diversity are examined. The first addresses multiculturalism. While most teachers in western countries remain White, student populations are increasingly diversified, raising questions about teacher–student mismatches. Can a teacher overcome cultural differences and teach a class of students from diverse cultural and religious backgrounds? When cultural differences overlap with systemic inequities, can a teacher make a difference? The research says yes, but teachers need to reject the cultural deficit model, which suggests that members of some cultural groups struggle in school because their culture is deficient in some aspects deemed important to the dominant societal group. Instead, researchers urge teachers to view all cultures as a strength and an important aspect of identity for each student. Rather than critiquing some cultures, these researchers and teachers, together with students, examine the power embedded in, for example, dominant language codes.

The second context of diversity discussed in this section concerns the different gendered experiences of both teachers and students in educational settings. While there are a variety of gender issues to address within a classroom, the authors share stories and research regarding popular stereotypes linking a "masculinity quotient" with teacher authority and problematic gendered student experiences in classroom talk.

15
TEACHER AUTHORITY AND CULTURALLY RESPONSIVE TEACHING

Margaretta Patrick

As the 21st century loomed, educational authorities around the world considered how to provide learners with relevant knowledge, skills, and attitudes. Ontario, Canada's most populous province, created a Royal Commission on Learning in 1993 to examine how to prepare students adequately. When the Commission released its report 20 months later (Government of Ontario et al., 1994), it included issues of equity, such as diversity within Francophone communities, ongoing gender discrimination, and the need for schools to implement anti-racist programs. The Commission called for more racist-free school materials, greater diversity among teachers, and less academic streaming, which tended to negatively impact non-White students. Its report also emphasized concerns heard from Indigenous and Black communities.

To meet some of these concerns, the Commission recommended the creation of schools for Black students. When the Toronto District School Board announced that it would establish an Africentric Alternative School, to date Canada's only such school, public controversy ensued, with some calling the idea segregationist, while others said it was necessary to address the higher-than-average school dropout rates for Black students (Teotonio, 2019). The school first opened its doors in September 2009 and today offers K-8 education. It continues to be the subject of discussion, and enrolment has dropped in recent years. A three-year study of the school, concluded in 2014, summarized its commitment to "cultivating a space that fostered a positive Black identity, set high expectations of students, and strengthened students' sense of belonging and self-confidence" (James et al., 2015, p. 29). Pedagogical approaches center the student and are described as "a component of being Africentric, teaching to the whole child, getting to know students, collaborating with students to co-create their classroom environment, providing opportunities for students to voice their opinions, and making learning relevant to students' lives and interests" (p. 39). The study detailed initial strong scores on standardized tests at grades 3 and 6 but went on to describe ongoing media coverage as "quite negative, biased, limited, disruptive, and damaging" (p. 44). A particular challenge was inadequate resources, including funding. Beginning in the 2013–2014 school year, the school's provincial test scores dropped below Board averages but have recently been rising (Teotonio, 2019).

The story highlights two aspects of teaching and classroom management developed in this chapter: 1) recognition that educational practices, including classroom management, must acknowledge students' cultural and ethnic backgrounds; and 2) the research emerging from this recognition has implications for teacher authority, particularly how it is both gained and lost in multicultural classrooms. This chapter opens with an examination of four teacher typologies originally developed to explain which type of teacher is most successful in cross-cultural teaching contexts. The model is then used to explore how a teacher loses classroom authority when they are: 1) insufficiently introspective about their own cultural assumptions, especially concerning "good" and "bad" behavior; 2) insufficiently warm and caring; 3) insufficiently aware of power in schools and classrooms; and 4) insufficiently engaged in cultural literacy.

Warm Demanders: Origin of the Term

If a visitor pops into a typical classroom throughout North America, they will likely see a White teacher with diverse students, raising questions about how White teachers learn about and incorporate their students' ethnic, cultural, and religious identities into the curriculum and their teaching. In our recent history, authorities responsible for education have addressed cultural diversity in oppressive ways. For Indigenous students, governments created residential schools to force assimilation (Truth and Reconciliation Commission, 2015), while American educational and societal institutions and structures denied African Americans "the codes of power that lay in literacy" (Butchart, 2010, p. 8). The American Civil Rights movement and subsequent legal decisions forced educational institutions to examine how curriculum and other educational processes create and maintain racism (Harmon, 2012). In Canada, the Truth and Reconciliation Commission (TRC) spent five years gathering testimonies from survivors of the Residential Schools. By incorporating survivor testimonies into their reports, the TRC ensured that Canadians learned about the schools from those who had endured them. Of ongoing political significance are the Commission's 94 Calls to Action for reconciliation.

Thankfully, assimilation and withholding language codes were not the only options for educators, and those seeking better ways to educate culturally diverse students in classrooms began investigating effective inter-cultural teaching. One of the earliest such studies resulted in the notion of "warm demanders." Working in Alaska, Judith Kleinfeld (1972) researched rural Inuit and Athabascan First Nation high school students as they transitioned from their villages to urban centers to complete high school, starting in grade 9. Students attended schools Kleinfeld described as integrated or Indigenous boarding schools. They experienced not only the culture shock of city life but also school systems and teachers markedly different from the small rural schools from which they had come. Kleinfeld sought to determine what types of teachers were effective at inter-cultural education; in other words, teachers who successfully taught all the students in their classes.

Kleinfeld (1972) observed and video-recorded teachers with diverse teaching styles, ran workshops on cross-cultural teaching methods, and interviewed teachers as well as both Indigenous and White students. Indicators of teacher effectiveness included the degree of Indigenous student verbal participation in class as well as the cognitive level of that participation based on Bloom's taxonomy. The first indicator was important because teachers reported that Indigenous students responded to stressful situations with silence. The second indicator revealed the degree to which the students were learning.

The data led Kleinfeld (1972) to conclude that two characteristics distinguished effective inter-cultural teachers. First, they created a warm classroom environment. They elevated personal relationships over professional formality and communicated their warmth nonverbally via facial expression (e.g., smiling), less spatial distance (e.g., moving toward a student to ask a question rather than asking it from the front of the room), and touch (an incredibly sensitive topic as Kleinfeld acknowledged, given the history of sexual abuse experienced by Indigenous peoples at the hands of White adults). Second, effective teachers maintained high levels of "active demandingness" that expressed teacher concern for students beyond sympathy.

Placing these two characteristics on an X- and Y-axis yielded four teacher typologies: labeled by Kleinfeld as the traditionalist with high demands but little warmth; the sophisticated with low demand and low warmth; the sentimentalist with low demand but high warmth; and the "supportive gadfly," with high demands combined with high warmth (Figure 15.1).

Although traditionalist and sophisticated teachers tend to be successful with urban students, claimed Kleinfeld, the Indigenous students of the study perceived them to be cold. The sophisticated teachers' use of irony, "fast paced classroom repartee," and playing the "Devil's Advocate" increased the Indigenous students' apprehension because they did not understand these language codes (p. 31). While both urban and rural students learned little in the sentimentalist's class, the Indigenous students faced the added barrier of hostility from other students who resented what they viewed as teacher favoritism toward Indigenous students based on sympathy. Kleinfeld argued that it was only with the supportive gadfly teachers that the Indigenous (and urban) students participated verbally and demonstrated high levels of learning.

Kleinfeld (1975) later replaced the term "supportive gadflies" with "warm demanders," a term now found throughout classroom management literature,

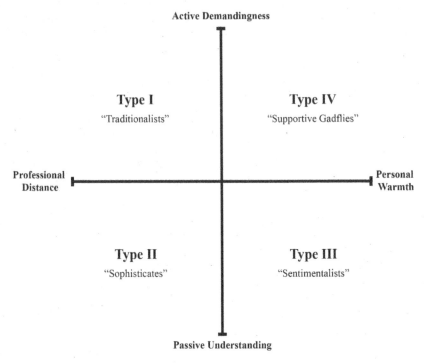

FIGURE 15.1 Kleinfeld's Typology of Teacher Types

Source: Kleinfeld (1972, p. 28), used with permission

especially related to culturally responsive teaching. The literature is replete with stories of classroom management and teaching going wrong and of teachers unable to gain students' consent to teach because they were not warm demanders.

Warm Demanders and Culturally Relevant/Responsive Teaching

The related research is expansive. For instance, scholars posed the idea of a self-fulfilling prophecy regarding teacher expectations (Brophy, 1983) and care ethicists such as Nel Noddings (2005, 2012) highlighted the importance of students' emotional health and feelings of belonging. Some scholars and practitioners focused on multicultural education, while others developed the concepts of culturally relevant pedagogy or culturally responsive teaching. Educators involved with culturally relevant/responsive teaching rejected cultural deficit explanations for why students from urban, poor, and diverse areas were failing in school and instead viewed culture and communication styles or language codes as an asset (Banks, 2010; Delpit, 1995; Gay, 2010). Commitment to culturally relevant teaching is both necessary and difficult for two reasons. First, Gay (2013) observed that teachers in the United States tend to be female, middle class, and of European ancestry, whereas students are increasingly diverse. While the data are more difficult to obtain in other jurisdictions, the situation is similar in several countries (Donlevy et al., 2015; Ryan et al., 2007; Vangool, 2020). Second, when culture, communication styles, and language codes are ignored, students who do not "assimilate, code switch, or culture switch" (Ware, 2006, p. 429) quickly fall behind academically.

Several justice and equity issues are immediately apparent. First, if some students must engage in cultural and linguistic switching to succeed at school, then the educational system works against them rather than with them, placing such students at a disadvantage through no fault of their own. Second, questions arise regarding both the responsibility of educators and schools to support students for whom the dominant codes in the school are unfamiliar and to discern the best means of implementing that support. Going even further, one may ask whether it is just to expect all students to fit into one model of education. And third, if schools continually fail some types of students more than others, then educators must determine the degree to which racism pervades educational systems.

Initially, researchers in the 1970s and 1980s worked to ensure that students received accurate information about diversity and argued for such education for all students (Gay, 2013). Then researchers moved to examine injustices within the system itself and how teachers could support the learning of all their students. Gloria Ladson-Billings (1995) studied successful teachers of African American students and theorized how "culturally relevant pedagogy" contributes to the academic achievement of all students, teaches cultural competence (meaning that students retain their culture while succeeding academically), and engages in cultural critique (especially the social inequities confronting many students and their communities).

Gay (2013) used the term "culturally responsive teaching," summarized as "teaching diverse students *through* their own cultural filters" (p. 50, italics in original). Promoters believe that culturally response teaching promotes equity, creates community among diverse students, and develops students' agency. The approach views diversity as normative and full of positive learning possibilities, requiring the reconsideration, if not abandonment, of many negative beliefs about students who are marginalized within society and educational systems.

Advocates for culturally relevant/responsive teaching often incorporate the two facets of warm demandingness. For example, in her book *"Multiplication is for White People": Raising Expectations for Other People's Children*, Lisa Delpit (2012) summarized the literature describing warm demanders as teachers who "expect a great deal of their students, convince them of their own brilliance, and help them to reach their potential in a disciplined and structured environment" (p. 77). Building on her own research and that of others, Delpit demonstrated how a teacher's quality of instruction and culture of learning are significant, especially for students living in lower socioeconomic settings. Insisting on high standards communicates to students a belief in their ability. But high standards must be accompanied by the social supports needed for students to take risks and make mistakes. Without one or the other, student gains in learning are diminished. Together, demands and supports create trust, provide security, build relationships, and develop cooperation. As Delpit wrote, "these students know that if the teacher is strong enough to control them, then the teacher is strong enough to protect them" (p. 86).

Research documents the potential of culturally responsive teaching. Papp (2020) described the improved graduation rates for Indigenous students (from 3 to 55 over four years) after a school in the Canadian province of Saskatchewan adopted traditional Indigenous pedagogy, which emphasizes holistic, experiential, and interdependent learning, respects oral traditions, and includes ceremonial and spiritual elements. Together with the Elders and the Indigenous community, the school decolonized the curriculum, honored the Indigenous worldview, and mapped the similarities between Indigenous ways of knowing and 21st-century learning. Papp noted how teachers in this school rejected hierarchical structures of power and knowledge and provided relational pedagogy, active learning experiences, and positive learning spaces.

Situations where the opposite happens—namely, low teacher expectations and low teacher support—negatively impact student engagement, academic self-concept, and motivation. Such is the documented experience of many Indigenous students in Australia, Canada, and the United States (Whitley, 2014). In the case of Indigenous Peoples in Canada, these challenges are layered on top of the negative effects of intergenerational trauma resulting from the residential school system that operated from the 1870s through 1996. The disconnect many Indigenous students encounter between the curriculum and their interests, lives, and ways of learning can be a significant barrier to their academic success. Sometimes the problems are difficult for teachers to identify. In Whitley's small study, teachers articulated several concrete steps they took to support their Indigenous students and they lamented the racism their students experienced in the broader community. While they admitted to a cultural mismatch with the Indigenous students, the teachers did not identify the racism students experienced within their classrooms or the school. For instance, teachers did not discern how particular pedagogical approaches, curriculum content, and behavioral expectations were discriminatory.

Teachers' lack of understanding and subsequent interpretations have significant impacts on students. The classification of poor and/or racialized students as "at risk" often masks negative and racist stereotypes (James, 2012). One study revealed that African American students as young as 11 and 12 years old were aware of whether their teacher maintained high expectations for them (Harmon, 2002). For decades, studies for the Toronto School Board (serving a highly diverse student population) revealed how Black youth, especially Black males, faced racial barriers such as stereotypes, low teacher expectations, and streaming practices that limited their academic achievement and ability to enter and graduate from university (Chadha et al., 2020; James, 2019; James & Turner, 2017). It is important to note, however, that students do not interpret these experiences in the same way. In studying the middle school experiences of Black students, James (2019) recorded how some of the students who encountered negative stereotypes of themselves from their teachers and peers, such as playing basketball, eating chicken, lacking discipline, and being troublemakers, viewed the constructs as systemic, while others saw them as the actions of individuals. Of central importance to the students was how teachers supported them through relationships and attending to their learning needs and questions.

While this type of research exists, it is often limited to small studies. Sleeter (2012) found the evidence of the efficacy of culturally responsive pedagogy on student academic achievement "thin" and the entire notion marginalized by the neoliberal promotion of individual responsibility, free markets and small government, and the application of business models to education, resulting in the foci of standardized tests and school choice. Sleeter (2012) identified three factors that contributed to the marginalization of culturally responsive pedagogy. First, simplistic conceptions of the concept result in reductions to cultural celebrations and/or a technique rather than a paradigm, with its embedded political analysis subsequently ignored. Second, there is limited large-scale research connecting it with increased student achievement, although the research that does exist is promising (for example, see Browning, 2018; Konold et al., 2018; Sandilos et al., 2017). Third, when its early uses resulted in higher achievement rates for Latinx and African American students, it engendered a backlash from some White elites who feared a corresponding loss of power and dominance. The consequence was the application of neoliberal principles to education, named by some as "backlash pedagogy" (Sleeter, 2012, p. 577).

Losing Authority

The literature on both warm demanders and culturally relevant pedagogy addresses the issue of teacher authority, a complex issue involving culture and power. To examine these issues, Ware (2006) studied two urban African American female teachers. Ms. Wills was in her final years of teaching, having spent her career teaching for an inner-city school district. One day Ware observed Ms. Wills emphatically reprimanding one of her classes because not all students had completed their homework assignment from the previous day. The students listened respectfully and then calmly carried out their next task, which Ware interpreted as a reflection of the caring relationship Ms. Wills had established with them and the students' acknowledgment of her authority. Both Ms. Wills and the other teacher participant, Ms. Carter, demonstrated care by maintaining high expectations, with Ms. Carter articulating the necessity of listening skills.

They believed that poverty did not excuse "a lack of academic achievement" (pp. 443–444). Their "'fussing, mean talk or verbal discipline' . . . is often misconstrued by people who lack a cultural sensitivity or emic perspective into the authoritarian style of parenting in the African American community," wrote Ware (p. 452; see also Cosier, 2019).

Irvine and Fraser (1998) told the story of how a highly successful, passionate African American teacher of 23 years in her largely African American community reprimanded a grade 1 student. The researchers recorded Irene Washington, the teacher, saying "That's enough of your nonsense, Darius. Your story makes no sense. I told you time and time again that you must stick to the theme I gave you. Now sit down" (para. 1). Many educators found the words overly harsh. After all, Darius was only 6 years old. Irene explained that her response was driven by her cultural context. "You see, you've got to know these students and where they're coming from—you know, 'talk the talk.' He knows what's expected during these activities, but he's trying to play the comedian. I know he knows how to develop a theme, and I won't let him get away with ignoring my instructions" (para. 3). As a warm demander, Irene was maintaining high expectations, but she was also being culturally responsive.

> "Darius is street-smart, streetwise. You see, he has older brothers who are out there on the streets, selling and using. I know if I don't reach him, or if I retain him, I may lose him to the streets this early. That's what I'm here for, to give them opportunities-to get an education and the confidence. I certainly don't want them to meet closed doors." She ends in a pensive and reflective mood. "When I look at these children, I see myself. I know what it is to grow up Black."
>
> (para. 4)

Irene knew the culture of her students and used the same culture codes in her classroom management.

Not everyone agreed with Washington's response (Milner, 2006), and Irvine and Fraser (1998) were quick to add that they were not advocating for different sets of standards for different teachers. Rather, they questioned whether the standards themselves were culturally insensitive. In a similar discussion, Delpit (2012) wrote, "What I am saying is that real concern about students' not living up to their academic potential should be transmitted in the teacher's genuine mode of emotional expression" (p. 81), including the use of humor or a quiet conversation.

Using authoritative language runs counter to European-based language codes and ways of conversing. These "direct discourse style 'mean-talk,' and other culturally specific communicative practices" (Ford & Sassi, 2012, p. 43) tend to be cultural and are the subject of much debate within the literature on warm demanders. The use of language codes raises significant issues for White teachers in culturally mismatched scenarios; in other words, contexts in which a teacher differs in cultural background from their students. In their comparison of a Black teacher and a White teacher with predominantly African American students, Ford and Sassi documented how the White teacher discovered she could not utilize the "mean talk" of her Black colleagues. Instead, she employed what Ford and Sassi identified as a form of signifying, "a discourse genre particular to the African American community that relies on indirection and wit to make a commentary on someone's behavior" (p. 55). For example, she used cultural tonal variations and indirection with a student looking at herself in a compact mirror when telling the student she looked "beau:utiful, dár↑lin↓" (p. 55). Ford and Sassi discerned warmth in the compliment yet detected a demand in the unstated expectation that the mirror would be put away. As the teacher explained to Ford and Sassi, she recognized the importance of first building trusting relationships with the students "before they would authorize her to 'teach the tests' and discuss race" (p. 56). Students first needed to see that the teacher cared about them before they would legitimate her authority to discuss issues of race with them. As Ford and Sassi concluded, "Her warmth warranted her demand . . . despite her White identity" (p. 56).

Although the indirection of this teacher was closer to the indirect discourse patterns of European Americans, its utilization for demands and the teacher's willingness to act authoritatively distinguished her from many White teachers. Ford and Sassi stressed the importance of White teachers incorporating racial justice as an integral element of their care. If White teachers are to become allies, they must first acknowledge their own biases. However, Ford and Sassi wondered if White teachers can truly be warm demanders due to the lack of a common shared history and traditions with their African American students. Not all scholars agree, with Gay (2010) believing that teachers can be "cultural and ethnic border crossers" (p. 241).

Expressions of the need for teachers to examine their biases are ubiquitous in the literature on education. Scores of research studies document how students' cultural responses are misinterpreted as defiance, resulting in harsh punishments (Milner, 2006). At issue is the fact that not all students accept or reflect the White middle-class cultural codes inscribed onto behavioral expectations. Because teachers "typically have good intentions, the differential treatment that the teachers display is located in their subconscious, and they are not able to critically examine these behaviors because they are not aware that the behaviors exist" (p. 503). This lack of awareness is one cause for teachers' losing their authority.

Not Doing the Work of Cultural Introspection

Gloria Ladson-Billings (2006) defined culturally relevant teachers (CRTs) as those who "assume that an asymmetrical (even antagonistic) relationship exists between poor students of color and society. Thus, their vision of their work is one of preparing students to combat inequity by being highly competent and critically conscious" (p. 30). They recognize how students in such contexts are "school dependent" (p. 31), meaning that school is a significant institution for social advancement and equity. When a school does not provide these opportunities, students experience life-long impacts, and when teachers have different expectations for students based on the color of their skin, they are practicing racial discrimination (Linton & McLean, 2017). CRTs recognize that all curricula are ideological and that some instructional strategies are harmful, such as tracking, excessive lecturing, and even cooperative learning when it is poorly managed. They understand how self-esteem is the outcome of engaged learning rather than an end to be taught (Ladson-Billings, 2006). Indeed, providing students with the knowledge, skills, and tools to become more independent is a social justice aspect of culturally responsive teaching (Hammond, 2015).

Thus, CRTs acknowledge that their beliefs and behaviors are informed by their cultural backgrounds. Such knowledge helps teachers monitor their responses to student behavior and consider how culture shapes normative views of "good" and "bad" behavior. Bondy and Ross (2008) told the story of a young Egyptian student who was punished in school after pushing a classmate. After talking with the teacher, the boy's parents discovered that pushing is viewed negatively in North America, whereas in Egypt, it is an act of affection. It was the teacher's lack of knowledge, concluded Bondy and Ross, that prevented her from conveying care to the young boy. The problem continues. Miller's (2021) research with teachers who strove to remain warm demanders when teaching online due to the COVID-19 pandemic revealed that some were unaware of how their own cultural backgrounds influenced their views of teaching and care.

One cause for the lack of awareness is the media. In their article advocating for "radical care" for Black boys, Howard and Howard (2021) wrote,

> Black boys are curious and complex, and they have dreams just like all other children. Unfortunately, these dimensions are often overlooked because of the persistent negative depictions of Black boyhood in the media. The result is often that educators dedicate their time and focus to controlling, surveilling, and punishing Black boys rather than caring for them.
>
> *(p. 25)*

The radical care advocated by Howard and Howard requires working with Black boys, avoiding tokenism when incorporating them or Black culture into the curriculum, ensuring that the classroom is safe from racism and that Black boys know they are seen, and avoiding curriculum materials that present Black boys as a single, and negative, story.

Cultural introspection is difficult work. Indeed, the process of "unpacking our implicit bias" is far more difficult than learning about the culture of others (Hammond, 2015, pp. 54–55). It is about examining how one's culture shapes the "normal" against which we measure all that we encounter. Although cultural understandings are ingrained in social habits and they influence why we value what we do, they operate invisibly, beneath the surface, so that we are not even aware of them. Yet it is very important for teachers to take the "emotional risk" (p. 56) of examining them so that cultural differences regarding "talk and discourse patterns, volume of interaction, time on task, collaboration or individual work" (p. 58), and so much more are not misidentified as student misbehavior or defiance.

The task is made more difficult when the teachers involved do not understand that they are the ones in need of introspection. As one teacher educator reflected, it is "some of the most difficult work imageable" to break through White privilege and convince White Pre-Service Teachers (PSTs) they need to think through their attitudes and ideas about race (Cosier, 2019, p. 68). Such reflection involves a process of "shedding the armor of 'niceness' and leaning into the sharp points of race work" (p. 68), of shifting beginning teachers' self-perceptions as caretakers and saviors to becoming warm demanders. It is the second word that is difficult because, in their European-American (or Canadian) culture, the PSTs view demanding as "so aggressive and assertive" (p. 69). As Ford and Sassi (2014) boldly pronounce, "Teachers' conceptions of authority are influenced by race" (p. 41). While Ford and Sassi condemn essentialism, which claims that all members of a racialized group think about authority in the same way, they also point out that ignoring the impacts of race will "render cultural incongruence inconsequential" (p. 42).

Not Teaching With Warmth and Care

In his doctoral dissertation studying high school graduates' perceptions of what constitutes teacher care, Jared Rodger Smith (2017) began with a narrative from his early teaching experiences, documenting his difficulties with classroom management. As a result of his self-professed lack of connection with approximately 25% of his students, Smith encountered behavioral issues and a general disengagement from this segment of his students. In his reflection, Smith identified specific decisions that contributed to the problem. First, in adopting the adage "don't smile until Christmas," Smith wrote, "I would intentionally choose to distance myself from students and was careful not to over-engage myself in conversation with students" (p. 3). Second, he lacked procedures for assignment and test redos, providing students with only one opportunity. As a result, he admitted to "[showing] little sympathy and was unwilling to listen to what [he] deemed to be 'excuses'" (p. 4). Third, when students broke a classroom rule, their names were put on a "naughty list" on the board, and subsequent misbehaviors meant checks after their names. If Smith perceived the entire class to be misbehaving (such as engaging in too much talking), all students were assigned homework or had to stay in after the bell, despite the protestations of those who had not been talking. Finally, Smith believed at the time that a silent class represented good classroom management, and after discovering how quickly collaborative work led to noise and off-task behavior, he resorted to more lectures.

Smith (2017) identified the main problem with his early management approaches as a lack of care toward his students, even though he described himself as a "caring and compassionate person" (p. 8). Despite his personality, he had adopted the idea from his personal experiences with teachers, popular culture, and his teacher preparation courses that teachers were to be tough. After many more years of teaching and being a principal, Smith set out to discover how recent high school graduates perceive teacher caring.

Twenty participants between the ages of 18 and 22 (mostly Caucasian) identified five aspects of teacher caring.

1. Caring teachers provide descriptive feedback on student work.
2. Caring teachers provide assistance when students struggle to understand course content.
3. Caring teachers engage students in conversations about post-high school ambitions.
4. Caring teachers display a positive and optimistic attitude.
5. Caring teachers honor student interests and perspectives.

(p. 79)

Statements 2 and 5 received the most references in the interviews. They mirror Kleinfeld's research into warm demanders: believing in students, building relationships with them, and supporting their academic success.

Research into warm demanders and culturally relevant teaching reminds us that caring and warmth have cultural components and perceptions. Delpit (2012) recounted the story of two teachers who taught about the American Civil War. One, an African American, told the story, stopping occasionally to ask students related personal questions. The second teacher, a White male, assigned groups of students a problem to resolve, related to the causes of the Civil War, with each student given a specific role. He then sat on the window ledge while the students puzzled over their respective problems. The university assessors scored the second teacher higher, but students within an African American community chose the first teacher as the "real teacher" because they viewed him as more caring. The second teacher, they said, "wasn't even teaching; he was lazy; he didn't care about his students; he was just sitting over there on the window sill" (p. 148). Delpit's point was not to support lecturing for African American students but to note how professional interpretations of teaching behaviors are culturally formed and can impede good teaching in the classroom.

Not Teaching About Power

How teachers demonstrate care can look different from teacher to teacher. Irene Washington, the teacher discussed by Irvine and Fraser (1998), had inequity in mind when she talked about the options facing Darius. In her two-year study with eight teachers, Ladson-Billings (1995) noted that care was not always in the form of affection. What the teachers did share was a commitment to "preparing the students for confronting inequitable and undemocratic social structures" (p. 474). Ladson-Billings described how several teachers used students' realities to engage in cultural and political critique.

When students perceived that their teachers were not preparing them for the world and its inequitable and undemocratic structures, they lost trust in those teachers. Delpit (1995) quoted several students who viewed their teachers as not teaching enough, if indeed they believed their teachers taught anything because the chosen pedagogies relied on students possessing certain cultural capital. Students without that cultural capital from home felt cheated because they were not taught the skills to "make it" in the dominant culture. As Delpit concluded, the students "seem to be saying that the teacher has denied them access to herself as the source of knowledge necessary to learn the forms they need to succeed" (p. 32). Delpit believed one of the reasons was the "teachers' resistance to exhibiting power in the classroom. Somehow, to exhibit one's personal power as expert source is viewed as disempowering one's students" (p. 32). Delpit found this view deleterious to the non-White students, although she hastened to add that teachers can never be the only expert in the room and direct instruction can never replace purposeful writing for real audiences. What teachers cannot do, Delpit insisted, is overlook their responsibility to teach all students, so that all students can function in the dominant culture. In her words, "pretending that gatekeeping points don't exist is to ensure that many students will not pass through them" (p. 39).

Delpit (1995) hastened to add that there is a difference between supporting all students in the manner described here and supporting the notion that everyone must follow the rules of the game as established by the powerful. She insisted that cultural groups have the right to maintain their own language style. But "to act as if power does not exist is to ensure that the power status quo remains the same. To imply to children . . . that it doesn't matter how you talk or how you write is to ensure their ultimate failure" (p. 39). Delpit described her own advocacy work as "pushing gatekeepers to open their doors to a variety of styles and codes" (p. 40). And she calls on educators to encourage students to value their codes of power, embedded within language codes, and understand the existent codes of power in society in the hopes of changing and/or enlarging them.

Not Engaging With Cultural Literacy

Culture is highly complex and dynamic. It is constantly changing, but at the same time, it is a stabilizing force (Gay, 2010). It can be overwhelming for teachers to read what has been written here and conclude that they need to be cultural experts on numerous cultures. However, if teachers engage in cultural introspection, are aware of culturally hegemonic norms, and reject cultural deficit models as explanations for the difficulties some students encounter at school, they have already taken a major step toward cultural literacy. Teachers need to be aware of such cultural factors as the degree to which cultures are comfortable with ambiguity, tend toward individualism or collectivism, value the masculine or the feminine, hold a long-term or short-term orientation, etc. (Hofstede, 2011). Cultures have different communication processes regarding verbal and nonverbal signals. For example, North American and northern European countries tend to have what are called low-context cultures that emphasize the verbal over the non-verbal, whereas the high-context cultures of many Asian countries value the non-verbal when receiving a communication. This may explain why those from Asian countries are generally more comfortable with silence than North Americans (Inoue, 2007).

Communicating between cultures, then, requires cultural fluency, an "awareness of the ways cultures operate in communication and conflict, and the ability to respond effectively to these differences" (Inoue, 2007, Cultural Dimensions section, para. 5). Inoue (2007) defined cultural fluency as awareness of the following six cultural factors:

- Tolerance of ambiguity
- Behavior flexibility
- Knowledge discovery
- Communicative awareness
- Respect for otherness
- Empathy (Cultural Fluency section, para. 1)

Two White, female, experienced scholars (Pitard & Kelly, 2020) used these cultural fluency skills to evaluate their own cultural interactions with two groups of adult Indigenous learners. One group came from Timor Leste to study in Australia for 12 weeks, while another group left Australia to study in Greenland for 2 weeks. The instructor working with the group in Australia discovered that the learners did not eat during the field trip taken two days previously with a colleague because, according to their cultural customs, they do not often carry money with them, eating instead in people's homes. When invited to go somewhere, the person inviting provides food. Thus, they had no money to buy food in the cafeteria at the site of the field trip. In a second account, the instructor with the group in Greenland took the learners to a museum in which the labeling of the artifacts did not properly indicate which items were culturally limited to be properly viewed only by men and others only by women. When a participant asked to shower after the museum tour, the instructor did not recognize the cultural importance of cleansing oneself after viewing something inappropriate. Both Pitard and Kelly acknowledged the unpredictability of these cultural concerns and how such unpredictability can be unnerving. Yet they persevered in the relationships and developed a taxonomy for cultural fluency that moved from shock and dismay to questioning, listening, and gaining a new perspective in which they learned about their own cultural assumptions and what they did not know about the others' culture.

The stories and reflections by Pitard and Kelly (2020) demonstrate the kinds of things that can go wrong in cross-cultural communication, especially if teachers are not aware of culturally hegemonic norms and lack the desire for cultural fluency. But in the presence of such awareness and desire, the stories also demonstrate that when teachers are willing to persist through the uncomfortable emotions and ask clarifying questions, they can arrive at new understandings which benefit everyone. If teachers are active cultural learners, they can create a classroom ethos characterized by respect and empathy.

Conclusion

Contemporary classrooms are increasingly multicultural, requiring teachers to reflect on the degree to which the curriculum and their teaching methods encompass the diversity of learners in the classroom. Culturally responsive teaching requires a rejection of deficit explanations for why some students do not flourish in school, an embrace of cultural diversity, and a belief that culture brings vitality into a classroom and provides an entryway to learning. If teachers show openness to learning about their students, provide a warm and safe learning environment in which all students know that they belong and matter, and maintain high expectations for all, students will learn and, one hopes, flourish. On the flip side, if teachers do not acknowledge the cultural norms embedded in many behavioral expectations and rules, do not provide a warm environment, do not teach about power, and do not engage with cultural literacy, they will lose authority in the classroom. They will not gain the consent of their students to demand hard work. They will not be able to enter the difficult discussions that help everyone in the classroom learn more about how discrimination works and the steps that can be taken to achieve a more just world.

References

Banks, J. A. (2010). Series Forward. In G. Gay (Ed.), *Culturally responsive teaching: Theory, research, and practice* (2nd ed., pp. ix–xiii). Teachers College Press.

Bondy, E., & Ross, D. D. (2008). The teacher as warm demander. *Educational Leadership*, 66(1), 54–58.

Brophy, J. E. (1983). Research on the self-fulfilling prophecy and teacher expectations. *Journal of Educational Psychology*, 75(5), 631–661. https://doi.org/10.1037/0022-0663.75.5.631

Browning, M. M. (2018). Student perceptions of teacher cultural sensitivity and its impact on student achievement. *Education Dissertations and Projects*, 306. Gardner-Webb University. https://digitalcommons.gardner-webb.edu/education_etd/306

Butchart, R. E. (2010). *Schooling the freed people: Teaching, learning, and the struggle for Black freedom, 1861–1876*. University of North Carolina.

Chadha, E., Herbert, S., & Richard, S. (2020). *Review of the peel district school board*. Minister of Education of Ontario. https://review-peel-district-school-board-report-en.pdf

Cosier, K. (2019). On whiteness and becoming warm demanders. *Journal of Cultural Research in Art Education, 36*(1), 56–72.

Delpit, L. (1995). *Other people's children: Cultural conflict in the classroom*. The New Press.

Delpit, L. (2012). *"Multiplication is for white people": Raising expectations for other people's children*. The New Press.

Donlevy, V., Meierkord, A., & Rajania, A. (2015). *Study on the diversity within the teaching profession with particular focus on migrant and/or minority background: Final report to DG education and culture of the European commission*. European Commission. https://ec.europa.eu/migrant-integration/?action=media.download&uuid=944D5517-E793-1877-069B3150067FF4B8

Ford, A. C., & Sassi, K. (2014). Authority in cross-racial teaching and learning (re)considering the transferability of warm demander approaches. *Urban Education, 49*(1), 39–74. https://doi.org/10.1177/0042085912464790

Gay, G. (2010). *Culturally responsive teaching: Theory, research, and practice* (2nd ed.). Teachers College Press.

Gay, G. (2013). Teaching to and through cultural diversity. *Curriculum Inquiry, 43*(1), 48–70. https://doi.org/10.1111/curi.12002

Government of Ontario, Begin, M., & Caplan, G. L. (1994). *For the love of learning. Royal commission on learning report: Short version*. Ontario Ministry of Education. https://qspace.library.queensu.ca/handle/1974/6880

Hammond, Z. (2015). *Culturally responsive teaching & the brain: Promoting authentic engagement and rigor among culturally and linguistically diverse students*. Corwin.

Harmon, D. A. (2002). They won't teach me: The voices of gifted African American inner-city students. *Roeper Review, 24*(2), 68–75. https://doi.org/10.1080/02783190209554132

Harmon, D. A. (2012). Culturally responsive teaching though a historical lens: Will history repeat itself? *Journal of Teaching and Learning, 2*(1), 12–22.

Hofstede, G. (2011). Dimensionalizing cultures: The Hofstede model in context. *Online Readings in Psychology and Culture, 2*(1), Article 8. https://doi.org/10.9707/2307-0919.1014

Howard, T. C., & Howard, J. R. (2021). "Radical care" to let Black boys thrive. *Educational Leadership, 78*(6), 22–29.

Inoue, Y. (2007). Cultural fluency as a guide to effective intercultural communication: The case of Japan and the U.S. *Journal of International Communication, 15*. www.immi.se/intercultural/nr15/inoue.htm

Irvine, J. J., & Fraser, J. W. (1998, May 13). Warm demanders. *Education Week*. www.edweek.org/education/opinion-warm-demanders/1998/05

James, C. E. (2012). Students "at risk": Stereotypes and the schooling of Black boys. *Urban Education, 47*(2), 465–494. https://doi.org/10.1177/0042085911429084

James, C. E. (2019). Adapting, disrupting, and resisting: How middle school Black males position themselves in response to racialization in school. *Canadian Journal of Sociology/Cahiers Canadiens de Sociologie, 44*(4), 373–398. https://doi.org/10.29173/cjs29518

James, C. E., Howard, P., Samaroo, J., Brown, R., & Parekh, G. (2015). *Africentric alternative school research project: Year 3 (2013–2014) report*. Toronto. www.yumpu.com/en/document/read/54690686/africentric-alternative-school-research-project

James, C. E., & Turner, T. (2017). *Toward race equity in education: The schooling of Black students in the Greater Toronto Area*. York University.

Kleinfeld, J. (1972). *Effective teachers of Indian and Eskimo high school students.* Center for Northern Educational Research, University of Alaska. https://pubs.iseralaska.org/media/f12320af-100b-48a9-bf9c-8c7b43ad46b7/1975_02-EffectiveTeachersOfEskimoAndIndianStudents.pdf

Kleinfeld, J. (1975). Effective teachers of Eskimo and Indian students. *The School Review, 83*(2), 301–344. https://doi.org/10.1086/443191

Konold, T., Cornell, D., Jia, Y., & Malone, M. (2018). School climate, student engagement, and academic achievement: A latent variable, multilevel multi-informant examination. *AERA Open, 4*(4), 1–17. https://doi.org/10.1177/2F2332858418815661

Ladson-Billings, G. (1995). Toward a theory of culturally relevant pedagogy. *American Educational Research Journal, 32*(3), 465–491. https://doi.org/10.3102/00028312032003465

Ladson-Billings, G. (2006). "Yes, but how do we do it?": Practicing culturally relevant pedagogy. In J. Landsman & C. W. Lewis (Eds.), *White teachers/diverse classrooms: A guide to building inclusive schools, promoting high expectations, and eliminating racism* (pp. 29–42). Stylus Publishing, LLC. https://digitalcommons.georgiasouthern.edu/esed5234-master/37

Linton, R., & McLean, L. (2017). I'm not loud, I'm outspoken: Narratives of four Jamaican girls' identity and academic success. *Girlhood Studies, 10*(1), 71–88. https://doi.org/10.3167/ghs.2017.100106

Miller, K. E. (2021). A light in students' lives: K-12 teachers' experiences (re)building caring relationships during remote learning. *Online Learning, 25*(1), 115–134. https://doi.org/10.24059/olj.v25i1.2486

Milner, H. R. (2006). Classroom management in urban classrooms. In C. M. Evertson & C. S. Weinstein (Eds.), *Handbook of classroom management: Research, practice, and contemporary issues* (pp. 491–522). Routledge.

Noddings, N. (2005). *The challenge to care in schools* (2nd ed.). Teachers College Press.

Noddings, N. (2012). The caring relation in teaching. *Oxford Review of Education, 38*(6), 771–781. https://doi.org/10.1080/03054985.2012.745047

Papp, T. A. (2020). A Canadian study of coming full circle to traditional Aboriginal pedagogy: A pedagogy for the 21st century. *Diaspora, Indigenous, and Minority Education, 14*(1), 25–42. https://doi.org/10.1080/15595692.2019.1652587

Pitard, J., & Kelly, M. (2020). A taxonomy for cultural adaptation: The stories of two academics when teaching Indigenous sojourners. *Forum: Qualitative Social Research, 21*(2), Article 11.

Ryan, J., Pollock, K., & Antonelli, F. (2007). *Teacher and administrator diversity in Canada: Leaky pipelines, bottlenecks and glass ceilings.* Paper prepared for the Annual Conference of the Canadian Society for the Study of Education, Saskatoon. http://home.oise.utoronto.ca/~jryan/pub_files/Art.April09.numbers.pdf

Sandilos, L. E., Rimm-Kaufman, S. E., & Cohen, J. J. (2017). Warmth and demand: The relation between students' perceptions of the classroom environment and achievement growth. *Child Development, 88*(4), 1321–1337. https://doi.org/10.1111/cdev.12685

Sleeter, C. E. (2012). Confronting the marginalization of culturally responsive pedagogy. *Urban Education, 47*(3), 562–584. https://doi.org/10.1177/0042085911431472

Smith, J. R. (2017). *Student perceptions of teacher care: Experiences and voices of recent high school graduates* (Graduate Theses and Dissertations. 15425). Iowa State University. https://lib.dr.iastate.edu/etd/15425

Teotonio, I. (2019, July 28). Canada's only Africentric school was launched amid calls to better support Black youth. Ten years on, has it fulfilled its promise? *Toronto Star.* www.

thestar.com/news/gta/2019/07/28/canadas-only-africentric-school-was-launched-amid-calls-to-better-support-black-youth-ten-years-on-has-it-fulfilled-its-promise.html

Truth and Reconciliation Commission. (2015). *Honouring the truth, reconciling for the future: Summary of the final report of the truth and reconciliation commission of Canada.* Author. www.trc.ca/about-us/trc-findings.html

Vangool, H. (2020, September 3). Schools need BIPOC educators now more than ever. *CBC.* www.cbc.ca/news/canada/saskatoon/op-ed-sask-diversity-teachers-bipoc-1.5703711

Ware, F. (2006). Warm demander pedagogy: Culturally responsive teaching that supports a culture of achievement for African American students. *Urban Education, 41*(4), 427–456. https://doi.org/10.1177/0042085906289710

Whitley, J. (2014). Supporting educational success for Aboriginal students: Identifying key influences. *McGill Journal of Education/Revue des sciences de l'éducation de McGill, 49*(1), 155–181. https://doi.org/10.7202/1025776ar

16
MALE AUTHORITY
Assumption Busting

Genie Kim

I invite you to ponder two questions: How would you describe the appearance of a person with authority? Based on your criteria, would people look at you and presume authority? It can be easily argued that most individuals ascribe power to those who possess a physically commanding presence, coupled with a deep, strong voice. In a nutshell, there is an assumed correlation between one's "masculinity quotient" and one's measure of power. Rarely, if ever, would someone who is described as slight in build and soft in volume be imagined to wield real authority. Yet, let us take a look at two historical giants: Mother Teresa and Gandhi. Notwithstanding their being diminutive in size and soft-spoken, they were thunderous, dominant, and far-reaching in their global influence and legacy. The immense authority they exerted contradicts their physical qualities. Both figures endure remarkably in their ability to mesmerize, confound, and subdue. How? Mother Teresa and Gandhi, seemingly effeminate and frail, are reminders to all educators that authority and impact do not derive from one's masculinity quotient but instead from one's character and conduct.

Setting the Stage

To begin this chapter, I would like to engage you, once again, in an exercise of reflection: why is it that male teachers have greater authority in the classroom than female teachers? You may have grasped that I presented a misleading question. Regardless, it would be unsurprising to know that the wider population holds this very assumption that male teachers inherently possess greater classroom control than their female counterparts.

In this chapter, I hope to dismantle the pervasive belief that a direct relationship exists between the gender of a person and one's ability to manage one's class.

Appreciating that *gender* is a nuanced, convoluted, and contested social construct, for the purposes of this chapter, I will make reference to the male/female gender dichotomy, as it relates to the perception of unequal power relations.

This chapter seeks to dispel the ubiquitous misconception that male teachers are more apt to secure authority and respect from their students in comparison to female teachers. I hope to debunk this misapprehension, which sadly results in many female teachers adopting a self-defeating and injurious mindset. My purpose in this chapter is twofold: 1) to offer four vignettes, which will serve as empirical illustrations; these portrayals were culled to reassure teachers who do not fit the masculine bill that credible authority can be achieved, irrespective of one's size, vocal range, and masculinity quotient and 2) to provide some gleaned tips and strategies one can utilize to exercise constructive authority in one's classroom.

I have chosen to employ factual vignettes of four female educators, all vastly dissimilar, to demonstrate that it is not one's gender but rather the individual who determines the scope of one's classroom authority. Rather than appealing to scholarly research conducted in this area, I believe my vignettes should compellingly turn on their head the notion of male preeminence as it relates to classroom authority. My own personal story of navigating classroom management is interwoven throughout and figures prominently; I go into depth foregrounding my vignette, with one express purpose: to illustrate that anyone, notwithstanding gender and apparent physical liabilities, can become triumphant with classroom management. At the conclusion of this chapter, I will address key strategies that I have distilled and adopted over the years.

Genie's Story—Part 1

Cautionary words, expressed by many well-intentioned teachers, contain this conventional message, "You can't teach, unless you master 'classroom management.'" No doubt, such words provoke anxiety for aspiring teachers. They forcibly conjure up images of pandemonium, often exaggerated and mockingly portrayed in the media. This happened to be what nearly foreclosed my chance of becoming a teacher. To explain, despite being encouraged by many of my trusted friends and family members to enter the teaching profession, I stubbornly and emphatically refused. My reluctance stemmed from what I privately feared would become a reality: losing utter control of my class. These fears were not without merit.

A brief self-description is necessary to help capture and justify the reasons behind my deep-rooted angst. As a short and small-framed Korean female, with an even smaller voice that often squeaks and croaks without warning, I questioned the following: "If my friends have difficulty hearing me, what chance would I have of surviving a class of 25+ students?" Despite my profound insecurities, through a series of unanticipated events, I awoke one day newly minted as a high school English teacher. Given this school's small class sizes, my overwhelming apprehensions of losing control completely vanished. In fact, in short order, I developed a strong sense that I was in my element and in full control, that is, until a jarring afternoon shook me to the core and left me stupefied. Herein, Vanessa's vignette begins.

Vignette One: An Uncommon Encounter and Paradigm Shift

At first, I was indifferent, and then I was intrigued. Finally, I became awed and mystified by a very thin, 5'3 bookish teacher in her late 20s, who always had her hair pulled back in a ponytail. Vanessa was her name, and I don't quite remember whether we had been formally introduced. She appeared solitary and unassuming, and she did not capture my attention, at least, not until our first staff meeting. Vanessa sat diagonally to my left, such that I was able to clearly see her profile. I remember that she sat with a bowl of fruit. It was with interest that I watched her as she casually picked at her grapes. I was fascinated merely by the fact that in my twenties, the idea of indulging in fruit for one's snack was, in my mind, bizarre and unnatural. But soon, Vanessa was to capture my attention and astound me for a reason I would never have imagined. Slouched and sitting quietly, Vanessa slowly raised her arm. I will never forget what followed when she began speaking. Everyone turned to look at her. And to my astonishment, the teachers appeared to hang onto every word Vanessa uttered. Without anyone having to tell me, on an intuitive level, I knew that this nondescript teacher had somehow earned the respect of everyone in the room. Vanessa spoke with calm and clarity. There was nothing special about her speech or its delivery. Yet, there was an unequivocal command she possessed, an inscrutable authority she somehow seized. Each individual willingly gave Vanessa their full attention, which, conspicuously, was not offered to any other speaker. It must be noted here that there was a disproportionate number of male teachers in this high school. Bearing witness to Vanessa's mysterious impact on the entire teaching staff caused me to feel intimidated, which sadly hindered me from getting to know her and the secret behind her noteworthy power. Yet, little was I aware that greater intimidation was awaiting me.

A Sucker Punch With Some Humble Pie

On a fateful day, it turned out that I would need to cover one of Vanessa's English classes. It was in her class that two unforgettable things were to occur. First, I would become better acquainted with Vanessa's mysterious authority and, second, my deepest fear would come to pass. Not knowing what would soon transpire, I blithely stepped into Vanessa's English class.

Vanessa's students sat silently, unmistakably focused on each word emerging from her lips. The tranquility in her room didn't stand out as anything exceptional, that is, until Vanessa left the room. I introduced myself and reiterated

Vanessa's instructions. I quickly noticed that the more I spoke, the apparent tranquility I had earlier experienced was fast evaporating. First, it started with quiet sidebar murmurs, and then, in no time, it escalated to full-blown conversations, with students hollering across the room to one another. A number of Vanessa's male students, who towered over me, gave me looks as they sauntered by me, which overtly signaled that I shouldn't "bother" with them. Exasperated, bewildered, and fearful, I stopped talking and allowed the students to do whatever they wanted, essentially to run the class. It struck me that I had lost complete control over Vanessa's students. Something within my gut knew that if I attempted to reclaim Vanessa's authority, I would risk making an even bigger fool of myself. If Vanessa's students had any doubts about letting me know about their complete disregard for my presence, they would soon punctuate this for me.

Upon Vanessa's re-entry, the entire room became hushed and everyone instantaneously transformed into virtuous saints. In a short space of time, I had the proverbial "rubbing salt into one's wound" feeling. Oblivious to all this, Vanessa kindly offered me her thanks. Being mortified by this comedic sequence of events, I hastily exited, with my pride battered and emotions crushed. Yet, I also walked out experiencing a heightened sense of curiosity about this waif and ordinary-looking teacher. I wanted to understand the quiet authority Vanessa exercised so effortlessly over what I believed were her devious and diabolical students. That one-period nightmare was horrifying, and I chose to repress it from my conscious memory—until it resurfaced through a trigger—the writing of this chapter.

Sadly, my sense of inferiority concerning Vanessa resulted in two negative consequences: it hindered me from getting to know her and I was never to unravel the secret behind her mysterious power, which the male teachers failed to exert.

Genie's Story—Part 2

Subsequent to teaching at the high school, I restarted my career in the elementary teaching level and was to become a grade 5 teacher. My re-initiation was to be at a very challenging inner-city school.

At the conclusion of my first year of teaching grade 5, I was beside myself with grief and despondency; anxiously, I was reconsidering my career options. When probed as to why I believed I had to leave this noble profession, my response was simple, "How can I teach when I have zero control over my class!" Through great coaxing and intense prayer, I found myself returning to this school the following year.

The Heavens listened and my prayers were decisively answered. My classroom environment went from chaotic to calm. I did not fully comprehend the extent of my transformed "teacher-stance" until a few years after my first-year fiasco. An event occurred that would become seared into my memory. A large proportion of the students were bussed in from what people called the housing projects. One winter afternoon, due to inclement weather, the busses were delayed, thus leaving about 120 grade 4 and 5 students strewn throughout the hallway, creating what people would call a ruckus. A male teacher, well-built, with a booming voice, menacingly charged down the hall, bellowing his demand for silence. The too-cool-for-school students, unfazed, blatantly ignored him. After a few more failed attempts, exasperated, he raised up his hands acknowledging defeat. Crestfallen, he slunk away from the epicenter of the disorder.

Appalled by the disrespect just witnessed, and unnerved by the ongoing inappropriate behaviors and loud noise, I stood up and called for the students' attention. I indignantly uttered some words, and the fracas and aggressive jostling stopped. The mayhem ceased, and the students compliantly engaged in quiet chatter. Shortly thereafter, the school custodian entered our hallway. Walking past me, these were his words, "Thank goodness 'Mr. Rambo' is here. If it weren't for him, this place would be a zoo right now!" I didn't respond. I felt numb. I needed to process the custodian's utterance. Some context needs to be added. When the custodian arrived on the scene, I was standing in the middle of the hall, in front of the students, while Mr. Rambo was disengaged from everyone. When I was able to collect my thoughts, two things rapidly rose to my consciousness. First, I was incredulous that it was in fact pint-sized me who commanded control over the 120 students, many of whom were hyper and unruly. Second, I was annoyed that the custodian assumed, despite the context, that Mr. Rambo was responsible for the resulting calm. This left an indelible mark on me.

I was to become consciously aware of the powerful role gender plays in influencing erroneous presumptions and perceptions. Admittedly, I too was equally guilty of this presupposition: I was deeply shocked by the unexpected difference in outcomes between myself and my colleague. Why? It centered solely on one key point: our gender difference. The social construct of gender and its supposed intersection with authority now took on a whole new meaning for me.

Vignette Two: The Curious Case of an Improbable Principal

I am acutely aware that convincing others effectively of the legitimacy of female authority requires more than scholarly theorizing; it requires concrete evidence. Well, this gift was inadvertently offered to me by someone who serves as my professional mentor and has become my beloved and treasured friend. Anne Lee is her name, and her stellar reputation as both a human being and as a principal of a middle school is more than justified. However, it was not until I saw Anne in action that I came to comprehend fully the quiet yet impressive power she wields. As a genuinely humble, graceful, and soft-spoken Asian woman, Anne exudes gentleness and femininity that beguile and conceal her intrinsic authority and commanding presence. I went to supply teach at Anne's school and asked her to keep our friendship secret; this way, I could poke around without drawing attention to myself.

A full day in a school can unearth a lot, especially when one is undercover. My sleuthing began even before the bell rang to signal the start of the school day. I actively sought out teachers from whom I could extract information. I asked a few available teachers about Ms. Lee. As expected, the comments were all glowing and replete with exuberant praise—nothing that surprised me. The real test came with my next unsuspecting targets. My radar turned to the students considered difficult and rebellious, students whose appearance and body language loudly communicated, "Don't come near me, especially if you're a teacher." Near a shady tree, a group of five males formed a loose circle, emitting an intimidating vibe. Brazenly, I slipped into their group, and without introduction, I simply asked, "So, what's the principal of your school like?" The coolest-looking boy, who was a head taller than me, spoke first. Despite having a menacing appearance, he enthused, "Ms. Lee! She's the best! Everyone loves her!" Taken aback, I responded, "You actually like the principal?" I knew I was being judgmental, but these grade 8 boys looked like they would frequent the principal's office and for all the wrong reasons. The students then gave me a list of why Ms. Lee was so highly esteemed. They focused on how she genuinely cares and looks out for them. Following my self-assigned detective work, two other significant events would consolidate my understanding of Anne's deep authority and impact that reverberate throughout her entire middle school.

An Anecdote Worth a Thousand Words

An event that baffled me took place during a lunch hour. I slipped into the school office, mid-lunch, to make a quick inquiry about my afternoon schedule. It was eerily quiet and empty. I casually struck up a conversation with the office administrator (OA), remarking on the oddity of the office being so quiet during the lunch hour. I further added that she must be feeling relieved by this auspicious moment of calm. The OA locked eyes with me and soberly stated that the office was always quiet. I physically reacted to this impossible-to-believe statement. My response was visceral, "You're kidding me!" to which the OA explained how prior to Anne's arrival, the office was pure bedlam all day. However, with Anne's presence as the school's principal, everything dramatically changed. The kicker was this statement, "Now, it's strange when students come to the office." This simple interchange with Anne's OA solidified my appreciation of the subtle and quiet power wielded by a petite, female principal.

Anne's impact felt particularly exaggerated, and it stirred my curiosity, especially when contrasted with the approach of many of the male principals I had met. Several male administrators, all of them burly, frequently ended up screaming at misbehaving students. Without fail, their crimson-faced hollering was met with defiance and unrestrained spewing of expletives. Misusing their overbearing size and overbearing personalities, these male principals erroneously believed that misbehaviors could be quashed. Sadly, I have witnessed a number of my male colleagues implement the same counterproductive approach, all with the same humiliating and damaging effect. Rightfully, many call this approach *bullying*.

Another Telling Anecdote About Anne

One day, I was instructed to take a grade 7 class to the cafeteria for an assembly. It was here that Anne demonstrated the nature of her authority. From the outset of the assembly to its conclusion, I witnessed order, respect, and decorum being exhibited by the entire grade 6–8 student body. When the noise level rose, it was Anne who stepped in. Using a gentle yet commanding tone, Anne brought the assembly to an immediate hush. Just like Vanessa, Anne spoke with calm yet with a weighty presence that exuded genuine care. I will take a detour at this moment to shed light on the noteworthiness of what I experienced during the assembly.

Puzzled by the rare sense of order that permeated Anne's cafeteria during the assembly, I was compelled to make a phone call. I needed to be certain I was not misguided in believing that school assemblies are commonly associated with a fair level of disorder. This was my personal experience for over 15 years. Hence, I decided to solicit the insights of a fellow educator friend, Rona. At that time, Rona had worked in education for well over 20 years, both as a teacher and as a vice-principal in various K-8 schools. As a no-nonsense, unfiltered, and refreshingly forthright leader, I knew I would receive a frank and reliable overview of the state of affairs within our schools. Without providing Rona any context, I asked her point-blank about experiences with assemblies and the customary office traffic occurring during lunch and recess times. As I anticipated, Rona generalized about the ubiquitous din during assemblies and the disorderly tumult inside the office during lunch and recess times. At this point, I disclosed the context of my query. I then inquired about Rona's thoughts pertaining to gender and classroom management. Rona, in typical fashion, was unequivocal and raw in her reply, "Regardless of gender, some people have *#!@ classroom management. I've seen it both ways." I then asked if she believed females were at an automatic disadvantage when it came to classroom authority. Rona offered a brusque response, "No, it's all about classroom management." Rona offered me what, based on my own experiences, I already knew on a gut level: her many years as a VP doing walkabouts throughout her schools clearly revealed a nonexistent relationship between gender and one's ability to manage one's class. Having access to Rona's trustworthy bird's-eye view helped reinforce my intuitive assumption: gender and classroom authority should not be conflated. With these points of contrast in view, let us return to Anne.

Having been accustomed to witnessing students and teachers openly chatting during assemblies, of which I too was culpable, I became fascinated watching students and staff give Anne their undivided attention. As I described earlier, Anne is a soft-spoken, feminine, and mild-mannered principal, who, during the assembly, carried herself with conviction, composure, and serenity. It was evident that the entire school had somehow come under her poised and amiable spell.

When I asked about the difference between male and female teachers in relation to classroom management, Anne was categorical. She started with "Male stereotypes are out there . . . that men have greater authority." Yet, as had Rona, Anne asserted that as a principal she has encountered way too many male teachers with **no** (emphasized by Anne) classroom management skills. Anne then presented an idea that all educators must heed: "Students' behavior is a way of communicating." Anne provided a few examples to make her point: "If students act out, it could be that they are communicating that the curriculum is too hard, they don't feel safe, or they are having issues at home or with their peers." Clearly, Anne gets students.

I then probed about her perspective on what she considers to be critical to teachers having strength in classroom management. Anne was emphatic in her response. Central for Anne is a deep and appropriate rapport with students. Anne believes, rightly, that students need to know that their teachers care about them and are invested in their lives. According to Anne, "This relationship piece is how difference is made, which is why teachers have been called into the profession." I unreservedly concur.

Anne's words, corroborated by the unsuspecting boys, signal that she genuinely cares about her students and not about imposing her authority. Anne's responses help uncover how she has earned respect and authority from her entire school community.

Vignette Three: The "Julia Carter" Effect

In life, you may have the great fortune of encountering someone who is not only inimitable but also a rare breed. Well, I happened to be blessed and cursed to have such a person become my unlikely mentor. Why unlikely? Julia Carter was a dreadlock-sporting, Caribbean force to be reckoned with. Julia is the diametric opposite of me, in every way possible. Humor is not my strong point, and people seem to have this unrestrained urge to tell me that my voice is barely audible. Conversely, Julia has this belly-aching humor. She is loud and intense, in a way that captivates and enchants. Unrivaled are Julia's charisma, wit, and energy. Once again, we're complete opposites.

No doubt, I will be indebted forever to Julia for voluntarily offering to mentor me, but, as I noted earlier, my knowing her was also a liability, at least at first. I will endeavor to make a very, very long story short. Julia was highly effective with students; in fact, the whole school was mesmerized by her. She was the *it* teacher whom all students wanted to have and all teachers wanted to be. This is how Julia unwittingly became my liability: trying to be like Julia Carter became my undoing. Earlier, I shared how I almost left the profession, the direct result of my impersonating Julia. I instantly became loud, intense, and then eventually unhinged. My students had no qualms about letting me know I was ineffectual, an imposter, and a bona fide joke. Defeated and desperate, I turned to the damaging approach I reported previously: bullying. I quickly degenerated into an unloving and unkind teacher. I succumbed to chastising, dominating, yelling, and bribing, all of which fueled anarchy within my class. I was prepared to leave the profession when a wise woman challenged me to restart in September by being myself while invoking various lessons I had learned during my hellish year. With hesitance, I took this Godly woman's advice. Counterintuitively, in being my authentic self, with my scratchy, small voice, I experienced authority and exhilarating joy, to the point where I would often close my classroom door at the end of the day, whispering, "I can't believe I get paid to teach!"

A 180 Degree Metamorphosis

Licensed to be my authentic self, along with implementing a host of critical teacher moves and strategies modeled by Julia, I saw my classroom environment take a dramatic turn, with a surprising twist. To understand the extent of the transformation, let us revisit one of the burly principals, whose berating style proved ineffective (similar to my own former misguided approach).

This physically large, blustering principal, periodically sent educational assistants to my classroom to take over my class. Why? This principal needed me to de-escalate situations that he had himself inflamed. This was the typical scenario: a Supply Teacher requiring assistance would call for the principal to help restore order. The principal would enter the class, only to exacerbate the problem. The unruly students would insolently refuse to listen to the principal while further wreaking havoc. Therein, I would arrive on the scene to remove the students—without raising my voice. At first, I was privately irritated by these interruptions; I knew this principal was responsible for precipitating these unnecessary standoffs with students. Then, one day, it dawned on me: a little female teacher, with a tremulous voice, was solicited by a large, male principal, to rescue HIM. Ironic? No, it is a reality that must become widespread knowledge: women are capable of exerting strong authority in schools, with high efficacy. I relate this anecdote to disabuse everyone of the spurious notion that males inherently have more authority than females. I hope this juxtaposition proves useful in uncovering a reality that some find difficult to understand.

Six Plus One Strategies for Garnering Classroom Authority

I shared my mortifying and triumphant experiences, along with three compelling vignettes, to highlight a fundamental truth: female educators can and do exert powerful authority, without the need for loud, masculine posturing. I would be naive and remiss if I did not acknowledge the reality that male educators, in general, are afforded greater respect from students at the outset than female teachers. However, achieving lasting authority in one's class is a different matter, one not contingent on gender. To earn and sustain legitimate authority requires the adoption of key strategies, techniques, and mindset.

The principles and practices for obtaining authority in one's class are largely consistent, which are described in many classroom management literature. A full-bodied and comprehensive understanding can be found through reading the entirety of this book. There exist general tried-and-true principles that must be adhered to, of which I shall heretofore list 6, "plus 1." These have been gleaned from my personal experiences and observations.

Relationships, Relationships, Relationships

Just as location helps determine real-estate value, fostering caring and authentic relationships with students determines classroom authority. Fostering such relationships begins with treating every student with dignity and respect. The male principal I mentioned failed to build genuine and positive relationships with students. During his self-defeating standoffs, he defaulted, disingenuously, to using a friendly and good-natured approach. This principal neglected to spend time cultivating authentic, respectful, and humble interactions with students. Consequently, when it mattered, this principal became a toothless sitting duck.

Be Consistent and Fair

Trust, we all know, is the foundation of any meaningful relationship. Students especially need to know that they can trust their teachers. Trust is manifested primarily through two tangible experiences: consistency and fairness. When rules, expectations, and the treatment of each student demonstrate integrity (consistency) and a sense of what is just (fair), loyalty naturally and powerfully ensues.

One Size Does Not Fit All

Believe it or not, ALL students want to learn. As Anne astutely and compassionately pointed out, students who misbehave do so for innumerable and often heartbreaking reasons. One such reason I frequently encounter is that students fear they will be exposed as incapable. Such students would rather be sent to the office for being disruptive than be labeled dumb by their teacher and peers. The implication of this truth is obvious: make learning accessible and engaging for all students. Ensure that your lessons invite all students into the learning, prioritizing the culturally relevant and responsive pedagogical approach (Ladson-Billings, 2006, 2021).

Establish Clear Expectations and Appropriate Boundaries

Kids are kids, no matter their size and age. Students need explicit and consistent opportunities to learn the appropriate boundaries and expectations. You can be fun and friendly with your students, but they must recognize that you are their teacher and should be treated respectfully. More often than not, I have seen male teachers endeavor to be cool and chummy with students, only to end up experiencing a downward spiral. Apparently out of nowhere, they have allowed the professional boundaries to become blurred and their authority diminished.

Take Off Your Mask and Be Authentically "You"

Again, we must acknowledge that when students first meet a tall, burly, masculine teacher, they immediately sit up taller and suppress their inclination to misbehave. But we need to add a caveat to that acknowledgment: This does not last long unless the teacher embraces the strategies, critical teacher moves, and attitudes I have listed. The authority with which many males are instantly endowed can just as quickly melt away. Vanessa, Anne, and Julia are all different in their natures, style, and approach; yet, a common thread I have observed in them is that they never postured or sought after power. Still, in all three cases, they gained and retained authority and respect to exceptionally high degrees.

Aspiring teachers need to operate according to how they have been uniquely designed and created. As earlier illustrated, the more I tried to mimic Julia's style and approaches, the more I lost control over my class. After a full year of futility and failure, I learned that I needed to adapt many of Julia's strategies to suit my personality, idiosyncrasies, and strengths. This meant, for example, that I needed to adopt techniques to compensate for my quiet voice. Using sign language along with some self-made quirky signals that amused my students is one example of how I was able to gain my students' respect without having to yell or bribe. I know that I am neither an anomaly nor an exception to the rule. I am what teacher candidates can look to and can boldly conclude: gender does not determine one's impact in the classroom. In essence, anyone who is committed to implementing the key strategies listed can effectively wield classroom authority.

Seek to Empower and Not Take Power

The case of the burly principal, in contrast with Anne, is sufficient evidence that one's motivation and heart matter. The burly principal sought to wrest power from grade 4 and 5 students by imposing his authority upon them. In doing so, he actually forfeited his authority. In contrast, Anne, in her selfless and other-centered ways, strives to equip and empower her staff and students to become their best selves. In seeking to empower her staff and students, Anne has inadvertently ended up wearing a superhero cape, especially in the eyes of her grade 6–8 students. We see again the potency of juxtaposition. At this juncture, I want to note there exist many effective male teachers who never resort to posturing or imposing their socially/physically ascribed power to wrest control. It was heartening to have witnessed a number of my male colleagues "empowering" their students, thus, naturally garnering respect and admiration.

"Plus 1": Mindset Matters

This *plus 1* piece of advice is targeted to female teachers. The preceding six offerings apply to all educators, regardless of gender. It may surprise you, but there's only one strategy that applies specifically to females. Ultimately, the legitimation strategy for female teachers begins with one's mindset. All educators, regardless of gender, race, or physical stature are capable of powerfully and positively creating a classroom environment conducive to learning. Mindset matters; therefore, a mental pivot is essential. Why? Perception becomes reality. Despite anecdotes and assumptions that delegitimize female teachers, we must believe we can exert influence and control. One's beliefs about classroom authority will largely determine one's success or failure.

Conclusion

Establishing credible authority is complex and nuanced. Like all other areas of expertise, there is a complexity of moves, learnings, understandings, and practices needed. I must note my awareness that this chapter merely scratches the surface.

In conclusion, educators will do well to reflect on William Glasser's sage words: "When you study by great teachers . . . you will learn much more from their caring and hard work, than from their style" (1998, p. 40). While this chapter has made clear the problems of linking teacher authority with gender, one thing is clear. *All* teachers possess an enormous capacity to influence students' lives positively. One's principled character and conduct, as powerfully evidenced by Mother Teresa and Gandhi, become every teacher's hidden superpower.

References

Ladson-Billings, G. (2006). "Yes, but how do we do it?": Practicing culturally relevant pedagogy. In J. Landsman & C. W. Lewis (Eds.), *White teachers/Diverse classrooms: A guide to building inclusive schools, promoting high expectations, and eliminating racism* (pp. 29–42). Stylus Publishing, LLC. https://digitalcommons.georgiasouthern.edu/esed5234-master/37

Ladson-Billings, G. (2021). *Culturally relevant pedagogy: Asking a different question.* Teachers College Press.

Glasser, W. (1998). *The quality school: Managing students without coercion.* Harper.

17

LOOK WHO'S TALKING

Gender, Teacher Authority, and the Use of Linguistic Space

Allyson Jule

The amount of talk in classrooms is remarkably gendered while many teachers are unaware of how their authoritative voice can limit the learning opportunities for students at all ages and stages of school life (Biggs & Edwards, 1991; Cameron, 2020, 2021). The silence of female students has been well documented (Coates, 2018; Coda et al., 2021; Gal, 1991; Jule, 2004; Lakoff, 1995; Myrick, 2021; Sunderland, 1998, 2000). Clearly, silence in the classroom by any participant—girl or boy—could mean a host of things, such as respecting the speaker, paying attention, using good listening skills, and deeply concentrating. Silence could also signal fear, intimidation, disinterest, or lack of concentration, but it could mean *silencing*, which is quite a different thing altogether. Silencing is to be made silent, to be kept quiet, and to be required to be a listener in the conversations of others. Much of my research has focused on silence in classrooms, on girls and women in particular being silent, and what the smallest classroom moments reveal about what may be silencing girls and young women in classrooms. As an educator, I have come to understand that it is too often the teachers themselves who limit girls' contributions to classroom discourse, and this silencing of girls is revealed in certain teaching methods and the use of an authoritative teacher voice that privileges some speakers over others.

This chapter explores the intersection of gender, classroom silence, and teaching methods in relation to female participation in various classrooms—one grade 2 classroom and two college classrooms. Specifically, I explore what I call "linguistic space." Linguistic space is the counting of words used by various speakers in any given situation: who speaks more? As a high school English teacher in the 1980s and 1990s, I noticed gender as a variable in classroom discussions. How were my students engaging in conversation? Talking more seemed to align with more authority or social power so that who talked was not a minor detail in

DOI: 10.4324/9781003140849-20

classroom life. When I first started researching linguistic space in the late 1990s, others were skeptical about its usefulness. Surely counting words was too simplistic: there are non-verbal cues, pauses, speed of talk, tone, volume, intonation, etc., that might be more significant than the amount of language spoken. Nevertheless, the counting of words used by each speaker in any classroom setting can reveal something about the female experience of schooling. Classrooms are often gendered spaces where teachers (often) inadvertently rehearse students into sexist stereotypic behaviors (McDowell & Klattenberg, 2019; Skelton, 2001).

Gendered Speech Patterns

There are gendered speech tendencies, patterns we perceive as masculine or feminine. Many of us see classrooms as key sites of gender role rehearsals, often with the teacher serving as a kind of gender coach. The value of silent girls seems to persist in spite of a perceived feminization of the classroom over the last 30 years or so and an effort to make successful many female students at various levels of education (Tannen, 2021; Thomas, 2021; Toohey, 2000).

Current gender scholars understand sex as the biological/physiological reality of the body as either male or female; sex is usually static and perhaps more aligned with personality and identity than the term *gender*. Gender is a sociological term that focuses on the behaviors that often (not always) align with one's sex: "masculine" behaviors for males and "feminine" behaviors for females—and these behaviors are not static, fixed, or unchanging. Gender appears vastly different in different settings and is always located in particular communities (Walkerdine, 1990; Cameron, 2006, 2020). We know that gender varies because of the ways gender plays out in various cultures across the world, across generations, in various school groups, in various age groups, and how it is influenced by socioeconomic status, race, ethnicity, level of education, membership in religious communities, and so on. Gender is something that reveals itself in response to certain situations and for certain effects, often for the basic need to belong and to feel accepted by one's surrounding community; including classroom communities.

When discussing gender, it is important to understand that we are not born masculine *or* feminine; we are born male or female (in most cases), and we perform a combination of many characteristics that could be understood as either or both masculine and feminine depending on culture and context. Of interest is what is known as "gendered speech patterns." In 1973, Robin Lakoff wrote *Language and Woman's Place*. Here she articulated some characteristics of feminine speech strategies that were located in her time and community, which was 1970s White New York Upper East Side. However, she presented these tendencies in speech as if these tendencies were universal to all women—an essential quality of the female sex. She identified a heavy use of backchannel support, more lexical hedges or fillers (e.g., "you know," "sort of," and "well, you see"), more tag questions (e.g., "she's very nice, isn't she?"), and more rising intonation on declaratives to sound like questions. She saw the use of intensifiers, hypercorrect grammar, and emphatic stress as feminine ways of speaking. Needless to say, the 50 years of research since Lakoff have challenged her list as limited and narrowly located in a particular community and not universal. Silence was not identified in Lakoff's original list, but researchers that came afterward did look closely at female silence. Lakoff's defense for not focusing or not noticing silence was that she couldn't focus on things that were not said; but more than a few of us have gone looking for exactly this: what isn't being said. Who isn't speaking? (Lakoff, 1995).

Looking for different gendered patterns of speech in classrooms—comparing girls and boys—is problematic because it is based on a troubling presupposition: different from what or from whom, exactly? Maybe the better question is when are they different from each other? And why? Importantly, why does this seem to matter so much to us as teachers? Girls and boys in classrooms may speak, write, read, think, and therefore learn in distinct ways. Could well be. But it is impossible to identify clearly specific or consistent gender patterns across all communities and in all various subsets. Most important to me is this: if a teacher holds the assumption that important thinking and behavioral patterns exist differently and distinctly for boys and girls and, later, for men and women, and that these differences are caused by biology or innate brain patterns, then that teacher is quite likely to use sex essentialism and narrow gender stereotypes as a guide to teaching rather than considering the complexities of gendered expectations or simply the complexities of each individual learner and the particular setting in which their students are located. Also, why create differences or magnify them or, at least, why reinforce them? For teachers in classrooms, an awareness of the complexity of gender roles and expectations is fundamental to creating safe learning spaces for all children. Teachers have the authority to influence such messages. What follows are the case studies: the three classrooms where a linguistic space analysis has been used to understand gendered patterns of speech in some classroom settings.

The Classrooms

Classroom #1; A Grade 2 Classroom: 11 Female Children and 9 Male Children

This school was unique. I had done research on this same group of students the previous year in their first grade that focused on literacy among young language learners. But, by grade 2, the group of children was quite different. What stood out quite clearly to me was how chatty the children were in grade 1, but how quiet they were by grade 2: the same children but different teachers. I was curious as to why. I took notes, videotaped the teacher-led lessons, transcribed classroom language, and engaged with the community in general over one school year.

What do teachers do that prompts certain students to speak more than others? The teacher in this classroom was a certified teacher, educated in one of

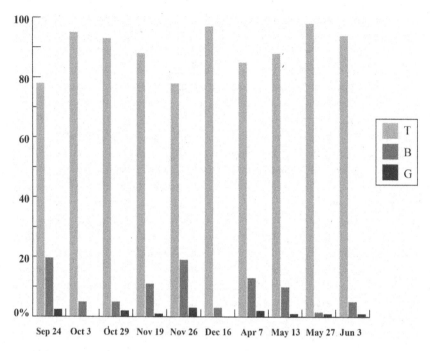

FIGURE 17.1 Linguistic Space by Word Count; Random Sampling of Teacher-Led Lessons, Including the Teacher

Canada's teacher education programs. What stood out immediately when viewing the transcripts was the significant amount of time the teacher spoke. In the first graph, the number of words spoken by Mrs. Green (not her real name) is represented by the light gray T bar: she speaks the most. Such a teacher-dominated discourse pattern is not surprising because the segments were pulled from the teacher-led lessons (see Figure 17.1).

In each of the ten segments randomly selected from the entire set of transcriptions, the teacher used 80%, on average, of the linguistic space (that is, she spoke 80% of the words spoken). In some lessons (such as December 16 and May 27) she spoke 100% of the words spoken. The students divided the remaining 20% (Boys are B; Girls are G). When removing the teacher's talk from the analysis, it is much clearer how many words the boys (B—light gray line) spoke compared to how many of the girls (G—dark gray line) spoke (see Figure 17.2).

It is almost a 10 to 1 word ratio over the course of the school year. Of these contributions, up to nine words were spoken at one time by the boys, while the girls only reached five word responses to questions or prompts from Mrs. Green. The linguistic participation on the part of all the students was minimal, but the

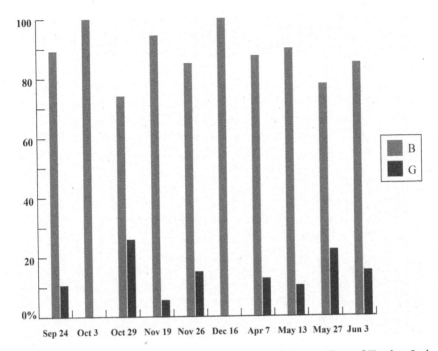

FIGURE 17.2 Linguistic Space by Word Count; Random Sampling of Teacher-Led Lessons, Excluding the Teacher

girls in particular appeared almost non-existent, certainly not necessary, for classroom lessons. It appeared to be the boys who spoke in response to the teacher significantly more often than the girls did in this classroom, and they said more when they did.

The most common teaching method anywhere is the IRF method, and it is seen here. Mrs. Green used this method during the teacher-led lessons: direct questioning (or Initiating—I), then a student responded in some way (Response—R), and then the teacher would offer feedback or follow up (Follow up—F). What I witnessed in this classroom by measuring linguistic space during the IRF lessons was a pattern: after each student response, Mrs. Green spoke more words to boys than to girls.

With a girl, she would affirm with a simple yes or nod of her head, but with a boy, it went differently. For example, Mrs. Green asked, "What is the capital city of the US?" If a girl answered correctly, "Washington, DC?," then Mrs. Green said, "Yes, that's right." With a boy with the same sort of questions, it was different. Mrs. Green asked, "What is the capital city of Canada?" If a boy said, "Ottawa," the teacher said, "Yes, That's right. Ottawa is the capital city of Canada. People think it's Toronto, but it's not." Both are considered positive feedback speech acts (Searle, 1969), but the more words used in interaction with her male students seemed to correlate with more talkative boys. That is, Mrs. Green seemed to prompt boys to contribute and, in contrast, seemed to offer minimal responses that dismissed the girls' contributions. Few of us as teachers are aware of how our speech mirrors and impacts gender roles and expectations within our own classrooms, and Mrs. Green was no exception. The classroom conversations, as seen in the transcripts, seemed to reveal that this classroom was often a conversation of the teacher with her male students. The girls were usually quiet listeners. Not all the boys spoke, but the majority of girls did not.

There were other hints of silencing apart from the formal IRF lessons, such as when the students presented their show and tell stories each day. Here's what happened to Zara when it was her turn:

[Zara gets up and tells a story. She has nothing to show but does have a story; there is no actual ball. She comes up to the front of the group and sits on the show and tell chair. Her classmates are seated around her; Mrs. Green is standing to the side—but still at the front of the classroom with her.]

ZARA: Um, uh, on Tuesday, I was, uh, at the store. It was Canadian Tire and my brother saw this, a baseball and then he started to bounce it, and then, um, my dad was calling my brother, and then, um, uh, when he was bouncing, my brother was bouncing the ball, and you know that fishing that where you catch fishes in?
TEACHER: A net?
ZARA: Yeah. And it went in there and then my brother went to my dad and then they both went like that and then I tried to, um, pull it down, and then the ball just came out.
TEACHER: Was it a basketball?
ZARA: No, uh, a baseball.
TEACHER: I didn't think baseballs bounce.
ZARA: No, uh . . .
TEACHER: A volleyball?
ZARA: Uh, yeah [nods]
TEACHER: Ah, cause I'm not sure. A tennis ball? A little Smith thing?
ZARA: Yeah. Yeah, that one. [Zara gets up and walks back to her desk.]
TEACHER: Okay. Cause I don't think baseballs bounce. But those little guys do. The tennis balls do. They go all over the place.
BOY: A soccer ball does.
TEACHER: Yeah, but she knows what a soccer ball is. It must be a ball that she's not, uh, sure of. Great. Okay.

In this example from Classroom Visit #29, Mrs. Green seemed uninterested in Zara's story, but rather in figuring out, what ball was used. Also, notice that Zara was referred to in the third person by the teacher, saying "She knows what a soccer ball is," a discussion she picks up with a boy who offers his suggestion that maybe it was a soccer ball. The teacher quickly moves her focus to the boy while Zara slips away from the front of the room with no other engagement with the teacher or with her classmates. The boy here gets more teacher engagement. Has Zara been silenced? I suggest she has been silenced by her teacher's minimal response to her contribution.

By contrast, a boy's show and tell went more like this:

JOE: On the weekend, I went to the hockey game and got this puck.
TEACHER: Oh my! The actual puck?
BOY: Which game?
JOE: The Canucks. I went with my dad and uncle.
TEACHER How fun! Do you go to all the games?
JOE: Just sometimes.
TEACHER: Who has a question for Joe?
BOY: Who was playing . . .?

Notice the teacher engagement, the use of his name, and the interaction with some classmates to follow in Classroom Visit #31. The larger question is: are girls inadvertently being educated to do their work correctly and sit quietly and follow all the rules and, hence, are not given the same opportunities to speak aloud, to try out ideas, or to contribute freely to the dynamics of the class? Does this matter? I wonder if missing out on public discourse results in girls not learning how to speak out in such circumstances and so are more hesitant to do so. When I discussed these observations of the quiet girls in her classroom with Mrs. Green herself, she offered an explanation: that these girls were like that, she said, "they are nice quiet girls." She felt that the boys were naughtier and needed more interaction to stay focused. This caused me to wonder: do we think that girls are nice when they're quiet? Or the inverse: do we think boys' calling out is the expectation of boys?

Researchers, such as Valerie Walkerdine (1990), have explored thousands of classrooms and found patterns (such as teachers holding the eye gaze of boy students longer, using boys' names more than they used girls' names). Example: "Peter, be quiet; girls, shush." Many teachers say this pattern is because boys need more attention to stay on task and that the girls are usually paying attention and doing their work. This may be, but it also may be that there are sexist assumptions teachers hold—some more than others—and that these assumptions influence class participation. Teachers, as the authoritative voices, matter significantly in guiding classroom conversations.

Classrooms #2 and #3: Two College Classes

Another example of the authoritative teacher's voice is seen in a very different setting: university. Classrooms #2 and #3 are graduate classrooms that also reveal a gendered educational space where authoritative speakers are valued (Apriyanto & Anum, 2018), and gender appears to influence classroom participation (Aziz et al., 2018; Sunderland, 2000). This graduate college markets itself as "an international graduate school of Christian studies" (school website). It also advertises itself as a "trans-denominational graduate school," not affiliated with any specific Christian denomination. At the time of the study, 40% of the student population were Canadian with 40% from the United States; the remaining 20% were from other areas including Britain, Australia, Asia, Africa, and Latin America. There were 350 full-time students and approximately 350 part-time students. Because the college is only for graduate students, most were over the age of 25 and all had one degree behind them. There were roughly 60% male to 40% female students.

The college employed 19 full-time faculty members: 17 were male and two were female. The large lecture classes at this college were taught exclusively by male faculty. I focused on two large classes in particular because they shared the male:female ratio that existed in the college at largely 60 male:40 female with 120 male students and 80 female students. I attended the classes for a full term, measuring the linguistic space of the women in these courses. Both courses were compulsory, and both filled the lecture hall with 200 students. Both classes were held once a week during the Fall term. Both classes ran for three hours with one or two breaks. Both male lecturers were known as senior scholars in their fields; both were well published and well known.

The Male Lecturers

Dr. MacKay began each class with approximately five minutes of announcements (such as where to collect graded assignments) before beginning his lecture. Sometimes one of the tutorial assistants (all of whom were male) would announce something (such as the sale of Christmas party tickets) before Dr. MacKay would ascend the podium. A microphone was usually clipped onto the lapel of his suit by a sound technician to record the lecture and to allow the entire lecture hall to hear adequately. Dr. MacKay would lecture with notes. He spoke in a clear, steady voice; he rarely used humor or personal anecdotes, and he demonstrated a more "aloud reading" style of performance discourse. At the end of the three hours (including one half-hour break), 20 minutes would be given over to questions from the students. For the 12 weeks of lectures in Dr. MacKay's class, not one woman asked a question. Three to five male students would ask suitable but often long and rambling questions between one and five minutes, all higher-order questions spoken into standing microphones. Each week, different male students would ask questions; there were a few repeat speakers. Dr. MacKay's responses would follow the amount of linguistic space used by the questioners, generally running four to eight minutes. All students who asked questions during the question time were male.

Dr. Jones's class appeared less formal than Dr. MacKay's. Dr. Jones's manner appeared quite natural and relaxed. He was warm and friendly and was very welcoming to me as a visitor/researcher in his room. He did not wear a suit and often arrived late and with scattered papers. He usually began his lectures with a joke or humorous anecdote from his family life. He used PowerPoint images that would include particular Bible passages under examination in the lecture or photographs of Biblical sites or maps. Dr. Jones used a more "fresh talk" lecture style that is more spontaneous and less structured. Dr. Jones gave a very long one-hour break. During the hour, Dr. Jones would retreat to his office; the students ate their lunches or went to the library. He also gave time for questions at the end of the lecture, sometimes ten minutes but averaging only seven minutes most weeks. In the 12 weeks I spent sitting in on Dr. Jones's lectures, one woman asked a 20-second information/clarity question: "Why did St. Paul journey there first?" It was brief and answered just as briefly, but it stood out to me because it illustrated a lack of presence for women in this context. In spite of the fact that there were 80 women in the class (40%), they consumed almost no linguistic space whatsoever.

The one speaking aloud in public contexts often connects closely with power. In classrooms, the most vocal speaker is usually the teacher. It is the teacher's prerogative to hold the floor or allocate turns to students; the teacher's centrality and power are revealed through such language practices. Some suggest that the one talking is perceived as the valuable one, the one knowing (Skelton, 2001). Those who serve as listeners appear to be the ones seeking the knowledge. What is said aloud in groups sets up the speaker as significant and of greater value: the speakers perform power, status, and significance; the listeners perform an attentive and supportive role.

I asked six women who attended both courses why they had not asked any questions while in these classes. Ruthie was the woman who asked a short question in Dr. Jones's class; her response to my question is recorded here first:

RUTHIE: I was actually really nervous when I got up to ask Dr. Jones that question but I really wanted to know and he didn't seem to be getting close to saying what I wanted to understand.
LOIS: I have noticed that most lecturers respond to people who are most like themselves so I think the guys asked the questions all the time because they respond better to the men as professors. I ask questions all the time in the classes I take led by women. I think this is because I relate to them better.
BETHANY: Dr. MacKay is fairly aggressive and if you don't sound intelligent, he makes no excuses for you. It's his pedagogy, not his personality as such. He is just very masculine and old-school.

SARAH: I don't know why I didn't ask a question in Dr. Jones's class. Maybe I did feeler weaker—I am weaker! They are the experts.

JUDITH: I never ask questions in such a large space. I'd have to get up and stand by the mic and I'd never do that. Besides, I didn't know what I would have asked. It was all new to me.

PRISCILLA: I would rather someone else asked for me that doing it myself. I usually wait it out and usually my question gets answered without my having to ask it. I also think that the men knew what they were talking about and so I was in learning mode, not speaking mode.

Their responses to my observation were illuminating. The use and support of an authoritative discourse—lecturing and speaking out in large groups—appear to be a way men engage more easily with academic life. The profiling of power and significance as something understood as masculine seems to be at work here. Is it that the legitimate participants are male with the females present only to listen? The women themselves seem to suggest as much. The female experience here seems to be a quiet one and experienced differently in various contexts—at least this is how it appears in this group and was described as such by Lois. "I think the guys asked the questions all the time because they respond better to the men as professors."

Both Dr. MacKay and Dr. Jones clearly used most of the available linguistic space during their respective lectures. But, of the remaining linguistic space, men used disproportionately more. It wasn't even close to the 60:40 ratio of men to women in the student population. The women did not speak. For the entire term, the women attended and listened, but they did not say anything aloud during the Q & A. Why was this? The responses given by the women themselves offer some possible reasons as to why they remained silent. Clearly, not all the male students asked questions; some of them also remained silent all term as well. However, all the female students here were silent (the exception being Ruthie, but her contribution was minimal). Instead, the women appeared as consistently supportive listeners. When the women responded to my observation that they had not asked questions during the term, in general, they seemed not to see themselves as equipped or ready or not able to perform in such a circumstance. Judith said, "I never ask questions in such a large space," and Priscilla said, "I'd rather someone else asked the question." That she sees listening as learning and speaking as something else (a performance of something else) highlights the messages girls and women receive about their role in classrooms; their silence is affirmed, encouraged, and valued.

To belong fully here, all members have accommodated themselves to the gender expectations of women to be quiet participants and supporters of hegemonic masculinity. It seems to be that those who participate have made such accommodations with little, if any, conflict. Also, because of the transference of information/knowledge that lecturing presupposes, the silence of female students during the question-answer time (a time they could speak) affirms the possibility that women behave quietly as a way of performing a specific and understood femininity.

Discussion

A domination of linguistic space (Christine Skelton, 2001, calls it "the school and machismo") appears to be a way male students experience or use educational opportunities: their speaking aloud is valued, using skills that they have learned and developed throughout their education. Female students learn other skills, however, such as how to be attentive and quiet, not to be too aggressive or overly independent in their thinking, and to be sure to give space and attention to the teachers and/or males speaking around them. There are millions of other classrooms around the world that would each reveal certain gendered performances—and likely with silence as a key element of classroom life for many students—often girls (Walkerdine, 1990).

Important for teachers to understand is that talk is central to a good education. It is central to the learning process, regardless of the subject or level—all classroom learning is based on talk: teacher talk and student talk. Talk is a tool of learning—maybe the main tool of learning. We talk our way into understanding things. It's not just the listening to lessons (or lectures or stories) but the conversations that propel thoughts, attitudes, opinions, and knowledge. Some say we start to talk by mimicking others and that we continue to do so. We sound things out; we try things on through spoken words, becoming more of who we are through speaking. What happens if gendered expectations on the part of the teacher slant these opportunities?

Many researchers, such as Deborah Cameron (2006, 2021), Jennifer Coates (2018), and Jane Sunderland (1998), have suggested that all age groups seem to reveal this similar pattern of a more male-dominated linguistic space. And this has now come into the public eye, including mass media: who talks more signals who matters more. We see the rise of Beyoncé's Ban Bossy campaign and Sheryl Sandburg's (2013) bestseller, *Lean In*, as based on this reality that many women say very little in public spaces, in public roles. Hollywood actor, Geena Davis, and her See Jane research company has been keeping tabs on how Hollywood portrays male and female on the screen. Most recently, Hannah Anderson and Matt Daniels (2016) explored film dialogue from over 2,000 Hollywood screenplays. They said they wanted some "real data" (online) on the possibility that it might be true that males speak more than females in our society. They googled thousands of screenplays and matched each character's lines to the actor. From there, they compiled the number of words spoken (i.e., Linguistic Space) by male and female characters. They discovered that men speak more often than women in 15 Disney's princess films, an observation which seemed counter-intuitive. Surely the girl-centric stories would have more girls speaking, but no. Anderson and Daniels validated the claim and doubled the sample size to include 30 Disney films, including Pixar. Their results: 22 of 30 Disney films have a male majority of the dialogue. Even in films with female leads, such as *Mulan*, the dialogue swings male. Mushu, her male protector dragon, has 50% more words of dialogue than Mulan herself. Anderson and Daniels ultimately looked at 2,000 screenplays and declared that "white men dominate" (online).

As was the case with both Mrs. Green's classroom and the college students, counting the number of words is a helpful way to understand who has significance. As educators, we need to understand better how gender and education are inevitably and reliably linked and intimately connected. It may be that silence among female students functions as a way of being in classroom communities that prepare them for continued silence in the workplace. Being silent serves female students well in many ways (good grades, school success), but this silence also rehearses them into silence, participating in their own learning environments by saying nothing much at all and, as a result, limiting a full learning experience that engages in group discussions and future public roles.

Conclusion

Effective teachers demonstrate a sensitivity toward gender issues in their teaching, carefully and intentionally choosing methods that will further their students' growth and learning. The careful choice of words used to communicate with students and the creation of warm, open, and conversational spaces are part of what good teachers do. Students, including girls, must be prepared, coached to talk in class; they need teachers who use their authoritative voice to encourage their contributions.

Whatever one's age or temperament, speaking aloud in public discourse reveals significance. Attending to linguistic space is important, not only so that girls and young women can invest and learn in the communities but also because all voices can contribute to learning, to the sharing of ideas, to the necessary discussions, and to relevant new ways of thinking and knowing. If girls don't speak, everyone is diminished. Students need teachers who pay attention to who is speaking, and they need to know that their teachers—and society more generally—want to hear from them, not in a "what kind of ball is it" way of listening but really listening.

Because speaking during teacher-directed lessons is an important way for students to engage with ideas, thoughts, and creativity, teachers need to be thoughtful about the impacts gender has on speaking and learning opportunities. Classroom experiences are important in revealing who matters; everyone's voice needs to be heard to create meaningful educational settings.

References

Anderson, H., & Daniels, M. (2016). Film dialogue from 2,000 screen-plays, broken down by gender and age. *Pudding* (April). https://pudding.cool/2017/03/film-dialogue/index.html

Apriyanto, S., & Anum, A. (2018). Gender dynamics on speaking interaction in the college classroom. *Journal of English Language Teaching and Applied Linguistics, 4*(2).

Aziz, F., Quraishi, U., & Kazi, A. S. (2018). Factors behind classroom participation of secondary school students (a gender based analysis). *Universal Journal of Educational Research, 6*(2), 211–217.

Biggs, A., & Edwards, V. (1991). 'I treat them all the same': Teacher-pupil talk in multi-ethnic classrooms. *Language and Education, 5*, 161–176.

Cameron, D. (2006). Theorizing the female voice in public contexts. In J. Baxter (Ed.), *Speaking out: The female voice in public contexts* (pp. 3–20). Palgrave Macmillan.

Cameron, D. (2020). Language and gender: Mainstreaming and the persistence of patriarchy. *International Journal of the Sociology of Language, 2020*(263), 25–30. https://doi.org/10.1515/ijsl-2020-2078

Cameron, D. (2021). The impact of language and gender studies: Public engagement and wider communication. In B. Angouri & J. Baxter (Eds.), *The Routledge handbook of language, gender and sexuality*. Routledge. https://ebrary.net/147559/education/impact_language_gender_studies_public_engagement_wider_communication

Coates, J. (2018). The rise and fall (and rise) of Mars and Venus in language and gender research. In G. Olson, D. Hartley, M. Horn-Schott, & L. Schmidt (Eds.), *Beyond gender: An advanced introduction to futures of feminist and sexuality studies* (pp. 25–50). Routledge.

Coda, J., Cahnmann-Taylor, M., & Jiang, L. (2021). "It takes time for language to change": Challenging classroom heteronormativity through teaching proficiency through reading and storytelling (TPRS). *Journal of Language, Identity & Education, 20*(2), 90–102.

Gal, S. (1991). Between speech and silence: The problematics of research on language and gender. *Papers in Pragmatics, 3*(1), 1–38.

Jule, A. (2004). *Gender and silence in a language classroom: Sh-shushing the girls*. Palgrave Macmillian.

Lakoff, R. (1973). Language and woman's place. *Language in Society, 2*(1), 45–80.

Lakoff, R. (1995). Cries and whispers: The shattering of the silence. In K. Hall & M. Bucholtz (Eds.), *Gender articulated: Language and the socially constructed self* (pp. 25–50). Routledge.

McDowell, J., & Klattenberg, R. (2019). Does gender matter? A cross-national investigation of primary class-room discipline. *Gender and Education, 31*(8), 947–965.

Myrick, C. (2021). "Men could get up in front of a classroom and say any old thing . . .": Faculty perceptions of language and gender in higher education. In G. Clements & M. J. Petray (Eds.), *Linguistic discrimination in U.S. higher education: Power, prejudice, impacts, and remedies* (pp. 110–138). Routledge.

Sandburg, S. (2013). *Lean in: Women, work, and the will to lead*. Knopf.

Searle, J. R. (1969). *Speech acts*. Cambridge University Press.

Skelton, C. (2001). *Schooling the boys: Masculinities and primary education*. Open University Press.

Sunderland, J. (1998, January 1). Girls being quiet: A problem for foreign language classrooms. *Language Teaching Research, 2*(1), 48–82.

Sunderland, J. (2000, April 1). New understandings of gender and language classroom research: Texts, teacher talk and student talk. *Language Teaching Research, 4*(2), 149–173.

Tannen, D. (2021). Three decades in the field of gender and language: A personal perspective. *Gender & Language, 15*(2), 232–241.
Thomas, R. N. (2021). Elementary teachers' contributions to classroom gender climate: An exploration of teacher attitudes and classroom behaviours. *Ball State University. Dissertation*, 28414320.
Toohey, K. (2000). *Learning English at school: Identity, social relations and classroom practice.* Multilingual Matters.
Walkerdine, V. (1990). *Schoolgirl fictions.* Verso.

18
INTERROGATING THE RELATIONSHIP BETWEEN A TEACHER'S RACE AND CLASSROOM AUTHORITY

Malini Sivasubramaniam

With reference to classrooms characterized by racial differences, some researchers point out that race plays an important role in productive teacher–student authority relationships (Dickar, 2008; Ford & Sassi, 2014; Pace & Hemmings, 2007). It is argued that teaching and learning suffer when racialized teachers' authority is contested within the classroom context (Pace & Hemmings, 2007). Lisa Delpit points out that in the United States, the cultural knowledge of Black educators is often devalued, and she calls this lack of communication related to race, culture, learning, and the teaching profession a part of "the silenced dialogue" (1995). Given the racial, linguistic, and cultural diversity of student populations in many immigrant-focused countries, including Canada, and a lack of concomitant diversity in the teaching profession, there is much consensus that giving voice to this silence is crucial, and a large body of research supports the assertion that "Students who share racial and/or gender characteristics with their teachers tend to report higher levels of personal effort, happiness in class, feeling cared for, student-teacher communication, post-secondary motivation, and academic engagement" (Egalite & Kisida, 2017, p. 14).

In response, researchers have largely endorsed the call for hiring more racialized teachers to yield more cultural and racial alignment between teachers and students (Hopson, 2013; Solomon et al., 2005), a call reflected in changing policy. Some have argued that such a policy approach is reductionistic because the assumption that racialized educators will automatically be effective teachers or role models for racialized students ignores differences among students, attending only to their skin color (Martino & Rezai-Rashti, 2012). Instead of trying to create race-based role models, it is more important to acknowledge that conversations about race and authority are complex and multi-faceted. In this chapter, I interrogate the relationship between race and teacher authority by examining

DOI: 10.4324/9781003140849-21

the dominant discourse about race and teacher authority as it relates to racialized educators and I show that reducing race to notions of racial matching between teachers and students can be disempowering, resulting in a superficial treatment of these difficult conversations, and creating tensions within educational contexts.

Demographic Gap

In Ontario, the largest province in Canada, the 2016 census reported about 250 ethnic origins represented in the population. Of those living in Toronto, the largest city in the country, 51.4% self-identified as a visible minority, representing 77.5% of Ontario's total visible minority population. However, data from the Toronto District School Board (TDSB), the largest and most diverse school board in Canada, showed that of the 213 students who were expelled over the five-year period (2011–2012 to 2015–2016), 48% were Black students. Further analysis of the expulsion data showed that Black, Aboriginal (or Indigenous), Mixed, and Middle Eastern students are disproportionately expelled from TDSB schools when compared to their representation among all students (James & Turner, 2017). The vast majority of the TDSB's expelled students were males in secondary schools. Similarly, Black students also have the highest dropout rates (20%) compared to White (11%) and other racialized students (9%). Concurrently, according to the 2016 census, only 1.8% of elementary and secondary teachers in Canada were Black.

Such disparity in numbers has been identified as a factor in the well-documented race-based achievement gap. With reference to Black parents' disillusionment with the public education system, Brown noted that of those "students born in English-speaking Islands in the Caribbean who entered Grade 9 in 2000, 40 per cent had dropped out by 2005" (Brown, 2006, para. 17). The report stated further that this high dropout rate "applie[d] more to male second–generation Caribbean students than their female peers" (James, 2011, p. 193). These findings corroborate the 1994 Royal Commission on Learning in Ontario (RCOL) report that used the term "education in crisis" to describe the state of the Toronto public school system (RCOL as cited in James, 2011, p. 199). In this volume, Patrick (Chapter 15) points out that the Afrocentric school system was created in response to these faltering efforts to integrate African culture and learning better within the education system. Such race-based data have enabled school boards to address in more focused ways systemic racism and racial discrimination in their efforts to improve student performance.

A demographic gap clearly affects many school systems, including the Toronto school system. Black and racialized students are reportedly disenfranchised within school systems in both Canada and the United States (Delpit, 1995; Egbo, 2009; Sharp, 2020). However, it is important to be aware that issues of race and class are also inextricably intertwined. A recent paper, "*Teacher Diversity in Canada: Leaky Pipelines, Bottlenecks, and Glass Ceilings*" (Ryan et al., 2009), reported that

18.6% of Toronto's education labor force were teachers of color that year in a city that was 42.4% non-White (Sharp, 2020). This chapter takes as its starting point Giroux and McLaren's (1990) idea of critical pedagogy; they argue that "school practices need to be informed by a public philosophy that addresses how to construct ideological and institutional conditions in which the lived experience of empowerment for the vast majority of learners becomes the defining feature of schooling" (p. 156). Within this context, teachers and learners are viewed as change agents who, when empowered, have the potential to (re)address issues of race and class within the classroom.

Authentic Authority

Effective teaching requires teachers to assert and negotiate issues of authority in the classroom to ensure improved student learning and achievement. While teachers have traditionally been esteemed and respected in the classroom, Chesler and Young (2007) contend that in present times this authority relationship requires continuous negotiation. According to Chesler and Young (2007), two areas where students often covertly and overtly challenge teacher authority are subject-area expertise and the teacher's role. However, both these areas are also impacted by the intersecting social group identities of teachers, particularly that of race-ethnicity and gender (Black, 2021; Wright & Weeks, 2003; Pace & Hemmings, 2007). For example, Black (2021) notes that despite increasing numbers of female and minority teachers in predominantly White and male-dominated community colleges in the United States, empirical research reveals that the former group of teachers often experience high levels of stress because of how they are treated by students in the classroom. When teachers' authority is not valued within the classroom because of either their race or gender, then teaching and learning are inevitably negatively impacted.

Further, social expectations of teacher authority also vary cross-culturally (Choi & Lim, 2021; Lai et al., 2015; Pace & Hemmings, 2007; Subedi, 2008). For example, in comparing teacher authority in Chinese and American cultures, Lai et al. (2015) reported that

> Teachers in the United States are expected to behave in a more impersonal manner in fulfilling institutional roles and upholding impartiality, and their roles are to support students' development and encourage students to initiate communication and voice intellectual disagreement. In contrast, teachers in China are regarded as experts in the subject areas, role models and moral agents, and are expected to be respected by students and parents both inside and outside the classroom as authority figures. Intellectual disagreement and student-initiated free expression and thinking are regarded as disruptive behaviours and a challenge to teacher authority in this context.
> *(p. 13)*

Teacher authority is thus viewed differently in different sociocultural contexts. Teachers with an Asian background teaching in schools within a Western culture face unique challenges to their authority (Lai et al., 2015). Correspondingly, teachers who teach in a different cultural context may encounter more challenges in establishing authority than in teaching in one's own cultural context.

Racialized Teaching

Ford and Sassi (2014) point out that race influences teachers' conceptions of authority. The examination of this authority involves not only the relationship between teachers and students in the classroom teaching and learning context but also between teachers in the school environment. An examination of the literature reveals three relevant conclusions about these configurations, conclusions that demonstrate how problematic these relationships can be.

Caught in the Crossfire

Wright (1998) used the metaphor "caught in the crossfire" to describe the dual pressures that Black teachers experience who are caught between professional obligations to colleagues and a sense of loyalty expected by students. Black students sometimes demand that teachers of similar race act in solidarity with them and be their advocates by raising issues with the principal or use their institutional power on their behalf. The same can be inferred for other racialized students. Such demands inevitably create various dilemmas for racialized teachers. Dickar (2008) noted how the Black teachers she interviewed pointed out that the "demands of solidarity expose them to insult as well as creating conflicting demands on their allegiances" (p. 122). Such demands, as Dickar (2008) observed, place racialized teachers in a precarious position or "in the crossfire" because while students expect solidarity due to their shared race, teachers also have professional roles that demand solidarity with their colleagues.

Similarly, Chesler and Young (2007) described the discomfort that some teachers feel when students encroach on professional boundaries by virtue of race. As one teacher related:

> I've had students [of color] after class come up to me and hug me. I'm not a touchy-feely person . . . It makes me very uncomfortable. I think they mean it positively, but I also wonder if they mean it as, "Well, we're both black, and there's some connection." So . . . I simply say, "I'm not unreasonable, [but] look, I'm your teacher; you're my student; we're not friends."
>
> *(p. 15)*

In her doctoral research, Hopson (2013) heard teachers express similar sentiments in her interviews with 21 racialized teachers. A consistent theme that emerged from her interviews was that racialized teachers face more challenges when working with students from similar cultural backgrounds. Challenges arose because "these teachers have felt as though their authority was undermined by the fact that students viewed them as an uncle or auntie, and that their approachability in this regard enabled students to treat them with less respect or formality" (Hopson, 2013, p. 44). In light of her findings, Hopson (2013) suggested that any teacher can be a role model for students, and, in fact, trying to match students racially to teachers had the deleterious, reductionist effect of reducing individual differences to race and did not serve the interests of the teachers or the students. Another theme emerging from the interviews with Hopson's participants was the desire to be recognized first and foremost as a good teacher, and not as an individual who is a good teacher because of their racial background. One participant voiced it in the following way:

> If you're a good teacher, and a good teacher is a good teacher, good leader, you can be a role model to all kids because you have a certain core set of values. And I think that those core set of values to me is universal . . . If you have these universal values, humility, caring, equity, justice, you can be a role model to a lot of different students.
>
> *(p. 133)*

While racialized teachers were cognizant of the complexities of race in the classroom, this teacher's comments also suggest that they did not allow it to define their professional role nor constrain it.

Navigating Marginality and Authority

Institutional norms and culture can also contribute to how teacher authority is devalued or affirmed. In acknowledging their marginal positions as Asian, immigrant, female, or educators of color, Choi and Lim (2021) point out from their teaching experience that they experienced many moments of self-doubt and were unsure how to position themselves in relation to students who bluntly dismissed their authority because of their accented English or their racial or immigrant status. Such disrespect threatens classroom authority. In response, they describe how they learned "to vigilantly seek and intentionally exploit a point of connection with students in order to achieve [their] teaching goals" (p. 11). Such connections involve sharing references to their homeland experiences in their classrooms, despite experiencing some cognitive dissonance when they do so. For example, Choi and Lim (2021) often made reference to their educational and professional experiences in South Korea and how that changed coming to the United States as a point of shared connection with students when discussing marginalization and privilege.

However, race and teacher authority cannot be simply reduced to a racial affiliation between a teacher and a student. Martino and Rezai-Rashti (2012) interviewed racialized students specifically about their perspectives on the significance of teacher race and gender and concluded that most minority students do not place inordinate importance on racial matching. On the contrary, according to the same study, students expressed negative feelings about having a teacher with a similar racial background because they felt that these teachers would have more rigid behavioral expectations of them.

(Re)conceptualizing the Warm Demander

Teachers may hold different conceptions of authority than their students (Delpit, 1995). For example, Ford and Sassi (2014) suggested that in racially diverse classrooms, racial differences may affect how classroom authority is constructed. Much of the educational research supporting this claim is drawn from the notion of warm demanders initially developed by Kleinfeld (1975). Applying the concept to teacher authority in classrooms and schools with a large Black student population, Ford and Sassi (2014, p. 41) contend that a warm demander teacher is one who "provides a tough-minded, no-nonsense, structured, and disciplined classroom environment." Similarly, in her chapter on culturally responsive teaching in this volume (Chapter 15), Patrick claims that warm demander teachers, those who are open to learning about their students and provide a warm and safe learning environment while maintaining high expectations for all students, will more likely enable students to thrive.

However, this warm demander approach is often premised on the notion of a shared cultural and racial heritage, in other words, Black teachers teaching Black students. Using a comparative analysis of one White and one Black teacher, Ford and Sassi (2014) compared a White teacher's approach to authority with that of an African American warm demander and offered a reconceptualization of the warm demander approach to describe what White teachers might need to do differently to employ the warm demander's stance effectively. Ford and Sassi (2014) suggested that the warm demander's approach is applicable to other contexts if teachers understand and employ culturally relevant pedagogy. In addition, they found that the teachers who were successful in transferring the warm demander approach across the cultural divide "maintained high expectations for their students' academic achievement and behavior and created structured learning environments characterized by effective disciplinary strategies, warmly demanding that their students change their behavior" (p. 59).

Implications and Conclusion

Teacher education programs are important sites for discussions related to race and classroom authority. Critical dialogues about race and equity in education should prepare Pre-Service Teachers to carry on these conversations about race and authority and to acknowledge the tensions these expectations produce (Egbo,

2009). The professional development of teachers must continue to attend to the impacts that race and other social identities have on their work, particularly for racialized teachers who need to negotiate tensions between individual, racial, and professional identities. However, in increasingly diverse classrooms, it is important to go beyond tokenism. While increasing the number of racialized educators visibly increases diversity and representation in schools and classrooms and helps to build rapport with students and families, in and of itself such an increase does not necessarily translate into more effective teaching. Nor does it give due credence to the multiplicity of teacher social identities that shape their teaching. The reality, however, is that "having the same or a similar background to the children is not a sufficient condition for winning their respect or gaining recognition as a 'role model'" (Martino, & Rezai-Rashti, p. 43). Ultimately, it is far more important for teachers to be trained to be able to disrupt the dominant discourses, to (re)connect and (re)conceptualize their roles as warm demanders of students and be teachers who are committed to demanding excellence from all students, and to focus on issues of equity and inclusion rather than rely only of racialized representation on the teaching staff.

References

Black, M. (2021). Exploring relationships between a teacher's race-ethnicity and gender and student teaching expectations, *Education Inquiry*, *12*(2), 202–216. https://doi.org/10.1080/20004508.2020.1824343

Brown, L. (2006, June 23). Dropout, failure rates linked to language: Study compares countries of origin Spanish-speaking parents worried. *The Toronto Star.*

Chesler, M., & Young, A. A. Jr. (2007, Fall). Faculty members' social identities and classroom authority. *New Directions for Teaching and Learning*, *111*, 11–20. https://doi.org/10.1002/tl.281

Choi, J., & Lim, J. (2021). Knowledge, authority, and positionality in Asian immigrant female faculty teaching diversity classes. *Multicultural Learning and Teaching*, *16*(2), 103–117. https://doi.org/10.1515/mlt-2019-0007

Delpit, L. (1995). *Other people's children: Cultural conflict in the classroom.* The New Press.

Dickar, M. (2008). Hearing the silenced dialogue: An examination of the impact of teacher race on their experiences. *Race, Ethnicity, and Education*, *11*(2), 115–132. https://doi.org/10.1080/13613320802110233

Egalite, A., & Kisida, R. (2017). *The effects of teacher match on academic perceptions and attitudes* (Department of Educational Leadership Working Paper Series). North Carolina State University.

Egbo, B. (2009). *Teaching for diversity in Canadian schools.* Pearson, Prentice Hall.

Ford, A. C., & Sassi, K. (2014). Authority in cross-racial teaching and learning (re) considering the transferability of warm demander approaches. *Urban Education*, *49*(1), 39–74. https://doi.org/10.1177/0042085912464790

Giroux, H. A., & McLaren, P. (1990). Critical pedagogy and rural education: A challenge from Poland. *Peabody Journal of Education*, *67*(4), 154–165. ttps://doi.org/10.1080/01619569009538705

Hopson, R. L. (2013). *"People like me": Racialized teachers and the call for community* (Unpublished doctoral dissertation), OISE/University of Toronto. https://tspace.library.utoronto.ca/bitstream/1807/43595/1/Hopson_Robin_L_201311_PhD_thesis.pdf

James, C. E. (2011). Multicultural education in a color-blind society. In C. A. Grant & A. Portera (Eds.), *Intercultural and multicultural education: Enhancing global interconnectedness* (pp. 191–210). Routledge.

James, C. E., & Turner, T. (2017). *Towards race equity in education: The schooling of black students in the Greater Toronto Area.* York University. https://edu.yorku.ca/files/2017/04/Towards-Race-Equity-in-Education-April-2017.pdf

Kleinfeld, J. (1975). Effective teachers of Eskimo and Indian students. *The School Review, 83*(2), 01–344. https://doi.org/10.1086/443191

Lai, C., Hu, J., & Mingyue, G. (2015). Understanding legitimate teacher authority in a cross-cultural teaching context: Pre-service Chinese language teachers undertaking teaching practicum in international schools in Hong Kong. *Journal of Education for Teaching: International Research and Pedagogy, 41*(4), 1–18. https://doi.org/10.1080/02607476.2015.1081717

Martino, W. J., & Rezai-Rashti, G. M. (2012). *Gender, race, and the politics of role modeling.* Routledge.

Pace, J., & Hemmings, A. (2007). Understanding authority in classrooms: A review of theory, ideology, and research. *Review of Educational Research, 77*(1), 4–27. https://doi.org/10.3102/003465430298489

Ryan, J., Pollock, K., & Antonelli, F. (2009). Teacher diversity in Canada: Leaky pipelines, bottlenecks, and glass ceilings. *Canadian Journal of Education, 32* (3), 591–617. www.jstor.org/stable/canajeducrevucan.32.3.591

Sharp, M. (2020, June 18). Breaking the cycle of racism in Ontario's schools. *National Observer.* www.nationalobserver.com/2020/06/18/analysis/breaking-cycle-racism-ontarios-schools

Solomon, R. P., Portelli, J. P., Daniel, B.-J., & Campbell, A. (2005). The discourse of denial: How white teacher candidates construct race, racism and 'white privilege'. *Race Ethnicity and Education, 8*(2), 147–169. https://doi.org/10.1080/13613320500110519

Subedi, B. (2008). Contesting racialization: Asian immigrant teachers' critiques and claims of teacher authenticity. *Race, Ethnicity, and Education, 11*(1), 57–70. https://doi.org/10.1080/13613320701845814

Wright, C. (1998). Caught in the crossfire: Reflections of a black female ethnographer. In P. Connolly & B. Troyna (Eds.), *Researching racism in education: Politics, theory and practice* (pp. 67–78). Open University Press.

Wright, C., & Weeks, D. (2003). Race and gender in the contestation and resistance of teacher authority and school sanctions: The case of African Caribbean pupils in England. *Comparative Education Review, 47*(1), 3–45. https://doi.org/10.1086/373962

PART 4
Narratives From the Field and Special Situations

For most chapters in this section, Badley and Patrick tapped colleagues or former students in their respective programs to write about their experiences teaching in a variety of contexts. Each teaching context is unique, shaped as it is by the community in which it is situated, the vision of its leaders, and the role of specific teachers in it. Each context requires teachers to navigate a complex set of relationships, cultures, and authorities. Teachers begin to develop their ability to be flexible and to interact with diversity and complexity in their teacher preparation program when they complete at least one but usually several school practicums. For each practicum, student teachers, also known as Pre-Service Teachers (PSTs) or Teacher Candidates, begin as guests in another teacher's classroom and must build a relationship with their MT based on trust and communication. Wise PSTs take the opportunity to explore the nature of trust-filled student–teacher relationships and what shared classroom authority might look like.

The practicum experience is not the only time teachers draw upon their inner resources of resilience and adaptation. This occurs when teachers move from one school or school district to another, or they start working with a new principal who operates with a different vision. Other changes demand even more. For example, a Substitute Teacher, also known as a teacher on call or a Supply Teacher, regularly needs strategies to build relationships with new students, perhaps every day of the week. Those who choose to work in a new country often find themselves having to learn a new culture while navigating new educational philosophies and learning to work with different instructional and assessment philosophies. And those who take positions in rural and remote communities may also experience culture shock as they enter communities where important relationships were established long before their arrival. It can be difficult when the teacher is one of only a few new people in the school.

But as all the contributors to this section describe, when teachers commit to doing their best for all their students and when they work on building relationships in new contexts, trust happens and relationships blossom. While the challenges of teaching or changing teaching contexts cannot be minimized, the rewards can outweigh the challenges by far. When teachers are open to the possibilities, willing to grow and demonstrate the same growth mindset they ask of their students, they too become a valuable part of the community they are building. At the end of their career, they too will be able to reflect on their career and share the insights they have gleaned.

19

THE STUDENT TEACHER'S RELATIONSHIPS

Mentor Teachers and Students

Rebecca Clarke, Tiffany Chung, and Maegahn Smith

Pre-Service Teachers (PSTs) face many challenges, among them working successfully with the students they meet in their in-school placements and working together with their Mentor Teachers (MTs) in those MTs' classrooms. We asked three relatively new teachers to reflect on how they negotiated classroom authority during their internships. Tiffany Chung and Rebecca Clarke focus on PSTs' relationships with MTs and sharing classroom authority with MTs. Maegahn Smith describes the importance of building trust with students. (Eds.)

Mentor–Teacher, Student–Teacher Relationships
Rebecca Clarke

As a PST, you must navigate many complexities: creating in-depth lesson plans that accurately reflect how you will reach your learning objectives, figuring out dynamic ways to help your students connect with the learning content, capturing your students' attention and maintaining flow throughout the lesson, building strong pedagogical relationships with students, and the list goes on. One piece that is often overlooked—and is arguably one of the most important—is navigating the relationship between PSTs and their mentors.

You spend day after day in your education courses learning the most innovative ways of teaching, all while building your own philosophy of what being a teacher means to you. Through theoretical situations offered in textbooks, you begin to find your feet and become a little more confident about how you might approach your own classroom. Along with a deepening well of knowledge and a newly developed philosophy of education, comes a strong passion to bring everything you learned from those lectures into the field in a way that compliments your own philosophy. You eagerly head into your first day of practicum, excited

DOI: 10.4324/9781003140849-23

to try out your new knowledge in a practical setting. As the day proceeds, you might begin to feel a little bit of tension building between the two of you. You are not sure of the source of this tension and you begin to worry that it might ruin your overall experience. This is the beginning of many PSTs' stories as they embark on their practicum journey.

When entering a practicum, you have many pieces to consider in relation to creating and maintaining a positive relationship with your Mentor Teacher. The themes that appear most often in interns' stories are personality conflicts and differing teaching styles and philosophies.

Differing Teaching Styles and Philosophies

It is not always easy to develop positive relationships with your Mentor Teacher, especially if your educational values do not align. Being asked to teach in a way that does not align with your philosophy has the potential to create tension between you and your mentor teacher and to give you the feeling that you are not getting what you need out of your practicum. Heading into a classroom with up-to-date strategies and teaching theories can, at times, feed into your PST's ego, especially if you enter a classroom that is characterized by a more traditional teaching style. You will naturally want to jump in and implement your own teaching strategies, but if you do, I can promise you that your relationship with your MT will be rocky, even if you have the best of intentions. Trust me, I've been there!

The biggest lesson I learned while in this situation was to be humble. Instead of trying to change the world, focus on the basics. Remember that you are only there for a short time, and MTss need to maintain a classroom environment that works for them after your departure. I am not suggesting that you abandon all your ambitions and conform to a version of teaching that goes against everything you believe in. You can absolutely bring who you are into the classroom, just do so tactfully, while being mindful of your MT. It won't always be easy, but communication is key. If there is something you want to implement, document why you want to implement it and how it will benefit the classroom, and then pitch the idea to your mentor teacher. Be willing not only to hear their feedback, criticism, and suggestions, but be eager to implement what you hear. Though you may feel somewhat unseen and stagnant in this situation, remember that there are always opportunities for growth. It was in this situation that I learned the most about my beliefs as a teacher and what drives me to get up and teach every day. It is, in fact, what shaped me into the teacher I am today.

Personality Conflicts

Many stories about the challenges involved in forming positive relationships involve personality conflicts. You can do everything correctly and things still feel strained. Each person is unique, and it is only natural that some people do not jive with others. Navigating these differences is a skill set that everyone needs to develop, and it is no easy feat. The benefit of working with someone whose personality differs from your own is that you will learn new instructional techniques and strategies and new ways to connect with students. Here's the thing, you do not have to be best friends with your MT. You just have to keep an open mind and be willing to look at things from a new perspective. Take the time to eat lunch in the lunchroom with your MT and the other staff, every day, even if you are feeling overwhelmed with work. Go out of your way to be helpful to your MT and remember to communicate openly and effectively. If you can do that, you will make the most of your practicum experience, and potentially come out with a more wholesome way of teaching, including instructional approaches you might not have tried previously.

Communication

Communication is key! Communication alone has the power to make or break your practicum. It is shocking how many relationships fall apart because of ineffective communication. MT to PST relationships are no different. If I could give you one bit of advice, this is it: take the time to communicate with your mentor. If you are like me and struggle to communicate clearly, go in prepared. Write down the items you need to discuss, get clarification on, and want advice or feedback on. Bring up one point at a time, and repeat your MT's answers to ensure that you are both on the same page. At the beginning of practicum, ask your MT what time of day works for them to meet with you daily. Even if you don't have anything set to discuss, meet with them anyway. Creating a consistent and safe place for effective communication will help to eliminate any misunderstandings and will aid in the development and maintenance of a positive relationship.

It May Be Hard, but It's Worth It!

Though some situations make it challenging to develop a positive relationship with your mentor, there are many benefits to building such a relationship. Creating a safe learning environment for yourself is just as important as creating a safe learning environment for your students. It is difficult and usually impossible to learn in a toxic environment. A positive relationship with your mentor allows you to take intellectual risks in your own learning because you know that your mentor is right there, willing, and able to give you advice, feedback, and their expertise. Everyone has something to offer, but you have to be willing to see what that is. Once you have gained your MT's trust and acceptance, they will happily give you the authority in their classroom (such as creating more space for you to make decisions, build relationships with students within a lesson, and take pedagogical risks).

When Everything Aligns or Doesn't

On the flip side, your MT's philosophy, personality, and teaching style might compliment your own so intensely that your beliefs and instructional approaches are pushed to a whole new level, to a place where you have never felt more in *your* zone. To use the language of Vygotsky (1978), this is your zone of proximal development, a wonderful place where you feel challenged but safe enough to take chances and advance your learning. I am grateful to have been in this situation and, looking back, I am amazed by my own self-growth. I learned how to use the methods and strategies that I knew I wanted to use but had not yet had an opportunity to try. I learned how to take my theoretical knowledge and apply it to real-world circumstances. My relationship with my MT, though positive, still took work. Like every relationship, I needed to attend to that relationship daily. I showed up early, I took her feedback and constructive criticism eagerly, I met with her daily, and I immersed myself in extra-curricular activities both with her and with the other staff. I put in the work, and it truly paid off. I wanted to end on this note because this experience is one that almost all of you will find yourself in. This is the situation we all hope to encounter during a practicum.

Sometimes everything does not align. When that happens, try not to panic. There are things you can do to create a positive relationship, no matter the situation. The intent of this is not to scare you but rather to prepare you in case you find yourself in a less than ideal situation and to encourage you to keep an open mind. It is very likely that you will read this, go through your practicum, and have absolutely no issue relating to your MT. However, in case you do encounter difficulties, here is a list of strategies that will aid you in developing and maintaining a positive relationship with your mentor teacher, while maintaining who you are as an individual:

- Communicate openly, both with your MT and with your Faculty Advisor.
- Be open to feedback and constructive criticism, and act on the suggestions of your MT and Faculty Advisor.
- Make time for daily check-ins. Plan these for times that favor the MT's availability.
- Be flexible.
- No matter how busy you are, eat your lunch in the lunchroom and communicate with the other staff.
- If there are new strategies you want to implement, be clear and concise on why you want to try them and how they will benefit the students.
- Arrive early, put together, and eager to teach and learn.
- Remember that you are only temporarily teaching in that classroom, so do not try to change everything. Focus on the basics.
- Offer to help in any way possible.
- Ask questions and lean on your MT for support.

- Most importantly, be authentically you.

You could act on all these suggestions and still run into issues in your practicum, but try to go in with an open mind. Whoever your MT is and whatever philosophy they have, you will undoubtedly leave with more knowledge than you started, and that is exactly why a diverse range of field placements is so important for you as a PST. They give you a chance to learn from a wide variety of people, all with differing views. Each person is unique, and that uniqueness is what shapes their teaching philosophy, just as uniqueness shapes yours. This exposure to different teaching philosophies and personalities is what will eventually fine-tune your own teaching philosophy and aid in your ability to be a well-rounded teacher. Though these relationships might be difficult to form, there are so many benefits in taking the time to develop and maintain them. If we all taught in the same way, what a boring classroom that would be!

Shared Classroom Authority Tiffany Chung

It was clear to me that my goal during teacher's college was in a short period of time, to achieve the daunting task of learning current research-based pedagogy in order to put my knowledge to work in a real classroom with real students. The idea of learning a variety of effective pedagogical approaches was exciting; however, for someone like myself, inexperienced in maintaining classroom control, the anticipation was tempered by the scenario whereby a large number of unknowns could drastically affect my success (or lack thereof). Leading up to my first practicum, my concern for classroom authority grew. It was difficult to comprehend how an inexperienced teacher candidate like myself could effectively teach students given the shared classroom authority and temporary nature of each placement.

Being in the unique position of a PST meant I would practice new skills under the supervision of an Associate Teacher (another term for Mentor Teacher). This meant I had to harmoniously juggle faculty demands, curriculum expectations, student needs, and goals my Associate Teacher had for their classroom. With many variables at play, every inch of my being longed to take the reins on any factor that I could control in order to complete all three of my practicums successfully. To manage the complex dynamics of such a teaching environment, I came up with an approach to obtain classroom authority not for my own gain, but ultimately, to provide the best learning environment for the students.

Inspired by the four 21st-century competencies to improve student success and well-being (critical thinking, communication, collaboration, and creativity), I came up with my own approach to improve a PST's success and well-being in a scenario where classroom authority is both temporary and shared; shared with my

Associate Teacher, administrators, as well as specialty and resource teachers. My approach contains the three "C's" of competence, confidence, and care.

Competence

I went into my first practicum aware that my temporary presence affected how the grade 5 students viewed my importance and authority in the classroom. The plan laid out by my faculty was to observe the class once a week for two months followed by three weeks of student teaching. The observation period was helpful in creating a framework of classroom structure. Unfortunately, with minimal leadership and teaching involved during this phase, students naturally redefined my role as teacher and diminished it to the role of "helper." This demotion was confirmed by several students who asked me if I was in the classroom to help their homeroom teacher.

Aware of what I was up against, I knew that competency would help me gain some authority in the classroom. I knew the only way to become a competent, experienced teacher was to teach (and teach some more) and that the opportunity given to me as a guest in another teacher's classroom would be limited. Knowing that I would not be able to acquire great levels of experience in such a short period of time, I created a strategy to achieve the goal of being a competent teacher.

In my first step toward competency, I connected and met my first Associate Teacher weeks before the school year began. I took this opportunity to understand her teaching style and review her short- and long-range plans. It gave me an opportunity to ask questions, coordinate curricular goals for the term, and understand her expectations, regardless of whether they differed from the expectations set out by my faculty. This information helped me prepare for my first three-week practicum.

The vast number of curricular expectations can be overwhelming for any new teacher, so asking questions before and early on in the school year helped me focus on the specific expectations I would be teaching during my three-week immersive. This gave me ample time to prepare and become well versed in the subject areas I would teach; no more and no less. I understood that this phase of practice teaching was not a time for me to master skills but to get a glimpse of the work, art and craft that goes into teaching, managing, and facilitating students. This meant I intentionally focused my attention on topics I would be teaching and filtered out unnecessary information. Doing so allowed me to become proficient in the subject matter I taught. As a result, students became comfortable with my role as a teacher and looked to me for the next direction. Gaining the trust of the students and Associate Teacher during the first week of my three-week practicum created more opportunities to teach and, thus, develop greater authority in the classroom.

Confidence

This leads me to the second "C": confidence. Becoming competent in subject matter gave me the confidence to walk into a classroom, excited for students to learn. With the stress of content aside, I could confidently lead students in activities, discussions, group work, and independent work. It freed me to focus on their learning and tend to the challenging task of discerning the next steps based on their understanding.

Even so, confidence in a temporary teaching setting did not only come from being prepared with a few polished lessons. It also came from knowing my learners. Given the information provided to me in a short period of time, I took into consideration each students' ethnicity, socioeconomic status, general topics of interests, and more. Some of this information I obtained from speaking with my Associate Teacher; some I gained during my observation period; the bulk of it was gained while teaching the students. Regardless of when I gained information, responsive teaching helped inform my lessons so as to better cater to each student's needs.

The confidence I write of is not one that is egocentric. Rather, it is one that helps create a safe environment where students feel comfortable to learn. In both knowing my learners and the subject matter, I could confidently connect with the students in meaningful ways. This did not mean my lessons went without a hitch. I had students ask me questions to which I felt I should have known the answer. However, even in my shortcomings, I let them know that we could research information together, with the intent of modeling what it means to be a lifelong learner.

Care

The last strategy and arguably the most important is the last "C": care. If I did not care about the curriculum content, the quality of the lesson, or student well-being, authenticity would dissolve along with any chance of classroom authority. Exuding care meant I was intentional to tend to the whole child. This was shown through conversations at recess; attending volleyball games after school; showing up for homework club before school; spear-heading Student Vote to align with that year's federal election and build up student leaders; and the simple act of paying attention to a student's book of choice to help them find more in the school library.

In my final practicum, which spanned several months, I used three different-sized rubik's cubes for a Math lesson on scales. The rubik's cube became a point of challenge weeks after the lesson. Students happily struggled to solve the cube before school, after school, at recess, and any chance they could get their hands on the world famous puzzle. At the end of my practicum, I purchased each student a mini rubik's cube as a parting gift. The point of the gift was not to win the students over with toys. It was a continuity of the customized care I offered them in the classroom; one that encouraged them to learn long after the lessons were over.

I had the opportunity to teach grade 5–8 students across three separate practicums. Regardless of age, academic level, or social-emotional need, I found that students responded to a teacher who led with competence and confidence enveloped in genuine care for their academic success and well-being. With some hard work but more importantly, *heart work*, shared authority can be achieved so that students *benefit* from the partnership of multiple teachers in the classroom.

Building Relationships With Students During Practicum
Maegahn Smith

Creating relationships with your students is fundamental to your success as a teacher as well as to the success of your students. As a PST, creating relationships can be challenging when your time in a classroom is limited, but it is possible as long as you put in the effort to create relationships with each one of your students.

A trusting relationship is not one-sided. Students need to trust their teachers just as much as we need to trust them. Trust in our students is more than getting them to behave properly, come to school prepared, or do what we ask. It is trusting them to want to be there and have the motivation to learn. We are trusting them to be open and willing to have their minds changed. As teachers, we can forget what it is like to *really* learn; it can be stressful or confusing when the discoveries we make change our understanding of the world around us. That is why, as teachers, we need to create trusting relationships with our students, so that we can trust them to show up with a willingness to learn. In return, our students can trust us to provide them with the security and support required to be open to new ideas.

In the following, I explore and define trust-based relationships. If, as teachers, we do not recognize that trust-based relationships are multi-faceted, complicated, and a lot of work, then we will limit our own classroom success because we have limited our relationships.

Elements of a Mutual Trust-Based Relationship

The elements discussed in the following are focused on you, the PST, as the relationship-building process must be initiated and cultivated by you. Once you have started to engage in the building of relationships, the students will likely reciprocate. With some students, you will quickly form a bond, likely because you have things in common. With others, it will take time and effort to see even the smallest return. These small returns can be frustrating and challenging, and at times you may be tested to your limits (and might even fail), but you must never give up.

Predictability

Predictability is key to keeping your students at ease, especially those who are nervous about another adult coming into their life. Predictability establishes that you are a calm, level-headed person; with such a person in charge, students can anticipate what will happen based on your previous actions. It does not mean that you are a boring teacher who only uses worksheets and rote memorization. Predictability is particularly important in the early elementary grades as the students are still learning what is expected while navigating the differences between school and home.

Predictability in your actions helps establish trust-based relationships by minimizing the fear students have when they put themselves in a vulnerable situation, such as when they try something new or answer a question. If students know that they will be accepted and celebrated, that an incorrect answer will not be ridiculed, and that you will protect them and their growing minds, they will feel more willing to put up their hands to offer answers and pose questions that can stimulate in-depth discussions and further learning.

Showing Interest in Their Lives Through Questions and Conversations

In order to facilitate the creation of trust-based relationships, students need to feel that you are interested in them and their lives. This feeling grows in the soil of authentic conversations where you ask questions and spend time listening.

Too many times, teachers ask questions to get a pre-established answer or ask questions to lead the conversation toward the subject of themselves. Instead, questions should be crafted with the intention of listening to students and learning about them. A connection can be created between you and students simply by showing interest in them and what they have to say, even if you have little in common.

The stories and anecdotes evoked from questions provide vital information about what your students are interested in and who is important to them. You can use this information to shape future lessons and thereby promote intrinsic motivation and natural engagement. It will also help with future conversations where you can ask more questions about your students and their lives. Your students will be so thrilled that you remembered, they will often start asking you questions about your life and interests, reciprocating the effort you have put in, and starting to build the foundation for a mutual relationship.

Honesty in Actions and Character

Another facet of trust-based relationships is the ability to be open and honest with your students first so that they will be open and honest with you in return. As is true of many other classroom skills and behaviors, teachers model and the students follow. PSTs should be willing to be open and honest with their students from the beginning, knowing it will take time for a relationship to be formed.

Such honesty is especially important regarding how we represent ourselves. Students can smell a lie miles away, and any inauthenticity in character will leave a nagging doubt in the back of their minds. This doubt will cause them not to trust you fully and will limit the relationship that you might otherwise build together. Being honest does require some vulnerability, but being willing to go to that level and really be yourself with your students opens the playing field for them so that they can also be themselves and be accepted regardless of who they are.

Honesty also translates into admitting to your students when you have made a mistake and demonstrating to them that it is okay for them to make mistakes. The important part is what happens after the mistake is made: learning from it and trying again. Modeling honest, open, and reflective behavior helps students learn from your actions as a trusted role model in their lives. It can also help diminish perfectionism and anxiety within the classroom.

Communication

Communication is a two-way process, and you must provide opportunities within the classroom for students to communicate with you. Allowing time for open conversation allows students to express ideas, uncertainties, and questions to you without disrupting lessons. An option for this is to allow students to communicate in writing. Journaling is a great way for students to communicate feelings that they may not feel comfortable expressing aloud. Your job is to then read these reflections and reply with appropriately honest comments. Used properly, journaling can help develop relationships with students who have some lingering fears about you or who prefer to be quiet in class.

Conclusion

As a PST, what you are doing is daunting. You are tasked with going into classrooms for a short period of time and making them your own. It may only be your classroom for one lesson, maybe for one day a week, or perhaps for a full three months. In that time, you are charged with building relationships with each of your students while also teaching them. This is no easy feat. There will be times when you are absolutely lost and have no idea what to do next because the students are denying every opportunity that you have provided to create that relationship. They are not interested in trusting another adult who will leave or disappoint them. It is your duty to ensure that these students understand that you trust and appreciate them and that you need them just as much as they need you.

Focusing on these elements of trust-based relationships with every student in your classroom will help to create a classroom community. Students will take what they have learned from the positive relationship modeled by you and use it to create their own relationships with each other. Such an interconnected community allows for further exploration of ideas and growth in knowledge that may not be possible without such a foundation of trust between teachers and students. Knowing that their ideas will be taken seriously, their comments will be acknowledged, and their contributions appreciated will encourage students to participate more, learn more, and know more.

Let the students in your classroom know that each and every one of them is valued and has something to contribute beyond their physical presence in the classroom. They can contribute ideas, knowledge, passion, interesting facts, and a joyous atmosphere to the classroom, all of which make others in our learning community want to learn. Spending the time to form relationships characterized by openness, honesty, trust, two-way communication, and consistent predictable behavior will reduce students' fear and wariness and will help you, as a PST, be the most successful teacher you can be.

Reference

Vygotsky, L. S. (1978). Interaction between learning and development. Translated by M. Cole. In M. Cole, V. John-Steiner, S. Scribner, & E. Souberman (Eds.), *Mind and society: The development of higher psychological processes* (pp. 79–91). Harvard University Press.

Editors' Note

We recommend the 2019 book that Rebecca Clarke, Maegahn Smith, and several classmates produced about how to flourish during school placements: *So, You have a Teaching Practicum?* Amazon Independent Publishing.

20

REFLECTIONS OF A BEGINNING TEACHER

Who Am I Going to Be?

Ashley Ryl

High school was a time in my life when I was faced with the realization that I would soon need to decide what to do with my life. This was a big decision, and not one that I took lightly. When I looked around my environment, I contemplated what career path would fit me. What would I want to do for the rest of my life? How could I make a difference and how could I incorporate the things I enjoyed doing? As I entered my grade 11 English course, things started to become clear when I ventured through the pages of many great books and had discussions that felt deep and meaningful. That was it. I wanted to teach high school English. It felt good knowing that I had a path to venture along, and I started to observe my teachers. It was fun to daydream about my own classroom one day. I thought about vocabulary work I would have my students complete and I even dreamed about how I would want my classroom to look. Reflecting on those early dreams, I am now aware that I did not consider one of the most important aspects of being a teacher: what kind of teacher did I want to be and how would my being impact my classroom management? Little did I realize that my journey to become a teacher would consist of many reflections on these topics as I struggled to be myself—not a carbon copy of my mentors—and to incorporate structure through classroom management in the many different classroom settings I would face.

Trying to Be Someone Else

As I began the first year of my two-year after-degree BEd, I was still thinking and reflecting on what I wanted my classroom to look like and what I wanted my students to learn. The only real change was that I was now connecting the novels I hoped to teach to the Program of Study outcomes. I longed to get my future students excited about English Language Arts the way that my teachers did for me. I wanted them to find themselves in the books they would read.

As the first-year practicum drew near, the horror stories started to be shared—stories of students acting out or undermining their teachers. As I heard more stories, I became increasingly nervous. I had never stopped to consider a classroom management system. All I had ever reflected on is what I would say to students' one-off comments, so I would sound confident and in charge. I wanted my future students to respect my authority and I secretly wanted them all to like me, but I had no idea how I would achieve this—I was naive but excited.

The day of my first-year practicum finally approached and although I was nervous, I was excited to get to know my Mentor Teacher (MT) and students. As I sat down with my MT for our first conversation, I was wanting to make a good impression—I brought a notebook and came with questions preprepared, so he knew I was taking this very seriously. I thought I was ready for this—until he asked his first question: what is your philosophy of teaching? I was stunned and not quite sure how to answer. Sure, I had written a paper about my educational philosophy, but that seemed like years ago. I did not expect this to be his first question. I thought he would ask me about what my teachable major and minor were and fill me in on the classes I would teach. I understood that maybe he asked this question to try to get to know me better, but as I reflect on it now, I understand that knowing who you are as a teacher dictates how you teach and manage your classroom—it affects not only yourself but also all the students you teach. I was still so concerned with the content that I had not yet tried to understand who I was as a teacher and what I believe about students—which translates into how you treat and manage the students in your classroom.

As I observed my MT in the first week, it quickly became apparent that we were very different people. He loved teaching physical education and was very experimental in his teaching. He commanded respect from his students—as soon as he used a serious tone, the students knew to behave. I observed and wrote down everything I could about how he taught and ran his classroom. I thought that maybe if I did exactly what he did, that I could command the same respect from the grade 7 and 8 Social Studies students I was about to begin teaching.

As I began teaching, and my MT handed over the authority to me, I realized I would need to focus more on my classroom management than my content. I would plan out nine-page lessons that were detailed and interactive, only to have my students derail it. They would talk to their friends, fidget at their desks, and even try to sneak onto their phones. It felt frustrating that I could not simply teach my lesson to my students. I then understood why my MT briefed me so heavily on his classroom management systems. He would stay after school with me to talk about what he would do to manage such behaviors, so I started implementing his style of classroom management, which consisted of group rewards and punishments, moving students who were off task, and writing down those students' names on the board. I wanted so badly for this to be the fix—I thought that because the students were accustomed to my MT's management style, I just needed to do exactly as he did, and they would listen to me. I realized that it was not this easy. When I tried to implement classroom management, the students did not respond like they did to my MT.

I remember one event clearly. I was teaching a lesson on Japan to my grade 8 class. Throughout the lesson, I reminded a particular student to stay on task. Each time I would go back to his group, he was either doing nothing or talking to his friends. Out of frustration, I sent him into the hallway so that I could talk to him. Just like my MT, I used a stern and serious tone to explain to the student why we were having the conversation. Just as I was midway through talking to him, he burst out laughing, which only made me angry. I told him that he was being very disrespectful and sent him back to class. At that moment, I realized that this student did not take me seriously—even after I tried to be like my MT. This made me want to work harder to gain respect and authority in the classroom—I just was not sure how I could do this. The way I was managing thus far did not feel right—it did not feel like it aligned with who I was—but I did not know what else to do other than mimic what my MT had done.

Moving forward, I felt defeated, but I was not ready to give up. I was having a hard time gaining control of an unruly group of 34 grade 7 students. I had initially tried group punishments like my MT suggested, but the girls in the classroom were upset that they were getting in trouble even though they followed the rules. I then started individually punishing students by moving them to a different desk if they were being a distraction. This soon took a turn for the worst after I moved a girl who was then unhappy. After class, she questioned why I would move her and even accused me of being a racist. I was trying so hard to be like my MT and adapt to the pre-established classroom environment, but it was not working. I felt as though I was not treating or managing the classroom in a way that felt authentic and true to who I was, but I was not sure how else I would run it.

At the end of that practicum, I felt as though I was good at planning but a failure at classroom management. I could not get the students to listen, and it affected the way I thought of myself as a teacher. I was determined to get better at management, and when registration for year 2 opened, I quickly enrolled in a classroom management course—hoping that I could learn the secret to management. I was still holding onto the idea that there was something I was missing.

Walking into my second-year classroom management course, I expected to learn about practical solutions for management that I could add to my suitcase of knowledge and skills. Like numerous times before, I was surprised to find out that I was wrong. There was an emphasis on learning about educational philosophers. I was a bit disappointed that I was not learning about easy tips and tricks. At the end of the course, we were asked to write our own classroom management philosophy based on the philosophers we had studied. As I began writing and thinking, it started to become clear why this was such a large assignment. I was finally forced to think through and articulate what I believe about teaching and managing classrooms. At the end of the course, I felt more confident in my abilities because I was more confident in myself and my beliefs.

I brought this new learning into my second practicum in which I taught AP English in a highly academic high school. This time, I knew that I needed to be myself and not just copy the management style of my highly knowledgeable, veteran MT. My MT commanded respect based on his appearance alone. He was a tall and commanding figure. After seeing him teach, I knew that what worked well for him would not necessarily work well for me—an average height, young, inexperienced, female Pre-Service Teacher. In the school, students knew that he was a tough teacher, and he did not take any disrespect from students. As I began to take over the English 10AP class, I did not try to be my MT. I introduced myself with a get-to-know-me slideshow. When students were off task, I would kindly, but sternly, ask them to pay attention. The school took academics seriously, which meant there were fewer management concerns than in my previous practicum, but in this environment, I was able to build the necessary confidence in my abilities. I knew that this would not likely be the environment I would teach in for my first contract, but the space allowed me to practice being myself and using pre-emptive management tools instead of letting issues become so large that the first step would be a punishment. I also started to realize that there would never be a one-size-fits-all solution to management as each school and class are very different. What did work was being confident and aware of my management philosophy.

Becoming Comfortable With My Own Management Style

My dream of becoming a teacher had finally come! After applying for jobs, I was offered a position at a small, low socioeconomic, rural school, teaching all subjects to a grade 5/6 class. I was nervous because I had dreamt of teaching English to secondary students, but I was excited to start my teaching career. I knew that this was going to be a very different teaching journey from what I had previously experienced. I would be working with high-needs students; almost half my class had an individualized program plan, and I would also have students with behavior plans. When I went into school to set up my classroom, I was greeted by two teachers who were eager to help and filled me in on the students I would be teaching. They also informed me of the behaviors I could expect, and I became nervous. Everything was so new to me, and I was now in a new school environment that I needed to learn how to navigate. Many of the students had extended family as their primary caregivers, and many of the homes were largely unstructured. It quickly became apparent to me that it was the school environment that provided students with structure and expectations.

When the students walked into my classroom on the first day of school, I was surprised by how well-behaved they were. It appeared to me that the behavior was because of the structure and expectations within the school environment.

Students did not get away with any misbehavior and it was quickly dealt with by the educational assistants, teacher, or principal. This was unlike any learning environment I had previously experienced. During my practicums, I alone was responsible for behavior management, and I had never had to bring in the support of the principal. Looking around me, I observed how well the students listened to the other staff in the school.

When a student did not listen to my direction the first time or misbehaved, I thought maybe it was because I was not being hard enough on the students—perhaps they were taking advantage of my kindness. While the students' behavior was no more challenging than the students I encountered in my practicums, I became embarrassed when the students did not listen to me as well as they listened to the other staff in the school. I felt internal pressure to be stricter and slowly decided that I needed to be harder on them and maybe raise my voice in order to gain their respect. However, each time I would raise my voice at a student, I felt frustrated and angry. I did not like how it felt and, to be honest, I still had the same number of management issues. I did not feel as overwhelmed as I did in my first practicum as I had control over my grade 5/6 students, but I felt like I needed them to listen to me as soon as I gave direction. I was not sure what to do, but I did know that I did not feel like I was being authentic to who I am—and that felt wrong.

As a new teacher, I had a learning coach who would come help me in areas I felt I needed to grow in. She was someone who consistently saw me teach throughout the year as we collaborated on lessons. In my head, I assumed she probably thought I needed to be doing more for management, but she had never commented on this. One day, she made a passing remark that she thought I had control over my classroom and the students. This was huge for me. I was comparing myself to the other authority figures in the school and assumed that I was doing something wrong because I did not manage a classroom like them. This was now the validation that I needed to feel like my easy-going self could fit into this environment. One outsider's perspective was all I needed to remind myself that I could stay true to who I was and my philosophy of teaching, regardless of the environment I found myself in. After that, I decided not to raise my voice or get upset so easily if my students did not start work immediately. I allowed myself to have more fun with my students and take those off-task moments to talk, even if we were ignoring the curriculum for a bit. I was happier, and I no longer felt the same levels of frustration and anger. The students could see and feel that I cared for them, and they ultimately showed me more respect because of this—more respect than I could gain by yelling and handing out unnecessary punishments.

Thinking back to my teaching dreams as a high school student makes me smirk as I consider how naive I was. I assumed the tough part of teaching would be preparing lessons. As I reflect on my short career so far, I now know that the most difficult part of teaching, for me, is exploring who I am as a teacher. There are many different types of teachers, and there is no one-size-fits-all solution to being a good classroom manager. I tried to become copies of my MTs or emulate the school environment but quickly realized that if I tried to become something I was not, I was not happy, and the kids saw right through me. My advice for other new teachers: the important thing is to reflect deeply on who you are and what you believe about kids. This is a process that will never be complete. It is ongoing because things change; you change, your school may change, and your kids will change. As a young teacher, it can be so easy to become lost or distracted. Just know that reflecting on your beliefs and staying true to them will allow you to be the best classroom manager that you can be.

21
ESTABLISHING YOURSELF AS A TEACHER IN A FOREIGN SETTING

Nicola Campbell

Many teachers have an anecdote to share about time spent abroad teaching and developing their teaching philosophy further in a new environment. Traveling often challenges and expands an individual's worldview, and teaching abroad can mean an opportunity to learn and practice new pedagogies that will expand your understanding of education and the school classroom; however, it will perhaps also challenge your own beliefs and values. As Pre-Service Teachers, we are taught to examine many ideas related to teaching and learning, and from this examination to develop a teaching philosophy before we have really had the chance to establish authority in a classroom of our own. I found that teaching in a foreign setting can feel quite similar. Inundated with new information, theories, and educational values, I quickly attempted to create a place for myself as a teacher while grappling with many policies and protocols that made me feel completely uncomfortable.

I interviewed and received a job offer in the fall of 2017, six months before I was set to graduate from my Bachelor of Education program. After attending a university job fair presentation put on by a hiring agency, I was set on the idea of traveling and teaching abroad after I graduated. While other members of my cohort applied to local school boards, I was thrilled and excited by the thought that I would be experiencing a new place while teaching, not to mention that I had a job secured already. However, I was not prepared for the feeling of being completely lost in a foreign city while establishing my teaching career in an unfamiliar place. Establishing yourself and your teaching presence in a new place has its challenges: however, reflecting on these challenges can be a powerful tool in developing further your own teaching philosophy and approach to classroom management. In what follows, I recount what I learned about establishing authority in a new teaching environment, and I describe some of the concepts that I continue to work with as my teaching career progresses.

DOI: 10.4324/9781003140849-25

Navigating New School Policies, Practices, and Values

When graduating from a BEd program, you take your newfound understandings with you, confident and hopeful that you can tackle a new school's environment and find a place where you fit. In this new place, I experienced an immediate shift in educational paradigms and, in turn, held on tighter to my own values and understandings of education as a security blanket. I quickly realized that my own values were not going to align as closely as I had hoped. At that time, I thought I would need to put aside much of my BEd, at least for the time being, as its focus on contemporary teaching practices and open pedagogy felt somewhat irrelevant. The foreign teaching setting to which I had come, so different from my own experience in the Canadian education system, was rooted in traditionalism, with a keen focus on meeting academic achievement targets. Strong assessment policies, including even the color of pen you were to use to grade student work and the frequency of oral and written feedback, were monitored and frequently discussed. High standards for student behavior were valued; I have never seen a group of children so quiet. I realized quickly what the norms were and, while I had been anxious to establish a classroom climate suited to my own ideals, it was clear I would need to readjust.

Letting go of some of my own values, at least for the present, ended up being both freeing and draining. Freeing, because I could throw myself into my day-to-day teaching and tell myself that by meeting expectations, I was doing a good job in the eyes of my employer, and therefore was doing right by my students. I was drained because every day I left work feeling like an inauthentic educator. I struggled with school policies regarding behavior, lunchroom etiquette, and lesson plan scope and sequence, and I increasingly felt that neither I nor my students had any real room to fail and learn from our mistakes in this environment. I felt like a misfit, and if I wasn't buying in, then how could I expect my students to?

Navigating school policies can feel intimidating, and you may feel at times as though you are departing from your own ideals, ideals that are a fundamental part of who you are as a teacher. In establishing myself in a new setting, I worked to determine what was integral to my evolving teaching practice, and what I could and could not sacrifice while observing and respecting school policies that were valued in this school culture. Perhaps one of my most important takeaways was that while I felt that these school policies could be harsh or stifling, students were thriving in the routine and clear expectations that every teacher in the school set out and maintained. Working in an environment with these policies did not come without challenges or frustrations. However, a willingness to shift my own approach is what made me successful in establishing myself as a good colleague, a successful teacher, and a respected employee at this school.

Classroom Climate and Behavior Management

As a new teacher in a new setting, it can be intimidating to establish yourself in a classroom for the first time and to determine your classroom management style.

You might have a list of goals, routines, and a certain idea of what you want your classroom to feel like. In my new context, I found establishing my teaching presence, classroom routines, and management techniques to be made more difficult by the policies I was asked to follow. As a new teacher, I knew the importance of students' feeling secure and safe in my classroom. However, the behavior policy enforced strict rules that sometimes made me suspect that the underlying belief was that children were better off seen than heard. This concern about behavior and noise meant that a lot of time and effort was spent managing the classroom noise level and enforcing expectations through behavior charts. These practices allowed children to compare themselves to others and even had the effect of shaming children for their behavior. Furthermore, students lived under the threat of a behavior note going home to parents to encourage positive choices. This was a far cry from the warmth, security, and understanding that had become intrinsic parts of my teaching philosophy.

The staff member's understanding of these behavior rules and values came before the value of building classroom relationships, another startling realization, and adjustment in my first few weeks. Students seemed to thrive in this environment that had been established in the years prior, and since we taught collaboratively, this meant that I found greater success in establishing myself as an authoritative figure if I followed the example of my colleagues and supervisors. Therefore, in establishing my classroom climate, I let go of my own values to meet the collective norms. I gained respect from students and initially found it easier to manage the different classes I taught with these newfound techniques. Eventually, I found a middle ground where I followed these policies and behavior models but found room for my own approaches and values as well.

Curriculum and Expectations

One of the challenges of teaching abroad is quickly learning a new curriculum and the values woven through it. While you are navigating a new place, you are also orienting yourself in a new educational landscape. As I noted earlier, high expectations for student achievement were communicated at the school and were prominent in the school's values and mission statements. The curriculum scope and sequence had been developed by curriculum leaders, and I was handed what I was to teach each term from start to finish. That meant I was being told what to teach, when to teach it, and how to teach it. This system felt jarring, especially considering that I had naively expected something similar to what I was accustomed to at home. It can be difficult to release expectations, control, and input into how you are delivering instructional material, and it was in this area that I felt most inauthentic. I found myself using many worksheets, presenting new information to young children only by using PowerPoint presentations and using less and less innovation in the delivery of my lessons. I often struggled with finding a way to invest my interest and enthusiasm in a lesson that, in my opinion, put a constraint on student creativity and choice. I am confident I would not have always been able to answer "why are we doing this?" in a meaningful way had anyone asked me the question. These feelings made me question my perceived authority as a teacher immediately and often, and I worried that my students, supervisors, and colleagues might be able to detect this inauthenticity.

Although I was faced with many challenges related to curriculum and instruction, I did benefit greatly from learning new strategies and approaches to literacy and numeracy instruction. I found great success in the delivery of a structured literacy program, with roots in phonics, repetition, and early development of reading comprehension skills. While the delivery of the material was driven by traditional methods and direct instruction, this seemed comfortable for students, and they thrived with high expectations and goal setting. I began to see strengths in the delivery of these programs, and it was difficult to ignore the quick growth I witnessed when assessing students in their reading and writing skills.

Assessment Practices

My understanding is that assessment is one area of pedagogy that teachers perpetually discuss and debate. In this new setting, I found a common understanding of the purpose and effectiveness of traditional assessment practices. This understanding left little room for discussion or questions. Student achievement was primarily assessed through standardized tests, and my colleagues took great pride in student success and meeting government standards. This understanding of assessment was foundational to the instructional framework of each subject area, and it also determined how students were placed in classes to target gaps in achievement. All students valued their own achievement in these streamed classes, and it was clear they had high expectations from home as well as from school. However, I observed a lack of intrinsic motivation, with students craving the approval of their teacher, of their headmaster, and of their parents. This craving led to the young students I was teaching already being hyperfocused on the product of their learning, rather than the process of it. While I could assert the importance of making mistakes and learning from them, the assessment practices in place did not reflect this value. These practices often challenged my understanding of meaningful assessment, providing little opportunity for students to represent their learning in different ways, as I had learned to value through my BEd degree.

What I Took With Me

While new experiences like this can be challenging, teaching abroad also brings the opportunity to learn educational values in a new context and allows you to choose what you will add to your teacher toolkit. Teaching abroad allows you to experience new perspectives on education, and it gives you unique insights into a culture.

One thing I took with me is a collaborative mindset. Establishing yourself as a trusted, reliable team member is just as important as establishing yourself in a classroom, and having this experience allowed me to be a stronger team member as I moved forward in my career. A teacher in a new setting can contribute to the group's work by sitting back, absorbing new information quietly, digesting that information, and asking questions later. I found it easier than trying to jump in with my "expertise." However, because my educational background was somewhat different from that of my colleagues, we had ideas and perspectives to share that became invaluable to one another's teaching practice.

As I mentioned, I brought a large number of literacy strategies back with me from my time abroad. I learned invaluable approaches to teaching phonics and early reading skills. I quickly learned just how much I did not know about teaching literacy, and I have woven these approaches and strategies into my current classroom to help readers at every level. While some of them are very structured and traditional approaches, I have found ways to reconcile these with the more balanced literacy approach more typical to a Canadian classroom.

Every day will not be filled with innovative lesson plans that you have spent hours crafting. While my university journey set me up for success and led me to have high expectations for myself, one of my key take-aways from my time abroad was how a lesson can come together quickly and simply, using materials and resources you did not create yourself. I learned the power of the statement "don't reinvent the wheel," and I now benefit by regularly reminding myself of this saying.

My current classroom climate is an amalgamation of things I have learned along my journey as a teacher; however, I have also had to unlearn habits from my experience. Upon arriving back in Canada, some aspects of my classroom management strategies immediately seemed overzealous and strict. In my time teaching back in Canada, I have been reminded that great learning and social-emotional development can happen when a classroom is noisy. In my school setting abroad, silence represented a successful classroom management system. I have found in Canada that silence can result in students' being anxious to ask questions, to be curious, and to take risks. A quiet classroom has its place, but some of the best learning happens in the midst of classroom noise. Furthermore, in a vibrant learning community and comfortable classroom climate, students feel more confident in making their next move, and most students are intrinsically motivated to make good choices and take risks in their learning. In an effective classroom, students feel safe enough to take risks and they see the value in everyday mistakes and imperfect test scores.

In any setting, finding space for yourself as a teacher has its challenges, triumphs, and growing pains. No matter the teaching context, there are invaluable take-aways from each experience that will influence and shape you as an educator. In establishing myself as a new teacher, finding the parts of my teaching philosophy that aligned authentically with the framework in place in my new school setting allowed me to find common ground. The differences in ideas and values in an educational setting may challenge your own; however, they will also likely affirm your own best teaching practices. I continue to welcome opportunities where I can challenge and expand upon my own teaching philosophy with new ideas, knowing I have the opportunity to learn as an educator and find joy in the parts that fit for me. Such growth can be daunting and uncomfortable, but I do believe it is a great opportunity to continue to develop a reflective teaching practice. Adopting this reflective mindset has enabled me to approach new educational settings with more confidence, perseverance, and authenticity, making me a stronger teacher as a result of the cumulation of experiences I have had.

22
SUCCEEDING AS A SUBSTITUTE TEACHER

Bina Ali and Douglas Laing

In many locations, after graduating from one's education program, one needs to spend some time being an Occasional Teacher (also called Substitute or Supply Teacher) before landing a permanent position. In Ontario, it is very competitive not only to secure a permanent position with a school board but even to get on the supply list. If you are lucky enough to get onto the supply list, you will need to gain recognition and impress permanent teachers and principals so that you can increase your chances of getting consistent bookings with schools and eventually be recommended for a long-term position (covering a teacher on leave) or for a permanent position. I outline later what, after five years of supply teaching, I have learned I need to incorporate into my teaching practice to help find supply work.

Safety First

As a Substitute Teacher, it can be quite a scary situation to walk into a new school each day not knowing any of the students or staff and being unaware of the school routines. To manage some of the unpredictability and stress before a day of substitute teaching, I arrive early and take the time to look over the plans the teacher has left and to read the emergency binder. I like to be cognizant of any allergies or health issues of any of the students in the classroom and to ensure that I understand what to do in the case of a fire or lockdown. Additionally, as educators, we know that each classroom is diverse and there are students with different needs and learning styles. Along with reading the teacher's day plans, I check to make sure if there are any individual education plans or safety plans I need to follow. I have found this to be extremely important because I have been in many classes where I needed to wear an assistive device or where a student requires assistive technology. Instilling this routine into my day-to-day teaching has made me a more effective Supply Teacher, one who puts the safety and needs of the students first. As well, when I take the time to learn this information about every classroom I enter, I generally feel more prepared and confident to teach the class, and therefore, my day runs more smoothly.

Classroom Management

In teacher's college, we learn about our teaching presence (which is treated at length in Chapter 5 in this book). My teaching presence derives from me respecting students, building connections, and establishing authority. When I walk into any new classroom, I start the day by communicating the rules and expectations I have of the students (for example, be kind, be respectful, stay on task, etc.). I like to be clear with students that while I may be a guest teacher in their class for only the day, there are behaviors I expect and there are consequences for those who do not follow the rules. I often bring some games and fun activities as motivation and rewards, for example, "If I see that everyone is doing their work, we will play a game at the end of the day or we will go outside to play." In addition, when students are working, I like to circulate around the classroom to ensure students are following and understanding what they are being asked to do and to be nearby to answer any questions or help any students. I have found that any other educators or assistants in the room are excellent sources of knowledge, especially when it comes to following the established routines, and I also do not hesitate to contact the office and ask for help if I am facing some challenging behaviors and need assistance with a student.

Be Flexible and Prepared

For a Substitute Teacher—and, really, for any educator—no two days are ever alike. I have learned that while I often walk into a classroom with lesson plans laid out for me, the day can still be unpredictable and there can be many interruptions. I strive to be flexible as a teacher so that I can respond to the students' needs, abilities, and interests. As well, sometimes students may finish a task quickly or there is additional time left before the next block. Being prepared means that you want to maintain student engagement and classroom order, so you have activities and games at the back of your mind for these situations. When I supply teach in the primary grades, if there is extra time, I often have students draw a picture for me or I will take some coloring pages for them to work on. I like to go to each school with a bag of my own personal teaching materials such as a book to read aloud, some music, and some worksheets. I have found myself in situations where I have walked into a classroom and there haven't been any plans for me so having these materials has made me successful.

Communicate and Advocate for Yourself

At the end of any supply teaching day, I like to leave a note sharing with the teacher how the day went. It is important for the regular classroom teacher to understand if there were any tasks that did not get finished or students who were having a hard time or behavioral issues. These notes also allow me to provide recognition of helpful students or students who had a great attitude. It is important to describe exactly what happened and what actions I took.

As a new face walking into any new school, I like to introduce myself to the principal, the office staff, and nearby teachers. I also leave a business card at the office when I hand in my keys at the end of the day and thank the staff and the classroom teacher. This is not only a professional thing to do, but it presents the opportunity for others to have your information to call you again, especially if you have done a good job. From my experience, once you have established yourself as a hardworking Supply Teacher who is conscientious and promotes safety in the classroom, the calls will start coming in and you will find yourself as a school's go-to Substitute Teacher.

Do What You Would Expect a Substitute Teacher in Your Class to Do

A good mindset to have as a Substitute Teacher walking into any classroom is to do the same job that you would expect a Substitute Teacher in your class to do. That is, follow the plans the teacher has left as best as you can and if there are disruptions or if you don't complete the planned lessons, communicate this information. As well, respect the classroom setup and leave it the way you found it. In addition to having the students take the time to put things away where they found them and continue their end-of-day routine (clear desks, put chairs up, etc.), I also take a few minutes at the end of the day to walk around the classroom and do a last-minute check. I ensure that any work students have completed and handed in is on the desk so that it is accessible to the teacher.

Learn Something New

I often feel very lucky that I get to go to different schools and classrooms each day. I embrace this opportunity to experience how different schools are run and how classrooms are set up. And I embrace the opportunity to learn different teaching styles and become exposed to the different instructional approaches evident in the lesson plans the teacher has left behind. Any idea I like, I make a note of, knowing I can adapt it for my own future classroom. I sometimes find myself taking pictures of bulletin board designs I like and making a mental note about lessons that went really well. At the end of the day, I often reflect and ask myself what the take-aways are and what I have learned, and I add these ideas to my personal toolbox to become a more informed and experienced teacher.

Meshing Like Gears by Douglas Laing

When a teacher (whether contract, seasonal, or temporary) enters a classroom, there needs to be a *meshing* between the new instructor and the students in the class. This is even more important for the relationship between a class and a Substitute Teacher. Sharing classroom authority is understanding that sharing the responsibility for learning is up to both the teacher and students working together. If the Substitute Teacher is unwilling to share authority with the students, then optimal learning will not be achieved.

This meshing is how gears work in machines; they all share the work and move together. It helps to imagine that both the teacher and students are gears working together toward the goal of learning. If one gear isn't turning in the same direction as the class, whether it be the teacher or the students, then the classroom isn't running effectively and can eventually cause the entire system to grind to a halt. If a car transmission doesn't go into gear smoothly it can have lasting consequences for the vehicle . . . and the same can be said for a classroom. If a Substitute Teacher doesn't mesh with the classroom, then the students' learning may suffer in the short term or even the long term. If a gear or a student's interest in school gets ground down, it will not work as well as it once did either. When students associate a school subject with a bad experience, they will not do the best they can in school, which is why it is so important that educators be flexible and willing to change on the fly. In a classroom environment being able to compromise with others is an important skill to have and one that can be taught to others simply by demonstrating how to mesh with others in a classroom.

23
CREATING POSITIVE CLASSROOM CLIMATE IN REMOTE SETTINGS

Kristen Tjostheim

My first teaching job was in a tight-knit community in Northern Alberta. Like many rural communities, it was very small and isolated; the hamlet had roughly 30 trailers, with the nearest traffic light over 100 km away. Its members were united by a shared culture: not only were they mostly farmers, but they also were members of the same religious community and shared a common history and language.

Being in such a unique context, I received several crash-course lessons on classroom management. I learned about framing student actions in the proper context; focusing on strengths rather than deficits; building trust through negotiation and flexibility; explicitly teaching proper behavior; and creating connections regardless of the teaching medium.

Practical Jokes and Perceived Malice

In the weeks leading up to my first year of teaching, I was trying to set my classroom up for the first day of classes. At one point, after momentarily stepping out of the room, I found part of my classroom equipment missing. I confess I went into a miniature panic. My first instinct was that this had been done purposefully and maliciously. I jumped to several unfair conclusions about my community and my future at this school. After a minute, however, I began to think rationally again, and I returned to the hallway in case I had somehow simply misplaced the equipment. While investigating, I ran into some of my future students (it was common for families to be in and out of the building throughout the summer holidays). I forced a smile on my face and talked with them as pleasantly as I could. During the conversation, I asked them if they had seen my missing equipment. When they denied it, my instinct told me they were lying, but I left it at that, reminding myself that everyone deserves a chance at a good first impression. When I returned to my classroom a few minutes later, the missing equipment had been returned.

I later learned that my predecessor had been a favorite teacher of many students, especially those I had met that day. When they saw teachers returning to school, they assumed that teacher was also coming back and had hidden the equipment as a "welcome back" practical joke. There had been absolutely zero malice in their actions, and by not overreacting or accusing them on our first encounter, we laid the foundation for a great year together.

It is common for practical jokes to arise inside and outside the classroom in small schools, particularly when students know each other well. In my community, I learned that most of my students were cousins, related through one of two major families. This diminished certain classroom management considerations, such as speaking in front of their classmates, but magnified others, including roughhousing, teasing, and practical jokes. Whenever I or one of the other teachers tried to address such an issue, we received a shrug or an eye roll along with the statement, "It's okay: that's my cousin."

That line underlies the importance of context when attempting to establish an environment conducive to learning. Two students shoving in the hallway is never appropriate, but if the two students are best friends, my reaction needs to be very different than if the two students actively avoid each other in class. Treating a moment of goofiness like a dangerous crime and treating an act of malice like a joke are equally destructive to students' feelings of safety in the classroom. Students need to be able to trust their teachers, to know that they are safe and free to learn without being treated unjustly by their classmates or their teachers.

For some student behaviors, such as those disruptive to learning, choosing the appropriate reaction is arduous. Any teacher invested in their students' success fiercely protects their ever-precious instructional time, viewing unnecessary interruptions as a threat. It becomes easy to assume that student disruptions come from a place of malicious—even personal—intent, especially when performed by those students who know exactly what buttons to push. Students are seen as either short-sighted and unaware of the long-term consequences of their behavior or as young usurpers who enjoy picking fights and making the teacher's job harder. Truthfully, students of either bent are extremely rare, but my assumptions can turn students toward either path. Was the tape under my mouse someone trying to destroy my lesson, or was it a student wanting to include me in an April Fool's Day tradition? Does the student without their notes not care about their learning, or are they having a hard time focusing due to something going on at home? The actions still need to be addressed, but how I view the surrounding contexts affects how I address them.

In my rural community, I mostly needed to help students understand the appropriate time and place for their behavior, especially for practical jokes and roughhousing. Nearly their entire peer group were family members, so it was hard for the students to understand that certain family behaviors could offend other people. And people were offended. While most of the students in the school were within two degrees of relationship to each other, each class had a handful of students with no family connection to their classmates. When these students were teased or pranked, they felt bullied, even though the classmates were rarely trying to hurt them.

Gratefully, because the intent was not malicious, it could usually be corrected using a smile, a please, and a thank you (Wong & Wong, 1998). If I was pleasant in a correction or request, using the student's name, all I had to do was wait with an expectant smile and the students would get back on track. Sometimes, I would have to wait a while, and when that happened, I only had to repeat the request once more, and students would comply. Thirty seconds of wait time feels OK for a teacher but is nearly unbearable for students, especially when their teacher is standing right next to them and listening to everything they say. I learned very quickly that I could easily outwait a reluctant student. Once they corrected their behavior, I thanked them and moved on. At times, a truly defiant student would balk at this strategy, but it worked with many issues because, in the end, most students do not intend to be malicious or defiant.

However, sometimes a simple explanation or request is not enough. Management is mostly preventative, but there are times when students require reactive discipline. When that happens, my assumptions about students become that much more important. I remind myself of my mentor's advice: these students meant the world to someone. No matter how much trouble a student causes or how often they get under my skin, someone somewhere believes they are a good kid.

There is an adage that says students would rather be called bad than stupid, but students would rather be seen as neither. From a young age, their dignity and pride are both real and fragile. I must, even in discipline, protect that dignity. If I react punitively, students rarely learn anything: they focus on protecting their pride and justifying their actions, making them more likely to repeat or escalate their misbehavior. My first move, therefore, must be to remove any threats to their dignity. I invite them into the hallway before the conversation, always using "Please" and "Thank you." I then begin the conversation with earnest questions: "Are you okay? What just happened?" By starting with questions rather than statements, I establish that I am ready to listen, thereby disarming most defensiveness. More stubborn students deflect the concern, but regardless, they know that they will be heard in the conversation ahead. I then ask them if they know why I am concerned about what they did. We walk through it, step by step, discussing how their actions might have hurt others or themselves. Funnily enough, students are often quick to recognize how their actions might have injured another person, but they rarely consider how they could have hurt themselves until it's pointed out to them.

Then comes the most important line of the conversation: "I know you didn't mean to . . ." It does not matter if the student's actions were intentional or not.

Somewhere in our conversation, we identified an injury they had not considered. I immediately follow it up with "You are not the type of person who wants that to happen." Many students have trouble disassociating doing a bad action from being a bad person, and for those raised in ethical homes, being called bad is one of the worst labels they can get. They would rather defend actions they know are wrong than concede that they are bad people. With those two reassuring sentences, students no longer need to worry about protecting their honor: I have done it for them. Likewise, when we finish discussing my concerns and the consequences of their actions, I say, "You are a good kid; I don't want to see you go down this path." The result is, even when students are being disciplined, they are willing to work with me, sometimes even thanking me. I am often surprised to see students who were highly defiant when confronted in front of their classmates break down in tears when we have a conversation in the hallway.

There have been a few times in my career when I have regretted being too harsh on students when they have misbehaved; however, I have never regretted taking a breath and giving them the benefit of the doubt before reacting.

Strength and Flexibility

Another foundation to building a trusting and engaging classroom environment is focusing on strengths rather than deficits, not only in individual students but also in the community as a whole. It can be easy to see only the challenges: where I worked, the parents had a rocky relationship with public schooling, sometimes for political reasons and other times because of previous hurtful encounters. The school environment also clashed with their culture: students started school without exposure to English or even to books; religious, family, and farming responsibilities made homework impossible; and parents viewed technology suspiciously until only recently. Pursuing higher education was also contrary to the community's values: students were reluctant to sever their familial and cultural ties to go to university in the city; and the honest and humble, blue-collar jobs they sought were rarely part of university curricula.

Focusing on the lack, however, can result in missing extraordinary gifts: spending the entire day at school and then working for hours on the farm produced a strong work ethic; putting aside a day each week for family created humor and proportion; and their religious upbringing instilled a strong ethical code, intrinsically motivating them to do what was right. However, families were perpetually concerned that the school would try to strip their students of these strengths in order to assimilate them into public schooling. To allay these fears, teachers had both to recognize the strengths students brought to the classroom and to help students recognize that school offered a way for them to use their strengths to help their community.

Capitalizing on students' strengths sometimes felt like exploitation, and I was uncomfortable with the idea at first. For example, our school always had the older students set up and take down the chairs and tables needed for assemblies, concerts, science fairs, and other such events, which at first felt like forced labor. I soon learned, however, that the students loved the opportunity to contribute in this way. There were three boys in particular who eagerly volunteered whenever anything heavy needed to be moved, and there were two other students who would light up whenever we needed help with the sound equipment. None of these students was strong academically but when they realized that they were a valued part of the school, they wanted to stick around and persevere. All five students continued on to high school and four of them graduated, setting an example for their entire community.

Students cannot always control what happens to them or what resources are available to them, but they still deserve the best education possible. The best way I as a teacher can provide that is by focusing on what both I and they can offer, rather than what we cannot change.

Personal and institutional flexibilities are essential in this process. In a smaller school, teachers have a lot of freedom to try new things, and it is a significant boon to students. At a deeper level, teaching and management is also a game of negotiation. This was especially true in my tight-knit rural school, where none of the teachers had the same cultural background as the community and so were viewed with suspicion. Regardless of what teachers believed or how they were raised, we were all considered outsiders. Even though the community was very friendly and welcoming, there was an innate sense of distrust between teachers and students. We were to be indulged but not necessarily believed because our outsideness gave us a "false" perspective on certain matters. Whatever we taught had to go through the "home filter" before it could be considered correct.

The most effective counter to this distrust was negotiation. The idea of negotiating and giving up what little authority I had went against my intuition as a teacher, especially with misbehaving students. It frustrated me that a student sent to the office for misbehavior usually got exactly what they had been demanding. What I learned, however, was that being willing to sacrifice some of my authority in order to empower the students and community enabled me to make a difference in both. Negotiating demonstrated to students that I valued their perspective and modeled how they could do likewise. This involved asking questions and apologizing, going to parents' houses to examine controversial curriculum, attending school council meetings to listen to community concerns, and running ideas by highly respected community members before causing unintentional offense. Having these conversations and then following through on what was advised went a long way in building trust with the parents, which in turn, built trust with the students.

Letting students make decisions where it was appropriate further builds trust by instilling in students a sense of ownership. Students know I will say yes to their ideas whenever I can, allowing them more readily to accept when I say no. An example of this was when the traditional junior high week-long camping trip was discontinued, replaced with a day trip to the city. Understandably, the students felt cheated, and it could have resulted in weeks of sullen passive-aggressiveness. Instead, I put aside a class to plan the day trip together. Students came up with a list of educational experiences and a list of leisure activities they wanted to do in the city, and then we took a vote and built an itinerary. By the end, the students were not only excited for the trip they had helped create, but they were looking forward to the next year when they could complete the activities that did not make the list the first time. Students would often give me an inch when they realized that I was giving them an inch as well.

On the other hand, when students believe their choices are being taken away from them, they become uncooperative and defiant. Their powerlessness-bred rebellion can come from any circumstance, from playing a game to considering post-secondary education. Whenever a student feels that options are unfairly out of their reach, they create their own justifications for the deficit. Usually, it sounds like "that is stupid, anyway." Negotiation helps students understand that they still have choices. When I hear a negative attitude starting to form in a student, we have a conversation about what they need and feel they are not able to have. After listening, I give students a choice. The choice must be meaningful, reflecting both their strengths and their expressed needs. I am also determined to accept whichever option they choose, even if I think it is not the best one. For example, a student acting out because they are not ready for a quiz that day gets a choice between attempting the quiz with the opportunity for a rewrite later or studying during class and writing the quiz at the end of class. Sometimes, students counter my choices with one of their own, and I welcome it, explaining its implications so that they can make the best choice. Students have to know that the choice is truly theirs and that I will respect their decision. Suddenly, powerless students not only feel heard but believe they have options. Often, they make a positive choice.

Agency is very powerful in helping students make the right choice. When they are treated as valued, responsible, ethical people, that's who they become.

All for One and One for All

I frequently practice Universal Design for Learning (UDL), the idea that something that helps struggling students can benefit the entire class. I design my classroom and my teaching around the needs of students with challenges first, then add extensions for students without those challenges. For example, my junior high classes had no homework, since most students would be unable to complete it; however, I assigned "extension questions" to the in-class work so that those families which expected their children to do homework each night could explore the concepts further. If some students need to chew on something while working, I offer the whole class something to eat during a test. If one student reads a test better if it is on purple paper, I provide purple exams to whoever wants one.

Not only does it help normalize students' various needs, but it also puts a spotlight on tools students might not realize are available to them.

The benefits of UDL, however, go far beyond their uses as a curriculum tool. While on a basic level UDL builds engagement and trust by providing each student with an appropriate level of challenge, the principles are both efficient and effective in establishing classroom expectations. Secondary teachers especially tend to forget that proper behavior and socialization must be taught just as rigorously as any other skill. Lessons on empathy, responsibility, diligence, and respect need to be woven into the fabric of every classroom. Each fall, I prepare for my new classes by considering the students for whom these skills are most elusive. What do they need to be successful in my and future classrooms? If I can get them to engage meaningfully, not only will the whole class benefit from fewer disruptions, but their classmates should be able to engage better as well.

A major way I help these students is by frequently using explanations. Many times, when students ask "why," it is not out of defiance but out of a genuine desire to understand. They want to know that their teachers have a reason and a plan for their actions. Explaining my routines up front puts them at ease and reduces those questions later. I especially take time to explain my discipline system. Students need to be told explicitly that a correction is not the same as being in trouble. Without this understanding, a simple correction, such as "Please put away your phone," quickly turns into a defensive argument. Again, students' primary focus is to protect their dignity. So, when explaining my system, the first thing I discuss is all the ways students are *not* in trouble. I make it clear that, like a coach, I am trying to teach them good habits. Once they realize that my goal is their success, they become much more cooperative. I am also honest about my blind spots: I freely admit, for example, that I do not always notice when students wear a hat or hood, but if I notice it, I still expect them to remove it. This stops most arguments that I am unfairly picking on a student. Finally, I explain to them how they can approach me when they think I am being unfair. I make it clear that arguing with me is the quickest way to get in trouble, no matter how innocuous the initial situation, since it disrupts their classmates' learning. Then I model how to express their concerns respectfully. When they know they have an acceptable recourse if they disagree with me, students rarely cause major disruptions.

Another UDL tip related to behavior is to verbalize if a correction is being made for a second time. Before creating this habit, I assumed that I had made it clear to students that they needed to change their actions, but later realized that most of the time my "making things clear" was a stern look, or worse, something muttered under my breath. Many times, students were oblivious to my irritation. Once I started my requests with, "This is the second time I have asked you," and finished them with, "If I have to ask you a third time," however, it ensured I said it a first time and gave students fair warning that the consequences were about to escalate. "Three-strikes" is a common idea for most students; they remember I am serious but also realize that I have given them a second chance.

The consequences themselves are another area where UDL is essential, not by treating all students identically, but by designing consequences that are more about discipline than punishment. Natural consequences, where possible, are the best option: cleaning defaced surfaces; writing apologies to insulted parties; rewriting disregarded assignments; paying back wasted time from free time; or completing online ethics courses when technology has been abused. All these consequences require students to give up some of their recesses or lunch breaks but are more effective in reforming inappropriate actions than mere detention. When natural consequences are not available, proportion and explanations are again key to helping students take responsibility for their actions.

By treating classroom expectations, appropriate school behavior, and daily routines as a subject to be taught rather than demands to be met, students develop the tools necessary to be successful in school beyond the regular curricula.

Connection Beyond the Internet

Online learning is a challenge rural secondary teachers faced long before the pandemic that began in 2020. Small rural schools survive using split classes, but that is nearly impossible in high school due to the volumes of curriculum each course covers. To give students the best chance at a well-balanced education, my school division connected students online from multiple schools so that they could share a teacher and take their needed course. I became one of these teachers when a school smaller than mine and over 300 km away had an influx of 13 students entering grade 10 and no high school math teacher. Suddenly, my class of five students whom I had known for years had quadrupled into a class of strangers.

Each of our schools was equipped with a video conferencing (VC) suite that included cameras, monitors, a microphone, a dial-in connection, and software to share my screen with the other participants. The challenges that came with the set-up and maintenance of that suite were substantial, but as VC suites evolved into the Internet- and app-based "blended learning" suites, it became clear that the greatest challenge of teaching online was enabling students to make meaningful connections with their teacher and virtual classmates. I once booked a day to travel to and teach from my first satellite class. At this point, I had been teaching them for nine days. I knew all their names and many of their personalities and had spoken with them multiple times over the phone. Nevertheless, when I walked through the doors of the school and greeted one of my students by name, she acted like I had psychic abilities. "You know me?" This student had been one of the most engaged members of the class, but even she saw me as only a talking head until I stood before her as flesh and bone. After that visit, I noticed a dramatic difference in how the students interacted in class: they were more relaxed and a few more dared to speak up on the microphone.

Connection with students, regardless of the medium, is key to effective classroom management. When the teaching is done remotely, connection becomes twice as important even as it becomes twice as difficult. Many classic management tools are useless across hundreds of kilometers and a monitor. Every teacher knows how hard it is to keep students engaged during a video without deliberate planning, and that is when the teacher is present in the room. Until the students realize that they are active members of a conversation and not passive absorbers of information, inattention, distractions, and socialization plague the room. While there are things that can increase student engagement in class, it always starts with connection. With my blended learning classes, I made the extra effort to ensure that students knew they were both seen by and mattered to me. I prioritized visiting all my schools when I could, whether that meant twice a semester or twice a week. I made sure students could contact me via email, messaging apps, or one-on-one video calls if they needed extra help. But being available to my distanced students was not enough: I also had to initiate contact by sending the first email or, even better, by picking up the phone and talking to a student one-on-one. These conversations took extra time and would cut into my preparation times, but I saw these interactions as preparation of a different kind: laying the foundation for student success in the classroom. Once they saw me as their teacher and not a recording, their engagement in the class intensified.

It is not enough for online students to see me as their teacher, however; they must see the other students as their classmates. That means making time daily to allow students to talk. Speaking up in front of the class is frightening enough when students are all in the same room, but adding a camera to the mix increases many students' anxiety. No one wants to look the fool in front of the world, but by creating connections and building an intimate classroom environment, students are no longer in front of the world. And, students desire these connections as much as teachers do. The most common question I got when I visited satellite schools was related to the name of a classmate across the screen, and sometimes I would arrive at class to find students already connected to the VC and chatting. Once, as I was preparing to visit a satellite school, one of the students got on the microphone: "Can you take something back for me when you come?" When I said I could, he held up a pack of gum and said to one of the students across the screen, "This pack of gum is for you." It was reciprocated a few weeks later, when some students from my home classroom requested if they could come along on a final visit, they could play basketball with their new friends during lunch.

Connections are foundational for online classroom management, but they are not enough. Students still need structure and accountability to reach the high standards their teachers set for them, even more so online. I still explain my expectations and routines, but I now also explain the necessity of each student's being on camera and participating in online check-ins. I still get students to practice the procedures of my classroom, but now they also need to practice speaking in front of their classmates, usually through innocuous ice-breaker questions. I still need them to feel valued, but now I do it by calling students by name and honoring their courage for asking questions and attempting answers, making sure to say "thank you," "good question," or "good try." And I still need to preserve student dignity when addressing a concern with them, but now I do it through different off-camera methods such as emails and phone calls.

Additional structures are also necessary to maintain student accountability. The most valuable of these structures is having a partner on the other side of the screen. When there is a person who can print off documents, supervise exams, connect the VC suite at the start of class, provide proximity for students, and scan student work for me to mark, my job becomes so much easier. In the absence of that, and often in addition to it, I take time to train students on how to run the technology, submit their assignments, and access notes and assignments online. During tests, I use things such as different versions of exams and keeping the microphones and cameras live as deterrents to cheating. To maintain proximity, I require students to be visible in the classroom. Many online tools and apps allow for full-class participation and individual accountability, from online whiteboards and forms to random name pickers. Through them, I can ask any student to answer any question, and it allows me to spot check every student at once. With so many free options available, the issue becomes less about students falling through the cracks than figuring out which apps work best with an individual's planning and teaching style.

Teaching in rural communities comes with its own unique dynamics, some rewarding, others more difficult. But, whether teaching in a small school or a large classroom, in person or online, certain truths about classroom management remain the same: it must be founded on trusting relationships with students and their community, established early with clear expectations, and followed through fairly and consistently.

Reference

Wong, H. K., & Wong, R. T. (1998). *The first days of school*. Harry K. Wong Publications.

24
THE CHALLENGES AND REWARDS OF TEACHING IN REMOTE SETTINGS

Dena Palmaymesa and Natasha Steenhof Bakker

Perspectives of a One-Room Schoolteacher
Dena Palmaymesa

No one individual and no single class could have prepared me for the *gifts of simplicity* that awaited me as a one-room teacher. Early in my career in this remote setting, I loaded students into my car to travel several hours to cheer on a former student at his first basketball game. The call had come in around nine p.m. the previous evening. The father of this former student had suddenly died. The family had recently moved out of state for employment reasons. Early in his new employment, my student's father was attending training out of state, when he started to feel ill. The night before he was to return, he went to bed early and told his wife he would call her back in the morning. That call never came. He had an undetected heart issue and passed away that night.

On the day my student's mother traveled to escort the body of her husband home, their son, my former student, was a high-school freshman. He was starting his first varsity, basketball game. An impressive position for any freshman, but having come from a one-room school, it was even more impressive, and to carry on in the circumstances, unimaginable. Those of us in his old schoolhouse were excited for him and anticipated hearing all about his first game. However, when I heard of his father's passing, that his mom would miss this game, and he wanted to honor his dad by playing in the game, I knew he needed familiar faces and voices cheering him on that night.

Earlier that morning, I communicated with my principal the events that had transpired and what the day held for my former student. His closest friends, who had known this student and his parents since they were babies, sat before me grieving. I asked my principal to close school early and take this older group of boys to watch their friend play his first basketball game. She said, "As long as all parents agree, you have my support." My husband and I loaded his best friends into our truck and drove more than four hours to show our support. It was a night I will never forget. While he scored basket after basket, his mother was bringing the body of his father home. I sat in the stands watching my students cheer on their friend, and I asked myself how in the world I was blessed to witness such devotion. Years have passed, life has moved on, but their commitment to each other has remained. These boys are now married, have stood up for one another in their weddings, and have remained committed to sharing life's most precious moments. What an honor it is to have taught them.

At the beginning, it was foreign and unsettling to walk into a classroom as the teacher and the newest addition to the room. Typically, students are initiated into the classroom environment every year, and they rely on the teacher to acclimate them to the new surroundings. In my situation, it was the opposite. All my students, except one little boy—who was my ray of sunshine in those first months—had already attended that school. For a handful of years, students in the nine grade levels had grown accustomed to the school layout, the established routines, the locations of supplies, how to restart the printer when it acted up, and what time to begin their math lessons. They did not welcome any changes I might bring to the setting. For some, my presence was a constant reminder of the loss of the only teacher they had known. When volunteers came in, at times established by my predecessor, the students asked them questions rather than addressing me directly. And why wouldn't they? These women, all moms of students, were known trusted adults. To them, they were the surrogate auntie next door, where a child could enter in, unannounced, use the bathroom, or get a drink when out playing and her house was closer than their own. I had to work hard to earn their trust.

We experienced many bumps en route to the peace we now experience. In those first few weeks, students freely informed me that this was not how they did this or that and voiced doubts that I could teach both kindergarten and seventh-grade math simultaneously. It was not long before I realized that my desire to avoid rocking the boat and to honor their history by seeking out their understanding of the school had resulted in my giving my students most of the power. I was determined to show them, and myself, that I was up to the challenges of a multi-grade teacher. Instead of asking questions, I did a thorough inventory to memorize where supplies were. I read the manual on the printer and took math books home to remain at least two lessons ahead of my oldest students. Rather than compromising my style and addressing the need to rid myself of someone else's ill-fitting shoes, I took a pro-active stance. With the support and encouragement of my principal, I thoughtfully communicated, to my students and their families, that I would make some changes after the first grading period, to help us function more successfully and with a sense of unity. While I initially met resistance from the oldest students, parents gladly welcomed the adjustments and encouraged me as the new leader. I asked parents to pause their volunteer work in the classroom until I had the chance to establish myself and assess how volunteers would best serve students. Parents graciously stepped back and reentered when I made the areas of need clear.

I decided to *host* our classroom rather than *manage* it. I continue with these practices to this day. Each morning I greet my students by their first and last name. I ask them how they are feeling and if they have anything to share. I encourage students to take charge of their learning and voice how they work best: lights on, natural light, math or reading warm-ups first, music playing or silence, standing or sitting, working on a computer, or using paper and pencil. I play soft, instrumental music throughout the day. Students manage their personal needs when their body communicates the necessity. Rather than submitting to a specific schedule, they are empowered to develop agency and self-regulation. My students have never abused this freedom to self-manage. At the end of each month, there are awards for "self-managers" and a Fun Friday, the last hour of the last Friday given to games, to honor their hard work.

My expectations are clear and simple: *Do it nice or do it twice. Always do your personal best. In our classroom, we are safe, respectful, and responsible.* When there is an issue, be it workmanship or behavior, we measure the matter against these expectations and make necessary adjustments. Students also set quarterly goals and assess themselves. Behavior issues are rare.

As a community member, I live within walking distance of all of my students. I attend social gatherings, and many of my friends are also parents of my students. This is a delicate dance. While I do feel alone much of the time outside the school day, I have made meals when a family has had a baby, picked up items for community members while I was in town, and tended to plants or pets when someone is away. I am extended the same kindness in return.

When lines become blurred, and at times they do, I simply ask that I be allowed to wear my *neighbor hat* or indicate when it is time for me to don my *teacher hat*. This is usually respected. When there are issues, I remind myself to keep short accounts, extend grace, and tuck away the lesson to be learned. I also think about the differences between my current placement and the factors I dealt with in other settings. Both learning environments offer their challenges, some more draining than others.

Within the first months, I knew I was in a unique learning environment. Although I had experienced teaching a combined class of two grades, my education had not prepared me to teach nine grades. Classes on management or curriculum implementation, for example, did not cover how to create blended learning units, establish expectations, or design a classroom layout to span nine-grade levels. Likewise, my course work did not encompass how to manage the various roles I would play aside from just teacher: school nurse, recess attendant, janitor, registrar, and secretary. These additional responsibilities prove demanding and exhilarating at the same time, and they result in deep relationships. I know my students, their families, and the community well.

While I know my students, I often wonder if there is a better way. Am I doing all I can for my students and their families? This wondering led me on a road trip to visit similar multi-grade learning environments in my region and put me on the path toward my doctoral research. I found that, by common sense or by the grace of God, I do pretty much the same things as other multi-grade teachers: spin plates as best as we can. They too gave older students independent work while providing direct instruction to younger groups first. Then, once a group was able to work independently, they moved to the next group. This juggling act would go on all day, for all subjects. Older students, from time to time, assisted younger students when the teacher was unavailable. Strangely, all the teachers I visited also experienced resistance upon their arrival. It appears that some small communities are fearful of outsiders. Building trust is the best remedy, which takes time.

Interestingly, trust is now prevalent in my school setting, although it is difficult to identify the exact source of that trust. Does it come from the school and filter to the community or does it originate in the community itself and transfer to the school? I believe trust is rooted in the social capital we all experience. As one parent said to me, "It is just part of our community." This sentiment was echoed by a new family, "Trust transcended into us."

It is within this setting, where students trust other students, parents trust the teachers, and teachers trust the community, that I observe my students taking risks, regardless of their age. The multi-grade environment encourages older peers to set an example of how to ask questions, take risks, and persevere when a challenge arises. The stage is then set for endless exploration. I have heard that the factors that lead to trust are benevolence, reliability, competence, honesty, and openness. I am privileged to witness these factors daily in the interactions between my students.

I recall one of the purest exchanges between students I was privileged to witness. A grade 4 student had undergone a complicated surgery. She had to use a wheelchair for several weeks before transitioning to a walker. The boys in her grade group took the initiative to move desks and chairs to accommodate her wheelchair. They brought her school supplies, sharpened her pencils, delivered water and snacks to her, held the door, and volunteered to stay inside during recess to play a game with her, always of her choice. I was amazed by their inherent chivalry. It was beautiful, and it all happened naturally.

I remember feeling that their care for her was not necessarily a testament of what was taught in school, but evidence of the power of trust between them from having shared history. The fact that they were so secure with each other, that they had known each other since they were babies, meant they were more like brothers. Together, they were taking care of their sweet friend, a sister. She knew them and trusted them in her most vulnerable moments.

The inherent trust between students was evident to me from the beginning and shows up in students' creative play as well. Over one particular week, I witnessed students creating dinosaurs by laying out rocks on the covered patio area during recess. I was captivated that the children found enjoyment playing in the dirt with rocks. At that time, the school did not have much recess equipment, other than the tetherball. For an entire week, students worked on their creations, younger and older students altogether during morning and noon recesses. They told me I could not enter their work area until they were finished. I watched all week as students came out from the patio area in search of rocks, judged their treasures, and looked for symmetrical ones. When they finished, they walked around admiring one another's creations, giving out praise and compliments. At that moment, I hoped I would never lose my ability to notice these *gifts of simplicity* as I have come to call them. Thankfully, new students continue to bring such gifts before me.

In my 15th year, I witnessed a similar collaboration between children of various ages. Even with new playground equipment, these children freely create. Under the new dome play-structure, students designed gardens. For a couple of days, I watched them collect moss, sticks, and rocks. Each one carved out a little section, again, keeping their creations from me until they finished. As they worked, older students helped younger students with the Tonka Trucks to carve paths or carry larger rocks. Thankfully, the beauty in their simple gifts still does not escape me.

Relationships in this setting are deep. I know my students beyond a single school year. These long-term connections save time with assessments in September. In addition, when there are family issues or needs, I am kept in the loop and can offer extra comfort and support. Knowing my families, and having a shared trust between us, equips me to help my students process these stressors. I was not always privileged with this kind of information in other settings, and too often issues manifested themselves as negative behaviors or lack of attention.

In a rural setting, I perceive many benefits, as well as deficits. The addition of a teaching partner has been extremely beneficial. Together, we can focus on specific grade-level content without putting other grades on hold for extended periods. In the early days of teaching all grades, I often felt I was operating from the shallows. Now the school is divided into two groups, upper and lower elementary, and we serve students at a deeper level. Having a colleague has also addressed some of the perceived deficits of the school. Together, we combine our strengths to give students a well-rounded education despite our limitations. While we are somewhat limited in our academic offerings to older students in advanced placement courses, for example, we have the flexibility to explore various electives when community members volunteer to share with students their passion and expertise in areas such as orienteering, Spanish, or sign language. Our remote location limits extra-curricular activities as well. The trade-off for most families is the absence of many negative issues, such as bullying. However, these topics are addressed within the safety of a classroom of known peers. With a little creativity, the value of team sports is not overlooked. Community volunteers have come forward to teach soccer, basketball, and baseball. Practices are as well attended as the games between teams, with students and various community members all coming to watch. Serving students with special needs also takes creativity and collaboration and gives us the opportunity to partner with specialists over Zoom. Often, the good and the hard are one and the same here.

The most difficult aspect of teaching in a rural, remote setting is isolation. Having a true confidant and colleague is invaluable, and the feeling of constantly being on duty is somewhat reduced, but not eliminated. I recall a comment made to me in my first year. During a community social event, some of the students were roughhousing in the middle of the gathering. One older gentleman from the community asked me, "Hey, Teach, whatcha gonna do about those boys?" In a lighthearted response, I exclaimed, "I am off the clock." To which he said something that sticks with me to this day, "Didn't anyone tell you? You are never off the clock out here." While this is true, for the most part, I have found familiarity, balance, and awareness of the *gifts of simplicity* before me.

Moving From the City to the Country: Classroom Management in a Small Rural School Natasha Steenhof Bakker

During my two years in my teacher preparation degree, I heard the phrase "know your students" at least once every day, in innumerable settings, and repeated by every one of my professors. This simple expression became a slogan and a battle cry that our cohort rallied around and it even became part of our graduation celebrations. I admit that at times I scoffed at the simplistic nature of this motto that seemed to be given as at least part of the solution for every classroom management issue that was discussed. When considering matters of disruptive behavior, apathetic attitudes, and classroom clowns, we were always told that the key to solving these difficulties was to have knowledge about our students. We were encouraged to invest deeply in our relationships with students in order to understand what motivated them, to predict how they would respond to certain situations, and to assess if there were underlying factors that contributed to their behavior.

This motto was in the back of my mind as I approached the first of my two practicum experiences and I quickly realized that it was not an oversimplification. Having an understanding of my students, recognizing their strengths and areas for improvement, and knowing how they would respond to different learning activities were imperative for effective classroom management and for meaningful learning to take place. I also quickly recognized that most students will respond to displays of authority and discipline in a more positive way if there is first mutual trust and respect between the teacher and student. However, I also came to realize that knowing my students and forming relationships with them would look quite different depending on the context. In my short time as a teacher, I have experienced very different settings and classroom sizes; in my practicums, I taught at large secondary schools in urban centers with up to 35 students in a classroom. Since finishing my degree, I have taught at two small, independent, religious schools in rural communities. These experiences have allowed me to reflect on the impacts rural and urban settings have on my approach to classroom management.

My experience in urban settings consisted of two practicums: a six-week session at a junior high and an eleven-week period at a senior high school. This will focus on my final practicum, as this experience was much longer and more intensive than my first practicum. My second practicum took place at a large high school where I taught English in grades 10, 11, and 12. Class sizes ranged from 20 to 35 students and, due to the two-day calendar, I taught semester courses every day and linear courses two or three times per week. I had over a hundred students, many of whom I did not see very often. Despite my best intentions, it was difficult to build relationships with all students; my natural shyness and introverted nature did not help in this process, and I often felt intimidated by students who were sometimes physically bigger than me. In the semester courses, it was somewhat easier to find a natural rapport with some students, but I always felt that students were falling between the cracks. It was easy to miss students who were quieter, English language learners, and students who regularly skipped classes. The large number of students and the size of the classroom meant that sometimes students were quite literally hidden from my view, either behind other classmates or even because pillars blocked my view. These factors meant that it was difficult to have expectations of students whom I did not know well, and sometimes my classroom management strategies strayed into the areas of bribery and threats. Because I was unable to anticipate how students would respond to different situations and activities, it was sometimes difficult to plan learning strategies.

Reflecting on this experience, I can also appreciate the aspects of working at a large urban school that contributed to positive relationships between my students and myself. From the very beginning of my practicum, I felt that I was viewed as a professional by the students. A lack of previous personal connections meant that I approached the experience with no preconceived notions about the students, and they had no assumptions about me. This meant that I could build relationships with students and earn their respect and trust based simply on our interactions in the classroom. There were no outside factors such as mutual friends or involvement in different community groups that interfered with this process. In this process of building rapport with students, I never observed students questioning my authority because I was a female teacher, and I felt respected as a professional.

Another factor that positively impacted my ability to manage classrooms during this practicum experience was that the majority of my students were focused on attending post-secondary institutions and thus quite invested in their education. Many of my students were focused on completing their work well and finding success in my class because it would have a direct impact on their ability to enter the programs they had chosen.

It was this desire for post-secondary education that distinguished my urban and rural students. Although many of my rural students did want to pursue a post-secondary education, a large percentage also had ambitions outside the academic world. Some students were driven by a desire to do well in my class and they worked hard to receive top marks, but there was not the same expectation that students would inevitably attend a university that I experienced when teaching during my practicum experience.

After I completed my teaching degree, I accepted a temporary maternity leave position in a rural area, teaching high school English at the school I had previously attended. I knew that this position would be extremely different from what I had experienced during my practicums, not only because of the rural setting but also because I would be returning to a school where I knew all the teachers and many of the students. I taught students who I had grown up with, including younger siblings of my friends, classmates of my younger siblings, and students who were family friends. This meant that some of my students had preconceived notions about who I was, something that impacted my approach to authority in the classroom as I had to navigate these previous relationships. For some students who were more familiar with me, I had to work hard to establish a student–teacher relationship by differentiating between who I was as a friend outside the school and my position of authority inside the classroom. I struggled to navigate this complex situation, making sure that I asserted myself in the classroom without becoming overbearing or domineering. Building trust was still at the center of my classroom management style and I knew that completely alienating my students would not set me up for success.

Teaching at an independent religious school also meant that I now faced issues of gender that were not part of my practicum experiences. Although many of my students at this smaller school had females in their life who did not conform to typical gender roles, I did encounter a different atmosphere related to what it meant to be a female in the workplace. There were discussions in my classroom about the appropriateness of women having spiritual authority over men, either in teaching roles or as pastors of churches. These conversations made me aware that my leadership was possibly not accepted by all students in my classroom. I sensed that my authority was being challenged in a way that I had not previously experienced, and this did affect how I approached certain situations and specific students. Although I made a conscious effort to overcome these worries, I know at some level that my approach to classroom management shifted as I considered the fact that some of my students might be uncomfortable with a female in a position of authority. I worked hard not to feel intimidated by this or to compensate by becoming completely authoritarian, but instead continued to develop trust by investing in relationships and spending time with students.

Another aspect connected to gender that I noticed was that students were much more willing to inquire about my personal life; students would ask when I was going to have children and one student even asked if I was pregnant. During my practicum experiences, questions about my personal life were directed toward who I was as a professional; these questions centered on themes about my university experience, how I chose my profession, and advice I had for students entering post-secondary institutions. In this urban center, students knew me only as a professional and therefore my identity was formed entirely around this role. However, in a rural setting, I felt the unspoken expectation that beginning a family was an inevitability and that teaching was a secondary occupation for married women. Some of these questions might have been a result of the fact that some of my students knew me personally, but most of the questions and comments actually came from students with whom I did not have a previous relationship. The irony is that the willingness of students to enquire about my personal life had a positive impact on my ability to build relationships within my classroom. As I felt more comfortable sharing about who I was as a person, there was more intimacy between my students and me.

This leads to the biggest shift that I noticed when moving from teaching in an urban center to a rural setting: the prioritizing of creating a sense of community. In both schools I have worked at since moving from an urban center, I have observed an effort to build relationships not only in classrooms but across the school as a whole. Conversations in staff meetings are often focused on planning activities and events to strengthen community; all school assemblies are planned so that teachers can interact with students who they do not regularly teach. I recognize that moving from a large high school to a small independent school adds nuance to this situation as it is much easier to build relationships with a student body of 250 students compared to 2,500 students. In addition, teaching in religious schools adds the element of chapels and assemblies focused on worship that add to this community building. However, the reality of simply living in smaller communities also has a dramatic impact on the level of relationships and familiarity with students. In rural settings, teachers and students are often involved in the same community events outside the school; it is almost impossible to spend a day simply running errands without encountering at least one student. Teachers attend events such as games and musical recitals not because they are expected to, but because they are deeply invested in the lives of their students outside the classroom.

However, the tight-knit community found in rural communities can be both a blessing and a curse. Interacting with students in activities and community events outside the classroom can of course lead to the quick formation of relationships. But this closeness with students and their families can also cause fatigue; sometimes, it can feel as if there is no space between my workplace and my home life.

In some ways, I miss the anonymity that I experienced when teaching in an urban setting; leaving work on Friday afternoon and not interacting with my students or colleagues until Monday morning created a separation that contributed to a true sense of rest. It was easier to create a balance between work and life because they were not connected as intricately as they are in rural settings. The familiarity and closeness between teachers and students can also be difficult to navigate in terms of classroom authority. In my practicum experiences, my connection to students was only as a professional; in rural settings, I have had friendships with my students' siblings and parents and I have had to rethink what authority looks like; I give students a more intimate look into what my life is like outside of school. Some of this is unavoidable as I have connections to their parents through the church, community groups, and even social media.

The differences go beyond urban and rural, however. After completing the maternity leave, I moved to another small community where I accepted a job at another small independent school. I need to acknowledge that these two experiences had structural differences. In this second rural school, I was an elementary teacher; this meant that I directly taught only two classes and only 23 students with whom I interacted on a daily basis. Spending more time with each student was much more conducive to building relationships with the members of my classes. However, I could still observe the same differences between the culture and community that I had previously experienced in an urban setting. It was clear from my first interaction with this school that community building was an integral part of the school's identity. Administrators and teacher colleagues encouraged me to build relationships with my students, noting that sometimes academic goals needed to be secondary. This was an incredible gift for me, as my classroom management style is based on creating trust with students. The school I currently teach at encourages teachers to use initiatives called *CREW*, which stands for greetings, readings, games, discussion protocols, and trust-building activities. The purpose of these activities is to develop a classroom culture where students feel like they belong, are supported, and develop confidence. Being intentional about *CREW* has helped me immensely in creating an environment where students feel respected by their classmates and by their teacher. These activities have also benefited my classroom program as students feel comfortable sharing their ideas and thoughts during discussions. The safe environment that we have created together means that students do not mock their classmates' answers or ridicule the ideas of others, leading to fewer discipline issues and more meaningful class discussions.

The average classroom size in rural schools, especially independent schools, is another aspect that deeply affected my approach to classroom management. My classes have ranged between 14 and 20 students, allowing me to interact with each student individually every day. These small class sizes allow me to tailor lesson plans to different learning needs and styles that I know are present in my classroom. I am also able to consider the interests of my students when planning activities, a freedom which contributes positively to engagement from students who are more attentive when they can relate to classroom material in meaningful ways. These small class sizes also allow me to use small, practical measures in my classroom management approach, such as physical proximity to students. I am able to check in with each student during classwork, assessing their abilities and ensuring that they understand the material. When I was teaching classes of 35 or more students, this level of connection was impossible; keeping students focused and on-task was much more difficult. An important part of my approach to classroom management is ensuring that students understand the classwork or assignment they are completing; such understanding significantly reduces the amount of student distraction.

One reason I was originally drawn to the profession of teaching was the rich diversity of experiences within this line of work. As I reflect on my teacher preparation and what my career has consisted of so far, I understand why teachers must be flexible and willing to adapt to new situations and contexts. My practicum experiences gave me a taste of the challenges facing teachers who have large classes and who teach many students whom they may see only two or three times a week. Forming relationships with over a hundred students in one term requires an abundance of effort; building trust takes intentional work that can often be overlooked when teachers focus only on the curriculum they need to cover. Because I believe that classroom management is about building a space where students feel that they are heard and respected, the small classroom sizes I have experienced in rural schools have had a positive impact on my classroom management approach. Another aspect of teaching in rural communities that I have come to appreciate is the emphasis in rural schools on building community and the way it leads to more positive relationships between teachers and students. However, the small community characteristic of rural schools can be both a blessing and a disadvantage because of the level of fatigue that often results from the closeness and proximity in these settings.

Although classroom size, school size, and the rural versus urban school setting have had impacts on my approach to classroom atmosphere and management, one essential element has not changed: the pursuit of healthy relationships with students based on mutual trust and respect. The mantra of "know your students" is a piece of wisdom that I continue to repeat and reflect on despite the move from teaching in urban centers to rural communities. As I continue in my teaching career, I expect that building relationships with my students, developing trust within my classroom, and creating a safe space will be the center of my approach to classroom management.

25
REFLECTIONS OF A VETERAN SECONDARY TEACHER

Ron McIntyre

To my embarrassment, I admit that for over 30 years, I suffered from mild sleeplessness on Sunday nights, which regularly escalated to severe insomnia on the night before school start-up in the fall. Classroom management was usually the cause of my restlessness, but I learned over time that I was not alone. Even the most experienced teachers with impeccable reputations had a similar experience of dread upon their imminent return to the classroom. With time, teachers acquire and refine their management practices, but those butterflies—although diminished—linger. Classroom management presents a serious challenge for beginning teachers, but they can meet that challenge with good mentorship and honest self-reflection. When I was a beginning teacher, exemplar teachers had a profound effect on developing my belief that good classrooms should have three things: a strong sense of purpose, with optimism, and humor.

It is important to understand that while good pedagogy includes these three elements, they can be practiced by diverse personalities with varied leadership styles. For example, some teachers are extroverts who dominate a space with their presence and nature. Others are more subdued in their demeanor and manage their students accordingly. Schools have room for many types of teacher personalities and approaches, but one must always remember that the goal is for students to develop the knowledge, skills, and emotional attributes that will help them contribute to their communities. Furthermore, teachers must ensure that their leadership style is sensitive to the diverse beliefs and values of students.

Purposeful Leadership Planning: About Content and More

Exemplary teachers use curriculum as the vehicle to develop students' emotional, social, and intellectual development. The educator's job is to help students become more self-aware, resilient, and able to take responsibility for their actions. If, along the way, students also acquire skills that allow them to work with a diverse group of coworkers, then the teacher has served the community well. Good leadership, then, fosters the emotional growth of the student and delivers the curriculum through strong unit and lesson planning.

Teachers generally enjoy a great deal of freedom in crafting and delivering their lessons, and most teachers learn early in their careers that a well-planned lesson goes a long way toward ensuring that students will remain on task and be engaged. The key is to make the lesson resonate with the learner and this usually happens when it is delivered with energy and passion. Having a strong understanding of the methodology of their subject matter gives teachers the ability and flexibility to be spontaneous. Teachers well versed in their subject and connected to their students can roll with unexpected questions or interests, thus avoiding the issues associated with disengaged learners.

Lessons with clearly communicated goals display confident leadership as preparation is clearly evident. Special care should be taken to include both content and skill development in a lesson's objectives. Clearly, communicating goals has three primary functions: it lets the student know that the teacher is prepared with a plan, it reminds the teacher during the lesson what the goals are for the day while serving as a contract that will be fulfilled, and it provides a summary at the lesson's end. Student discipline inevitably suffers in classes without clear curricular and skill objectives.

As important as daily lesson plans are, the purposeful teacher must remember that the lesson fits into the greater arc of the unit. Units, like paragraphs, help organize students' thoughts and provide welcome breaks when they end, generating enthusiasm for the start of the next one. The American author, Stephen King (2000), argues that the paragraph is the foundation of good writing. While the sentence is usually considered a more basic unit of meaning, the paragraph allows the mind to process a central idea before moving on to the next theme. The comparison can be made that units in a subject serve much the same purpose as paragraphs in a story and bring continuity to a series of lesson plans. The lesson serves a similar role within a unit as the sentence does within a paragraph.

Knowledgeable teachers who prepare their lessons and units fulfill their obligation to fellow faculty members. Shirking the responsibility to prepare well can have repercussions within departments and institutions as it undermines the efforts of other teachers who must reteach content or skills that were not adequately covered in previous grades. Schools are more efficient when students transition easily from one grade to another and where the expectations are consistent. By setting high expectations for instruction and engagement, you do a great service to your pupils and teacher colleagues.

Assessment: The Power of Peers

An important element in the planning of a unit is formative assessment practices that help students understand the evaluative process. Peer comments and editing can be a very effective strategy to help improve student's work. Students sometimes care more about what their peers think of their work than what grade the teacher might assign it! For example, when debating the merits of a particular government policy or character in a story, students can take contrary positions and exchange papers with their partners to write a rebuttal. I tried this type of lesson quite late in my career and discovered that students often took such formative assignments more seriously than my weighted summative exams. The opinion of their peers clearly mattered, and their written projects improved dramatically.

When assessing learning, one must remember that quiet classrooms with desks in a row and a stern-looking teacher walking up and down the aisles banging a yardstick in the palm of their hand are not necessarily efficient. Students working with their peers may appear to be rather raucous, but on closer examination, one realizes that the students are clearly engaged. Carefully planned lessons with clear goals should occasionally include opportunities for students to engage with each other to achieve desired outcomes. A healthy byproduct of well-executed lessons with strong expectations is a student who understands that life tends to reward those who are willing to work toward an objective.

Building Relationships: Developing Student Resiliency

Students' ability to handle difficult situations and build resiliency is greatly enhanced in classrooms where encouragement and support are readily available. Teachers who choose not to build connections with their students will find their ability to manage undermined by students whose growth is not being supported or nurtured. This can lead to confrontations and ongoing discipline issues which will distract others in the classroom and perhaps the wider school community. The results can be highly detrimental for schools because morale will suffer, and some teachers will increasingly be drawn to the negativity expressed by their struggling colleagues. Teachers who are compassionate and help students move through their insecurities and fears leave an indelible mark, and their commitment is not forgotten by those fortunate to have experienced it.

Teachers who are compassionate, build relationships, and embrace a growth mindset foster the emotional growth and resiliency of their students. The concept of personal, social, or intellectual growth is a difficult concept to grasp for young learners as they, like most people, see themselves as either "good or bad" at something with little room for improvement. People who are inclined toward this way of thinking give up easily when presented with a difficult task, as they see themselves inherently weak in particular areas. This character trait is present in all levels of student ability, and it has long-term implications. At some point in everyone's life, challenges will appear that demand courage and the determination to improve. The student's first steps toward improving in an area of weakness are greatly facilitated by a teacher who understands the reluctance to move forward, which is deeply rooted in the psyche.

The resilience required to bounce back from disappointment and adversity is a much admired and necessary character trait. With recently gained knowledge in psychology and the neurosciences, it is increasingly important that we nurture adaptability and flexibility in our young people. One way to do this is through the teachers' insistence that students push themselves to reach the objectives for the course. The teachers' belief in the students' ability to persevere despite the obstacles they might face is an important yet often overlooked way to instill confidence. This is not only a problem for young people, and teachers need to be reminded that they too will stumble and need to model the resiliency they wish to instill in their students.

Optimism

A strong sense of purpose coupled with an optimistic mindset is a formidable combination for any teacher or educational leader. In fact, they are non-negotiable in well-managed classrooms or school activities. A philosophy of life that refuses to go down the road of cynicism and instead embraces positivity best serves the teacher and sets the students on the correct path. Teachers must be cognizant of the complexity of human behaviors and know that making connections through best practices give students the optimal learning environment.

Importance of Being/Appearing Confident

You often hear the language of confidence/positive energy mentioned in discussions about people who are very adept at their vocations. A well-prepared lesson will fill the teacher with a self-assured presence that the students will quickly recognize and to which they will respond positively. Conversely, there is little chance that an unprepared teacher can be confident. Through positive body language such as good posture, physical proximity, eye contact, and deliberate pauses, teachers are more likely to engage their learners. Another important behavior that exemplar teachers should always aim for is to "never flinch" in the face of adversity. Good leaders are adept at keeping their emotions in control and not letting adversaries know their weak spots. Challenges to the authority of the teacher are unavoidable in the classroom, but teachers can greatly reduce the chances of this happening through preparation and positive body language.

Confidence and optimism are further aided by a heartfelt greeting for those entering your classroom. Such greetings are a courtesy that pays dividends in building relationships. They also serve as a good chance to encourage, compliment, and get to know your students. Being at the door provides an opportunity to chat briefly in private with students who are not meeting the standards of behavior. Before the door closes, a quick smile and wave to a colleague can lift the spirit of optimism and positivity.

Human Nature Is Complex but Rules Should Be Simple

Teachers filled with optimism tend to have very few specific rules regarding classroom discipline yet have very high expectations for behaviors and student deportment. There are three rules that seem to resonate with students and they are quite simple: attend class and be on time, be prepared for class, and respect yourself and others. The first two rules seem easily attainable, as is the third with the exception of the student who likes to bemoan their lack of ability or is resentful of others. Fewer rules are better because most students are equipped with a moral compass that simply needs to be linked with the goals of the classroom. The teacher should remain optimistic that slight corrections are generally all that will be required.

Well-grounded teachers are aware of the potential as well as the limitations of their students when it comes to behaviors such as self-control, empathy, and critical thinking. Teachers who see their students as either forlorn little devils or perfect little angels neglect the reality of human nature. The truth about young people is that they are usually found somewhere in the middle on the continuum between selfishness and altruism. Teachers must not be surprised by both positive and negative behaviors in a classroom and must pursue a solution-based mindset to whatever transpires.

Teachers with an unrealistic view of their students risk being bitterly disappointed when the latter do not respond to positivity and optimism. Unfortunately, this can lead to self-doubt on the part of the teacher and a crisis of confidence. Teachers must always be introspective but sometimes the proper foundation in a classroom is not enough for a student who has issues with hierarchy or authority. For students with issues taking direction or following the dictates of the classroom, it is imperative that the behavior be addressed in a calm, hopeful manner with clear expectations on the standards that must be met. To react to the rebelliousness of a student with rancor usually serves to reinforce the stereotype of negative authority that the student has seen before. By addressing the actions and not the personality of the student, there is a better chance that the negative behaviors can be changed.

An approach rooted in positivity or a growth mindset is especially important with defiant students. As mentioned earlier, some students have a significant problem with negative hierarchy and authority figures. This may be deeply rooted in a cognitive behavior that has served them "well" over the years and has allowed them to control the classroom narrative. An experienced teacher knows that approaching these students in a way that emphasizes the power dynamic between teacher and student is usually not an effective strategy. Students who come to the classroom with a set of behaviors that have allowed them to get their way and control their classrooms rarely react well to negativity or heavy-handedness.

Some adolescents' predilection to cynicism is easy to understand for those of us who despaired over our own futures during our teen years or for that matter at any point in our lives. It can be emotionally crippling for a young person to succumb to the notion that the chance of a good future is not within reach. The role of teachers in recognizing the strengths and interests of their students can be life changing for those especially prone to despair. Optimism fuels the spirit, and young people will be drawn to the teacher who lives and communicates that ideal.

Humor

Purposeful and optimistic settings will often include a dose of humor to help fuel the spirit of both teachers and pupils. Through neuroscience and psychology, we know that laughter and smiles can have a positive affect on individuals and groups. "Playful" classrooms are often critiqued as lacking in purpose but in over 30 years of teaching and observation I found that the atmosphere in such settings allowed the teacher to switch gears easily between friendly banter and getting the job done. On a cautionary note, the types of humor that stereotype and demean groups of people are to be avoided as there is no shortage of content that is appropriate from which to draw funny stories. Teachers should steer clear of the type of humor that elicits a response of "That's not funny!"

The Biology Behind Laughter

With the advent of neuroscience, we know that laughter releases serotonin which facilitates risk-taking as the individual is made more comfortable by its release. Another positive side effect of a connected classroom is that students will be less self-conscious about asking for clarification of difficult concepts. Through neuroscience, we know that laughter in the classroom also serves to stimulate and foster an environment where creative thinking is more likely to flourish. A relaxed atmosphere where students are free to experiment through higher-level thinking and questioning produces better critical thinking than an environment devoid of joy and optimism.

The physiological effect of a stressful classroom or environment is well documented as it produces heightened cortisol levels which produce a fight or flight response in all of us. This evolutionary adaptation is a great short-term strategy in times of an emergency or perceived threat but is not a good way to morally or culturally advance an individual or community over the long term. A classroom that is oppressive runs the risk of losing students who will choose the flight response or be filled with daily confrontations for those students who choose to fight the imagined or real threat. Humor can thereby serve to relieve the need for a negative emotional response from the student and greatly facilitate a healthy learning environment.

Laughter Contributes to a Pleasant Atmosphere

Humor draws students together with the teacher in a common experience that makes going to class a more joyful experience. Laughter and smiles connect people. As positive energy resonates throughout a room, insecurities and self-doubt are diminished as life is seen through a different lens. Students in these types of atmospheres feel freer to make mistakes and learn from them as the class feels more like a family than a group of individuals competing against each other for grades. Another positive side effect of having a classroom that incorporates humor is that students are more inclined to attend. Seasoned teachers are aware that at times they must compete with outside distractions for the student's attention and attendance. The enthusiasm that students exhibit on entering your classroom sends a clear message as to the type of environment you have established. Sometimes, course corrections must be made if there are several days strung together where the students look as though they are headed to the gallows upon entering your room. The choices for the teacher to rectify a grim atmosphere are to become punitive or to create a more welcoming atmosphere. Attendance in a classroom should matter if the pedagogy is sound, so facilitating good attendance through an uplifting atmosphere should be part of a well-managed schoolroom.

Critics of some types of humor see it as a way for the powerful to poke fun at the weak. Comedy is seen by them as falsely upholding the superiority of a particular race, religion, political ideology, etc. People rightfully cringe at the comedy of this sort as there is much to laugh at in the world that isn't inflammatory. Satire is one way to do that. Satire as a form of social critique has huge value by exaggerating and highlighting contradictions in the ideas being discussed. Teachers must be careful that the satire they use regarding religion or politics is not constantly being aimed at a particular group or idea. The teacher must avoid indoctrinating students to a point of view and must remember that the goal is always to facilitate critical thinking in the classroom. Humor used properly can help us see the nuances in particular stances that the students or society may fiercely hang on to or reject out of hand.

An interesting byproduct of making students laugh is the positive affect it can have on the teacher. Any time you can make a student smile it will make your day as well as theirs. There are a variety of ways that teachers can show a lighter side of themselves both in and outside the classroom. Student Union events often give teachers the opportunity to engage in intramurals, silly dance routines, a teacher's choir, or comedic sketches. For the less adventurous a cartoon, joke, or humorous story to start a class can be an easy ways to elicit a few smiles. Dressing up for Halloween never fails to arouse a positive reaction from students. Bringing joy to a classroom has a huge affect on the teacher–student relationship and should not be dismissed.

Conclusion

Guiding a classroom is not for the faint of heart. It takes courage to stand and teach content which your students may or may not welcome. To look students in the eye in the hope of seeing the tell-tale signs of engagement takes mettle because it is an instant reflection on how you are faring as the classroom leader. You can meet the curriculum requirements in a variety of ways but never lose sight of how purpose, optimism, and humor can be the bedrock of a good classroom.

The apprehension that teachers feel upon entering a classroom is as natural as the solutions to help quell those emotions. When teachers are scrambling for answers to problems that seem formidable, they may find the answer in the three basic values that are older and more deeply seated than we can imagine: being a purposeful leader, being optimistic, and using humor.

Reference

King, S. (2000). *On writing: A memoir of the craft*. Pocket Books.

CONCLUSION

Margaretta Patrick and Ken Badley

It seems appropriate that in our conclusion we return to the title of this textbook: *The Complexities of Authority in the Classroom: Fostering Democracy for Student Learning*. In the following, we focus on the terms *complexities* and *fostering democracy*, because many of the chapters herein explore the complex layers of classroom authority and because a key function of classroom authority is fostering democracy as a classroom ethos in which students learn.

Complexities

Classroom authority involves dynamic relationships. A typical classroom comprises a teacher, anywhere from 18 to 40 students, perhaps a teacher's assistant, and various other professionals who enter and exit a classroom from week to week. There are myriad relationships, from teachers with their students and their students' caregivers, to peer relationships, to teachers with their administrators. While much can go wrong, it is a miracle that so much usually goes right, due to the hard work and dedication of educators and to the desire of students to learn. But even when things are going relatively well, the complexity underlying all the relationships and identities in the classroom remains. Issues of confidence arise for myriad reasons, even for seasoned teachers. From time to time, all educators have challenging classes, meet students with whom they must work extra hard to build a relationship, or face internal and external barriers they must overcome before they can fully authorize themselves to teach. These factors not only contribute to the complexity of teacher authority, but they are also foundational to the stories teachers tell about themselves, about their teacher identity, and about the processes by which they authorized themselves and their students to teach and learn together.

DOI: 10.4324/9781003140849-30

As various authors in this textbook have testified, it can be difficult for teachers to authorize themselves to teach, especially, but not exclusively, beginning teachers. Although teachers come into the classroom bearing their legal certification, self-doubts creep in and can destroy their confidence or feelings of authenticity. Ashley Ryl (Chapter 20) identifies the tensions of trying to become someone else, of attempting to adopt a successful Mentor Teacher's approach to classroom management. In the early months of her first position, she thought she needed to become stricter to be like the other teachers in the school. As Ashley and everyone else who has tried to emulate another teacher has discovered, trying to be someone else is rarely, if ever, successful. The lack of authenticity ultimately wears a teacher down. Ashley overcame the barrier and, as a result, was able to build deeper relationships with her students.

Others faced the barrier of disappointment, of a new experience not being all that it could be. Nicola Campbell's move to a new country to start her teaching career (Chapter 21) immersed her in various approaches and practices with which she was initially uncomfortable. This was not what she had signed up for when she became a teacher, and she felt she had to abandon, at least temporarily, her visions and dreams of the type of teacher she wanted to become. But Nicola overcame the barrier of disappointment, coming to appreciate aspects of the approaches and practices she encountered overseas and even incorporating some of them when she returned to Canada.

Another barrier we witness in the stories is that of disappointment, of wondering whether the decision to become a teacher was the right decision. Nadine Ayer (Chapter 9) shares her story of working with students in a high-needs classroom. Initially, she found her students' needs and behaviors overwhelming, and it was all Nadine could do to hold herself and the classroom together. But she persevered, sought solutions, and educated herself, and through conversation and valuable insights gleaned from professional reading, Nadine shifted her perception of her students and together with those students, turned the classroom around.

Malini Sivasubramaniam examines the barrier of cultural mismatches between diverse student populations and the largely White teaching profession. The "race-based achievement gap" has rightfully prompted parents and school boards to hire more racialized teachers. But Malini cautions readers against thinking that changing hiring practices, while incredibly important, are the panacea. Research indicates that some racialized teachers may face dual pressures from their professional responsibilities and students who overly identify with them or view them more as family than as the teacher. Teacher authority may be difficult to maintain. While Malini emphasizes the need for teachers to recognize the impacts of race and social identities on their work, she concludes that good teaching is good teaching. All teachers have the potential to reach all their students, but they need to do the work of disrupting dominant discourses, (re)conceptualizing their role as warm demanders, and addressing issues of equity and inclusion.

At other times, barriers are rooted in gender stereotypes, some of which we internalize. Genie Kim weaves her story through several vignettes to bust the myth that to have authority in the classroom teachers require a certain type of stature and voice, usually associated with male teachers. Instead, Genie urges teachers to adopt strategies and principles that enable all teachers, regardless of gender, to gain authority in the classroom, strategies such as fostering caring relationships with students, developing trust through consistency and fairness, making learning accessible to all the learners in the class, establishing clear expectations, being one's authentic self, and empowering students. For female teachers, Genie adds another practice: believe that every teacher can create a classroom in which learning occurs.

Genie Kim is one of several contributors to emphasize classroom relationships. As Iriel Jaroslavsky Rindlisbacher (Chapter 12) so eloquently stated, "Relationships must be the most important aspect of teaching because, well, we're simply human." Reanna Jordan (Chapter 11) observed that "your classroom authority is only as strong and effective as the relationships you develop in your classroom." Some might consider this relational approach too soft, but those who research effective teaching and high-functioning classrooms keep arriving at the same conclusions as do the contributors to this book: relationships are key.

Most of the teachers in Part 4 highlighted relationships, whether they were Pre-Service Teachers (PSTs) (Rebecca Clarke, Tiffany Chung, and Maegahn Smith, Chapter 19), taught in small or remote settings (Kristen Tjostheim, Chapter 23; Dena Palmaymesa and Natasha Steenhof Bakker, Chapter 24), or served as Substitute Teachers (Bina Ali and Douglas Laing, Chapter 22). Several of these teachers described classroom relationships as gifts, finding joy in the simplicity of their relationships with students and of students with each other. The PSTs understood how authenticity was the bedrock of their relationships with students. Others came to value the opportunities of small communities, where their lives as teachers intersected with their students' lives both in and out of the classroom. Throughout all these narratives from the field, it was clear that in widely varying contexts, these teachers came to practice what Kristen articulated so well: to focus on student strengths rather than their deficits. The commitment to focus on students' strengths and see the best in students is the path that offers hope for frustrated teachers, broken classroom relationships, and struggling students. The sense of optimism described by Ron McIntyre (Chapter 25) serves a similar purpose.

Relationships are foundational to classroom authority, the subject of this textbook. That the concept of classroom authority requires an entire textbook to elaborate, and that chapters discussing it spend as much time detailing what it is not as describing what it is, attests to the conceptual complexity of teacher authority, student consent, and how teachers authorize their students. As Badley and Hughes portray in Chapter 3, teachers need to authorize themselves to teach. They do so by showing up and teaching, developing confidence by taking stock of their internal and external resources, sharing authority, and building courage. Mason Steinke (Chapter 8) shares how a study of the teacher character in a film taught him the value of employing various types of authority in his own teaching practice. In Chapter 4, Badley explores the role of moral authority in gaining students' consent to teach.

Teacher authority involves presence which, in Chapter 5, Badley says is necessary to teacher authority. Presence is another complex term, in part because it has been overly romanticized and prescribed in Hollywood teacher films. However, it can be learned, insists Badley, through effort, enthusiasm, listening and conversation, empathy, humor, humility, authenticity, self-awareness, tact, and professionalism. Emily Robinson and Shae Nimmo (Chapter 6) develop the listening element of teacher presence further, speaking from their respective professions as a family nurse practitioner and an elementary teacher. Emily and Shae describe listening as a gift and they emphasize the physical and bodily process of preparing to listen. Active listening has its own set of skills, demonstrated in professional examples from both Emily and Shae, skills which can be compromised if one is not alert to the roadblocks of listening, which they identify as judging, suggesting solutions, and avoiding the other's concerns.

We have presented several barriers to the development of healthy classroom authority, of teachers authorizing themselves, because the conceptions are complex and involve multiple people. There is nothing easy about classrooms or about teaching. But the stories told in the various chapters, and even the summaries provided here, remind us that teachers regularly meet the challenges that come their way, that they can and often do overcome frustrations and disappointments, and that they can and do learn how to be successful educators and create classrooms where students flourish.

Indeed, as the contributors to this volume demonstrate, teachers can learn the knowledge and skills and can live into the dispositions and attitudes needed to authorize themselves and to authorize their students. Beginning with their on-campus courses, PSTs can learn how to authorize students by creating student-based learning opportunities and planning for differentiation (Jacqueline Filipek, Margaretta Patrick, & Wendy Stienstra in Chapter 14). Reanna Jordan (Chapter 11) extends the authorization of students to include the development of their inquiry and decision-making skills in everyday life events. Ken Badley (Chapter 11) describes how teachers might authorize their students by providing them with choice in how they demonstrate their learning, thereby allowing students to "play to their strengths." Iriel Jaroslavsky Rindlisbacher (Chapter 12) authorized her grade 4 students to take ownership of their learning by choosing which subjects they were going to study when. Classrooms are already beehives of activity, and having students do different things at the same time adds to their complexity. But, as these teachers insist, the added activity is structured, not chaotic as long as expectations and routines are clear. The added work is worth every moment of work because students thrive when they have some choice and agency.

Fostering Democracy

Fostering democracy is staggeringly complex, as we can attest by looking at many of the world's present democracies. There is nothing easy or obvious about participating in and sustaining a democracy. Citizens have an array of expectations of their democracy, and they have diverse views of the role of governments within them. When a fundamental right of democracy is freedom of speech, then even those who speak against democratic values have their rights protected (to a point; we know there are limits).

We are not claiming that classrooms are, or can be, completely democratic. But we do believe that all students deserve to be treated with dignity in the classroom, that they are able to engage in and develop the skills of citizenship, and that they can and should be taught the value of caring for themselves and others, which involves probing the thorny issues of equity. As do many students, we catch the irony when teachers in democracies teach about the benefits of democracy but operate undemocratic classrooms.

Theory helps us create caring classrooms that foster democracy. The invitational approach to classroom management outlined by Sean Schat (Chapter 7) poses invitation as an ethical process in which teachers believe in their students. If the reader takes anything away from this textbook, it should be the importance of teachers' belief in their students. The invitational theory reminds teachers that they are modeling how to do the right thing, how to respond to both mistakes and misbehavior. Invitational theory helps teachers understand the roles that perception and self-concept play in behavior and it provides opportunities for students to participate in democratic practices within the classroom. If a decision has an impact on students, they should have input into what happens to them.

The theory of place applied by Jacqueline Filipek (Chapter 10) to the classroom is helpful in that it outlines how space can be imbued with meaning and how students come to define themselves in relation to a place. When students know that they belong in a place that is safe, great things happen. Relationships are established and fostered, and identities may be formed or strengthened. The helpful and rewarding aspect of place for teachers is that the transition from space to place is not some magical process but can be achieved through everyday classroom structures, rules, and routines, as well as the intentional development of relationships.

As has been said so often throughout this textbook, the importance of relationships cannot be overstated. Fostering democracy requires that all students be treated with dignity. Paige Ray links a democratic approach to classroom management with student voice and agency, the work of dignifying students, and critical theory. As she works with university students from rural communities who are often culturally marginalized due in part to their limited use of privileged academic English, Paige dignifies the students by asking them to share a literacy in which they have some expertise, such as fly-fishing, working with resin, dairy and beef farming, and hunting skills. Members of the class then critically examine dominant conceptions of literacy, discuss who they are *as members of language communities*, and explore their delight in gaining literacies. In this manner, Paige dignifies the students by valuing their literacies and their agency.

Critical theory asks teachers to examine both their individual and societal assumptions and assess how those assumptions enable some students to flourish while hindering others. As Margaretta Patrick outlines in Chapter 11, researchers who study multicultural classrooms and have developed culturally sensitive teaching practices are aware that unconscious bias often limits students from marginalized communities from participating fully in democratic societies. Some educators blame the educational difficulties facing these students on their culture. Promoters of culturally sensitive teaching reject this deficit model of culture and instead view culture as an asset by which teachers and students can enrich teaching and learning. Of particular interest to many of these researchers are language codes because those who do not adopt the dominant culture's language codes face discrimination and limitations inside and outside the classroom. If all students are to have agency and participate in a democratic society, then educators need to recognize the power that lies in dominant language codes, unpack this power with students, and educate students in both their own language codes and those of the dominant culture.

Language codes can also be gendered, as described by Allyson Jule (Chapter 17). When educators dominate the talking space and when they interact with male student responses more deeply than with the responses of female students, female students receive the message that the space is not for them, that only males may find their identity in public space. When those messages are sent to students as young as 7 years old, it is no wonder that they do not ask questions in a university classroom. As Jule concludes, public space is diminished when girls and women do not speak. And, if we may add, democracy is limited.

Critical theory returns us to the introduction of this textbook. As Margaretta Patrick (Chapter 2) traced the history of classroom management as an area of research, critical educators continued to raise questions about power and coercion. They worried that the concept of *management* was inherently problematic because one can never *manage* students without coercing them. As this section indicates, the concerns raised by critical educators were deeply connected to the desire for equitable and democratic education. Democratic education in which all students flourish will help prepare citizens for what will likely be some difficult times ahead. Indeed, it may well be an increasingly important antidote for sustaining our democracies. We hope this textbook contributes to that endeavor in some way.

INDEX

5 primary domains, invitational theory 83

ability groups and mixed ability groups 145–146
acting, and presence 74
active listening 75–76, 270
advice, as roadblock to listening 78
African American students, 157–158, 160–167; *see also* race
Africentric Alternative School 157–158, 202
agency, for students 242–243
Ali, Bina 14, 234–237, 269
Anderson, Hannah 197–198
"apprenticeship of observation" (Lortie) 46
Arend, B. D. 64
Arinto, P. B. 64
Aristotle 67
assemblies, behavior during 181
Assertive Discipline: A Take-Charge Approach for Today's Educator 23
Assertive Discipline program 18
assessment: choice in assessment 11, 121–125; in foreign settings 231; as part of classroom management 148–151; peer assessment 260–261
attentive teachers, portrayed in film 59–60
authenticity: contrasted with entertainment 62–63; as quality of teacher presence 66, 185
authority: authentic authority 203–204; classroom strategies 183–186; as collaborative work 137–139; and cultural introspection 165–167; and cultural literacy 169–171; and dignity 132–139; Genie Kim's personal classroom experiences 176–183; loss of 163–165; and male teachers 175–176, 182, 183–184, 194–197; and marginality 205–206; misunderstandings regarding 2–4; moral authority 40, 44, 48–52; and power 168–169; and race 157–158, 165–171, 201–207; relationships as foundational to 269–270; research 23–24; and *The School of Rock* 92–94; shared authority 38–39, 105, 215–218; and social questions 24–26, 28–29; and teachers' physical appearance 175–176; types of 1–2, 93; and warm demanders 158–163; warmth and care 167–168
authorization *see* self-authorization; students, authorization of
Ayer, Nadine 9–10, 95–103, 268

Badley Ken, 1–16, 33, 44–70, 84, 121–125, 267–272
Bakker, Natasha Steenhof 15, 253–258, 269
Bandura, Albert 61
Barlowe, A. 58
beginning teachers 141–144, 222–227
behaviorism 23–24, 29
behavior management *see* discipline
Benne, Kenneth 2

Beyoncé 197
Beyond Behaviorism (Freiberg) 23–24
bias, privilege, and listening 79–80
Bigatel, P. M. 56
Black, Jack 37, 59, 63, 92–94
Black, M. 203
Black identity 157–158, 160–167; *see also* race
blended learning 245–247
body language and listening 75–76
Bondy, E. 166
book clubs 143–144
boring teachers, portrayed in film 59
boundaries 138–139, 185
boys, girls, and gender differences *see* linguistic spaces
Brach, Tara 74
Brantlinger, Ellen 29
Brophy, J. 23, 26, 27
Brown, L. 202
Brown v. Board of Education 22
Bryson, Tina Payne 99–100
bullying approach to discipline 181, 183
Butchart, Ronald 24–25

Calvinism and approaches to discipline 19, 21
Cameron, Deborah 197
Campbell, Nicola 14, 228–233, 268
Canter, Lee 18, 23
Canter, Marlene 18, 23
care: and culturally responsive teaching 167–168; in invitational theory 83; and moral authority 49; and a student teacher's relationships 217–218
Carrington, Jody 98
Carson, Robert 25–26
Carter, Joe *(Lean on Me)* 60
Carter, Julia 182–183
Carvill, B. 52
case study of a high-needs classroom 95–102
Casey, Z. A. 28–29
Catch Me if You Can (film) 37
certification/licensure process 47
charismatic teachers, portrayed in film 58–59
Chesler, M. 203, 204
child study, and changes in classroom discipline 22
Choi, J. 205
choice: in assessment 121–125; and student agency 242–243

Chung, Tiffany 13, 211, 215–218, 269
cinematic depictions of teachers *see* film depictions of teachers
Civil Rights movement, U.S. 158
Clarke, Rebecca 13, 211–215, 269
class, social, and restorative justice 134–137
classroom climate 3
classroom ethos 107; and invitational theory 84–85, 88
classroom management: alternative disciplinary measures 21–23; as an educational specialization 26–29; and assessment 148–151; "Big Five" strategies 17; and complexity 267–270; corporal punishment 18–21; and democracy 271–272; emerging principles 26–27; in foreign settings 229–230; and lesson planning 144–148; misunderstandings regarding 3; in small rural schools 253–258; for student teachers and beginning teachers 223–227; for substitute teachers 235; and teacher anxiety 259; and teacher authority 23–26; trust and self-authorization 141–144
Classroom Management that Works (Marzano) 27
classrooms and sense of place *see* place-making
class sizes 257–258
Coates, Jennifer 197
code switching 161
cold starts 36
co-learners, teachers as 124
collaboration: and authority 137–139; collaborative grading tasks 150
college classes, gender, and classroom participation 194–197
Collier-Meek, M. A. 28
colonialism 28–29
command, contrasted with counsel 2
communication: for student teachers, in classrooms 220; student teachers with mentor teachers 213; for substitute teachers 236; *see also* conversation
community, sense of, in remote schools 256–257
competence, for student teachers 216
compliance, as unsuccessful disciplinary approach 96–97
confidence: and optimism 262–263; for student teachers 217

Index

conflict: 6 Cs approach to conflict management 89–90; and restorative justice 134–137
connectedness, as quality of teacher presence 66
connection, fostering 98–99
consent of students 8, 44–52; *see also* place-making
consistency and student relationships 184
control, as unsuccessful disciplinary approach 96–97
conversation: importance to learning 197; as quality of teacher presence 64–65; to show interest in students 219; *see also* communication
Cook, A. 58
Cook-Harvey, C. M. 145
corporal punishment 18–21
counsel, contrasted with command 2
courage and self-authorization 41–42
Courage to Teach, The (Palmer) 62
COVID-19 pandemic 8, 41–42, 46, 76–77
Crang, M. 108, 113
Critical Pedagogy 134
Critical Theory 272
Csikszentmihalyi, Mihaly 129
cultural codes 164–165
cultural fluency 170–171
cultural introspection 165–167
cultural literacy 169–171
culturally relevant pedagogy 160–163
culturally relevant teachers (CRTs) 165–166
cultural switching 161
Cumming, Alan 21–22
curriculum, in foreign settings 230–231
curriculum planning 151
curriculum standards *see* standards, curricular

Danforth, Scot 29
Daniels, Matt 197–198
Darling-Hammond, L. 145
Davis, Geena 197
Dead Poets Society (film) 58, 64, 135
Death of Expertise, The (Nichols) 46
decision-makers, students as 118–119
degree, as starting condition for professional job 45–47
Delpit, Lisa 137, 161–162, 164, 168, 169, 201
democracy: in the classroom 271–272; Democracy in Ancient Athens unit case study 121–123, 124; and restorative justice 134–137
democratic ethos and invitational theory 87
Deschanel, Zooey 60
Dewey, John 21, 25, 29
Dickar, M. 204
Dickens, Charles 133
differentiation and diversity 145
dignity: and authority 132–139; and students in remote settings 240
"Dignity of Man in the Classroom, The" (Raths) 132–133
discipline: alternatives to corporal punishment 21–23; behavior management in foreign settings 229–230; boundaries as discipline 139; bullying approach to 181, 183; corporal punishment 18–21; rules in the classroom 263–264; *see also* classroom management
Discipline and Group Management in Classrooms (Kounin) 24
Disney princess films 198
diversity and differentiation 145
Donehower, K. 135
Dreikurs, Rudolf 6, 18, 24
Duke, Daniel 26
Dweck, C. 42
Dworkin, Gerald 57
dysregulated students 95–102

effort, as quality of teacher presence 63–64
elementary English language arts 146, 149–150
elementary mathematics 143
Ellis, J. 107, 108, 110–111, 116
Ellis, T. I. 86
Emmer, Edmund 27
empathy: projective contrasted with receptive 85; as quality of teacher presence 65
empowerment and classroom authority 185–186
English language: and academic language 136–137; NES (native English speakers) 136
enigmatic teachers, portrayed in film 58
entertainment contrasted with authenticity 62–63
enthusiasm, as quality of teacher presence 64

Escalante, Jaime 60
Escalante: Best Teacher in America (Matthews) 37, 60
Ethics, The (Aristotle) 67
ethos of place 107
Evertson, Carolyn 27, 29
expectation effect 37, 39
expectations 185
expertise, distrust of 46–47
extraversion/introversion 63
Eyles, J. 110, 111, 112

fairness and moral authority 51, 184
Farber, J. 62, 66
Farrington-Thompson, Angela 50–51
fear: effect on learning 61; in students' experience 50
female teachers, increase in numbers 22
femininity, masculinity, and gender differences *see* linguistic spaces
feminization of education 22
Ferris Bueller's Day Off (film) 59
Filipek, Jacqueline 10, 107–117, 141–153, 271
film depictions of teachers 36–37, 38, 58–61, 135
flamboyance, effect in classroom 62–63
flexibility, personal and institutional 241–243
flow (Csikszentmihalyi) 129
following, as listening skill 76
Ford, A. C. 165, 167, 204, 206
foreign settings, teaching in 228–233
Fox, P. 56, 66
Fraser, J. W. 164, 168
Freedom Writers (film) 36, 60–61, 135
Freeman, Morgan 60
Freiberg, Jerome 23
Freire, P. 134

Gallie, W. B. 57
Gandhi 175
Gardner, Howard 122
Gay, G. 161, 165
Geddes, Patrick 22
gender: and authority 175–176, 179, 181–182, 183–184; gendered speech patterns 12–13, 187–189; gender roles in independent religious schools 255–256; and restorative justice 134–137; *see also* linguistic spaces
"gifts of simplicity" 15, 252, 253
Ginott, H. G. (Haim) 33, 40–41

girls, boys, and gender differences *see* linguistic spaces
Giroux, H. A. 203
Glasser, William 186
"good discipline sequence" 88–89
Good Discipline Sequence, The (Purkey and Strahan) 88
grading *see* assessment
Graham, E. 134–135
Greene, Maxine 66
greeting students at classroom entrance 52, 257, 262–263
grouping strategies, student 145–146
"growing from the inside out" 42
growth mindset 42, 262–264; *see also* optimism
Gruwell, Erin 36, 60–61
Guaspari, Roberta 60
guided reading 146–147
Gurley, Lisa 66

Halonen, J. 62, 64
Handbook on Classroom Management (Evertson and Weinstein) 27, 29
Hard Times (Dickens) 133
Harry Potter and the Deathly Hallows (film) 61
high-needs class, case study 95–102
High School Musical (film) 42
Hobbes, Thomas 2
Hollis, J. 62
honesty, and trust-based relationships 220
Hopson, R. L. 204–205
Hosler, K. A. 64
hospitality, and moral authority 52
Howard, J. R. 166
Howard, T. C. 166
Hughes, A. 75, 269
Hughes, Michelle C. 8, 35–43, 269
humility, and moral authority 50–51
humor: and classroom management 264–265; as quality of teacher presence 65

imposters and self-authorization 37
Indigenous students 158–159, 162
Inheritance (Shapiro) 78
inner work (growing from the inside out) 42
inquiry learning 10–11, 118–120
integrity, in invitational theory 83
interest groups 146
interest in students' lives 219

International Association for Invitational Education (IAIE) 83
Internet-based learning 245–247
Intrator, S. 62
introspection, cultural 165–167
introversion/extraversion 63
invitational theory: and classroom ethos 84–85; 5 primary domains 83; foundations of 85–87; overview 9, 33, 82–84, 271; in practice 87–90; *The Six C's Approach to Conflict Management* 88, 89–90
"Inviting Positive Classroom Discipline" (Purkey and Strahan) 88–89
IRF method (initiating-response-feedback) 191
Irvine, J. J. 164, 168
isolation in remote settings 253

James, C. E. 163
Jaroslavsky Rindlisbacher, Iriel 11, 126–131, 269, 270
Jesuit approaches to discipline 21
Jewett, James 19
Johnson, F. H. 17, 21
Jones, Vernon 26
Jordan, Reanna 10, 118–120, 269, 270
judgement, as roadblock to listening 77–78
Jule, Allyson 12–13, 187–200, 272
junior high English language arts 143–144
junior high mathematics 147–148, 150–151

Kabat-Zinn, Jon 73–74
Kelly, M. 170–171
Keyes, T. S. 49
Kids These Days (Carrington) 98
"kidwatching" 149–150
Kim, Genie, personal experiences of authority in classroom 12, 175–186, 269
King, Stephen 260
Kleinfeld, Judith 158–160, 206
Kounin, Jacob 18, 24, 27

Ladson-Billings, Gloria 161, 165, 169
Lai, C. 203–204
Laing, Douglas 237, 269
Lakoff, Robin 188–189
language and dictionary definitions 57
Language and Woman's Place (Lakoff) 188–189
language codes 164–165, 272

language communities 272
laughter 264–265
leadership groups in the classroom 113–114
Lean In (Sandburg) 197
Lean on Me (film) 60
learning outcomes *see* standards, curricular
learning styles 122–123, 126
Lee, Anne 179–181
lesson planning: content and goals 259–260; in foreign settings 230–231; student grouping and diversity 144–148
Leviathan (Hobbes) 2
licensure/certification process 447
"lid-flipping," management of 99–100
Lim, J. 205
linguistic spaces: and classroom practices 197–198; college classrooms 194–197; elementary classrooms 189–193; and gendered speech patterns 187–189
linguistic switching 161
listening: active listening 75–76, 270; elements of listening 75–77; in healthcare settings 72, 76–77, 78, 79–80; impact of listening 71–73; impact of power and privilege on listening 79–80; and mindful presence 74; and moral authority 52; preparation for 73–74; qualities of a good listener 75; as quality of teacher presence 64–65; roadblocks to 77–79
literacy: alternative literacies 137–138, 271–272; cultural literacy 169–171; media literacy 148
Little Engine that Could, The (Piper) 35
Locke, John 8, 44–45, 48
Lortie, Dan 46–47

male teachers and authority 175–176, 182, 183–184, 194–197
management and neo-liberalism 28–29
Mann, Horace 19–20
Martino, W. J. 205–206
Marzano, Robert 27
masculinity, femininity, and gender differences *see* linguistic spaces
Mastel-Smith, B. 49
Matilda (film) 59–60, 61
Matthews, Jay 36–37, 60
McIntyre, Ron 15, 259–266, 269
McLaren, P. 203
media literacy 148
meditation 73–74

Meijer, P. 64
Meisner, Sanford 74
mental hygiene, and changes in classroom discipline 22
mentor teachers and student teachers 211–215, 223–225
Miller, K. E. 166
mindfulness 73–74
Mindfulness-Based Stress Reduction (MBSR) 73
mindful presence 74
mindset 186
mini lesson planning 146
minimization, as roadblock to listening 78–79
Mona Lisa Smile (film) 37, 135
Montessori schools 22
moral authority 40, 44, 48–52
moral education 20
Morgan's Passing (Tyler) 37
Mother Teresa 175
Mulan (film) 198
multiple intelligences (Gardner) 122–123
"Multiplication is for White People" (Delpit) 161–162
Music of the Heart (film) 60, 135
mutual learning 50–51

National Council on Teacher Quality (NCTQ): on classroom management strategies 17; report on classroom management 27–28
negotiations, with students 242–243
neo-liberalism and management 28–29
NES (native English speakers) 136
New Girl (television series) 60
Nichols, Tom 46
nicknames in the classroom 101–102
Nimmo, Shae 9, 52, 71–81, 270
Noddings, Nel 49, 160
Not One Less (film) 37
Novak, John (J. M.) 82, 87, 89, 90
Nwaubani, Adoabi Tricia 148

objectives, learning *see* standards, curricular
Occasional Teachers 234–237
Oliver, Henry K. 19
one-room schools 248–253
online learning 56, 245–247
Ontario, Canada, Royal Commission on Learning 157

Ontario, demographics 202–203
optimism 83, 262–264; *see also* growth mindset

Palmaymesa, Dena 15, 248–253, 269
Palmer, Parker 33, 42, 62, 67–68
Papp, T. A. 162
parent/teacher relationships 72–73
Patrick, Margaretta 3, 5, 12, 39, 141–153, 157–174, 202, 206, 267–272
peer assessment 260–261
perceptual tradition and invitational theory 85–86
personalities: personality conflicts 212–213; of teachers 40–41
person-centred paradigm 23–24, 26
Pestalozzi, Johann Heinrich 22
pioneer rhetoric 135
Pitard, J. 170–171
Pixar films, 198
place-based theory 105
place contrasted with space 108
place-making: and classroom life 108–111; planning for 116; and relationships 115–116; and resources 115; and routines 113–115; and rules 112–113; and structures 111–112
planning, lesson 144–148, 230–231, 259–260
"playful" classrooms 264–265
Portier, Sidney 58–59
positivity 83, 262–264; *see also* growth mindset
Postman, Neil 52, 67
power 2–3, 79–80, 168–169
practicums *see* student teachers
predictability, and trust-based relationships 219
preparation, teacher 39–40; *see also* lesson planning
presence *see* teacher presence
pre-service teachers (PSTs) *see* student teachers
Pressure Cooker (film) 61
privilege/power, and listening 79–80
professionalism, as quality of teacher presence 67
progressivism and classroom discipline 22, 25
projective empathy 85
Purkey, W. W. (William) 9, 82, 83, 84, 86–87, 88–89, 89–90

Index **279**

race: attitudes about 167; privilege and listening 79–80; racialized teaching 204–206; racism and Africentric Alternative School 157–158; racism in health care 79–80; and restorative justice 134–137; and teacher authority 201–207
racialization of management 28–29
Radd, T. 86–87
random groups 146
Raths, James 132–133
Ratio Studiorum 21
Ray, Paige 11–12, 132–140, 271–272
Read, V. 75
reading, guided 146–147
reassurance, as roadblock to listening 78–79
receptive empathy 85
Reddie, Dr. Cecil 22
reel teachers (film depictions) 36–37, 38, 58–61, 135
reflecting, as listening skill 76
Reimer, K. E. 134
relationships: with families 72–73; as foundational to classroom authority 269–270; gender differences and authority 184; mentor teacher/student teacher 211–215; and place-making 115–116; in remote settings 252; and student resiliency 261–262; student teachers/students 218; through authorizing students 126–131; trust-based relationships 218–220
religious views on corporal punishment 19
remote settings: and class sizes 257–258; one-room schools 248–253; and sense of community 256–257; small rural schools 238–247, 253–258; teaching in 14–15, 238–247; *see also* rural communities and education
reputation of teachers 40
residential school systems, for Indigenous students 21, 162
resiliency, student 261–262
respect 49–50, 83
restorative justice 134–137
Rezai-Rashti, G. M. 205–206
Rickman, Alan 61
Robinson, Emily 9, 52, 71–81, 270
Rock, Chris 55
Rodenburg, P. 66
Rogers, Carl 75, 76, 77, 124

Ross, D. D. 166
Rossetti, J. 56, 66
Rousmaniere, K. 22
Rousseau, Jean-Jacques 22
routines, and place-making 113–115
Royal Commission on Learning in Ontario (RCOL) 157, 202
rules: in the classroom 263–264; and place-making 112–113
rural communities and education 135–136; *see also* remote settings, teaching in
Ryerson, Egerton 20–21
Ryl, Ashley 13–14, 222–227, 268

safety concerns for substitute teachers 234–235
Sage Encyclopedia of Classroom Management 22
Sandburg, Sheryl 197
Sassi, K. 165, 167, 204, 206
Saturday Night Live (SNL) and cold opens 36
Scarlett, W. George 22, 25
scary teachers, portrayed in film 61
Schat, Sean 9, 82–91, 271
Schlechty, Phillip 39
Schmidt, J. J. 86–87
School of Rock, The (film) 9, 37, 58, 63, 92–94, 135
Scouting movement 22
Sebastien, L. 108, 109–110
secondary social studies 144, 148
See Jane (Geena Davis Institute) 197
SEL (social-emotional learning) 73–74
self-authorization: and imposters 37; for students 105, 141–144; for teachers 33, 35–42, 105
self-awareness, as quality of teacher presence 66
self-concept theory and invitational theory 86–87
self-discipline 21–22
self-regulation 99–100
self-selected groups 146
Self-Talk/Self-Pictures 86
sense of place *see* place-making
sex contrasted with gender 188
shaming techniques in discipline 21
shared authority 38–39, 105, 215–218
Shaw, D. E. 83
Shin, N. 66

Siegel, Daniel J. 99–100
silence: female silence 189; "silenced dialogue" 201; silencing of students 187, 191–192
Simonsen, B. 27–28
Sivasubramaniam, Malini 13, 201–298, 268
Six Cs Approach to Conflict Management, The (Purkey and Novak) 88, 89–90
Sleeter, C. E. 163
Smillie, L. D. 66
Smith, D. I. 52
Smith, Jared Rodger 167–168
Smith, Maegahn 13, 211, 218–221, 269
Snyder, T. 135
social change, 20th century, and classroom discipline 22
social-emotional learning (SEL) 73–74
social structures 111–116
sociolinguistics 136–137
space contrasted with place 108
Stand and Deliver (film) 36–37, 60, 135
standards, curricular 121–125
Steinke, Mason 9, 37, 58, 92–94, 270
Stephenson, Wilma 61
Stiles, Julie 50
Strahan, D. B. 83, 88–89, 89–90
Streep, Meryl 60
student-centered pedagogies 141–142
student consent *see* consent of students; place-making
student engagement 124–125; and classroom management 148–149
"Student of the Day" 101
student resiliency 261–262
students: as decision-makers 118–119; dysregulated 95–102; fears students experience 50; student grouping strategies 145–146
students, authorization of: choice in assessment 121–125; inquiry learning 118–120; through relationships 126–131
student teachers: curriculum planning 151; elementary English language arts classroom 146, 149–150; elementary math classroom 143; junior high English language arts classroom 143–144; junior high mathematics classroom 147–148, 151; in large urban schools 254–255; mentor teacher/student teacher relationships 7, 13–14, 211–215;

overview 12, 269; reflections of a beginning teacher 222–227; secondary social studies classroom 144, 148; shared authority 215–218; strategies for student teachers 214–215; trust-based relationships 13, 218–220
substitute teaching 14, 234–237
Sunderland, Jane 197
Supply Teachers 14, 234–237
Swank, Hillary 36, 60–61

tact, as quality of teacher presence 67
Teacher and Child: A Book for Parents and Teachers (Ginott) 33
teacher authority *see* authority
"Teacher Diversity in Canada" 202–203
teacher presence: examples from films 58–61; and humility 50–51; learning process to develop presence 61–67; overview and importance of 8, 40, 55–57, 270
teachers: authoritative voice in college classrooms 194–197; authority of 23–26; beginning teachers 141–144, 222–227; as co-learners 124; substitute teachers 234–237; teaching abroad 228–233; time spent speaking in classroom 189–192; veteran teacher, reflections of 259–266
Teachers (film) 59
teacher tact 67
Teaching as a Subversive Activity (Postman and Weingartner) 67
teaching partners 252
teaching styles, differing 212
teamwork *see* collaboration
Ten Things I Hate About You (film) 50
three threshold conditions 45–48
Tjostheim, Kristen 14–15, 238–247, 269
Tomlinson, C. A. 145
Toronto, Ontario, demographics 202–203
Toronto Board of Education 21
Toronto District School Board (TDSB) 157–158, 162–163, 202–203
To Sir with Love (film) 58–59
tough love, film portrayals of teachers using 60–61
trust 40, 83, 138, 141–144, 184, 218, 251–252
trust-based relationships 13, 218–220
Truth and Reconciliation Commission (TRC) 158

Tuskegee Experiment 79–80
Two Treatises of Government (Locke) 44–45
Tyler, Anne 37

Universal Design for Learning (UDL) 14–15, 243–245
URStrong program 115

Van Manen, Max 49–50, 67
video conferencing (VC) 245–247
Vygotsky, L. S. 214

Walkerdine, Valerie 193
Ware, F. 163–164
warm demanders 158–165, 206

warmth and care toward students 167–168
Washington, Irene 164, 168–169
Weber, Max 33
Weingartner, C. 67
Weinstein, Carol 23, 27, 29
White privilege 167
Whitley, J. 162
Whole-Brain Child, The (Siegel and Bryson) 99–100
Williams, Robin 58, 64
Wright, C. 204

Young, A. A., Jr. 203, 204

Zelenski, J. M. 66

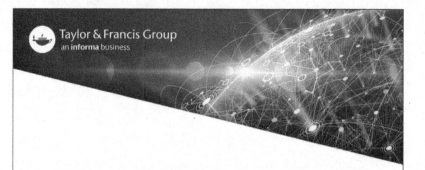